Children's Britannica

CHILDREN'S BRITANNICA

Volume 3

BEECH—BUILDING

ENCYCLOPAEDIA BRITANNICA INTERNATIONAL, LTD
LONDON

First edition 1960

Second edition 1969

Third edition 1973

ISBN 0 85229 099 3

Printed in England by
Hazell Watson & Viney Limited, Aylesbury,
Waterlow & Sons Limited, Dunstable,
Hazells Offset Limited, Slough
and bound by
Hazell Watson & Viney Limited, Aylesbury & Cymmer

BEECH. This handsome tree belongs to the Fagaceae family, which also includes the oak and the chestnut. It has a smooth, grey-green bark and reaches a height of 30 metres with a trunk 2 metres across, but sometimes it is cut and made into a hedge. It is a deciduous tree; that is, the leaves fall in the autumn. The common beech first appeared in southern England between 1000 and 2000 B.C. and it became the commonest tree of the chalk uplands, for the roots can take hold on quite shallow top soil.

Only a very few plants can grow in a beech wood, because the thick canopy of leaves keeps out the light and the roots of the trees spread out and take up the moisture. There are, however, two plants that grow on decaying beech leaves —the bird's nest orchid and the yellow bird's nest—and there is a special fungus that grows among the roots of the tree and helps them to absorb moisture.

The pale green young leaves have long silky hairs. Male and female flowers grow on the same tree and the fruit is known as beech mast —three-sided dark brown nuts which fall from their prickly husks in the autumn.

Beech wood is used for chair making and tools and, in some parts of western Europe, for the shoes of the peasant and farm worker. An oil produced from beech mast was sometimes used

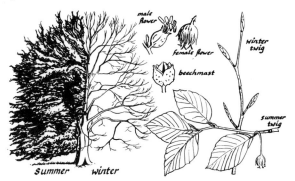

male flower
female flower
beechmast
winter twig
summer twig
Summer   Winter

No forest tree has richer foliage than the beech.

for butter, while dry beech leaves were once widely used to stuff pillows and mattresses.

The beech has a place in legend, history and superstition. One legend is that the first beech tree was stolen from heaven and brought to the Earth by an Indian hero named Arjuna. Joan of Arc is supposed to have seen visions under a beech tree. The leaves of the beech provide one of the most beautiful bronze browns in nature's autumn pageant of colour but—and this is the superstition—a famous 16th-century herbalist named Gerard warned his readers against taking the leaves into the house in case they brought death with them.

The copper beech, often grown in parks and gardens because of the beautiful colour of its leaves, is a variety of the common beech. Other cultivated beeches came from Europe, North America, China and Japan.

BEE-EATER. Among the most brilliantly coloured and graceful birds of the eastern hemisphere are the bee-eaters. The cock and the hen of the common bee-eater are alike, with chestnut backs, yellow throats and greenish-blue underparts. They are about the size of a blackbird, but more slender. Their bills are long and pointed and their tails are also long, with the two middle feathers longer than the others.

These birds live on insects—chiefly bees, of course, and they can be a great nuisance in places where there are beehives. They also eat wasps and dragonflies, and often they hunt for insects in the air, gliding about like swallows. They like to perch on dead boughs, telegraph wires or posts, darting off to catch a fly and then back to their perch again. They have a queer, single note which they keep on repeating.

Usually, bee-eaters keep together and nest in colonies. They dig out a tunnel in a soft sandbank, throwing the sand backwards with their feet as they peck it out. These tunnels can be 2 metres long and there is a round nest chamber at the end. The hen lays her five or six white eggs on the bare sand.

During the summer common bee-eaters are found in southern Europe from Spain to Bulgaria. Now and again an odd bird visits Great Britain and two pairs nested in Sussex in 1955. In the autumn they migrate in large flocks to Africa and India.

There are many different kinds of bee-eater. Most of them are found in Africa and one of these, the carmine bee-eater, often rides on the backs of large birds like bustards and storks, jumping off to catch the grasshoppers and other

S. C. Porter-Bruce Coleman Ltd.

The common bee-eater often chooses to perch on a dead bough while waiting to catch insects.

insects they disturb. It has also been seen to follow lorries, catching the insects that are disturbed by their passing. There is an Australian bee-eater, which is sometimes called the rainbow bird. Bee-eaters are close relatives of the kingfishers.

BEE-KEEPING. Wild honey bees, living in hollow trees or holes in buildings, usually make only small nests in which to store sufficient honey for their own use during the winter. In very early times bee-keepers kept their bees in hives made of wicker or in hollowed out logs, and later in straw baskets called "skeps", but in all such hives the bees fixed their combs to the hive walls and the honey could not be taken out without harming the colony. At the end of the summer it was then the custom to select the heavier skeps, kill the bees with sulphur fumes and then cut out the combs and press the honey from them; good use was also made of the beeswax. In the following year the bee-keeper filled the empty skeps with swarms from the remaining colonies.

Modern hives are larger, so that the bees have room to store honey for the bee-keeper as well as for themselves. They are made of wood and are divided into separate compartments—one called the "brood chamber" where the queen bee lays her eggs and others above it called "supers" for the storage of honey. In all the compartments the bees are provided with wooden frames across which are stretched foundations for the cells; that is, thin sheets of wax stamped with the shape of the cells. Then the bees have only to make wax to build the cells outwards on both sides of the foundation sheets. This wax is not gathered by the bees but formed by them in their own bodies out of honey and used for building the comb.

No doubt the bees appreciate the fine home provided for them, but they still object when the bee-keeper removes the roof of the hive to take their honey. To avoid stings, which can be painful, the bee-keeper must be able to quieten the bees when he attends them. To do this he makes use of an instinct which the bees developed a long time ago when, on smelling the smoke of the dreaded forest fire, they filled themselves with honey so that they were ready to leave for a new home. The bee-keeper uses a "smoker", which is a kind of bellows filled with burning sacking or similar material. By puffing smoke into the top of the hive he drives the bees to fill themselves with honey and this honey makes them feel good-tempered, so that he can then handle them with no more than an occasional sting. Most bee-keepers take the added precaution of wearing a veil; this is draped over a broad-brimmed hat so that the material is kept well away from the face. Some use gloves also, but these are rather a hindrance in handling the frames and other equipment.

The Bee-Keeper's Year

The colony of bees is small during the winter and the insects cluster tightly together for warmth on the combs of the brood-chamber, flying out only on warm days or when the sun is shining. Towards the end of January the queen begins to lay eggs and from then onwards the number of bees gradually increases. As soon as they are fully occupying the brood chamber the

Courtesy, *Australian News and Information Bureau*

A veil and "smoker" are essential tools for the bee-keeper. The brush is used to remove bees from the combs.

bee-keeper adds a "super", putting below it a metal frame which has slots through which the worker bees can pass but the larger queen cannot. This means that the queen can only lay eggs in the brood chamber, while the workers are free to store their honey "upstairs". As the colony continues to grow in size—and it may contain 50,000 bees or more by the middle of the summer—so more "supers" are added when needed. Whenever he handles the hive, the bee-keeper always takes care to work calmly and steadily, so as to avoid knocking the framework or disturbing the bees in any way.

The honey bees' habit of swarming during the summer has been described in the article BEE. The habit may be useful to the bee-keeper if he has an empty hive to fill, for a swarm first settles on a tree or bush nearby while scouts go out to look for a new home, and this is the time when the bees can be shaken into a box or a straw skep and then allowed to run into a new hive.

However, the loss of a swarm greatly reduces the number of honey gatherers in a colony, and swarming is often caused by overcrowding. So the bee-keeper usually does his best to prevent the instinct to swarm from developing. First he must make sure that the queen has plenty of combs in which to lay eggs and that there is

enough room up above for the workers to store honey. If this fails and he sees queen-cells appearing in the brood-chamber, he must take further steps. Some bee-keepers clip the old queen's wings to prevent her from flying with a swarm, but this alone is not enough, for the first young queen to hatch will soon be ready to leave. There are many different ways of preventing swarming, too complicated to be described here, but the aim is always to prevent more than one young queen from hatching, for bees will never swarm without leaving a queen behind them in the hive.

The honey stored in the combs during the summer is at first thin and watery, but after undergoing a chemical change gradually in the warmth of the hive it becomes thicker, or "ripe". The bees then cover the cells over with a thin capping of wax to preserve it. Towards the end of the summer, when the bee-keeper sees that all the honey has been sealed up, he places a board under the lowest "super"; in the centre of this board is a hole and a metal spring, called an "escape", which allows the insects to pass downwards into the brood-chamber but not upwards again. In some countries, particularly in the United States and Canada, the bee-keeper places a cloth sprinkled with carbolic acid in the "supers", for the bees dislike the smell of this intensely and quickly go below. The "supers", having been emptied of bees by one method or another, can then be removed with the combs from the hive.

The next job is the extraction, or removal, of the honey from the combs. First the wax coverings are sliced off with a sharp knife; this is sometimes heated so that the wax cuts more easily. The combs are then placed in the "extractor", a metal tank in which they can rapidly be whirled round either by hand or by means of an electric motor, until all the honey has been thrown out of the cells and collected in the bottom of the tank. The honey is strained, allowed to settle for a day or so in another tank, and then run off into bottles or tins. Finally, to make up for some of the honey taken from the colony, the bees must be fed with enough sugar syrup to last them until the spring.

When many hives are kept, the bee-keeper often moves them long distances in the summer, usually by road, to fruit orchards or to crops such as clover, lucerne or mustard, according to the time when these are in flower. There the bees do a useful job for man, quite apart from the honey they collect and the wax they produce, for, by carrying pollen from one flower to another, they fertilize the fruits and seeds of the trees and plants. In many countries in Europe the bees are taken to the moors in August so that they can gather honey from the heather. Australian bee-keepers practise what is called "migratory" bee-keeping, moving their bees from place to place to new sources of honey and taking their extracting apparatus with them.

BEELZEBUB. In the Old Testament Beelzebub or Baalzebub is the name of the false god or Baal of Ekron, which was one of the towns of the Philistines. The name means "Lord of the Flies". Ahaziah, one of the kings of Israel, fell sick, and instead of praying for help to the true God, Jehovah, he sent messengers to Baalzebub to ask whether he would become well again. Knowing this, Elijah the prophet told both the messengers and the king of Jehovah's anger at this sin, and the king died of his illness.

The enemies of Jesus Christ called Him Beelzebub, meaning that He was a devil, or accused Him of healing sick people with the help of "Beelzebub, the chief of the devils".

John Milton, in his long poem *Paradise Lost,* describes Beelzebub as an angel fallen from Heaven, next in power to Satan "and next in crime". In the *Pilgrim's Progress*, by John Bunyan, Beelzebub is a devil who lies in wait for the pilgrim Christian on his journey, hoping to kill him with arrows.

BEER AND BREWING. Beer is a drink made from the grains of barley and flavoured with hops. (Hops are described in a separate article.) The barley is first made into malt, and the process of making the malt into beer is called brewing. The making of beer is probably nearly as old as the growing of grain crops for food. It all started in the countries surrounding the eastern shores of the Mediterranean. Ten thousand or more years ago the men who lived there began to cultivate certain wild grasses, particularly wheat and barley, because their seeds could be used as food. This was much better than living on wild fruits and roots, for the corn could be stored and used all the year round. Grain-growing meant that the people were able to live in bigger groups because there was more food for them. In time they spread westwards over Europe and brought with them their skill in using the grain for baking and brewing. Bread made from wheat and beer made from barley are still the characteristic food and drink of such peoples as the Scandinavians, the Germans and the English.

Nowadays beer is usually made in great breweries which turn out thousands of barrels, but the process is very much the same as was carried on throughout the ages from the kitchens of Egypt to the abbeys of Europe in the middle ages. It must have been a happy accident that produced the first bread and the first beer, for both need yeast and yeast in its natural condition cannot be seen by the naked eye. (Yeast is a living substance, made up of cells so small that 4,000 of them in a row would just reach across a penny. It is described in a separate article.) Nobody could have guessed that the addition of yeast to flour before baking would produce a spongy loaf much more pleasant to eat than

4

bread without yeast, or "unleavened" bread; nor is it likely that yeast was deliberately added to wet sprouting barley to produce a sparkling drink.

The First Brews

No doubt yeast's first appearance in history was when, thousands of years ago, a man drank some grape juice which had been left standing and which in that warm climate had started bubbling. The bubbling was caused by the yeast from the skin of the grape; this turned the sugar of the grape juice into alcohol and carbon

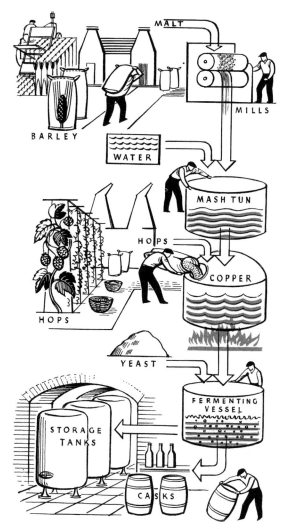

Stages in the brewing of beer. Malt made from barley is crushed and mixed with hot water in the mash tun. Liquid from the mash tun is then boiled with hops in the copper and fermented with yeast in the fermenting vessel.

dioxide gas, a process known as fermentation. This fermented juice was the first wine.

The accident that made the first beer is not quite so simple, for beer cannot be made directly from barley. The barley must be allowed to get wet and to grow a little. This is the first part of the process of making malt. As it grows, certain changes take place inside the corn which result in its containing more sugar than the dry barley.

Probably some barley corns were left about in a damp spot and started to grow or "germinate" as all seeds do if they are kept warm and wet. They must then have been crushed in water so that the sugar from the inside of the corn was dissolved in the water. Yeast from the outside of the corn started the fermentation and produced the first beer.

This beer had no hops in it. Throughout the centuries various herbs and other flavouring materials were put into beer but it was not until the 14th century that hops became commonly used. Even then for many years in England hops were not always used; the word "beer" was kept for the hopped variety and unhopped beer was called "ale".

Beer and Brewing Today

Today the name "beer" is applied to all kinds of beer, the chief types being pale ale, mild or brown ale, stout, Burton or strong ale, and lager. Sometimes in Europe and America the word "ale" is used for the English type of beer and "beer" is kept for the European type—called "lager" in Britain—which has less hops in it and is made somewhat differently.

The first step in making beer is changing the barley into malt at "maltings", which are usually in the country near the barley fields. After the barley has germinated, the malt is dried in a kiln. It is then brought to the brewery where it is crushed between rollers and mixed with hot water in a large circular vessel called a mash tun. Sometimes small quantities of other grains such as maize or rice are used; these are not malted but are specially treated before being added to the mash tun.

In this vessel the changes which started in the maltings continue until nearly all the contents of the barley corn have been changed into sugar.

This is not quite the same sugar as that sold in the shops but is very similar and is called "maltose". The maltose and small quantities of other substances dissolve in the water, which is now called "wort". This is then run off from the mash tun and boiled in a copper for one or two hours with hops. After this the hops are strained off, the hopped wort is cooled and yeast is added to start the fermentation. This continues for three or four days during which the yeast grows and multiplies.

Much of this yeast collects in a "head" on the top of the beer and is skimmed off; part is kept for the next fermentation and the rest sold for animal feeding or for making into soup, for yeast is a very valuable food. When the fermentation is complete the beer is allowed to settle for three or four more days and is then run into casks or storage tanks, where it is kept for various periods according to the type of beer and whether it is to be sold draught or bottled. Draught beer is sold to the customer straight from the cask.

The various kinds of beer depend on the mixture of malts used and different treatment throughout the course of brewing. Dark beers are made with malts which have been heated more strongly than the malts for the pale beers; stouts are made with roasted malt or roasted barley. Continental beers, including "lager", are fermented very cold with a yeast which goes to the bottom of the vessel and these beers are stored a long time before use.

BEET. The vegetables known as beets probably came from a plant called by the Latin name of *Beta vulgaris* which still grows wild along the shores of the Mediterranean and of the Canary Islands. Beets have thick, solid roots, and in the first of the two years of their growth only the roots and leaves appear. Farmers usually dig up the beets during the first year, so the flowers and seeds which develop in the second year of growth are not normally seen.

There are several different kinds of beets, some of which are grown for people to eat and others for animals. The beetroot, also known as the red beet or garden beet, has a round, purplish-red root which is usually cooked and served in salads. The Swiss chard (which is

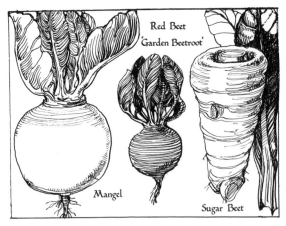

Red Beet 'Garden Beetroot'
Mangel
Sugar Beet

usually known as perpetual spinach or spinach beet) is grown for its leaves, which may be eaten and which taste very like spinach. The mangel-wurzel is valuable for feeding cattle and sheep during the winter, for it can be kept from autumn until late spring.

Perhaps the most important type of beet is the sugar beet. This is a white root and from it more than half the supply of sugar in the world is made.

BEETHOVEN, Ludwig van (1770–1827). When people talk about Beethoven today they think of him as a composer of great music of all kinds, yet in his own time he was admired more because he was a wonderful pianist. People especially marvelled at his astonishing power of playing a piece of music on the piano at the same time as he was actually composing it in his head (this is called extemporization), but his written music was often too difficult for them to listen to and too hard for them to play. Through the course of time, however, he has come to be regarded as one of the greatest composers that has ever lived.

Beethoven was born at Bonn, a town on the River Rhine in Germany which is now the capital city of the German Federal Republic. His cruel and lazy father was a singer at the court of the Archbishop-Elector of Cologne. When the little boy Ludwig showed signs of being musical his father thought he might get rich quickly by showing off his son as an infant wonder, as the great composer Mozart had been when he was little. (There is a separate article about him.) At the age of four Ludwig was therefore locked into a room with a harpsichord and violin and told to practise, and at the age of eight he was also learning the organ. When he was 12 years old he was appointed to a post in the court theatre where his duty was to accompany the orchestra on the harpsichord. In this way, in spite of an unhappy childhood, he gained valuable experience in music and was already trying his hand at composing music himself.

The first important event of Beethoven's life was his visit to Vienna in 1787. There he met Mozart, who heard him play and said: "Pay attention to him; he will make a noise in the world some day." The visit to Vienna was cut short by the death of Beethoven's mother and he returned to Bonn. This time life became happier for him than it had been before. He met the von Breuning family, his first real friends, and Count Waldstein, who provided him with a piano and helped him in other ways.

Beethoven was now 18, stocky and rugged in appearance, ill-mannered, hot-tempered and obstinate. When he was not occupied in the court orchestra or with teaching he would go for long walks alone in the country, jotting down tunes that occurred to him in a little notebook, something which he did all his life. From these little notes he would work out the themes for his sonatas and symphonies. All his life he was a lonely and sad man, and although many stories are told of his love affairs he never married.

In 1792 Beethoven again left Bonn for Vienna to study composition with the composer Haydn. Haydn did not take much trouble with his pupil and the lessons ended when the master went to England in 1794. Beethoven then studied with J. G. Albrechtsberger, a strict teacher who could not understand his pupil's rebellious nature.

On this second visit to Vienna everything at first went well. Beethoven was successful both as a pianist and as a composer, playing his own music at the court and at other important concerts, teaching many of the nobility and having new works published all the time. The Prince and Princess Lichnowsky provided him with money. However, he was always quarrelling, having difficulty over his servants and his lodg-

Beethoven-Haus Bonn, Bodmer Collection
A miniature portrait of Beethoven at the age of 32.

ings and indulging in practical jokes.

It was at this time that Beethoven became deaf. He had already had trouble with his hearing, but by 1801 it was becoming more and more serious and in the end he could hear nothing at all. It was a terrible thing to happen to a musician—and yet it was after this that he wrote some of his most wonderful music—music which he never heard himself. Gradually he withdrew more and more into himself and his music; his behaviour, too, grew more strange and difficult when he could no longer enjoy other people's company. At the first performance of his ninth symphony in 1824 he was so completely deaf that a friend had to turn him round to see the thunderous applause for his music. He remained in Vienna until his death at the age of 57.

Beethoven's Music

Before Beethoven's time the music of great composers like Haydn and Mozart was graceful and delicate, full of beautiful and charming tunes and perfectly planned. Beethoven's music was stronger and more romantic, full of personal feelings; it could express the most unbearable sadness, or joy and delight, or even laughter, as the composer wished. This seemed like a revolution in music at the time and was one of the reasons why people did not altogether realize Beethoven's greatness during his lifetime. His own strong and stubborn character comes out in his vigorous music.

He was chiefly a composer of music to be played on instruments rather than to be sung, although he did write choral masses and an opera called *Fidelio*, and the last movement of his ninth symphony is choral. His greatest works are his nine symphonies and 17 string quartets (pieces for four players). Musicians think of the nine symphonies of Beethoven in the same way as writers think of the plays of Shakespeare : they are among the greatest works of music.

Beethoven also wrote several overtures, five piano concertos and one violin concerto, 32 piano sonatas and a great deal of other music. (There are separate articles CHAMBER MUSIC; CHORAL MUSIC; CONCERTO; OPERA; OVERTURE; SONATA; SYMPHONY.)

BEETLE. Beetles are to be found in almost any place where animals exist, except in the sea. Something like 250,000 different species, or kinds, have been discovered in the world, of which about 4,000 have been found in Great Britain.

They are very easy insects to recognize, though they are all sorts of shapes and may be as small as a pin's head or as big as a man's fist. True beetles have the scientific name of Coleoptera, which means sheath-winged, and they all have one thing in common : what should be the front pair of wings are not wings at all, but thick, usually tight-fitting sheaths, or covers (called *elytra*), which completely cover the real pair of wings and so protect them. Only beetles have sheaths like this and they usually meet in a straight line down the middle of the back. Sometimes bugs are mistaken for beetles, but instead of the powerful biting jaws of beetles they have sharp-pointed beaks through which they suck their food. (See BUG.)

When a beetle flies, it lifts up its wing covers and then spreads out the wide, thin wings behind them. All beetles were, at one time, flying insects but many of them, like the common ground beetles, have given up flying and depend on their six legs for travelling about.

Although most beetles have eyes with which they can quickly see approaching danger, their most useful organs (parts of their bodies) are those with which they smell. These are chiefly contained in the antennae, called feelers by most people, and help them to find their food and recognize others of their own kind. However, there is little doubt that male and female fireflies and glow-worms, which are beetles in spite of their names, find each other partly by means of their lights. (See the article FIREFLY AND GLOW-WORM.)

Many beetles can make chirping or squealing sounds by rubbing one part of the body against another. Often this is done by scraping the legs over very fine close ridges on another part of the body, rather as a bow is used to scrape the strings of a violin. This noise is called stridulation. The deathwatch beetle makes a tapping noise by banging with its head, usually against wood. (See DEATHWATCH BEETLE.)

In one respect beetles are like bees and wasps, butterflies and moths. They are not born as little beetles which grow gradually into large ones, but instead start as eggs from which larvae, or grubs, hatch. These spend all their time eating and as they grow they keep on shedding their skins, which become too tight for them, until eventually they turn into pupae. In this stage, like the chrysalises of butterflies, they rest and when they hatch out they are fully grown beetles.

Most beetles are careful to lay their eggs where the larvae will find plenty of food. This is not difficult, for most of them feed on leaves, flowers, stems and roots of plants and even the wood of trees.

Some, however, have to go to much more trouble. The dung beetles make burrows beneath cow dung and stock the holes with dung for the larvae to feed on. The scarabs, once the sacred beetles of Egypt, first make balls of manure and then pull and push these balls into holes they have already prepared, after which they lay their eggs on top of them. (See SCARAB.) Burying beetles have much the same habit;

underneath small dead animals they make a pit into which they pull the carcase and on this they lay their eggs so that their grubs can feed as soon as they hatch. All these kinds lay only a few eggs because the food for their offspring is plentiful and they are all likely to survive.

The blister beetles and the oil beetles go to the other extreme and may lay as many as 10,000 eggs. Each tiny grub that hatches needs to feed first on the egg of a bee and then on honey and pollen. To reach the bee's nest it lies in wait for a bee visiting a flower. It then fastens itself to the insect's hairy body and so gets carried to the hive. No wonder these beetles have to lay so many eggs; it is surprising that even one in a thousand should find the right kind of flower and the right kind of bee.

Beetles that are Harmful

One of the most destructive beetles is the Colorado beetle which, having been brought across the Atlantic from North America by accident, has become a terrible pest on potatoes in Europe also. Both the beetle itself and its grub eat the leaves, stems and even sometimes the roots of potato plants. (See COLORADO BEETLE.) The Colorado is one of a very large family of beetles which feed on plants. The family includes the pretty little asparagus beetle, another pest, and also the tiny but troublesome flea beetles which eat the leaves of cabbages, turnips and other plants, often killing them when they are small. If it is disturbed it hops off the plant just like a flea.

Much bigger than this are the handsome long-horned beetles, whose "horns" are really antennae. The grubs of these beetles burrow into the wood of trees and often take years to grow up, so that they may not come out of the wood until it has been made into timber and used in houses and elsewhere. The bark beetles, which look just like the bark of the trees they live on, are among others that cause serious damage to valuable timber.

Although most weevils are quite harmless (see WEEVIL) there are quite a number which cause serious trouble by attacking corn, rice, cotton, palms, nuts and so on. In the old days they were often found in ship's biscuits. Among the harmful beetles which live in the house are the carpet beetle and the furniture beetle. Carpet beetles are pretty little oval insects and it is their larvae that do most of the damage to carpets and clothes as well. The furniture beetle, a relation of the notorious deathwatch beetle which causes such damage to the woodwork of old churches, lays its eggs in cracks or crevices of the furniture. When they hatch, the grubs may then turn the woodwork to mere powder inside. When nearly full fed the grubs bore their way outwards until they are just below the surface of the wood, so that when they turn into beetles they can escape easily through the holes known as "worm-holes". The so-called woodworm is in fact the grub of the furniture beetle.

The mealworm is really the grub of a beetle and so is the wire-worm, which is cursed by the farmer and the gardener in many parts of the world, for it lives in the soil and feeds on the roots of plants. Wireworms are sometimes found in such numbers that they do very great damage to corn and other crops. They turn into the rather attractive click-beetles, named from their habit of jumping into the air with a snap when they have fallen on their backs. Buprestid beetles, which are big brothers of the click-beetles and have no English name, live mostly in very hot countries and some are destructive to timber.

TIGER BEETLE (MALE)

LARVA

PUPA

The larva of the tiger beetle lives in a burrow. It lies in wait to catch and eat other insects that walk over it.

(1) Lady-bird. (2) Soldier beetle. (3) Cockchafer. (4) Burying beetle. (5) Bombardier beetle. (6) Goliath beetle from West Africa, showing its size compared with that of a lady-bird. (7) Tiger beetle. (8) Musk beetles. (9) Devil's coach-horse. (10) *Gymnopleurus sinuatus*. This beetle from Assam is related to the sacred scarab beetles of Egypt.

Nearly all of them are brightly coloured and many are so highly polished that they look like metal. For this reason, and because they are very tough, the natives of South America use them as ornaments.

Cockchafers are also a great pest in many cases, for their grubs feed on the roots of crops, the beetles into which they change feeding on the leaves of fruit trees and other kinds of tree. (See COCKCHAFER.) The Maybug, or June-bug, which is a cockchafer beetle in spite of its name, sometimes does great damage to the roots of strawberry plants.

Harmless and Helpful Beetles

After describing so many of the beetles which do harm it is only fair to state that most beetles are harmless and some actually helpful to man. The well-known ladybirds, which are also beetles and on which there is a separate article, are often very useful, for many of them eat huge numbers of the harmful greenflies (see APHID) and scale insects (see SCALE INSECT). Some ladybirds are so useful in this way that they have been taken from one country to another to help control these pests.

A great many beetles live by scavenging the useless rubbish that collects in houses, hedges, old tree stumps, birds' nests and similar places. Among these are many of the rove beetles which are very easily recognized, for they are narrow and their wing cases cover only about half their bodies. Most are very small, but the devil's coach horse, the best-known British species, is about an inch long and always cocks its tail up over its head when frightened. Other beetles, such as the burying beetles mentioned earlier, are useful in helping to clear away dead animals.

Among the most active species are the brightly coloured tiger beetles that may be found in hot, sandy places, flying about very actively in the sun. The grub lives in a tube-like burrow in the ground, lying in wait with its head sticking out over the top, to seize and eat other insects that walk over it. Ground beetles are very similar and might be called hunting beetles because, both as grubs and as beetles, they spend their time searching out other small creatures to eat. One of them has been taken from Europe to North America where it does good work by eating caterpillars of the harmful gypsy and brown-tail moths. The largest ground beetles are about two inches long and the smallest is only a little bigger than a pin's head. The smaller ones live amongst rotting leaf-mould, under stones and in caves, often being quite blind. When frightened some of them squirt out a nasty-smelling liquid from the end of the body; one in Great Britain, called the bombardier, sends out a liquid which explodes into a small amount of poison gas, under cover of which it runs away.

Water beetles form another very large group. They are all of the same rounded, "stream-lined" shape and propel themselves through or over the water with their hairy hind legs, which act like oars. The middle pair of legs is generally used for clinging to weeds and the front pair for seizing the beetle's prey, which may be an insect or even a large creature such as a tadpole or a small minnow. Other water beetles feed on plants, however. All water beetles have to come to the surface for air from time to time and often they leave the water and fly long distances to other ponds and streams.

Male stagbeetles have great jaws which look like antlers (see STAGBEETLE). They sometimes frighten people but in fact the jaws are not of much use for biting. In hot countries stagbeetles are common and it is there, too, that their cousins the Hercules and Goliath beetles live. These are amongst the biggest of all insects, as big as a man's fist and very hard and tough. It is not always the jaws which grow into "antlers"; sometimes other parts of the head or of the thorax (the part just behind the head) grow horns.

Many more beetles will no doubt be discovered in the world. There is much still to be learnt even about those known already.

BEETON, Mrs. Isabella Mary (1836–1865).

If you hear someone mention the name "Mrs. Beeton" you can be fairly sure that the person is talking about cooking. This is because Mrs. Beeton wrote a famous book about cooking and looking after a house.

The title of this book is *Household Management*. It took Mrs. Beeton four years to write it,

Radio Times Hulton Picture Library

A French kitchen of the 19th century. This was one of the pictures in Mrs. Beeton's book *Household Management*.

and although it was published about 100 years ago it is still used by housewives today. It contains hundreds of recipes all of which Mrs. Beeton is said to have tested herself. Here is one of them, for Farmer's Fruit Cake.

Ingredients. Take 1 cup of dried sour apples, 1 cup of golden syrup, 1 cup of sugar, ⅓ cup of butter, ½ cup of sour milk, 1 teaspoonful of soda, 2 teaspoonfuls of cinnamon, 1 teaspoonful of cloves, 1 egg, 2 cups of flour.

Mode. Chop the apples fine, and soak overnight; in the morning let them simmer for two hours with the syrup. Prepare the other ingredients as for any cake, beating well, adding the apple and syrup when a little cool, not cold. Bake in tins in a moderate oven.

Time. ½ to ¾ hour. *Average cost,* 10d.

Seasonable at any time.

People sometimes make jokes about Mrs. Beeton's recipes, saying that they start with a sentence like "Take a dozen eggs . . ." or "Take a pint of cream . . ." but it should be remembered that Mrs. Beeton wrote her book for large Victorian families which included servants, so the joints, cakes and other dishes had to be large enough to feed a good many people. In fact, Mrs. Beeton wanted her book to be really useful to people in running their houses well without being extravagant, and at the end of each recipe she put the approximate cost of the dish. Today

there are many labour-saving machines, like gas and electric cookers and refrigerators, that were not invented in Mrs. Beeton's time, but even though life is different now, many cooks still consider that her recipes are the best of all.

As well as cookery, *Household Management* gave information about such things as the duties of the housekeeper and other servants, the arrangement of the kitchen, table decoration and the management of the nursery and the sick-room.

Mrs. Beeton's maiden name was Isabella Mayson. She was born in the City of London and she married Samuel Beeton, a Fleet Street publisher, when she was 20 years old. She was interested in many things besides housekeeping—she was a clever musician, for instance. She also studied the fashions of her day, and invented probably the first paper patterns to be used for dressmaking at home. When making these patterns she used her own clothes, which she bought in Paris, as a guide.

She died, leaving a family of four children, when she was only 29 years old.

BEIRUT is the capital and chief seaport of the republic of the Lebanon, at the eastern end of the Mediterranean Sea. The town lies on a pro-

Camera Press Ltd.

The entrance to the Jewellery Market in Beirut. The shop signs are written in two or even three languages.

montory just south of St. George's Bay, where the saint is supposed to have slain the dragon.

Beirut first achieved fame under the Romans in the 3rd century A.D. when the chief school of Roman law was set up there. In 551, however, an earthquake destroyed the town and it never returned to its previous splendour. It revived a little under the crusaders in the 12th century, but it was not until the 14th century that it started to be a prosperous seaport. Even then the town did not grow very much until late in the 19th century, when French companies built the harbour and the railway to Damascus. French is the second language, after Arabic, and there are three universities, including a big American one. Beirut is the chief centre of trade and banking in the Middle East, with a busy harbour and an international airport. Many visitors come to the holiday resorts in the beautiful Lebanon Mountains, which rise steeply behind the town. The population is about 300,000.

BELFAST is the capital city of Northern Ireland and a great seaport, lying at the point where the River Lagan joins the arm of the sea known as Belfast Lough. It is the chief industrial centre of Northern Ireland.

Like London and many other cities, Belfast was founded at a point where a river could be forded, or crossed by wading. It was founded by Sir Arthur Chichester, then chief governor of Ireland, at the beginning of the 17th century. The centre of the city is low-lying, but it is surrounded by hills.

Although during the English Civil War Belfast was in 1648 occupied by Cromwell's forces under George Monck, it has had a fairly peaceful history. It was quite a small town until the end of the 18th century, but then grew rapidly. It first became industrialized by the establishment of cotton mills, but this industry died out when the American Civil War cut supplies of raw cotton. Belfast next became one of the world's chief centres of linen manufacture, and nowadays it is also a centre of the synthetic textile industries. (See SYNTHETICS.)

Belfast is also a great shipbuilding centre. The first ship to be launched there was the "Eagle's Wing", built in 1636 for some Presbyterians who wished to emigrate to America.

Crown Copyright Reserved

Belfast's huge city hall was built in 1906. The architect followed the Renaissance style used by Wren for St. Paul's.

Small shipbuilding yards were at work in Belfast at the close of the 18th century. In 1847 the River Lagan was deepened by dredging, and in 1858 was founded the great firm of Harland and Wolff, which in time grew to be the largest shipbuilding establishment in the world. It built a long succession of passenger liners and, later, aircraft carriers and other warships. More recently, the shipyard has launched tankers and bulk carriers, including some of the world's largest.

As well as textile factories and shipyards, Belfast has engineering works, a large aircraft factory, chemical, tobacco and clothing factories, one of the biggest ropeworks in the world, iron foundries and a large industry making mineral waters and soft drinks. Ginger ale was invented in Belfast. It was in Belfast, too, that John Boyd Dunlop invented the pneumatic tyre. (See TYRE.)

Belfast is also the chief transport and commercial centre of Northern Ireland. Much of Ulster's trade passes through the city, including many of the products of a big farming industry. Belfast Harbour, with its network of basins and channels, has ten miles of waterfront and occupies nearly four square miles. Regular shipping services link Belfast with ports in Britain and many other parts of the world. The civil airport at Aldergrove, about 13 miles west of Belfast near Lough Neagh, is one of the busiest in the United Kingdom. The city has three railway stations and several bus stations.

A ring road about half a mile from the centre of Belfast links it with motorways to various parts of Northern Ireland, including the M1 motorway leading southwest to Lisburn and Craigavon. There is much attractive countryside near by and several seaside resorts are quite close to Belfast. The city has some fine public parks. Three of these extend along the slopes of Cave Hill (1,188 feet) and give wide views over the sea to Scotland and sometimes as far as the Isle of Man. Three more large parks extend up the valley of the Lagan.

As the capital city, Belfast is also the seat of the Government of Northern Ireland. (See IRELAND, NORTHERN.) The Parliament House is at Stormont on a hill east of the city. Its grounds form another big public park.

The Ulster Museum and Art Gallery is situated beside the Botanic Gardens Park and the Queen's University. There are some fine modern churches, including the Anglican Cathedral of St. Anne, and a handsome city hall.

The population of Belfast is about 399,000. Planning and redevelopment in the 1960s actually reduced the population of the county borough of Belfast by causing people to move out of the central part of the city area. Many of them moved to Newtownabbey, Castlereagh and Holywood, a ring of growing districts around Belfast. Together with these districts, Belfast includes more than one-third of the population of Northern Ireland.

BELFRY. The part of a building where bells are hung is called a belfry, but the word does not come from "bell". It means a tower, and at one time a belfry was a movable wooden tower which was used by armies besieging a town.

Left: An Anglo-Saxon tower, now a belfry, at Sompting, Sussex. Right: The home of Bow Bells, St. Mary-le-Bow in Cheapside, London. This is one of the City churches built by Sir Christopher Wren. The bells came crashing down when the church was bombed in World War II.

Later it came to mean a tower built specially to contain bells, or the room at the top of a church tower where the bells are kept.

Bells are hung high up so that their sound can carry well, and for the same reason belfry windows have no glass in them. Instead, across the window spaces, there are boards called louvers which are placed a little way apart and sloping downwards and outwards. This means that the sound of the bells is sent downwards through the spaces and rain is kept out. Until wire netting was invented and could be put over the windows bats and birds used often to be found in belfries. This is where the saying "bats in the belfry" came from.

In northern Italy a belfry is called a campanile. It is a tall tower which often stands beside the church, but is not joined to it. One of the most famous of these is the Leaning Tower of Pisa, which was built in the 12th century.

The articles BELL and BELL-CASTING describe how bells are rung and how they are made.

BELGIUM. Wedged in between France on the southwest, Germany and Luxembourg on the east and the Netherlands on the north, with only a short coast on the North Sea, the little country of Belgium has suffered terribly as a battleground during wars among its powerful neighbours. That is why it used to be known as "the cockpit of Europe", the name being taken from the pits in which cockfighting was once held. In peacetime, however, such a central position has advantages for trade and business and Belgium has become one of the most heavily industrialized nations on the continent of Europe. It is also one of the most thickly populated.

Three rivers, all rising in France, form the main branches of a complicated system of waterways, including canals. The Scheldt helps to water the flat plain of Flanders in western Belgium and then flows on through a corner of the Netherlands to the North Sea. Entering Belgium halfway along the border with France, the Sambre flows through a hilly coal area to join the Meuse at Namur. The Meuse itself follows a northeasterly course through wild and beautiful country, passes Liège and further on becomes part of the boundary with the Nether-

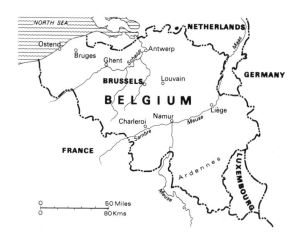

lands where that country juts southwards.

South of the Meuse are the Ardennes Hills and there the countryside is very like the neighbouring part of Germany, with woods, bogs and moors. The climate is dry and often cold instead of rainy as it is in Flanders. On the northwest the Belgians have been able to increase their grazing land by reclaiming a strip from the sea, just as the Dutch have done further along the coast. Between this reclaimed land and the sea is a belt of carefully protected sand dunes, about a mile wide.

Agriculture and Industries

To supply enough food for the dense population every acre of the precious soil must be cultivated all through the season, so the Belgian is first of all a gardener, whether he uses the produce himself or sells it. He may work in a factory or a mine all day but when evening comes he probably goes by railway or tram to his home outside the town and tends a little plot of ground.

In the northern part of the fertile central plain the farmers grow oats, rye, flax and potatoes for export to other countries, while in the south their main crops are wheat and sugar beet. The region near Brussels, the capital, is famous for its hot-house grapes. A large number of cattle and pigs and a great many chickens are raised in the country. One way and another Belgium obtains more agricultural products from each acre of land than almost any other country.

Although farming is so important, however, it is the coal deposits which have led to Belgium's chief wealth. The main coal belt lies towards the south where limited quantities of other minerals are found, such as iron, zinc, lead and copper. These supplies of raw materials, combined with Belgium's central situation in Europe, have encouraged the setting up of steel and glass works, sugar refineries, woollen and cotton mills and industries producing machines and chemicals. These are spread all over the country, with the main centres at Liège in the south and the ports of Antwerp and Ghent in the north. In the past, Belgian industry was greatly helped by supplies of zinc, copper and other raw materials which it obtained from what was then the Belgian Congo. For the size of her population, Belgium is one of the leading exporters of industrial products in the world.

Cities and People

Side by side with all the industrial activity, Belgium preserves in its cities the beauty and charm of the middle ages. Brussels and the great port of Antwerp, on both of which there are separate articles, together with Ghent, Louvain, Malines, Bruges, Ypres and Tournai were all built between the 13th and 16th centuries. Old gabled houses with red roofs line the clean, tree-bordered streets and often the carved house fronts are reflected in the clear waters of the canals that wind through the cities. Some of the mediaeval fortifications still remain and there are many beautiful Gothic town halls with tall belfries. The cathedrals with their famous carillons, or chimes of bells, contain paintings by the Flemish masters Hubert and Jan van Eyck, Peter Paul Rubens and Anthony van Dyck.

Much in Belgium's everyday life is picturesque. The country is famous for its many colourful carnivals. In the older parts of some of its cities, the women still sit outside in their white lace caps making the lace for which Malines, and in particular Brussels, have long been noted. Passers-by stop to admire the deftness of their fingers as they manipulate the dozens of bobbins, or spools, which carry the linen thread.

On the canals, barges float along carrying crowds of holiday-makers, while Ostend, which is a favourite holiday resort, looks from the sea as if it were composed entirely of glittering hotels and casinos (places where music and dancing and, sometimes, gambling are the amusements).

There are universities at Brussels, Louvain, Ghent and Liège, the last two belonging to the state. Primary schools and many secondary schools are also maintained by the state.

Although most of Belgium is Roman Catholic the people are free to choose their own religion. The country has two languages. In the northern parts Flemish is spoken—of all foreign tongues it is the most like English and anyone who speaks English can recognize many of the words. The fair-headed Flemings are much like the Dutch. (See the article FLEMINGS.) In the south French, and in some parts Walloon, a dialect of French, is spoken and the dark Walloon people are very like their French neighbours. (See the article WALLOONS.)

Early Belgian History

The earliest mention of the Belgians is that made by Julius Caesar in his account of his campaigns. Beginning in 57 B.C., it took him seven years to conquer these people, whom he called "the bravest of the peoples of Gaul". In the 4th century A.D. the Franks, crossing the Rhine from Germany, practically controlled the Belgians, and when Charlemagne was the Frankish emperor in the 8th century (see CHARLEMAGNE) they came under his rule and were converted to Christianity. Travellers between Aachen, Charlemagne's capital in Germany, and France, had to pass through Belgium and it soon became

FACTS ABOUT BELGIUM

AREA: 30,513 square kilometres.
POPULATION: 9,690,991.
KIND OF COUNTRY: Self-governing kingdom.
CAPITAL: Brussels.
GEOGRAPHICAL FEATURES: The country is a plain rising gently towards the southeast, the highest level being the plateau of Botrange (690 metres).
CHIEF PRODUCTS: Coal, iron, copper, zinc, lead, grain, sugar beet, hops, cattle, pigs and horses.
LEADING INDUSTRIES: Steel, machinery, glass, textiles, leather, carpets, diamond cutting, chemicals, food.
IMPORTANT TOWNS: Brussels, Antwerp (chief port), Liège, Charleroi, Ghent, Namur, Bruges.
EDUCATION: Children must attend school between the ages of 6 and 15.

the central market place of the vast Frankish empire.

In those days nobody spoke of Belgium, because Holland, Belgium and French Flanders made up what were called the Low Countries,

Courtesy, Belgian Embassy, London

The belfry at Bruges is famous for its chime of bells.

which were not much above sea level anywhere and even below it in some places. During the Crusades the towns gained in wealth and importance and in the 11th and 12th centuries became fairly independent. Bruges, Ghent, Ypres and Louvain imported wool from England and wove cloth for all Europe, while ships from Bruges and Antwerp carried the rich trade of the northern seas.

In 1385 the Low Countries came under the powerful dukedom of Burgundy. The peaceful reign of Philip the Good was a golden age for art and architecture in Belgium but it was followed by oppression and revolt under Charles the Bold. The towns recovered their liberties under the rule of his daughter Mary but it was her marriage to Maximilian, Archduke of Austria, that led to the Low Countries first becoming the battleground of Europe, for Mary's son married a daughter of the King of Spain and thus both Spain and Austria had a claim to the land.

The Protestant teaching of Martin Luther and John Calvin, on whom there are separate articles, made great progress in the Low Countries in the 16th century. However, their followers suffered cruelly under the Spanish Inquisition (see INQUISITION) and when the people were preparing to revolt against their Roman Catholic rulers the Spanish king sent an army under the merciless Duke of Alva to suppress them. Holland fought for and won its independence, but what is now called Belgium remained under Spanish rule for another 70 years.

From 1701 to 1713 the country was the battleground of the general European war known as the War of the Spanish Succession and by the Treaty of Utrecht it was given to Austria. Then in 1792 the Austrians were defeated at Jemappes, in Belgium, by the French republican armies and Belgium became a province of France, sharing all the horrors and glories of the French Revolution until Napoleon's career came to an end at the Battle of Waterloo, also on Belgian territory, in 1815. Belgium was then united to Holland but in 1830 the people revolted and the Dutch were forced to retire.

A year later the Belgians chose Prince Leopold of Saxe-Coburg, a German, as their king and in 1839, by the Treaty of London, the great European powers recognized the independence of

Courtesy, Belgian Embassy, London

Metal-working is an important Belgian industry.

17

Courtesy, Belgian Embassy, London

Left: A Belgian lace-maker at work. The threads, wound on ivory bobbins, are braided together in a complicated pattern around the little pins set out on the pillow. Right: Digging up chicory, a vegetable which is used in salads.

Belgium and promised not to invade it in time of war. This was the treaty the Germans broke in 1914 when they invaded Belgium; their chancellor called it "a scrap of paper".

During the 19th century Belgium made great progress. Leopold II personally started the huge Congo Free State in central Africa; in 1908 this was taken over as a colony by the government and named the Belgian Congo. Belgium obtained great wealth from the Congo. Though it was a sparsely populated country, it contained great mineral wealth in the Katanga district in the southeast, and was also a source of rubber and ivory.

Two World Wars

So strong was the Belgian spirit of independence that when the Germans demanded that their troops be allowed to pass through the country in 1914, at the beginning of World War I, the Belgians refused. They were, of course, overwhelmed and for four years most of their country was under German control, suffering bitterly at the hands of the invaders.

After the Armistice of 1918 the Belgians enjoyed a period of peace and prosperity but in 1940 war struck them again, the German troops marching in without warning this time. Neither the Belgians nor their French and British allies could withstand the fury of the German onslaught and within 18 days King Leopold III had accepted the German terms of surrender. Belgium was conquered and once more at the mercy of the invader. Two regions given to Belgium after World War I were taken back into Germany and King Leopold was taken prisoner, but the government fled to London and carried on the struggle from there.

When World War II was over the Belgians, for the second time within a generation, had to restore their land after the damage and ravages of the fighting and the German occupation. The country had been ruthlessly used by the Germans for their own advantage, 140,000 workers had been deported to Germany and 18,000 people had been sent to the grim concentration camps because they resisted the Germans. However, the armies of liberation, helped by the Belgians' own resistance movement, advanced so rapidly that the Germans were given little time to destroy important industries and means of communication, and the Belgians were able to recover fairly quickly from the effects of the war. Progress was especially good in the chemical and metal industries.

Belgium joined a customs union (see CUSTOMS

AND EXCISE) with Luxembourg in 1922 and with the Netherlands in 1948. This union, called Benelux, meant that there were no trade barriers between the three countries even before they joined the European Economic Community, or Common Market. The Common Market headquarters are in Brussels and the military headquarters of the North Atlantic Treaty Organization (Nato) are at Casteau, near Mons.

Belgium has no overseas possessions nowadays. In 1960, the colony in Africa called the Belgian Congo became an independent state, now called Zaire. Two years later the Belgian trust territory (entrusted by the United Nations to Belgian rule) of Ruanda-Urundi became the two independent states of Rwanda and Burundi. (See BURUNDI; RWANDA; ZAIRE.)

BELGRADE used to be the capital of Serbia but since 1918 it has been the capital of Yugoslavia. It has a magnificent position on a spur of the Serbian Hills which juts northwards into the plains where the River Sava joins the Danube.

Belgrade is in a very important position for it guards the gateway from the Balkans to central Europe and throughout the ages armies have fought for possession of it. Founded by the Celts in the 3rd century B.C., it has been held by

Yugoslav Tourist Office
Buildings in the centre of Belgrade, decorated with flags and portraits for a Communist party congress.

Romans, Greeks, Huns, Bulgarians, Hungarians, Turks and Serbs. The Serbian name for the city is Beograd, meaning "White Fortress", but the Turks knew it as the "Home of the Wars of the Faith" and the Hungarians as the "Key to Christendom". The city was half-ruined by the Austrians in World War I and heavily bombed by German aircraft in World War II.

The old fortress, now ruined, stands at the extreme tip of the hill spur, where it ends in a cliff 60 metres high. The outworks have been levelled and made into a public garden from which there are magnificent views of the two rivers and of the great plains which stretch away to the north. Behind the park, on the ridge of the hill, is the old city with the main hotels and shops, and the old royal palace. The slopes fall steeply to crowded commercial and industrial areas beside the rivers. Several bridges across the Sava link the city with New Belgrade, developed since 1945, and a railway bridge spans the Danube. The modern buildings of New Belgrade include one huge block that houses the headquarters of the Yugoslav government and the Federal Assembly, or parliament. The airport also lies on this side of the Sava.

In 1918 Belgrade was still half Eastern in appearance, with mosques and bazaars like those of Turkey. The large new buildings which have replaced them are more European in style, less attractive, though tidier, than the old. Nevertheless, thanks to its situation Belgrade is still one of the most impressive cities of Europe. It is the chief river port of Yugoslavia and is served by many railways and main roads. Its population is about 1,083,500.

BELIZE, formerly known as British Honduras, is a small, thinly populated British colony, approaching independence, on the Caribbean (eastern) coast of Central America. It is bordered by Mexico and Guatemala. It should not be confused with the republic of Honduras, farther to the south. (See HONDURAS.)

The story of Belize is largely the story of its forests. After Christopher Columbus had discovered Central America at the end of the 15th century, the Spanish settled at various points but saw little to attract them in this particular

FACTS ABOUT BELIZE

AREA: 22,963 square kilometres.
POPULATION: 119,645.
CAPITAL: Belmopan.
KIND OF COUNTRY: Self-governing British colony.
GEOGRAPHICAL FEATURES: Low and swampy coastline; northern part of territory is flat but in the south there are mountains; many rivers; most of the country is forest land.
CHIEF EXPORTS: Timber, chicle gum (for chewing gum), citrus fruits, sugar and frozen seafoods.
EDUCATION: Children must attend school between the ages of 6 and 14.

Paul Popper

Houses in Belize stand on piles above the river. The logs on the bank are of mahogany for export.

stretch of coast. Not only was it fringed with islands and reefs, making navigation difficult, but the coast itself was swampy and overgrown with mangrove trees. However, it was just these things which first drew Englishmen there in the 17th century, for they could have wanted no better base for their struggle against Spanish control of the New World. The buccaneers found that, although there were countless stinging and biting insects, the land was more hospitable than it seemed, for the climate was quite pleasant and they could spend their spare time cutting a timber known as logwood in the forests.

From logwood valuable dyes (colouring matter) were made and soon settlements grew up specially to obtain it.

The most important of these settlements was at the mouth of a river which, in spite of rapids, provided a way to the forests of the interior. Both the settlement and the river became known as Belize. The Spanish attacked the settlements from time to time, in spite of treaties signed in Europe, and eventually there was a major attack on Belize in 1798 which the settlers repulsed.

After that the settlers were left alone and, as Spanish power in America grew less, neighbouring Mexico and Guatemala became independent countries. The frontiers with these were gradually settled but the agreement about the borders with Guatemala was never confirmed and in 1946 Guatemala claimed the whole territory. Great Britain offered to put the legal question to the International Court of Justice, but the offer was not accepted. The claim was later put before the United States but the problem remained unsolved.

Logwood is no longer sent abroad; instead the colony exports mahogany, cedar, pine, and cane sugar. Another important export obtained from a tree is chicle, from which chewing gum is made, although nowadays the manufacturers also use synthetic, or artificial, ingredients. Recently a valuable citrus fruit industry has been built up, and both fruit and juice are tinned for export. Nevertheless, the country has difficulty in paying its way and Great Britain has provided financial help, including aid for the new capital. Roads have been built to open up valuable agricultural land and the outlook is brighter, although much food still has to be imported, as do most manufactured goods.

About one-third of the people live in Belize

City, the largest city and formerly the capital. This low-lying city was largely destroyed by a hurricane and tidal wave in 1961, when work was begun on the new capital Belmopan, farther inland. Maya and Carib Indians live in the interior, where, although it is still partly unexplored, the remains of massive stone buildings have been found, showing that at one time the Maya Indians developed an important civilization. In Belize and elsewhere there are many descendants of the African slaves who were brought over to the early settlements. There has been considerable intermarriage between the races. English, Spanish and American Indian languages are spoken. Most of the schools are Roman Catholic.

BELL, Alexander Graham (1847–1922),

was famous for his invention of the telephone in 1874. He was born in Edinburgh where his father was a teacher of elocution. In 1870, having become ill with tuberculosis, Alexander emigrated with his family to Canada. In 1872, at Boston in the United States, he opened a school for training teachers of the deaf. The next year he became a professor at Boston University, studying the science of speech.

Much of his spare time was spent in trying to discover a way in which people could talk to each other over long distances. He realized that the actual sound waves of speech travelled only short distances even through a speaking-tube, or through string or wire stretched between two hollow vessels. He therefore experimented with the vibrations caused by sound and at last found that these could be sent from one place to another by using electric currents (see Sound).

Bell's telephone consisted of two similar instruments each having an electro-magnet (that is, a piece of iron made into a magnet by a wire carrying an electric current coiled round it) with a very thin sheet of iron called a diaphragm supported near it. The coils of the electro-magnets were connected to the line wires, joining the transmitter to the receiver. Speech waves caused the diaphragm to vibrate and the vibrations gave different currents to the coil. The currents flowing round the coil of the receiving instrument caused its diaphragm to vibrate in tune with the

transmitting diaphragm and so the sounds delivered to the receiver were heard coming from the transmitter. Bell's instrument is still used as a receiver, but not as a transmitter. The first complete sentence was transmitted in 1876.

Bell's telephone consisted of two instruments like this.

Bell made several other inventions. One was the photophone, which used a beam of light to carry speech over a short distance. Bell's graphophone—a kind of record player—in 1883 played the first records, made of wax. Later he experimented with kites, and worked with Glenn Curtiss, an American, to develop an aeroplane. In 1918 the world water-speed record was taken by a hydrofoil developed by Bell and the Canadian inventor Casey Baldwin. (See Hydrofoil.)

BELL. A bell is a circular piece of metal, held or fixed in the centre, which is made to vibrate and give a musical sound by being hit near the circumference, that is, the outside edge of the circle. (The article BELL-CASTING explains how bells are made.) The "bell shape" most people know has been developed to make it possible to vibrate this circle of metal by means of a clapper hung inside which hits the circumference as the bell is swung to and fro.

Church bells are designed like this and are fixed to wheels which are turned from below by means of long ropes. As the wheels revolve the bells swing and are sounded. There are two ways of sounding church bells—by chiming or by ringing. Chiming is a gentle method in which the wheel moves just enough for the clapper to hit the side of the bell. Ringing is a vigorous method in which the bell is swung full circle, starting from an upside down position. Bell-ringing, or campanology, is hard work and each bell requires a person to pull the rope.

Bells are tuned to different musical notes according to their size, the largest bells giving the deepest sounds. Thus the different bells in a church tower can be used to play simple tunes. Bells, however, have a special music of their own known as change-ringing, based on varying the order in which the bells are sounded according to a complicated plan. For example, three bells can be rung in six different orders, or changes—123, 132, 213, 231, 312 and 321—and a mathematician can work out that 12 bells can give 479,001,600 possible changes. Changes have been given various curious names such as "Bob Major", "Oxford Treble Bob" and "Grandsire Triple".

Another method of bell-ringing is practised in some countries, particularly in the Netherlands and Belgium. In many cities there, a large number of bells (sometimes as many as 70) are hung in a special tower and are played by means of a large keyboard and sometimes a pedalboard as well, rather like an organ. These are known as *carillons*. The *carilloneur* (carillon player) plays on these bells by pressing down the keys with his fist, protected by gloves—hard work compared with playing the piano. The most famous carillon is that at Bruges; there are also carillons at London, Perth, Bournville, Saltley and other places in the British Isles. There is a school for training *carilloneurs* at Malines in Belgium and carillon playing has been recognized by Birmingham University as a subject for a musical degree.

In an orchestra the sound of bells is imitated

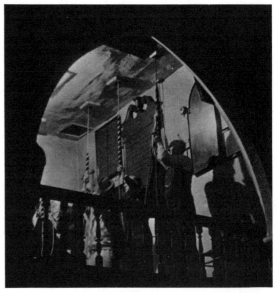

Radio Times Hulton Picture Library

Ringing the changes in an English parish church. There are said to be 10,000 peals of bells in England.

by metal tubes of different lengths hung on a stand and known as "tubular bells". Similar tubes are sometimes hung in church towers in place of true bells, particularly in America.

Bells in History

Bells are to be found all over the world and play an important part in most religions. Often they have also been important in history. In 1282 a peal of bells in Sicily gave the signal for a great massacre of Frenchmen known as the "Sicilian Vespers". (A massacre is the killing of many people.) Bells were again the signal for the massacre of the Protestant Huguenots in France on St. Bartholomew's Day in 1572. William the Conqueror ordered the curfew bells to sound at eight o'clock as a signal for putting out fires and

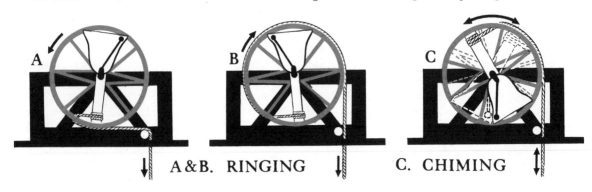

A&B. RINGING   C. CHIMING

the custom is still continued in some English towns although the law enforcing it was cancelled more than 800 years ago. (See CURFEW.)

In the United States the Liberty Bell, which hangs in Independence Hall, Philadelphia, in 1776 gave the signal for the war between the American colonies and their British rulers to begin. The Great Bell of Moscow, which was cast in 1733 and weighed 180 tons, was broken before it was ever rung, and was used instead as a chapel. Today the ringing of a special bell called the Lutine Bell at the headquarters of Lloyd's in London, the great insurance business, gives warning of important news—a ship has been lost or a missing ship found. In World War II it was planned to ring all the church bells in Great Britain if the country was invaded by the German armies.

BELL-CASTING.

For centuries bells have been used as messengers, calling people to church, warning towns or garrisons of danger and passing on glad tidings of victory. Much care has always been shown in making them and the well known bell-shape has always been used as it is the best shape for the purpose. The pitch, or note, depends upon the size and thickness of the metal and the tone upon the metal used. Bell metal is the name given to an alloy or combination of copper and tin in the proportion of four parts of copper to one part of tin, but in practice bells are commonly made with metal having a tin content of from 15% to 25%.

In casting a bell a core of loam sand is built round a framework of bricks and wood. This core is shaped by means of a "bell board" which rotates or spins about a central vertical post and is the shape of the inside of the bell. An iron moulding case is then taken and moulding sand and loam rammed into it to form the cope or outer case. The shape of the outside of the bell is then swept out in the cope in the same manner as was used for the core. Into this outside form may then be pressed any lettering or raised decoration that is required to appear on the outside of the bell. The cope is carefully placed over the core and the two are bolted together firmly, forming inside a space of exactly the same shape and size as the required bell. Molten bell metal is then poured into the mould, which stands with the bell-mouth downward.

After the metal has cooled the mould is broken up and the casting removed and cleaned. The pitch of the bell is then tested and, if necessary, a little of the metal is machined off the inside of the bell.

BELLINI, Giovanni (?1430–1516).

Between 1500 and 1800 the city of Venice produced so many great painters that they have been given a special name—the "Venetian School", typified by its portraits and rich scenes of processions and pagan subjects, painted in glowing colours, with a grandeur and nobility of design. The first of the great Venetians was Giovanni Bellini.

His father, Jacopo, had settled in Venice as a painter, and Giovanni and his brother Gentile, as young men, both assisted him in his work. The

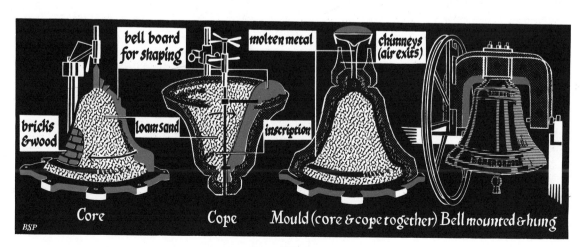

bricks & wood — bell board for shaping — loam sand — molten metal — inscription — chimneys (air exits)

Core — Cope — Mould (core & cope together) — Bell mounted & hung

BSP

Bellini's portrait of the Doge Loredan painted about 1501.

BENEDICT, Saint.

Benedict of Nursia laid down a rule or general plan for the lives of monks which was later followed in almost all the monasteries of Europe. Today there are still a great many Benedictine monasteries and convents in the Roman Catholic Church, and there is also the Order of St. Benedict in the Church of England. (See MONKS AND FRIARS.)

Of Benedict himself very little is known. He was born at Nursia in Italy in about A.D. 480 and was sent to be educated in Rome. However, Benedict was so horrified by the wickedness that he saw around him that he ran away, eventually coming to the ruins of one of the Emperor Nero's palaces at Subiaco, 40 miles from Rome. He made his home in a cave and ate food brought by a monk from a monastery near by.

Benedict spent three years alone in this cave, praying and eating only enough food to keep him alive. Seeing that he had given up everything to devote himself to God, the monks asked him to be their head.

Benedict consented and went to the monastery but the monks had grown so used to idleness and pleasure that they found him too severe, and it is said that they tried to murder him by putting poison in his cup. Before drinking, Benedict offered thanks to God and as he made the sign of the cross the cup upset, spilling the poison.

He returned to his cave, but still had many disciples, and in time he set up 12 monasteries in the neighbourhood of Subiaco, with 12 monks in each. Later he journeyed to Cassino, a town halfway between Rome and Naples. On the high mountain overlooking the town he built the great monastery of Monte Cassino, which became the centre from which his influence spread all over Europe.

It was probably in 529 that Benedict established what is known as the Rule of St. Benedict. The great difference between this rule and earlier ones was that the monks were taught that work and study have as much value in the eyes of God as a life of prayer. Between their services, Benedictine monks, wearing their black habits or robes, worked on the farms attached to the monasteries and in the vineyards, which became famous for their produce and orderliness. A fine liqueur (a kind of drink) first made by monks in

famous Andrea Mantegna married their sister, Nicolosia, and both Giovanni and Gentile were influenced by the harsh, probing nature of his paintings. Giovanni's early works are all of Christian subjects, and are full of religious intensity and pity for human suffering. Later his paintings became less pious and dramatic, and instead took on a noble serenity and splendour, and a greater warmth and charm.

Giovanni painted many frescoes for churches (see FRESCO). When his brother went to Constantinople at the Sultan's request, to paint pictures there, Giovanni became the chief painter in Venice.

In 1475 the new art of oil painting came to the city and Giovanni soon mastered its techniques, producing superb portraits of the doges of Venice. He had many pupils, and when he was over 80 he proved himself a rival to even the two most talented of them, Giorgione and Titian, by painting a magnificent pagan picture "The Feast of the Gods".

Normandy in the 16th century is still called Benedictine. Boys were, and still are, educated in the monasteries and much study and copying of manuscripts went on. An example of Benedictine learning is the *Ecclesiastical History* of the Venerable Bede, about the early English Church.

It is not known exactly when Benedict died, but it was probably in about the year 547. He had a sister, Scholastica, who is generally looked upon as having founded Benedictine convents.

BENGAL. At the mouth of the two great rivers Ganges and Brahmaputra lies the hot and steamy region of Bengal. The upper part is rich and fertile, but nearer the sea are vast, tiger-haunted mangrove swamps and dense forests known as the Sundarbans.

Bengal, once a kingdom larger than England and Wales, was a province under British rule. When India became independent in 1947 it was divided into two. West Bengal became a state of the Republic of India with its capital at Calcutta, while East Bengal, where about three-quarters of the population is Moslem, became a province of the new state of Pakistan. Its name was changed to East Pakistan with the capital at Dacca. East Pakistan became inde-

pendent as Bangladesh in 1971 (see BANGLA-DESH). It is a "land of rivers" which take the place of roads and is subject to floods. One in 1970, caused by a cyclone and tidal waves, resulted in enormous damage and perhaps 500,000 deaths—one of the worst natural disasters ever. Jute is grown here to be made into sacking. The chief product of West Bengal is rice.

The Bengalis have produced many scientists, writers and painters. The most famous is the poet Rabindranath Tagore, who was awarded the Nobel Prize for Literature in 1913.

BEN NEVIS is the highest mountain in Great Britain, rising 1,343 metres above sea level at the southern end of the Great Glen in Inverness-shire, Scotland. The top is not a peak but a plateau about 40 hectares in extent. An idea of the mountain's size can be seen from such a point as Corpach. From Corpach there is a magnificent view of the great precipices on the northern side of the mountain and there are glimpses of the snow which lies in the corries, or hollows, all the year round. There is a legend that the agreement by which certain land is leased, or hired out, in Glen Nevis is to last as long as snow lies on Ben Nevis, and folk in Fort

G. Douglas Bolton

Ben Nevis from Corpach, on the Caledonian Canal. At its base the mountain has a circumference of 40 kilometres.

William tell how in one very hot summer the remaining shreds of snow were protected by a tent.

By a remarkable piece of engineering a tunnel, 24 kilometres long and 4·6 metres wide, has been cut through Ben Nevis in order to bring water from Loch Treig to the aluminium works at the western foot of the mountain. The pipes carrying the water from the end of the tunnel to the turbines can be seen from the road which runs northward from Fort William.

BENTHAM, Jeremy (1748–1832).

The great service which Jeremy Bentham rendered to his age was to ask of everything, "What use is it?" This earned for him and his followers the title of "the Utilitarians" (utility means usefulness). It also helped him, when the Industrial Revolution was producing great changes in society (see INDUSTRIAL REVOLUTION), to reform many institutions and practices which were unreasonable and out of date.

At the age of 7 Bentham went to Westminster School, at 13 to Queen's College, Oxford, and before he was 16 he had taken a degree in law. Although he had been trained to practise as a lawyer, he quite soon turned his efforts to trying to reform both the law and the prison system. Between 1785 and 1788 he travelled in Russia with his brother Samuel. In France his reputation was so great that the Revolutionary assembly elected him a French citizen and in Spain his writings were printed at the public expense. In England he lived the life of a recluse, perfecting his philosophical theory that all human action, especially action by the government, should aim at the greatest happiness of the greatest number of people. He wrote many books and pamphlets.

Only gradually, and then largely through his disciples or followers, did his teachings bring practical results, but by the time of his death his influence was already great. He played an important part in sweeping away many stupid and brutal punishments, such as transportation to the colonies and imprisonment for debt, in getting rid of corrupt practices, in overhauling the law concerning paupers (very poor people without any means of getting a livelihood), in making the civil service more efficient and in hastening parliamentary reform. (The first great Reform Bill was passed in the year he died and others followed later.) In his will he directed that his body was to be dissected and his skeleton preserved (as it is to this day) in University College, London, which he had helped to found.

BEOWULF,

one of the oldest poems in the English language, tells of a powerful hero who alone, through physical strength, loyalty and courage, defeated evil and malevolent monsters. Though it was written probably 1,200 years ago the story goes back even further. Perhaps it was told among the Angles and Saxons before their arrival in England. A manuscript of the poem is in the British Museum. It begins at the court of Hrothgar, King of Denmark. He and his warriors would have been happy in their magnificent gold-roofed hall had it not been for the dreadful monster Grendel who came out of the lonely marshes near by. Every night for 12 years Grendel burst into the hall where the warriors were sleeping and dragged away one or more of them to devour; no one in Hrothgar's realm was strong or brave enough to tackle him.

Then at last Beowulf, who was the nephew of the King of the Geatas of Sweden, heard of Hrothgar's misery and came to Denmark with 14 chosen companions to help him. Hrothgar welcomed Beowulf with joy, but feared that even he would not be able to defeat Grendel. All evening the warriors drank and made merry together, but when night came fear fell on them at the thought of Grendel's coming.

Beowulf stood on guard waiting, and as usual Grendel came. Before the hero could do anything Grendel had seized and devoured one of his men. Then he came for Beowulf, and in the struggle between them Beowulf tore one of Grendel's arms right off. Howling and bleeding, the monster returned to the marshes to die.

The next night, however, Grendel's mother, an even more dreadful monster than her son, came to the hall seeking revenge, and carried off the king's chief counsellor. Beowulf followed her down to her lair at the bottom of a muddy lake. There was a terrible fight in which Beowulf was nearly killed, but in the end he slew the monster with a magic sword called Hrunting.

Some years later, when the King of the Geatas died, Beowulf succeeded him as king and reigned happily for 50 years. At the end of this time, however, a dragon appeared in his kingdom and began to destroy the land. Once more Beowulf took up his shield and sword and went out to challenge the monster. Beowulf, helped by his one faithful follower, managed to kill the dragon and so save his country, but in doing so he received such a terrible wound from the beast's poisoned fangs that he died.

BERING STRAIT. This is the narrow strip of water which separates the northeastern tip of Asia from the northwestern tip of America and so connects the Arctic Ocean with the Bering Sea and the Pacific.

Although America had been discovered by the end of the 15th century, it was not until about another 250 years had passed that people knew whether it was linked by land to Asia or formed a separate continent entirely surrounded by sea. Many believed that there must be a channel between the two continents making it possible to sail from the Pacific to the Arctic and thence to the Atlantic Ocean, and Russian explorers were among those who tried to find out whether this was so. By about 1697 they had reached Kamchatka in the far northeast of Siberia. Then in the early part of the 18th century Peter the Great (the Tsar of Russia) sent Vitus Bering, who was actually a Dane, to follow the coast northwards from Kamchatka and find out "where it joins with America". In 1728 Bering's expedition could find no such land link between the two continents. In 1741, with a second expedition, he found and followed the American coast northwards a little way but on the return journey his ship was wrecked and he himself died on a barren island which was named after him. His name was also given to the sea between the two continents and the narrow strait which joins this sea to the Arctic Ocean. Between them, these pieces of water do connect the Atlantic to the Pacific, although the ice and other difficulties prevent ships from using the route.

Bering Strait is only 90 kilometres across at its narrowest point. For many years Alaska, on the American side, was part of the Russian Empire,

but it was bought by the United States in 1867. The boundary between the two countries passes between the two Diomede Islands in the strait, so at this point there is only about a kilometre between American and Russian territory.

More important is the fact that the shortest air route from the United States to Japan passes over this region.

BERKSHIRE is an English county lying midway between London and the Bristol Channel. The River Thames forms the northern boundary line, running from near Faringdon in the northwest to Windsor in the southeast. Berkshire is a county whose boundaries will be greatly changed by the reorganization of local government. Its northwestern part will join Oxfordshire, but it will gain from Buckinghamshire an area including Slough. This article describes Berkshire as it exists up to 1974.

There are three distinct areas of Berkshire—the Forest, the Hill and the Vale, or valley. East of Reading is the Forest area, which used to be covered with woods where timber was obtained for shipbuilding. Today the woodlands are fewer but there is much scrub, or brushwood, and heathland. Through this area flow two rivers—the Loddon, once the western boundary of Windsor Forest, and the Blackwater. Two of Berkshire's most popular beauty spots, both controlled by the National Trust (see NATIONAL TRUST), are in this Forest area—Finchampstead Ridges, one of the stretches of sandy soil with heather and pine trees, and Maidenhead Thicket, once a favourite place for the highwaymen who preyed on travellers along the road to Bath and the West Country. In the Forest, too, is Ascot, famous for the horse races which began in the 18th century.

To the west of Reading is the old Hill division of the county, which includes the low-lying areas of the Kennet and Enborne valleys and also Inkpen Beacon, the highest point, in the far southwestern corner of Berkshire, and the rolling chalk downs. The White Horse, cut into the turf of the hill above Uffington some 2,000 years ago, is probably the oldest and largest of its kind in England (see WHITE HORSES) and appears to stand guard over the Vale, which spreads northwards from the slope of the Downs. Through this very fertile, and therefore well cultivated, area the River Ock flows to join the Thames at Abingdon. Here the landscape is flat and has a peaceful look, very different from the open-ness of the Downs and the wildness of the Forest.

With so many different levels and kinds of soil—water meadows and pastureland, sandy ridges and chalk downs—Berkshire has a wide variety of wild life. Fritillary plants can be found by the banks of the Thames and heather near Finchampstead and Ascot. The Kennet is well known for its trout and the Thames provides fishing of many kinds. The bird-watcher can find much of interest along the Thames and may still see stone curlews on the downs.

Industries and Towns

Sheep are still pastured on the Berkshire Downs, but far fewer than in the past; many of the downland slopes now produce rich crops of wheat and barley instead, as does the lower ground. Dairying concerns produce much butter, milk and cheese and a number of pigs are bred; the black Berkshire variety has white feet, arched back and a white mark on its forehead.

Until the middle of the 19th century Berkshire was almost entirely an agricultural county but after that there were many changes and new industries grew up. The centre of importance shifted from Abingdon, the county town since the 17th century, to Reading, for this was well placed on the road and rail routes. The gradual growth of London made east Berkshire into a place where people who worked in the capital liked to live or spend weekends and holidays. Maidenhead is a popular residential area as well as a starting point for boating and river holidays. Some of the old centres of activity have become quiet country towns, for the railways and important roads have passed them by—East Ilsley, once a great sheep centre, Wantage, and Wallingford, which, at the time of the Domesday Book, was more important than Reading.

Nearly one-quarter of the people of Berkshire now live in Reading, the present county town, which is famous for its biscuits and its seed raising grounds and has many other industries, such as boat-building beside the Thames and

Thames at Windsor

Ascot

stone curlew

black Berkshire pig

Harwell atomic research

white horse at Uffington

brewing. It has a university where many students study agriculture.

The most important new industry to come to Berkshire in recent times is nuclear energy. On the bushy heath at Aldermaston, close by the Hampshire border, is the Atomic Weapons Research Establishment and at the northern foot of the downs is Harwell, where scientists investigate the peaceful uses of nuclear energy.

Bracknell, once a small village, is now a new town containing the headquarters of the Meteorological Office. At Thatcham is one of the paper mills that were built on the rivers in the 19th century and at Aldermaston willows growing beside the Kennet provide wood for cricket bats. Didcot has a huge coal-fired power station and Abingdon, long famous for carpets and clothing, now produces motor cars. Wokingham is a quiet town which up to the 19th century was noted for silk weaving. At Newbury the Cloth Hall (now a museum) is one of the few reminders of the days when the town was important for the weaving of woollen cloth.

The Kennet and Avon Canal, built to link Bristol and the River Avon with London and the Thames, has been partially restored. It was neglected in the mid 19th century because of the building in about 1840 of the two main railway lines, one to the West Country and one to Wales. In 1874 an unusual steam tramway was built between Wantage and Wantage Road railway station, and it ran beside the road to Oxford; this tramway was used until 1946 and one of the old engines is now preserved in the railway station at Didcot. The Bath Road was first built properly in 1746. Its place as the route to the west has been taken by the M4 motorway through Maidenhead to Bristol and South Wales.

Some Berkshire History

Long ago, when much of England was marsh and forest, most people lived in such open, well-drained areas as the Berkshire Downs. One of the pleasantest ways of exploring these is to travel along the route known as the Ridgeway, on the spine of the Downs, which was made by these early people. On every hand is evidence that many people lived here—forts and earthworks of various kinds and many barrows, or burial places. (See BARROW.)

In Anglo-Saxon times Berkshire was part of the Kingdom of Wessex. Alfred, who was to become King of Wessex and later of all England, was born in A.D. 849 at Wantage, while it was on the Berkshire Downs that he won the Battle of Ashdown and so saved Wessex from the conquering Danes. In Saxon times, too, the Danes raided Reading and Wallingford. At Abingdon, in the 10th century, was founded what became one of England's greatest abbeys until it was suppressed by Henry VIII in 1538.

Near Windsor, King Edward the Confessor had a royal residence and at Windsor itself William the Conqueror built the first castle where the present castle stands. At Wallingford, then the chief town in the county, the Conqueror

built another castle which was besieged during the civil war between King Stephen and Queen Matilda, but it was pulled down in 1652.

In the days when Berkshire was noted for weaving, the most famous weaver of all was John Winchcombe, better known as Jack of Newbury. He is said to have taken a company of his weavers all the way to Flodden Field, in Northumberland, to help defeat a great Scottish army in 1513. At Cumnor Hall, just to the west of Oxford, in 1560 the Lady Amy Robsart, whose husband the Earl of Leicester wanted to marry Elizabeth I, died in mysterious circumstances; Sir Walter Scott used the story in his book *Kenilworth*. William Laud, later Archbishop of Canterbury and adviser of Charles I, was born at Reading in 1573. During the Civil War, Reading and Wallingford Castle were besieged and at Newbury two battles were fought between Roundheads and Royalists.

Famous men who lived later had more peaceful occupations. Alexander Pope the poet, for example, lived at Binfield in the early 18th century and a century later the poet Percy Bysshe Shelley lived nearby in Bracknell. Thomas Hughes, author of *Tom Brown's Schooldays*, lived as a boy at Uffington, also in the first part of the 19th century.

Riots broke out in the Hungerford area in 1830 when farm workers were afraid that new machines would throw them out of work.

The Royal Military Academy, where army officers are trained, has been at Sandhurst since early in the 19th century. At Pangbourne, on the Thames, is a nautical training college for boys which has its own fleet of boats, and once a year the parish of Remenham has a brief importance, for the races at Henley Royal Regatta start on the Berkshire side of the river by Remenham.

The old county hall at Abingdon, built by one of Sir Christopher Wren's master masons, is one of the finest public buildings in Berkshire, while the very wide St. Helen's Church, with its chapel ceiling painted in the middle ages, is one of the county's notable churches.

Near Maidenhead is the village of Bray, whose vicar in the 16th century changed his religion rather than be moved from his home and

29

so gave inspiration to the writer of the song called "The Vicar of Bray". Not far from the White Horse of Uffington is the spot known as Wayland's Smithy, where Weland, a swordsmith of German and Norse legend, is supposed to have had his forge; it is really a Stone Age burial place.

The royal borough of Windsor is famous for its castle, described in the article WINDSOR CASTLE. The town has many interesting sights including the town hall, completed in 1690 by the architect Sir Christopher Wren (who was once member of parliament for Windsor).

BERLIN is the largest German city and lies on the Rivers Spree and Havel, on a plain in eastern Germany. It used to be the capital of the whole of Germany but since World War II Germany has been divided into two and Berlin, which

Tourist Photo Library
Above: The fashionable Kurfürstendamm in West Berlin.
Below: The opera house, East Berlin.

suffered great wartime destruction, has lost a great deal of its importance. Much rebuilding has already been carried out, however.

Berlin probably started as a fishermen's settlement but the town was not built until the 13th century. Two hundred years later, when Germany was still a group of small independent states, the family of the Hohenzollerns established themselves as the rulers of the state of Brandenburg. Before long, they went to live in Berlin and made it their capital. In the Thirty Years' War (1618–1648) Berlin was practically destroyed and had to be rebuilt.

Berlin first became prosperous under Frederick William, who became ruler of Brandenburg in 1640. He developed the town into a city and built a canal to join the Spree and Oder Rivers, so that Berlin could trade with the Baltic Sea. Near the city he settled a number of French Huguenots who had fled from France, where they were being persecuted because of their Protestant religion, for France was a Roman Catholic country. They were hard-working, clever people and started some of the trades which were to be so important later. Frederick William's successor became the first king of Prussia, a much larger German state and the most powerful, of which Berlin then became the capital. (See PRUSSIA.)

When the separate states joined together in 1871, Berlin became the capital of the new German Empire and this made the city even more important. It grew very rapidly at the end of the 19th century and its population doubled between 1870 and 1890. The city was becoming the centre of a great web of railways and canals stretching in all directions. It was also a market centre to which barges carried wheat and rye and timber from Russia and Poland, while trains brought cattle and wool from central Europe. One canal joined Berlin to the River Elbe and the North Sea.

The city's own industries were also growing and among the things they made were railway engines, guns, electrical apparatus, chemicals, tools, cameras, sewing machines, bicycles and pens. When World War I broke out in 1914 Berlin was already Europe's third largest city.

Before World War II Berlin had many large

and imposing buildings. The royal palace, home of the last German Emperor William II, had more than 600 rooms, and the 19th-century cathedral was another grand building.

Berlin also had several fine museums and art galleries, and its zoo was one of the best in the world. Through the central park ran the Avenue of Victory, dominated by the 200-foot column of Victory and lined with statues of the Hohenzollern princes, kings and emperors who had ruled part or the whole of Germany until the end of World War I.

The busiest and most handsome street was *Unter den Linden*, which means "beneath the lime trees". This was one of the best-known avenues in the world, stretching nearly a mile from the royal palace to the Brandenburg Gate, a massive arch which was put up in 1784 and still stands. Along the avenue were the palaces of two earlier emperors, as well as the university, the opera house, luxury hotels and fine shops.

When the Nazis came to power in 1933, the Reichstag, or parliament building, was burnt down by the Communists. The Nazis built a magnificent sports stadium in western Berlin for the 1936 Olympic Games, and linked the city with other parts of Germany by *Autobahnen*, or motorways.

The Effect of World War II

During World War II much of the city was damaged by British and American bombs and when the Russians captured it in 1945, in desperate fighting, their guns caused more destruction.

Roughly one acre in every seven was ruined in the war and in some streets hardly a building, shop or house was left undamaged. The Chancellery was gutted by fire. (It was in a bunker, or air-raid shelter, of the Chancellery that Adolf Hitler committed suicide.) Almost every famous building was ruined and many of the factories destroyed. In one place the Germans were able to build a mound over 200 feet high after the war, making it of rubble from the ruins. Berlin lost much of its trade and its population is about 3,255,000 compared with 4,300,000 in 1939.

In 1945 Berlin was divided into four sectors —British, American, French and Russian. After the "Cold War" began in 1948 the Russian sector (East Berlin) was split from the other three and put under a separate City Council and Lord Mayor. East Berlin is now regarded as the capital of the German Democratic Republic (East Germany). West Berlin is treated almost as a part of the German Federal Republic (West Germany) but is separated from it by a 100-mile broad strip of East German territory. West Berlin still has garrisons of British, American and French troops.

In 1948 the Russians tried to obtain control of the whole of Berlin by stopping the trains, lorries and barges bringing supplies from the west. This Berlin blockade was broken by the American and British air forces which brought in food, coal and raw materials for the factories in the western part of the city. The airlift, as it was called, went on day by day for about a year, until the Russians allowed normal traffic to start again.

West Berlin suffered from the fact that many factories, banks and business firms moved to the Federal Republic. But gradually it regained its position as an artistic centre, with festivals of music and plays and many exhibitions. A new university was built in the western sector and the war-damaged buildings were rebuilt.

In August 1961 the East Berlin authorities put up barriers along the boundary with West Berlin. Later they built a wall along the boundary so that the two parts were completely separated. This was chiefly to prevent people leaving the Democratic Republic by going to West Berlin, as about 1,500,000 had done since 1949.

The most important industry in West Berlin is the production of machinery (especially electrical machinery). Other products include clothes, foodstuffs and chemicals. Coal, steel, materials and food are the chief imports. The links with the Federal Republic are three air corridors, three railways and three roads leading to Hamburg, Hanover and Frankfurt am Main. The railway to Hanover is the only one that may be used for goods, although goods traffic may also use the Mittelland Canal.

West Berlin can never have the importance it had as the capital of undivided Germany. Because it is isolated in the middle of East Germany, West Berlin gets a very large grant of money every year from the Federal Government. As a result it is reasonably busy and prosperous. The Kurfürstendamm, which is the main shopping street, is one of Europe's most glittering and luxurious thoroughfares. The West Berliners, living in a city ringed by walls and barbed wire, have felt rather shut in. Restrictions on travel from East to West, once very strict, have been eased, however, and talks between East and West on the future of Berlin have led to a lessening of tension.

Widespread rebuilding has been undertaken in both east and western parts of the city, improving its appearance and the general way of life of all Berliners.

BERLIOZ, Hector (1803–1869).

The composer Hector Berlioz was born in southeastern France, the son of a country doctor. He taught himself a great deal about music and composing while he was still a child. Later in Paris, and very much against his father's wishes, Berlioz gave up his medical studies and became a music student at the famous Paris Conservatoire. In 1830 he completed the *Symphonie Fantastique*, still his most popular work. It describes in music Berlioz' own life and his love for the Irish actress Harriet Smithson, who had come to Paris to act in Shakespeare's plays. Berlioz later married Harriet Smithson but the marriage was not a happy one.

In 1830 Berlioz won the *Prix de Rome* which enabled him to live and study in Italy. He wandered about the countryside with his guitar, making friends with bandits and peasants, but after 18 months he returned to France. Berlioz continued to write music but the Parisians did not really like it or understand what he was trying to do. His opera *Benvenuto Cellini* was a failure at the Paris Opera but his orchestral works were more popular and the great violinist Paganini was overwhelmed by the symphony *Harold in Italy*.

Berlioz was greatly attached to Shakespeare's plays and they inspired a number of his own works such as *Romeo and Juliet* and *Beatrice and Benedict*. He admired Beethoven, whose achievements in using the orchestra he continued. Sometimes Berlioz used a huge orchestra and in the Requiem Mass he brought in four brass bands. A "romantic" composer, Berlioz liked to work on a huge scale and used all the different sounds of the instruments to express feelings, ideas and strong contrasts. His music bubbles with exciting sounds and delightful melodies but some people are put off by the changes and irregular musical forms he often used. To make his music more popular and to make orchestras used to playing it, Berlioz spent much of his later life travelling throughout Europe as a conductor. His music has become better understood in the 20th century and nowadays some opera houses perform his massive opera *The Trojans*, about Dido and Aeneas.

BERMUDA is a British colony in the North Atlantic, about 1,200 kilometres southeast of New York, and it consists of about 300 small coral islands known as the Bermudas. The colony is fortunate, not only in the natural beauty of its lagoons (salt water lakes), which are ideal for bathing, yachting and fishing, but also in its climate which is sunny all the year round and yet never becomes oppressively hot. Being near the coast of the United States the delights of Bermuda are within easy reach of American and Canadian holiday-makers, many of whom come by air.

The chief islands, long and narrow in shape, are linked by bridges and raised roads called causeways. In the centre of the biggest island is

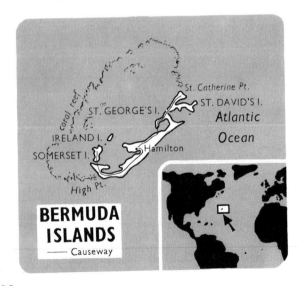

BERMUDA ISLANDS
—— Causeway

the capital, Hamilton, which has an excellent natural harbour. This island accounts for two-thirds of the area of all the islands, which is only 53 square kilometres. People often think of Bermuda as being in the West Indies but in fact the nearest West Indian island is 1,300 kilometres away and Bermudans do not think of themselves as West Indians at all. Well over half the total population of the islands are Negroes, descendants of slaves brought from Africa in the 17th and 18th centuries.

The people earn their living chiefly from the tourist trade. Bermuda was the headquarters of a British fleet from 1767 onwards and for a long while many people worked in the naval establishments, but these were partly closed down in 1950. Some employment is provided also by the United States naval and air bases, which were built early in World War II on land leased, or hired out, to the United States government for 99 years. Land has also been reclaimed from the sea for the bases.

Vegetable-growing and fishing (especially for lobsters, a popular local dish) are other important occupations and there is a valuable lily-growing industry. Lily bulbs and blooms from Bermuda find a good market in the United States. At Easter, the lily fields are a lovely sight. Drugs and perfume essences are made in several small factories and are among the main exports.

The Bermudas are said to have been discovered early in the 16th century by a Spaniard, Juan de Bermudez, from whom they received their name. The Spanish apparently made no attempt to start settlements and the Bermudas were uninhabited when, in 1609, the flagship of Admiral Sir George Somers, leading a small fleet

Bermuda Travel Office

A sunny beach in Bermuda.

to the new settlements in Virginia, was blown off its course and wrecked in the islands. The admiral and his men built boats to reach Virginia and the glowing accounts they gave of the islands (which are still sometimes called the Somers Islands in honour of the admiral) led to the arrival in 1612 of the first governor with 60 settlers. Since 1620 Bermudans have shared in their own government. In 1968 they were granted self-government, but Britain remains responsible for defence and foreign affairs.

FACTS ABOUT BERMUDA

AREA: 53 square kilometres.
POPULATION: 53,000.
KIND OF COUNTRY: British colony.
CAPITAL: Hamilton.
GEOGRAPHICAL FEATURES: A chain of about 300 small low-lying coral islands, about 20 of which are inhabited.
CHIEF OCCUPATIONS: Tourist trade, vegetable growing, fishing, dairy farming, cultivation of lilies.
EDUCATION: Children must attend school between the ages of 5 and 16.

BERNARD, Saint (1090–1153). Bernard, Abbot of Clairvaux, played an outstanding part in the church history of Europe in the middle ages. He was born at Dijon near Burgundy in France, and as a young man he and 30 other nobles became Cistercian monks at Cîteaux. In 1115 he became abbot, or head, of the monastery of Clairvaux. His preaching and the 68 monasteries he set up in northern Europe soon made him famous, and under Pope Honorius II he took part in many affairs of church and state. (See MONKS AND FRIARS.)

After the death of Honorius in 1130 there

was a dispute as to whether Innocent II or Anacletus II was the true pope. Bernard supported Innocent and travelled all over Europe to persuade several rulers, including the Emperor Lothair III, to come over to his side. Anacletus died in 1138 and his successor resigned, chiefly through fear of Bernard.

In 1145 one of the monks of Clairvaux became Pope Eugenius III, and this put Bernard at the height of his power. Eugenius was anxious to send a crusade to Jerusalem to drive away the heathen, and he commanded Bernard to preach on this subject throughout Europe. As a result of his sermons, crowds of people from France, Germany and Flanders, including King Louis VII of France and the German King Conrad III, formed a great army and set out for Jerusalem. This was known as the Second Crusade and lasted from 1147 to 1149. It was, however, a failure, and the two kings were obliged to return separately. The result of this crusade was a bitter blow to Bernard, and he did not live long after it.

He wrote many Latin hymns and books on prayer, and some of his hymns have been translated into English and are often sung in churches. Two of the best known are : "Jesu, the very thought of thee" and "Jesus, thou joy of loving hearts".

BERNE has been the capital of Switzerland since 1848, though Zürich and Basle are much larger cities. It is a charming place, built on high ground almost completely encircled by the blue, rushing waters of the Aare River. The main streets are decorated with gaily coloured and elaborate fountains, while deep arcades (covered walks lined with shops) branch off on each side.

Founded towards the end of the 12th century as a military post between German and French-speaking peoples, Berne seems to take the visitor back into the middle ages as no other Swiss town can do. Two buildings dominate the city, perched high above the river. The first is the *Bundeshaus*, the meeting-place of the national parliament, where delegates from all the Swiss cantons, or states, discuss national affairs. The other is the minster, or cathedral, with a tall, thin spire, from which a splendid view of the

Bernese Alps can be obtained.

There is also a famous gate-tower with a curious 16th-century clock from which a procession of bears and other figures comes out to mark the striking of the hours. The bear is the heraldic emblem or sign of Berne (see HERALDRY) and is to be seen stamped everywhere, even on the cakes in the pastrycooks' shops for which the city is renowned. Near the Nydegg bridge is a bear pit full of shaggy, shuffling creatures which pass their days eating the carrots, peanuts and buns thrown to them by visitors. Bears have been kept there since 1480.

Berne Tourist Association
A brown bear and cubs in the famous bear-pit at Berne.

Berne has a well-known university and many museums. The occupations of its 166,000 inhabitants include chocolate-making and engine-building. Berne is the headquarters of the Universal Postal Union, which is a branch of the United Nations.

BERWICKSHIRE is one of the smaller counties on the east coast of Scotland with East Lothian lying to the north, Midlothian to the west and Roxburghshire to the south. On the southeast the border with Northumberland in England runs mostly along the River Tweed.

On the western border is the valley of the River Leader, called Lauderdale, and in the north are the Lammermuir Hills. The coast is rocky, with fishing ports at Eyemouth and Burnmouth, though most of the county's fishing is done in the lower Tweed, where salmon are netted. The angler can find sport in the upper Tweed and its tributaries.

Farming is the chief occupation. Sheep and cattle are kept on the Lammermuirs and on the rich lowland area in the southeast known as the Merse, where cereal crops are also grown. (See CEREAL.) Boatbuilding is done at Eyemouth and knitwear is finished at Greenlaw. Near Duns, blankets are made and there are chicken hatcheries.

Duns is the county town. (Berwick-upon-Tweed is not in Berwickshire but in Northumberland.) Duns was the birthplace of the mediaeval philosopher and religious writer John Duns Scotus. More recently, the world champion motor racing driver Jim Clark (1936–1968) farmed near Chirnside.

Eyemouth was once a smugglers' town which was said to have more underground tunnels than streets. Its little harbour was reopened after improvements in 1965 and many people spend their summer holidays there.

The oldest building in the county is the ruined broch on Cockburn Law, north of Duns. It is one of those circular fortresses with double walls, between which there are rooms and staircases, built by the early inhabitants of Scotland, who were called Picts. At Coldingham there was once an abbey founded by St. Ebba in the 7th century, and in the period when Viking raids on the coast were frequent it is said that the nuns once cut off their noses to make themselves less attractive. No such thoughts entered the heads of the young Englishwomen who, in more recent times, rode in haste to Coldstream, for their object was to reach Scotland, where it was lawful for them to be married by simple declaration of witnesses and without their parents' consent. But Coldstream's greatest fame comes from the regiment of the Coldstream Guards which started as a force raised there by General Monk in 1660, just after the death of Oliver Cromwell. Seeing that the southeastern boundary of the county is with England, it is not surprising that many raids took place and there was much border warfare

salmon fishing

knitwear

Eyemouth

chicken hatcheries at Duns

boat building

along the boundary until the union of Scotland and England in 1707.

BESSEMER, Sir Henry (1813–1896).

The English inventor Bessemer discovered the first process for making steel cheaply and in quantities. He was born at Charlton in Hertfordshire, where his father had a small engineering works. Henry as a boy spent much of his time in the works and at the age of 17, when he had learnt all he could, went to London resolved to make his fortune. Among his earlier inventions were two connected with printing: one for casting type under pressure and the other for a typesetting machine. (See PRINTING.) In 1840 he invented and operated a secret process for making "gold" paint from bronze powder, and made a lot of money from it.

Bessemer's work on steel began in the Crimean War when he was trying to develop a new gun but could not find a metal strong enough. The cast iron then used was too brittle because of the large amount of carbon in it. Bessemer's remedy was to blow air through melted cast iron, so that carbon was removed by combining with the oxygen in the air. This left a soft steel that could be brought to the exact hardness needed by adding the required amount of carbon. The process was done in a Bessemer converter. (See IRON AND STEEL.)

Steel made by the Bessemer process was widely adopted from 1864 onwards and huge amounts were used in bridges, ships, railway rails, guns and machines. The process reduced the price of steel to about one-third of what it had been in 1860. It also made Bessemer a wealthy man and brought him a great reputation. He received honours from several countries and in the United States six towns were named after him.

BESTIARY.
Books describing animals were very popular in the middle ages, and were called bestiaries. They came originally from a collection of stories in Greek called the *Physiologus*. Each article in a bestiary generally began with a picture of the animal. Next came an explanation of why the animal had been given its name, and then a short description of its habits. Finally there would be a "moralization", or short sermon about its behaviour, for most bestiaries were written by monks.

Much more is now known about animals, and so bestiaries may seem full of very strange and funny ideas about them; but it is a mistake to laugh at them too much. They were lovingly written by monks who had not seen most of the animals but had had them described to them by travellers. Even if a "cameleopard" seems today an impossible and comic animal, it is less comic when one realizes that the writers were trying to picture a giraffe—as big as a camel and spotted

Stories were often told of the whale (left) and of the phoenix (right), which died and rose from its own ashes.

rather like a leopard.

The illustration below, from a 12th-century bestiary in the Cambridge University library, shows an amphisbaena. This "dragon", the writer says, is given this name "because it has two heads, one in the proper place, the other in its tail; it can run with either head first, and with its trailing body bent round." Much later, a man who

Amphisbaena.

was translating the bestiary thought that before he decided that this description was just nonsense, he would try to find out more about the amphisbaena.

So the translator went up to the British Museum in London and there discovered that it was a real creature which still exists, although of course it does not have wings and legs like the one in the picture. Amphisbaenas are lizards that live in the tropics, and can move along either forwards or backwards. The translator found that these creatures were blunt at both ends, and that people sometimes painted a head on the tail end as a practical joke; he also found that they did move along with their bodies in a wavy line, and lift their tails to threaten their enemies. So the old bestiarist was not so far wrong after all.

Many of the traditional characteristics associated with real or mythical creatures derive from the bestiaries and survive in folklore and literature. Examples are the stories concerning the phoenix and the parental love of the pelican.

Courtesy, Trustees of the British Museum

The belief that salamanders could live in fire grew from the mixture of truth and myth in bestiary accounts.

BETHLEHEM. On a hillside, five miles south of Jerusalem, stands the little town of Bethlehem. There Rachel, wife of Jacob, died. In the fields near by, Ruth gleaned after the reapers of Boaz. Later the town was the birthplace of David and the place where he was anointed king by Samuel. At the appointed time the shepherds keeping guard over their flocks by night were the first to know that in the stable of an inn at Bethlehem the baby Jesus was born. (There are separate articles DAVID; JACOB AND ESAU; JESUS CHRIST; RUTH; SAMUEL.)

After the birth of Christ, Bethlehem, together with Nazareth and Jerusalem, became a place to which Christian pilgrims went. In the year 330 the Emperor Constantine the Great built the Church of the Nativity to commemorate the holy birth. This church survived the Arab conquest of 636 and in it Baldwin, the first crusader king of Jerusalem, was crowned in 1100. In 1187 his kingdom fell, but even under later Arab and Turkish rule the town stoutly held on to its Christian importance. Captured from the Turks in 1917 during World War I, Bethlehem, like the rest of Palestine, became the responsibility of Great Britain until the state of Israel was formed in 1948 and then the town was taken by Jordan. It was occupied by Israel in 1967.

BHUTAN is a semi-independent state on the southern slopes of the Himalayas, lying between Tibet on the north and Assam, which is part of the republic of India, on the south. The country is exceedingly mountainous, with much forest, and in some parts the rainfall is very heavy. Many animals are found, including elephants, rhinoceroses, tigers, bison, bears and deer.

About two-thirds of the people are Bhutias and the rest Nepalese, with a few thousand Tibetans. The Bhutias are a Mongolian race and are very like their Tibetan neighbours; both peoples are Buddhist by religion, both regard the Dalai Lama as their spiritual head and they speak a similar language. Monasteries are dotted over the countryside (as they were in Tibet before the Chinese conquered it). The people grow maize and other crops in fields cut out of the mountain slopes. The houses are built

Modern Bethlehem is a well-built town, visited each year by many thousands of pilgrims.
Courtesy, Israel Government Tourist Office

Central Press

A Bhutanese wall painting. Tigers, not all as handsome as this one, are among the many animals found in Bhutan.

of mud painted white between the black wooden beams and roofed with wooden shingles.

The Bhutanese angered the British towards the end of the 18th century by making raids and kidnapping British people who lived in India. At length, in 1865, the British sent troops into the country to put a stop to this. Then they made a treaty with the Bhutanese who gave up, in return for a yearly payment of money, a good piece of land called the Duars at the foot of the mountains where, later, tea plantations were set up. In 1910 the yearly payment was doubled and the government of Bhutan then agreed to let the British handle its foreign affairs so long as there was no interference in its home affairs.

When the British left India in 1947 Bhutan made a new treaty of the same kind with the Republic of India. Since 1961 India has done much to help Bhutan by building roads and training the people in new skills as well as sponsoring the country for membership of the United Nations. The government is under a maharaja who is known as king, a position passed down from father to son. The capital is Thimbu and the population of the country is about 836,000.

BIBLE. The Bible gets its name from a Greek word meaning "books". It is divided into passages of various lengths which in their turn are also known as books. In the Bible used by Protestants there are 39 of these books in the Old Testament, which is the first and longest part of the Bible. The Bible used by Roman Catholics includes some additional books called the Apocrypha (see APOCRYPHA). These books are also used by some of the Protestant churches and are to be found in some Bibles used by these churches. Most Protestants, however, do not regard the books of the Apocrypha as having the same value as the other books of the Bible. The second part of the Bible, which is called the New Testament and tells the story of Jesus Christ and his followers, has 27 books.

The Old Testament

The Old Testament is many things in one. It is the Word of God and His promises to mankind, revealed through men's lives and through the sayings of the prophets. It is the history of a nation, the Israelites or Jews; their conquests, travels, the building of their cities and, most of all, the way in which the teaching of God was revealed to them and their struggles to keep faithful to it. The Old Testament is full of legends, poetry and hymns, many of which are among the finest ever written. Also, in all the world's literature it would be hard to find men and women who arouse more interest and sympathy than such Biblical characters as Joseph, Ruth, David and Jonah.

The first book of the Old Testament is called Genesis, a word that means "creation" or "origin". Genesis goes back to the beginning of time, with God's creation of the heaven and the earth. The first man and woman, Adam and Eve, disobeyed the commands of God and were driven out of Paradise. God promised to give Canaan (Palestine) to the descendants of Abraham, the father of the Jewish people. Abraham's grandson Jacob, who was also called Israel, had 12 sons whose descendants were known as the 12 tribes of Israel. It was the 11th son, Joseph, who took his father, brothers and their children into Egypt to live, as he thought, in safety.

The descendants of Jacob were so numerous that Pharaoh, King of Egypt, became afraid of them and made them slaves. So terrible were their hardships that in later years the highest praise they could give God was to say of Him that He "brought us out of the land of Egypt".

The second book of the Old Testament is called Exodus, which means "departure". Led by Moses, the Israelites left Egypt, but Pharaoh pursued them with his army to the shores of the Red Sea. There God divided the sea for the Israelites to cross and then the water rolled back again and drowned the Egyptians.

The Jews spent 40 years in the wilderness on their way to the Promised Land of Canaan. During this journey God gave the Ten Commandments to Moses. By following these commandments, and particularly the first two, which forbid the worship of idols or false gods, the Jews were set apart from all other nations of the world, and they had many struggles with heathen people who tried to make them turn away from the true God.

The first five books of the Bible—Genesis, Exodus, Leviticus, Numbers and Deuteronomy —are also known as the Pentateuch. Leviticus, called after the Levites, the Israelite priests, describes the religion of the Jews. Numbers contains the census or numbering of the Israelites. Deuteronomy, a word meaning law, describes the law that was laid down for the Jews, and the last chapter records the death of Moses.

The soldier Joshua succeeded Moses as leader of the Israelites and led them into Canaan, where the walls of the city of Jericho fell down before them. Victory after victory was won until the Israelite tribes were settled in the Promised Land.

The Book of Judges covers the period from the conquest of Palestine to the time when Israel began to be ruled by a king. It is a collection of tales of early Jewish heroes, amongst them Gideon the mighty soldier; Samson the strong; and a woman, Jael, who killed Sisera, a captain of the enemy.

During this time the Israelites had much difficulty in fighting against their heathen enemies the Philistines, so they asked the prophet Samuel to make them stronger by giving them a king. The two books of Samuel tell how Samuel chose Saul and crowned him the first king of Israel. But Saul disobeyed God, and Samuel chose the shepherd boy David to be king in his place. Eventually Saul and his son Jonathan were killed in battle against the Philistines. The passage in which David laments their death is one of the most beautiful in the Bible.

David ruled as king for many years, making Zion or Jerusalem the capital city of Palestine. His death is told at the beginning of the First Book of Kings, which continues with the reign of his son Solomon. Both David and Solomon ruled according to the law of Moses and so for a time God's promises were fulfilled. Solomon's reign was a long and peaceful one and he was remembered for his wisdom and wealth. He built the Temple in Jerusalem which became the centre of Jewish life and worship.

However, in his old age Solomon turned to the worship of idols, and so began the downfall of his kingdom. In the reign of his son Rehoboam ten tribes set up a kingdom of their own in the north of Palestine and only the tribes of Judah and Benjamin remained faithful to Rehoboam. This was the period known as the divided kingdom, with the kingdom of Israel in the north and the kingdom of Judah in the south.

The histories of the kings in the Second Book of Kings tell of the troubles of the divided kingdom until Israel was captured by the king of Assyria and, according to Jewish belief, the ten tribes vanished, although the Samaritans claim to be descended from them. About 100 years later the king of Babylon, Nebuchadnezzar, burned Jerusalem, robbed the Temple and carried the people of Judah into captivity at Babylon in Mesopotamia. This period is known as the Exile or the Captivity.

Although they were among heathen people and were grieving for their home, the Jews in Babylon continued to follow one God, and it was this faith that kept the prophet Daniel from harm when he was thrown into the lions' den. Another story of the Exile is the Book of Esther, which tells how Esther, a beautiful Jewish maiden, became queen to the Persian king Ahasuerus and so was able to help her captive people.

The books of Ezra and Nehemiah tell of the joyful return from exile to Palestine and of the rebuilding of the Temple.

The two Books of Chronicles repeat the whole

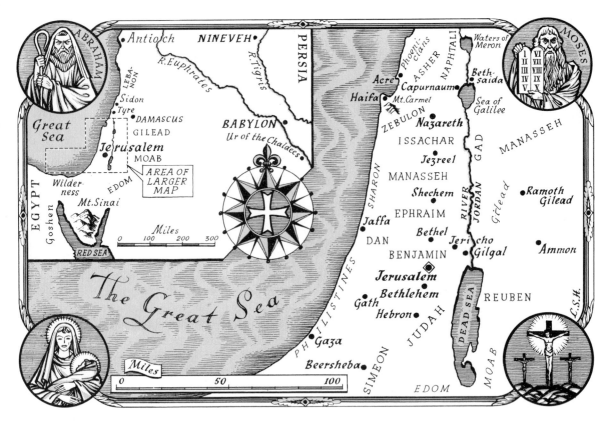

story, from a list of Adam's descendants to the announcement by Cyrus, King of Persia, that the Jews could return to their own country.

The other books of the Old Testament include the Book of Job, which seeks to explain the ways of God to men. The Psalms are a collection of hymns, many of them said to have been written by David. Proverbs, described as "the proverbs of Solomon", are wise sayings. The theme of Ecclesiastes is vanity; that is, the uselessness of men's lives if they do not remember God. The Song of Solomon, also known as the Song of Songs and the Canticles, is a collection of love songs. Perhaps the loveliest book of all is the Book of Ruth, which tells the story of the devotion of the foreign girl Ruth to her Jewish mother-in-law, Naomi.

The prophets were religious teachers who also advised the kings and people in political matters. Among the sternest, or grimmest, of the prophets were Amos, Hosea, Micah and Isaiah, who lived before the Captivity and knew how God would punish the people for forgetting his law and for

worshipping idols. Jeremiah preached to Judah after the conquest of Israel. The Book of Lamentations is an expression of sorrow for the fall of Jerusalem. Ezekiel was a prophet of the Exile; he spoke of the wickedness of Israel, but also comforted the Jews with the promises of God.

The Book of Jonah is unlike those of the other prophets, as it simply tells the story of the adventures of Jonah, who was sent to convert the heathen city of Nineveh, in Assyria. (See JONAH.)

The books of the prophets are full of glory and terror, but every now and then there is a verse that seems to refer in the clearest way to the story of Jesus as told in the New Testament. In chapters 40–55 of Isaiah there are whole passages about a servant of God who was sent to bring the Gentiles or non-Jews to God and who suffered for all people. No one knows who wrote these passages; the prophet is known as the second Isaiah.

The Old Testament ends with the Book of

Malachi and repeats God's promise of the coming of a great Messiah or teacher for the Jews.

The Four Gospels

The story of that coming is told in the Gospels of the New Testament. The word gospel means "good news". The four Gospels of Matthew, Mark, Luke and John, which tell the life of Jesus in different ways, were all written late in the 1st century after Christ. (See GOSPELS.)

Each gospel gives an account of the life of Jesus but tells it in a different way. The first three were written for Christians who did not know the full story of the life of Christ. John, who wrote his gospel last, took it for granted that the story was well known, and therefore explained the character of Jesus as the Son of God, instead of merely saying what He did.

The Gospels of Matthew, Mark and Luke tell more or less the same story, although Mark leaves out the account of the birth of Jesus. They tell how Jesus was baptized in the River Jordan and how He preached in Galilee, followed by the men who were later known as the apostles. Matthew tells how He taught His disciples the true way of life in what is now known as the Sermon on the Mount. Other sermons were told in the form of stories and are called parables. Many of the miracles of Jesus are told by Matthew, Mark and Luke, but we know of the marriage at Cana and the raising of Lazarus only from the gospel of John.

After about three years of preaching and performing miracles, Jesus rode into Jerusalem in triumph and a little time afterwards He and His disciples ate the Last Supper together. All four gospels tell how He was taken prisoner by His enemies and crucified and how on the third day He rose again from the dead. (See JESUS CHRIST.)

The gospels are the only trustworthy accounts of the life of Jesus that have come down to us, so there are many years of His life that we know nothing about, and many of His sayings that have been lost. John, at the end of his gospel, says that if everything Jesus did were to be written down, "Even the world itself could not contain the books that should be written."

Many times the writers of the gospels say that "the scriptures were fulfilled". By this they mean that the Word of God, spoken by the prophets, came true, thus proving that Jesus was indeed the Messiah. For example, Matthew, telling how Jesus entered Jerusalem, repeated the words of the prophet Zechariah, who foretold that the King (or Messiah) would come to Jerusalem riding on an ass.

The Acts of the Apostles

The Acts of the Apostles takes up the story of how God's promise to men, brought about by the life and death of Christ, began to be told to all men everywhere. The small band of apostles began the work of spreading Christianity, as the new faith came to be called. The Jews tried to prevent them, and among them was a man named Saul who threw many Christians into prison. While he was on a journey to Damascus to search for Christians there, a light shone round Saul on the road and the voice of Christ spoke to him from heaven. For three days he remained blind, but at the end of them his sight returned and he was baptized a Christian.

Saul, or Paul as he was later called, was the first of the apostles to realize that a man could become a Christian without first becoming a Jew. Nearly all the first Christians were Jews by birth and when they became Christians they continued to keep the Jewish laws handed down since the time of Moses. A number of people whom Paul met on his journeys to different countries objected strongly to keeping some of these laws, which they quite rightly felt to be nothing to do with the teaching of Jesus. Paul eventually persuaded the rest of the church leaders that when a Gentile became a Christian he need not also begin to keep the Jewish laws. With his friends Barnabas, Silas and the apostle Luke, he travelled through the countries of the Roman Empire, finally reaching Rome itself.

After the Acts there are 21 epistles, or letters. Of these, 13 were written by Paul himself to the new Christian churches in various cities, such as Corinth, Ephesus and Rome, helping them in their troubles or laying down rules for them to follow. The epistle to the Hebrews was written by someone unknown and the remaining epistles were written by James, Peter, John and Jude.

The final book in the Bible is the Revelation of St. John the Divine. This is the only book of prophecy in the New Testament and was written to comfort the early Christians in their troubles. It tells of the vision of the apostle John, who "saw a new heaven and a new earth".

How the Bible was written

The original language of almost all the Old Testament was Hebrew, the language of the Jews. Parts of it may have been first written in the 10th century B.C. More was added over the next few centuries and much was probably written at the time of the divided kingdom, about the 7th and 8th centuries B.C.

It was handed down in three different ways: (1) Hebrew copies, one dated A.D. 916 and one or two others, possibly of the 9th century; (2) the Samaritan collection of the Pentateuch; (3) the Septuagint. This is a Greek translation of the Hebrew Old Testament which was made for the Jews of Alexandria in the 3rd century B.C. It is called Septuagint, meaning 70, because it is supposed to have been written by 72 translators.

The books of the New Testament began to be collected together in the 2nd century and were finally declared to be the Word of God in A.D. 397 (after the Roman Empire had become Christian). They were probably written in Greek, though Jesus Himself spoke in Aramaic, a language very like Hebrew.

Both the Old and New Testaments were translated into Latin by Jerome, a 4th-century scholar. His translation is known as the Vulgate, and it became the Bible of the Roman Catholic Church.

The oldest English prose translation of the gospels that still exists was made by a priest called Aldred, who is believed to have been Bishop of Durham in about A.D. 950. Between the lines of his Vulgate he wrote an old English translation, now known as the "Lindisfarne Gospels". The earliest complete translation of the Bible was made from the Vulgate by John Wycliffe the reformer, or under his leadership. This was in the 14th century, before the days of printing, and many copies were made by hand.

One of the most important decisions at the time of the Reformation was that the Bible should be translated into English for everyone in England to read. For this purpose William Tyndale set to work on a Greek edition of the New Testament, published by the Dutch scholar Erasmus, and he also translated the Pentateuch and the Book of Jonah, using original Hebrew copies. The Roman Catholic Church at that time would not allow the English Bible to be used, and Tyndale was forced to leave England and go to Germany, where he had his translations printed and sent to England. In 1536 Tyndale was executed for heresy (holding opinions not taught by the Church) near Brussels in Belgium.

The first complete printed Bible in English was the Coverdale Bible, which was prepared by Miles Coverdale and finished in 1535. Four years later the Great Bible was printed, and for a time no other English Bible was allowed to be read. Passages from the Great Bible can still be read in the Book of Common Prayer.

In 1582 the Douai Bible, the authorized or approved Roman Catholic English translation, was published. Besides including the Apocrypha, it differs from the Authorized Version of the Bible in the spelling of some names; for example, Noah is called Noe.

The Authorized King James Version of the Bible was made with the approval of King James I and first published in 1611. A special staff of trained scholars prepared it, using Tyndale's and Coverdale's translations, as well as the Bishops' Bible, a translation made in the reign of Elizabeth I. The King James Bible is used by English-speaking Protestants everywhere in the world, and the stately beauty of the 17th-century English seems so well suited to the message it has to tell that many people will not read any other translations.

Modern Translations

In fact, however, the Authorized Version is often rather inaccurate, as well as being difficult to understand, and in order to correct these faults the Bible known as the Revised Version was prepared. The New Testament was published in 1881 and the Old in 1884. In the 20th century, however, it was felt that the Bible should be translated into modern English.

Many modern translations have been made. James Moffatt's translation of the whole Bible was published in 1926 and revised in 1935. Ronald Knox prepared a Roman Catholic version, publishing the New Testament in 1945 and the Old Testament in 1949. Meanwhile, the other churches in Britain helped with the New English Bible, of which the New Testament was published in 1961 and the complete text in 1971. The Revised Standard Version prepared by American Protestant scholars was published in 1952 and in 1965 was approved for use by English-speaking Roman Catholics. The Jerusalem Bible, prepared by Roman Catholic scholars, was published in an English translation in 1966.

In 1947 the very important discovery of the Dead Sea Scrolls was made in Palestine. These are religious writings, some of them much older than the Septuagint and others written during the lifetime of Jesus. (See DEAD SEA SCROLLS.)

There are separate articles on many of the important people in the Old and New Testaments. See also APOSTLES; CHRISTIANITY; PROPHETS; PSALMS; RELIGION.

BICYCLE. The mechanism of a bicycle is quite simple. The pedals are fitted to cranks which turn a chainwheel. When they are pushed round they give a pull on the chain, which in turn rotates a sprocket fixed to the hub of the bicycle's rear wheel. This causes the bicycle to move forward because of the grip of the rubber tyres on the road.

The steering is also quite simple. The front wheel is fitted with fork blades which come together in a single column made so that it is free to turn in the head of the cycle frame. To this column is fitted a pair of handlebars which steer the column and, through it, the fork and the wheel.

Most bicycles are made of steel, although aluminium alloy is used for some lightweight models.

One of the most desirable features of a bicycle is that it should be "lively". However hard some bicycles are pedalled they never seem to move along easily; they feel almost as if they were made of lead. A "lively" machine, on the other hand, makes the work of pedalling seem easy and effortless. This liveliness is the result of building the frame in such a way that it has two opposite features; it must be rigid and it must also have resilience or "give".

It must be rigid so that all the effort of the rider goes into the downward thrust. If after each push on the pedals some part of the frame had to straighten out again before the next push, energy would be wasted. That is why the racing cyclist rests part of his weight on the handlebars and the pedals and less on the saddle. He selects a narrow, hard seat so that his legs, moving up and down like pistons, will not waste energy by compressing the springs of his saddle with every up and down movement on the pedals.

Resilience or "give" is necessary because without it all the bumps or roughness in the road would be transmitted to the rider's seat and hands and a bicycle ride would be a most uncomfortable business. Having been knocked or pushed out of its normal straightness, the steel of which the frame is made should recover quickly. In the same way a steel girder on a railway line may "bend" to the wheels of a train but springs back at once into shape after the train has passed.

The gearing on a bicycle is designed to make the most efficient use of leg-power. It can best be explained by describing the effort used by a person walking up a flight of stairs. If he goes upstairs two steps at a time he doubles the size of the "gear" between his legs and the stairs; his body has to be lifted twice as high with each step as it would if he climbed only one step at a time. This makes twice the work, but the number of steps is reduced by half and climbing speed is quicker.

If the chainwheel of a bicycle were the same size as the rear wheel sprocket, the rear wheel would turn once to each complete pedal turn. If the chainwheel were twice as big as the sprocket then one complete turn of the pedals would turn the rear wheel twice; in other words it would be the same as having a direct drive to a road wheel twice the size.

The gear of a bicycle is calculated by multi-

Crown copyright, Science Museum, London

The Draisienne or hobby horse (top left) was ridden by fashionable young men in the 1820s. Later, in 1869, came the "boneshaker" (bottom left). A lady and gentleman are on "ordinary" bicycles, or pennyfarthings, of 1872.

plying the number of teeth on the chainwheel by the diameter of the rear wheel and dividing the answer by the number of teeth on the sprocket.

A bicycle needs to be taken care of just like any other machine. The most important thing to remember is to oil it from time to time. If you want your tyres to last for a long time always keep them well pumped up. When you know that you will not be riding for some time you should let out the air from them and hang the bicycle up. Nothing rots the rubber so quickly as having the weight of the bicycle standing on flat tyres. The article CYCLING gives you tips about riding your bicycle.

Pedalling Through the Ages

Many queer looking two-wheeled balancing machines were built before the modern bicycle appeared. The treadle used on foot-operated sewing machines and lathes, with rod and crank, was invented hundreds of years ago. Treadle propulsion was adopted by a Reigate schoolmaster who, in 1760, built a four-wheeled "travelling chaise without horses" which was propelled by footpower applied to a cranked axle. However, when in 1816 a Frenchman, J. Niepcé, who was also known as the father of photography, made a two-wheeled machine which was paddled along with the feet striking the ground in turn, the idea of applying the treadle principle to drive it along was not thought of. This "swift-walking" machine was called a celeripede. An improved model by Baron von Drais called the "Draisienne" came to England in 1818 and became known as the hobby-horse or the dandy-horse because the "dandies" or fashionably dressed men of the time rode it.

In 1839, however, a Scotsman, Kirkpatrick Macmillan, put a drive to the rear wheel of this hobby-horse by means of treadles, rods and

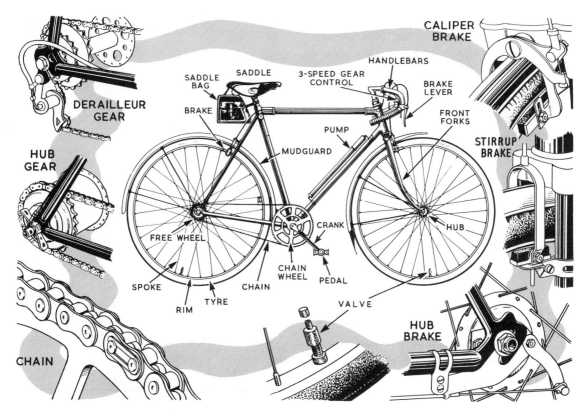

DERAILLEUR GEAR

HUB GEAR

CHAIN

SADDLE BAG

SADDLE

3-SPEED GEAR CONTROL

HANDLEBARS

CALIPER BRAKE

BRAKE LEVER

BRAKE

FRONT FORKS

PUMP

STIRRUP BRAKE

MUDGUARD

CRANK

HUB

FREE WHEEL

CHAIN WHEEL

PEDAL

SPOKE

CHAIN

TYRE

RIM

VALVE

HUB BRAKE

cranks and thus constructed the first real bicycle. He rode his machine from his Courthill smithy in Keir, Dumfriesshire, to Glasgow in 1842 and was fined for knocking down a child. However, this invention was forgotten and played no part in the development of cycling.

In 1861 Pierre Michaux (or his son Ernest, or it may have been a workman in the factory named Lallement) fixed cranks directly to the front-wheel hub of an old celeripede. It was shown at the Paris Exhibition of 1867 and was called a velocipede. This was the actual birth of bicycling. The Paris representative of the Coventry Sewing Machine Company brought home one of these French velocipedes and persuaded his firm to make some hundreds of them for the French people, but the coming of the Franco-Prussian War made it necessary for the sewing-machine company to sell them in England. Thus the bicycle industry came to be founded in Coventry; since then many developments in cycle design and construction have come from this city.

This type of bicycle with heavy wooden

wheels became known as the Bone-Shaker. Its disadvantage was that it travelled only one wheel's circumference with each complete turn of the pedals. To "gear it up" the front wheel was made larger and the machine was soon made into the High Bicycle of the 1873–1890 period which, years afterwards, was called the "Penny Farthing" because of its large and small wheels. However, a bicycle that depended on the size of its big wheel for its speed, was likely to be used only by tall athletes with long legs.

The "endless chain" drive patented in 1716 was applied to tricycles in the 1870s. It seems obvious now that the simplest way to drive a bicycle is on the rear wheel, leaving the steering wheel free of mechanism, but it needed imagination to apply a chain drive to a bicycle with a large front wheel and a small trailing wheel. A man named Lawson accomplished this in 1879. Six years later came the greatest advance in the whole history of bicycle design, when J. K. Starley made a machine, the Rover, shaped almost like the modern bicycle, with equal-sized wheels and a rear chain drive. The other great cycle invention was J. B. Dunlop's pneumatic tyre, introduced in 1888. (See TYRE.)

Since then the bicycle has been improved in many ways, including the use of the free wheel, variable-speed gears, lighter wheels and tyres, stronger and lighter steels, weather-proofing, much better brakes and lighting, better placing of the rider for using his legs to push the pedals, and saddle designs for comfort and speed. The small-wheel bicycle invented by the British engineer Alex Moulton was introduced in 1962.

BIG BEN, the world's most famous clock, stands beside the Houses of Parliament at Westminster, London. In European countries occupied by the Germans during World War II people used to listen in secret to B.B.C. broadcasts, this being forbidden, and the chimes of Big Ben which announced the news bulletins made them feel that they were linked with those whom the Germans had not yet conquered.

Strictly speaking, Big Ben is not the name of the clock but is the name of the bell on which the hours are struck. It was named after Sir Benjamin Hall who, among other things, was in charge of the difficult operation of hauling the bell up inside the tower. It weighs about $13\frac{1}{2}$ tonnes and was cast in Whitechapel, in the East End of London, in 1858.

The clock has four faces, one on each side of the tower, and they are about 6 metres across, the minute hands weighing 101 kilograms each. The wonderful thing about the clock is the way in which it keeps such accurate time. Standing among its great works, looking through the dial faces at the shadows of the enormous hands or down inside the tower at the huge weights which drive the machine, it is difficult to believe that it could be so finely adjusted. This adjustment is made by adding or taking away twopenny pieces on a tray attached to the pendulum and this method keeps the clock accurate to within a fifth of a second over 24 hours. The clock was designed by E. B. Denison (later Lord Grimthorpe, 1816–1905) and was erected in 1859.

The chimes of Big Ben can be heard up to 6 kilometres from Westminster. When the light shines above the belfry at night this shows that the House of Commons is still sitting.

Big Ben towering above the Houses of Parliament. The chimes of Big Ben are familiar to people all over the world.

BIG GAME HUNTING. "Big game" is the term usually used for large wild animals, living in their natural surroundings, which are the prey of hunters—whether with guns, or, more often today, with cameras.

At one time, man hunted animals for food, but as he settled and learnt how to grow crops, hunting gradually developed into a sport. The main areas of the world where big game hunting still attracts many sportsmen are Africa and Asia, though hunting also flourishes in the United States. Africa has lion, leopard, elephant, rhinoceros, hippopotamus, buffalo and many kinds of antelopes, while deer, tiger, bear, boar and bison live in Asia.

Many governments in different parts of the world now protect their wild animals. Official protection most often takes the form of game parks or reserves, where the killing of any animals by hunters is completely prohibited. The Serengeti National Park has the finest group of plains animals in Africa and the best grassland range in the continent. India's national parks protect many species, such as the Asiatic lion and the Indian rhinoceros, which exist nowhere else. Game wardens, responsible for the health and safety of wild life within the parks, are also responsible for seeing that poachers do not hunt any of the protected species. Outside protected areas the hunter of big game can travel in organized safaris, experiencing the traditional enjoyment of camping, tracking, stalking and the final kill. The hunting seasons even in the free districts are closely regulated, with no shooting allowed in the breeding months, and hunting is by licence only. Tourists, who form the main body of sporting hunters, usually employ the services of a professional hunter whose first job will be to obtain the necessary licences. In some cases, these will limit the number of animals allowed to be shot by each hunter, in order that the total amount of game lost each season can be regulated and re-stocked during the next breeding season. The professional hunter will then take his party to a remote area where game is to be found.

Hunting parties vary in size from small numbers of people who wish to follow and photograph big game, to convoys which include trackers, cooks, gun boys, tents and other equipment necessary to set up camp. On large expeditions, there will have been a great deal of preparation before starting for camp in gathering transport, equipment and guides. The smaller safaris are usually "photographic" ones. People join these to take close-up photographs or films of the animals, not to kill them. Although it is possible to photograph animals in the game parks, this must be done from inside a vehicle, whereas in the open range there is more chance of a dramatic or unusual picture.

The site of a camp has to be chosen with care because if the animals are alarmed, they may move away to continue their search for food and water. It is therefore better not to camp on the best hunting grounds in case scent is carried to the game. If the camp is too near the animals' water hole, it could be very dangerous. There are often established camps to which hunters are taken by their professional guide.

It may take some time before any game is sighted or before the animal being sought arrives to drink—a great deal of patience is required, but once the game has appeared, the hunt can begin.

One of the main methods used to hunt big game is stalking, which takes place in open

Courtesy, Satour

The African buffalo is a most dangerous animal when wounded.

country where the game can be seen from afar. The hunter moves slowly into the wind and under cover, using rocks and tufts of grass to avoid being seen, heard or smelt. In forests, bush or thick jungle where game can be seen only at close range, stalking is unsuitable. The hunter will come upon his prey suddenly so he must move silently and be prepared to shoot quickly before the animal is disturbed by his presence. Sometimes in dense jungle it is impossible to either sight or track the game. When this happens the animal has to be "driven" or "beaten" from cover out into the open.

The number of wild animals in the world has been drastically reduced in the past by indiscriminate hunting, but governments have realized the danger that some rare species may become extinct and heavy penalties are now imposed for breaking the hunting regulations.

BILBERRY AND CRANBERRY. Other
names for the bilberry are whortleberry and blaeberry. The bush has oval leaves with their edges turned back and grows close to the ground in order to avoid the winds which sweep across the moorlands and the open mountain woods. The bilberry is common all over Britain, except in eastern England, and can be found only 25 miles from London, on Leith Hill in Surrey.

The poet Wordsworth wrote that this plant was "never so beautiful as in early spring". The petals of the flowers are joined together, making little pink globes. When the fruit is ripe, in July or August, it is the colour of a very dark bruise.

Bilberries are about the size of currants and are good in tarts and as jam; they can also be pickled in vinegar and in some parts of the country people eat them raw with cream. In the highlands of Scotland, the grouse often help themselves to bilberries. In North America they are called blueberries, grow from 4 to 12 feet high and have large clusters of fruit.

The cranberry is a relative of the bilberry, but it grows in peat bogs. The leaves of the two plants are similar but those of the cranberry are evergreen, whereas the bilberry loses its leaves every autumn. In June, the flowers hang from slender stems and have four pinkish petals. When growing wild, the berries are about the same size as

Bilberry flowers, fruit and foliage.

bilberries, but they are bright red. In the United States there is a cultivated cranberry which grows in bogs and from it come the large, dark red and very sour berries sold in shops in Europe. The Americans and Canadians use them to make pies and drinks, as well as in the sauce for the turkey on Thanksgiving Day.

BILLIARDS AND SNOOKER are two
very popular games, both played on a billiards table. Of the two, billiards is by far the older—

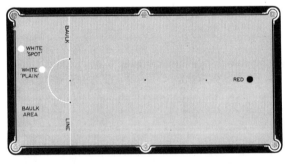

Above: A billiards game begins with the red ball on its spot.
Below: For snooker, 22 balls are set out on the table.

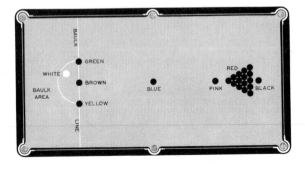

it has been played for at least 400 years. Serious snooker has been played only since the beginning of this century.

A billiards table consists of a slate bed, covered by a green woollen cloth and enclosed by a wooden framework. The playing surface is surrounded by rubber cushions which are also covered with the green cloth. A full-sized table measures 12 feet by 6 feet $1\frac{1}{2}$ inches although the actual playing area is smaller owing to the overhang ($1\frac{1}{2}$ to 2 inches) of the cushions. There are also smaller sized tables used. Six pockets are inset into the sides, one at each corner and one at the centre of each long side.

A straight line is drawn across the table near the bottom cushion and is called the baulk-line, the smaller area it cuts off being called baulk. A semicircle, with its centre on the baulk-line, is called the "D" and in both billiards and snooker all strokes, after the player's ball has entered a pocket, are made from this "D". This is called "playing from hand".

Billiards is played with three balls, one red and two white, one of which has two black spots to distinguish it. One player takes "spot", the other "plain". Each hits the ball with a cue, a long, thin stick with a leather tip, on which chalk is rubbed so that it does not slip on the ball.

To decide which player takes the first stroke, the two players "string" for their turn. That is, each takes one of the two white balls and, with his cue, strikes it so that it travels up the table, rebounds from the top cushion and returns, the player whose ball stops nearer to the bottom cushion, whether it rebounds from it or not, having the choice of opening the game by playing first, or of asking his opponent to do so.

The game is started with the red ball on its spot and the player's ball, called the cue-ball, in hand. The red ball and the other white ball (that is, not the player's ball) are called the object-balls. There are six spots marked on the table. Three are down the centre of the table—the Billiards Spot (on which the red ball is placed), the Centre Spot and the Pyramid Spot. The other three spots are on the baulk-line.

The aim of the game is to score points by "cannons", "pots" and "in-offs". (Pots are also called "winning hazards" and in-offs "losing

hazards".) For a cannon, which scores two points, the player has to make his ball strike the other two. For an in-off he has to make his own ball first hit one of the other two balls on the table and then enter one of the six pockets. If it goes in off red he scores three points, off white, two. A pot is made by the player sending one of the other balls into the pockets with his own ball. Potting white scores two points and red three. After the red ball is potted, it is placed on its spot, unless it is pocketed twice in succession, without a cannon or in-off being involved, in which case it is placed on the centre spot. The white, however, if potted stays in the pocket.

The skill of the game lies in the way the player leaves the balls after making a scoring stroke. He has to try to place them so that he will be able to score again. A series of scoring strokes is called a break. The official record break was 4,137 made by Walter Lindrum in 1932. Most ordinary players feel very pleased with themselves if they make one of about 30 but the best amateurs make breaks of 100 and more fairly frequently.

Snooker

Snooker is played with 22 balls: the players' ball (white), 15 red balls, valued for scoring purposes at 1 each, and the "colours", valued as follows: yellow (2), green (3), brown (4), blue (5), pink (6) and black (7). The only scoring stroke is the pot, referred to in billiards. The player tries first to pot a red ball, then a colour, then a red, then a colour and so on until all the 15 reds are in the pockets. Each time a red ball is sent into a pocket it stays there but the colours are replaced on their respective spots. In snooker, both players use the same white ball.

After the red balls have been potted, the player then tries to pot the colours in their correct order, starting with yellow and finishing up with black. When the black is finally potted the game, or "frame" as it is called (a match consists of a number of frames), is over. As in billiards, the skill of snooker lies in leaving the cue ball in a good position after making a pot, so that further pots can be made. In both games, when a player fails to score he loses his turn.

To "snooker" one's opponent means to make a stroke so that the ball the opponent has to strike at is obstructed by another ball so that he cannot strike at it. If the opponent then fails to hit the correct ball he suffers a penalty. The "snooker" is an important part of the game and can be used if no ball is in a good position for potting.

BILLINGSGATE MARKET.

London's most important fish market stands where it has stood for hundreds of years—down beside the River Thames, between London Bridge and the Tower. In the early days fishermen would come in their boats and lay out their fish on the shore and people could go and pick out a nice specimen for breakfast, but nowadays most of the fish arrives by train or lorry—much of it comes all the way from Scotland or Cornwall—and the market is attended by fishmongers or their

British Tourist Authority
Fishmongers, or their agents, select the best fish.

agents who buy great boxes of fish. Those who visit the market early in the morning can see how cleverly the porters balance these boxes on the special leather hats they wear.

BINDWEED belongs to the family of plants called Convolvulus, which means twining round. That is what the bindweed does to other plants: when it reaches a certain height it bends over and turns in an anti-clockwise direction until it finds a victim to which it can cling.

The lesser and the greater bindweed are the commonest kinds of convolvulus, growing all over Europe. The former is a nuisance to gardeners and farmers, for it creeps along the ground and winds around the plants and vegetables. To get rid of it, deep digging is necessary for its roots may go down as much as 20 feet and they spread fast. It is a beautiful little plant, however, with sweet-smelling

Bindweed.

white or pink flowers shaped like funnels.

The greater bindweed looks like a large version of the lesser bindweed, but has tougher stems, and the arrow-shaped leaves are larger. The flowers are like trumpets and are two inches long; they are usually pure white but have no scent. Sea-bindweed has similar flowers but its leaves are smaller, thicker and rounder. It creeps along close to the sand, binding it together with its long roots.

A relative of the bindweed, the beautiful morning glory, is grown in English gardens although it is not a native of England as it comes from tropical America.

BIOGRAPHY AND AUTOBIOGRAPHY.

Biography is the art of writing the history of a person's life. When people talk of "a biography" they mean the life-story of a particular person, told by someone else. An autobiography is the life-story of a person told by himself. People have always enjoyed writing and reading the "lives" of famous and interesting persons—one of the oldest known books of biography was written by a Roman author, Plutarch, nearly 2,000 years ago. Shakespeare used Plutarch's *Parallel Lives* to help him write the plots of his plays about Romans.

Many of the early biographies were written to praise the person who was the subject of them and so naturally the writer would leave out anything which might show the subject's bad points.

Obviously this meant that the biography was not a true portrait at all. The aim of most modern biographers, on the other hand, is to show the man or woman as he or she really was. A modern biographer tries to discover why a man acted as he did and is not satisfied with just writing down the things that happened to him. He tries to understand the mind of his subject thoroughly. A good example of this sympathetic kind of biography is Lord David Cecil's life of the poet William Cowper, called *The Stricken Deer*.

People's real lives can often be as exciting as any novel and many biographies are so well written that reading them is like reading a fascinating story. As well as getting to know the main character, the reader often meets many other interesting people and finds out what it was like to live in another time or another country. As well as all this, the life of a great man or woman can be an inspiration to the reader. Many a famous soldier, statesman, artist, lawyer or writer has admitted that his determination to succeed started because when he was young he read the biography of some successful person in his own chosen profession.

Two Kinds of Biography

Biography has grown and changed a great deal since Plutarch wrote his *Lives*, and today there are two main kinds.

First there is the plain straightforward "life" of a person. The book begins before he was born by telling of his ancestors and then goes on to give everything that happened in his life, year by year. Often it has many extracts from his own diaries and letters, and those of people who knew him, and from all sorts of books and papers which show something about him. This kind of biography sometimes fills three, four or even more large volumes. Even if it is not very exciting to read, the reader can usually find anything he wants to know about the man in it.

In more recent times, people who write biographies have thought that the things a man did every day—the meetings he went to and so on—are not as important or interesting as what he thought and what he felt and how he fitted in with the ways of his time. This kind of biography can make a man seem much more

real and the reader can often imagine him much better than from the kind of biography that gives every detail about him. However, if the author lets his imagination run away with him his book may seem more like a romantic story than a real life one. In order to make a better story he may put in all sorts of descriptions which may not always be true. So scholars and historians and other people who really want the true facts do not always trust this kind of biography, but the ordinary reader can enjoy it very much and it will often give him a good idea of what the person was like.

Here are some examples of both these kinds of biographies. James Boswell's *Life of Samuel Johnson* is probably the best known biography of all, and it belongs to the first kind; other enjoyable ones are *Sir Francis Drake* by Julian Corbett, Holmes' *Life of Mozart* and Robert Southey's *Life of Nelson*. Good examples of the second kind are some by Emil Ludwig—*Beethoven, Napoleon* and several others—which are all like novels to read; and Arthur Bryant's life of Samuel Pepys. Anyone who has ever read one or other of these will know how fascinating biography can be.

Of course, there are some biographies which do not quite fit into either of the two kinds. For instance, the life of *Thomas More* by R. W. Chambers has all the true facts, but is written so well that it is more interesting than many novels.

Autobiography

One might think that a person's autobiography, a biography of himself, would be able to show much more about him than one written by someone else. After all, nobody knows better than *you* do what is going on in your mind, what you did in your schooldays, what you thought of your parents and your friends, and all the other things that go to make up your life. There are some facts which you and only you can tell. For example, in Sir Winston Churchill's book *My Early Life,* he described how he escaped when he was a prisoner in South Africa during the Boer War. Nobody else could have told that story so fully, because for most of the time it was happening he was by himself.

However, a good biography contains more

than facts; it contains a lot about a person's character. So here there is a problem. Is anybody a good judge of his own character? Can anybody see himself as others see him? Perhaps most people are either too shy or too conceited about themselves to write really true stories of their lives!

Although autobiographies may not contain as much of the truth as biographies, there are a great many of them and they are usually very interesting and entertaining. Some good autobiographies to begin on are *Far Away and Long Ago* by W. H. Hudson, *Farmer's Glory* by A. G. Street and *The Autobiography of a Super-Tramp* by W. H. Davies.

BIOLOGY is the study of all living things, from the tiniest one-celled plant to the biggest tree, and from tiny one-celled animals to man himself —the most complicated of living creatures. The article LIFE explains the differences between living and non-living things. Scientists who study biology are called biologists.

The two main branches of biology are botany, which is the study of plants, and zoology, which is the study of animals. Many biological sciences apply to both plants and animals; for example, anatomy deals with the way they are put together while physiology deals with the way the different parts of plants and animals work. There are also various names for the study of different groups of animals. A person who studies birds is an ornithologist, one who is particularly interested in insects is an entomologist, and so on.

Man has always wanted to find out about the plants and animals round him and also how his own body works. The first people to write anything down about biology were probably the Greeks. Aristotle was the greatest of the Greek biologists and he dissected, or cut up, fishes and many other animals to see how they are made.

In order to find out more about the human body, Galen, a Greek doctor and philosopher, dissected apes and many other animals as well as the bodies of people. Galen was born in the year A.D. 130 and he wrote descriptions of what he saw, one of the most famous being his essay on the hand. After this, very little new work was done in biology for a very long time although artists were fascinated by the beautiful shapes of plants and animals and of the human form. One of the greatest of these artists was the Italian Leonardo da Vinci, who was also a scientist and an engineer and on whom there is a separate article. He made many wonderful drawings of such parts of the human anatomy as bones and muscles. At the same time books, especially on plants, were being illustrated by hand. People still read the old books but they never

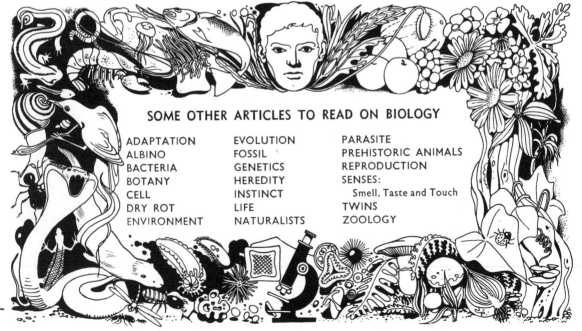

SOME OTHER ARTICLES TO READ ON BIOLOGY

ADAPTATION
ALBINO
BACTERIA
BOTANY
CELL
DRY ROT
ENVIRONMENT

EVOLUTION
FOSSIL
GENETICS
HEREDITY
INSTINCT
LIFE
NATURALISTS

PARASITE
PREHISTORIC ANIMALS
REPRODUCTION
SENSES:
   Smell, Taste and Touch
TWINS
ZOOLOGY

thought of finding out for themselves whether what they read was true. Then Andreas Vesalius, who was a Belgian, wrote a book on the anatomy of the human body. This was published in 1543 and it had a very great influence on biology because Vesalius showed that Galen had been wrong in many of his statements. This encouraged scientists to test things for themselves and not to believe everything they read in books.

The Microscope

By the end of the 16th century botany, zoology, anatomy and physiology were being taught as separate sciences in the universities of northern Italy. Then an enormous step forward was taken with the invention of the microscope. In 1624 the great Italian astronomer Galileo was shown a compound microscope (see MICROSCOPE), and four years later the English doctor William Harvey, who had earlier studied in Italy, made the important discovery that blood moves round people's bodies in arteries and veins and that it is kept moving by the pumping of the heart. By using the microscope the structure of insects was investigated, and also the existence of bacteria. Parts of plants and animals were examined, and in order to describe the smallest unit of any piece of living matter, the word cell was invented.

For more than 100 years after the discovery of bacteria people thought that these tiny plants were made out of decaying matter. In the middle of the 19th century, however, a Frenchman named Louis Pasteur proved that bacteria are found everywhere and that some of them are the causes of certain diseases. This great discovery inspired biologists to look at diseased parts as well as healthy parts of people, animals and plants under the microscope. At the same time the sciences of chemistry and physics were developing and people began to watch and understand chemical and physical changes in the bodies of plants and animals.

The examination of the minute structure of plants and animals led people to try to put them into different groups or classes according to how they are built up. In the 17th century John Ray and Francis Willughby put the flowering plants into different families and grouped animals according to the arrangement and structure of their fingers, toes and teeth. This work of classification, as it is called, was continued by Linnaeus of Sweden (on whom there is a separate article), who collected specimens of plants and animals from all over the world. By using his scheme it is possible to put any plant or animal into its class, its order, its family, then into a genus and finally into a species. So every plant and animal has two Latin names (one for the genus and one for the species) and by using these Latin names people all over the world can understand what plant or animal is meant. For example, the Latin for dog is *canis* and so Linnaeus called all beasts belonging to the dog tribe, or genus, *Canis* and gave each one a second, or specific, name to distinguish it from the others. The domestic dog is called *Canis familiaris*, the wolf is *Canis lupus*, and so on.

Evolution

In the Industrial Revolution coal mines were sunk and cuttings and tunnels were made for the railways. During these excavations fossil animals and plants were dug up and it was discovered that many of the fossils were of kinds of plants and animals that were no longer to be found. These discoveries led to the conclusion that living things must have existed and must also have been changing from one form to another for millions of years. This theory is called evolution because one form evolves, or develops, out of another; it is explained in the article EVOLUTION. A Frenchman, Jean Lamarck, produced the theory in 1809 that the changes in any animal or plant which lead to its becoming another kind of animal or plant are brought about by alterations in its surroundings.

Fifty years later Charles Darwin published in London a book called *The Origin of Species*. Darwin and Alfred Russell Wallace had thought a great deal about how so many different kinds of plants and animals had been evolved, or come into being. They came to the conclusion that every individual plant and animal is slightly different from every other when it starts life, and that the differences have nothing to do with its surroundings. One of the greatest of Darwin's supporters was Thomas Henry Huxley (there are

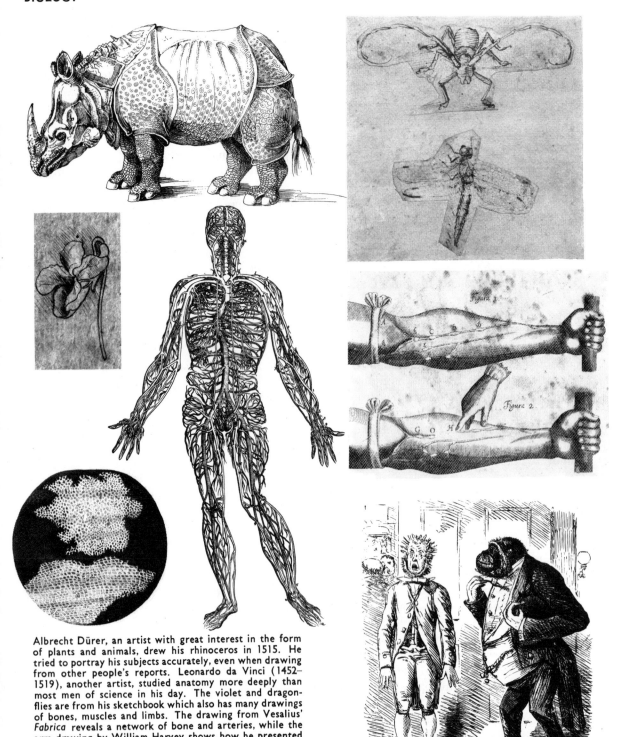

Albrecht Dürer, an artist with great interest in the form of plants and animals, drew his rhinoceros in 1515. He tried to portray his subjects accurately, even when drawing from other people's reports. Leonardo da Vinci (1452–1519), another artist, studied anatomy more deeply than most men of science in his day. The violet and dragon-flies are from his sketchbook which also has many drawings of bones, muscles and limbs. The drawing from Vesalius' *Fabrica* reveals a network of bone and arteries, while the arm drawing by William Harvey shows how he presented his ideas on blood circulation. The microscope helped in accurate observation, and magnified diagrams, such as the one of cork, could be made. Careful observation helped Charles Darwin to compile his theory of evolution. A Punch cartoon of 1861 made fun of the then-astounding idea that man was related to the apes.

articles on both), but the whole idea was very fiercely opposed at first, especially by people who took the biblical story of Adam and Eve to be true in every detail. There are still many arguments about what actually happened but almost everyone agrees that the process of evolution has taken place.

The work of Lamarck and Darwin led scientists to study both heredity, the passing on of characteristics from one generation to another, and environment, the surroundings in which they live. In 1865 a monk named Johann Gregor Mendel made some wonderful discoveries about the peas he was growing in the monastery garden. He showed how the height and other characteristics of different varieties of peas were passed on to their seedlings. (See the article on HEREDITY.) Mendel published his findings in 1866 but little notice was taken of them at the time. When microscopes had been improved enough to study living cells, it was noticed that inside the nucleus there were thread-like bodies. These are called chromosomes. When the cell divided, the chromosomes behaved in a way which agreed with Mendel's laws and suggested that these were the carriers of hereditary characteristics. (See CELL.) Viewed closely through a microscope, the chromosomes look like strings of beads. It is the beads, or genes, which hold the hereditary factors.

The 20th century has seen the development of biochemistry. Biochemists have discovered the stages in which the body acts on the complex chemicals it contains, in order to renew itself. The agents needed for each stage in this reaction are called enzymes and if an enzyme is missing, that particular link in the chain reaction cannot take place. The controlling factor which produces the right enzyme for a cell is the D.N.A. (deoxyribonucleic acid) present in the nucleus. Scientists have discovered both the structure of D.N.A. and the way in which it controls the build-up of enzymes.

Other fields of study in biology are directed to improving man's needs, especially his food plants such as wheat. The first agricultural station was founded at Rothamsted in Hertfordshire, England in 1843. Here plant biologists experimented with different soils and their effect on the growth of crops. Plant diseases and other problems were also studied to help farmers improve their production. There are now agricultural experimental stations all over the world.

Biological studies today include microbiology, the study of microscopic organisms, molecular biology, the study of molecules in biology and marine biology, the study of life in the oceans. In many of these fields, biologists are interested in the relation between living things and their surroundings (see ECOLOGY) and especially the effects of man on his environment. The threat of man's activities to the existence of other living things is now understood more clearly.

BIRCH. One of the most graceful of the woodland trees is the birch which belongs, like the alder, to the Betulaceae family. Unlike most of the other woodland trees the silvery-white bark peels off in thin layers round the trunk. The twigs of the white birch are smooth and hairy but those of the silver birch are warty.

Birch leaves are golden in spring, very green during the summer and yellow in the autumn, after which they fall and make good leaf-mould. The flowers are in the form of catkins and the male ones stay on the tree during the winter to scatter their pollen in the wind the following spring when the female flowers are out to receive it. The females then produce tiny winged fruits, often called seeds, and these are sometimes carried long distances by the wind, which is one reason why birches are found in so many places.

If they have room to grow, silver and white birches will rise to a height of 60 or 70 feet, but a third kind, the dwarf birch, is only a shrubby, creeping plant found on open mountainsides. In the Scottish highlands the silver birch is very common and it is also found in great numbers in the forests of Siberia in the U.S.S.R.

The Russians use the bark to make shoes and for tanning leather. In Great Britain the birch was once widely used for beating children but nowadays a commoner use for the twigs is on brooms. The trunk, being waterproof, can be made into piles for supporting bridges; when skilfully used it also makes an excellent charcoal.

There are many kinds of birch in the world and the wood of some can be polished until it looks like mahogany. The yellow birch of North America, which may grow to a height of 100 feet, is used a great deal for floor-boards. The paper birch, which grows as far north as arctic Alaska, has a waterproof bark used by the Indians of Canada for making canoes; there are references to these canoes in H. W. Longfellow's

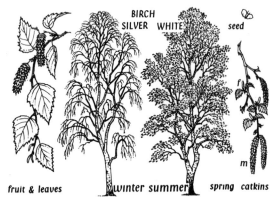

BIRCH
SILVER WHITE   seed

fruit & leaves   winter summer   spring catkins

The male catkin is marked m and the female f.

Hiawatha. The white wood of paper birch is used for spools, toothpicks and dowel rods. Birch wood is also used for making plywood.

BIRD. A bird is an animal with feathers. In other words, it is different from all other living things because it has feathers, but it still belongs to the animal kingdom. Animals are divided up into a number of different classes, or groups. Birds form one of these classes. The two classes nearest to birds are mammals and reptiles.

Birds are just like mammals in having warm blood and backbones; but their front legs have turned into wings which are very different from those of flying mammals like bats. In general, birds are more like reptiles than mammals. For one thing they lay eggs, and only one or two mammals do that. Also, their feathers have developed from the scales that reptiles have. You may not think a fluffy chick looks anything like a lizard or a snake; but there is something in the cold eye and shiny plumage of a farmyard cock that is more like a reptile than a mammal. Some birds are like reptiles in other ways. In the island of Celebes, in Indonesia, there is a bird called the malleo which buries its eggs in the sand and leaves the young to hatch out and look after themselves, just as baby reptiles have to do.

Birds did, in fact, develop from the reptiles which lived 180,000,000 years ago. (The dinosaurs had the same ancestors.) Gradually, over millions of years, some of these creatures lost their teeth and other reptile features, and began to grow feathered wings and tails. Nobody knows for certain how they began to fly. Some scientists think that they climbed on to perches and glided off from there: others say that they first took off by running fast on two legs in open desert country.

For the size of its body, a bird has a much larger brain than a reptile. A bird's whole body is specially made for flight. Its bones are partly hollow, to save weight; its muscles are very strong; and most of its weight is below its wings. This means that it acts like the ballast or weight low down in a ship and keeps the bird on an even keel. The tail helps in steering, acts as a brake and helps the bird to balance.

Different birds fly in different ways. Small land-birds have to beat their wings almost all the time, but many birds can sail or glide on currents of air. The large land-birds, such as ravens and hawks, use the upward currents that you find among the hills, and sea-birds like the albatrosses, petrels and shearwaters use the winds over the ocean. An albatross can race a ship without moving its wings and it may keep up this gliding for hours without seeming to make any effort. (You will find articles on most birds mentioned here.)

The different ways of flying help us to divide birds into different groups and to recognize them. Some fly straight with regular wing-beats—ducks and some waders, for example. Others, like the woodpeckers and many of the finches, rise and dip and rise again. Swallows and swifts always seem to be changing direction, and the big soaring birds glide or flap along in a lazy manner. (See NATURAL FLIGHT.)

As you would expect, birds' wings are designed for the kind of flying they have to do. Game birds have a short, round, "sprinting" type of wing. Eagles and vultures have the large, rounded, soaring and flapping type. Most sea-birds' wings are long, narrow and gliding. Hawks, swallows and waders have the long, narrow pointed "quick-change" wing. Finally, there is the "general purpose" kind of wing which most of the smaller land-birds have.

The way a bird is flying often shows you what it is doing. When the swallow flies overseas for the winter (or migrates, which is the right word for this), it flies much straighter than when it is darting about catching insects in the air. The same bird may fly in different ways when it is hunting or being hunted, moving alone or in a flock, and when courting a mate or defending its territory. (You will find these words explained further on in this article in the section called Song, Courtship and Territory.) Birds do not fly as fast as some people think. Speeds of more than 60 miles an hour are rare, and most small birds fly at 20 or 30 miles an hour.

The ostriches of Africa cannot fly, nor can the rheas of South America, the Australian emus, the kiwis of New Zealand and the penguins. In the Pacific islands of New Caledonia there is a bird called the kagu, which has normal wings, but only uses them to dance about. Perhaps the best-known flightless bird, and the only one in Europe, was the great auk, which died out in 1844. The dodo of Mauritius, an island off the east coast of Africa, became extinct (died out) about 200 years before that.

Usually, the birds which cannot fly have no natural enemies on the ground, and do not need to fly for safety. Unfortunately for many of them, however, man came on the scene and either he or the dogs, cats or rats which followed him became the birds' new enemies.

Plumage

This is the proper name for a bird's feathers. It has been explained that the body and wings of a bird are shaped to suit the way it flies. In the same manner its general plumage and its tail, beak and feet are fitted to play their part in its life.

A bird's plumage keeps it warm and, in the case of water-birds, keeps it waterproof too. Feathers have another job to do. Usually, the colour helps to protect a bird from its enemies and keep it in touch with other birds of the same kind. The colours and pattern often help a male bird to attract a wife or to frighten off a rival.

Very often the bird's colour acts as camouflage and helps it to fit in with its surroundings, but this does not always mean that it is drab and dull. For example, the oystercatcher lives on the shingly shore where there are strong contrasts of light and shade, and its plumage is strikingly black and white. You can read more about this sort of natural camouflage in the article PROTECTIVE COLORATION.

So far, nobody has really found out how the special markings or colours of a bird's plumage help it to recognize others of its own kind. However, we do know that the light markings round the tails of deer help them to follow each other through the woods. So it is quite likely that the white rumps of the bullfinch and the jay help in the same way. This is probably why many birds have white bars or stripes on their wings, although they may be used for display or showing off as well, for the same part of a bird often does several jobs. Tails, for example, are very important in flight and also in display, and the tree-climbing woodpeckers even use their tails to prop themselves up against the trunk of a tree.

There are many different kinds of tails among birds. They range from the short, stiff fringes of the sea-going auks to the wonderful plumes of the birds of paradise, which are several times larger than their bodies.

When a bird's plumage is designed either for courtship or for showing off to enemies in a threatening manner, it must be showy to be of any use. The pattern of the tail, the bars of colour on the wings and the decoration of the head and neck are all important. Good examples are the long tails of peacocks, lyrebirds and birds of paradise; the brightly coloured patch which most ducks have on their wings; and the handsome head ornaments of the great crested grebe and the farmyard turkey. Sometimes both males and females have these fine adornments—the grebes have, for example—but usually it is only the males. Of course, plumage like this makes such birds easy to see. That is why the most showy males do not help at all in bringing up the family. Then, even if the male is seen and killed, the mother and her young ones are safe. But many birds can hide their display feathers by closing their tails and wings and by lowering

THE PARTS OF A TYPICAL BIRD

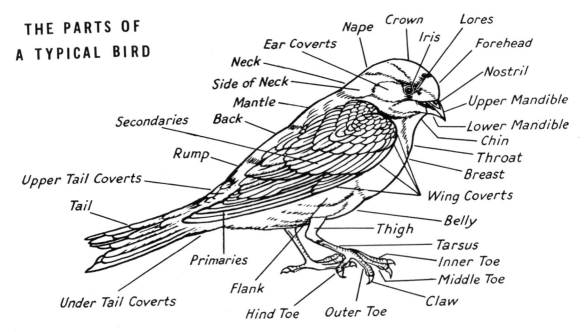

their ruffs and crests. In any case, they lose much of their finery when the feathers moult at the end of the breeding season, but by that time they have done their job. (See FEATHER.)

Bills, Legs and Feet

You can tell a bird by its beak or bill almost as often as you can recognize it by its plumage. Different birds eat different kinds of food, and they also catch it in different ways. The beaks of nightjars and swifts are rather like the clasps of bags and open just wide enough to catch flying insects. If you watch carefully you will notice the medium-sized "general purpose" bills of thrushes and robins, the long probes of the hoopoe and bee-eaters, and the tweezers of the woodpeckers. The extinct huia of New Zealand had a very odd arrangement. The male's beak was straight, with a sharp point for pecking beetle grubs out of wood, while the female had a long curved beak. Probably the male used to chip off flakes of wood to help his mate dig further into the trunk.

The long, needle-shaped bills of the hummingbirds were mainly developed to poke into the tube-like parts of flowers, but they can also catch insects with them.

As a rule, birds that dig for worms have long bills with sensitive tips. The wading birds are a

good example. Many of them breed in the northern hemisphere and spend the winter in the south. So they are well-known to bird-watchers not only in Great Britain and Canada, but also in South Africa, Australia and New Zealand.

Birds which take their food from the water have many different kinds of bill. Ducks which feed on or just below the surface of the water have a broad, dredging kind. One of the most handsome of these is called the shoveller. Petrels and shearwaters have narrower beaks, so that they can pick up morsels from the water and dive as well. The true divers and grebes have straight, spear-shaped bills; and there is a group of ducks called "saw-bills", which have toothlike knobs inside their beaks which help them to grip slippery fish. The skimmers, which scoop the surface of the water while they are on the wing, have the lower part of their beaks longer than the upper part.

Birds which eat fruit generally have shortish, straight bills that can do other jobs as well. This is because they can only find fruit at certain times of the year. But the large beaks of toucans and hornbills are believed to have grown as they are specially to help them reach for fruits. Seed-eaters have rather short, stout bills and the British finches have different sizes of beak according to the kind of seed they eat. They range from the powerful, outsize bill of the haw-finch to the neat bill of the goldfinch, which picks the little seeds out of thistle heads. The bills of the parrots are very powerful and hooked. Parrots are normally seed-eaters but the kea parrot in New Zealand has developed a taste for animal fat.

Although birds of prey have the sort of bills which are obviously useful for tearing flesh, most of them actually catch their victim in their talons. The gulls and skuas, which are sea-birds of prey, also have fierce-looking beaks.

The legs and feet of birds show just as many differences in length and shape as do their bills. Anyone could find out something about the life of a heron or a hawk or a duck by looking at its legs. Herons have long shanks for wading in ponds and rivers. Hawks have long talons for seizing their prey, and of course ducks have webbed feet which help them to swim.

Most birds walk or run on the ground, but many of the smaller ones hop along. Some birds spend most of their time flying or swimming, and these can only shuffle along on land, using their bodies as well as their legs. Nothing looks so awkward as a diver flopping its way from the water to its nest. Most of these birds cannot take off from the ground but need a ledge or the surface of the water to do it.

How different Birds live

Since the days of their reptile ancestors, birds have developed such different ways of living and rearing their young in different countries and climates that they are divided into a large number of kinds or species. The birds themselves seem to know about these, for usually a bird will only mate with one of its own kind. If two birds from different species do mate, their young ones may grow up, but these are usually unable to breed in their turn.

We do not know exactly how many true species there are in the world, but there are probably about 8,000, which is roughly the same as the number of new insect species discovered every year!

Each species of bird has its own way of living. Some move by day and sleep by night. Others move and feed mainly or entirely at night, and there are some which are affected by the moon and by the tides as much as by daylight and darkness.

Again, some birds, of which the European robin is a good example, live alone most of the

Bills and legs show the feeding habits of their owners. (1) Sea-bird beaks for fishermen and scavengers. (2) Special duck bills: the saw-bill (above) and the shoveller. (3) Wader bills: the spear (above) and the probe. (4) Bird of prey's hooked beak and strong claws. (5) Woodland bird's special beak, feet and tail. (6) Sweep-net beak (above) and a bark prober. (7) The tit (above) is an acrobat in the twigs, while the hedge sparrow feeds on the ground. (8) Seed-eating beaks.

time, only taking a mate in the spring when the breeding season starts. Others, like the bullfinch and the raven, are believed to stay with their mates all their lives. Some, like the tits, breed in solitary pairs and join little parties in the winter. Some nest in small groups and flock together in the winter. Many of the finches do this. Birds like rooks, and many of the gulls, not only breed in crowded colonies but spend the rest of the year in flocks, too. Some birds that nest in colonies—razorbills and guillemots, for instance —scatter into loosely connected parties when the breeding season is over. Cormorants and shags and others become solitary wanderers. Finally, there are birds like the warblers and some waders (the common sandpiper is one) which are more or less on their own both in summer and winter, but make up parties when they migrate abroad. Even in one day, a starling or a pied wagtail may feed alone or in a small party and then at night join a roost with hundreds or even thousands of birds of its own kind.

A bird-watcher who gets up early on a spring morning soon notices that different species of bird begin to sing at different times. This is the start of the famous dawn chorus. But on the whole (and unless it wakes at night) the length of a bird's day is the same as the number of hours of daylight. So a bird has to work harder to get food on short winter days than on long summer ones—but if it is feeding a family it has to work hard in any case. A few birds spend the winter in the Arctic Circle, and these have to feed during the hours of twilight.

Except during the nesting season, a bird spends its day in feeding, resting, preening its feathers and in moving from place to place. Some birds will sing a little. Others play about very like children do, and often time will be spent in chasing enemies or trying to avoid them. The time a bird spends doing each thing probably depends on how easily it can get food. When this is easy to find, it may spend hours just sitting or standing on one leg or flying about. As long as a bird is well fed, its warm blood and its feathers help it to keep alive and well in very cold weather. In Great Britain, birds do not usually die of cold; they become weak because of hunger in the first place.

After mid-winter, the first big change in a bird's life is the spring migration, or moving from one place to another. This may be only a short move from a regular winter food supply by a farmhouse to a better breeding place in a nearby wood. The arctic tern, on the other hand, makes a 10,000-mile journey across the equator from the Arctic to the Antarctic, and the swallow may fly from South Africa to Scotland. Some birds do not migrate at all. These are called "residents".

Why Birds Migrate

But tens of millions of birds do migrate every year, and for thousands of years naturalists have been puzzled by this as well as interested and excited. They have always been trying to find out how and why birds migrate and also exactly where they go to. Because birds can fly they are able to make long migrations more easily than other animals; for rivers and seas are not such obstacles to them. Some flightless birds, however, such as the penguin, travel great distances partly by swimming and partly by walking on the ice. Except for a few sea-birds which travel a long way, no species spend the winter in the northern hemisphere and breed in the southern hemisphere, but a great many species winter in the south and travel north to nest. This may be because there is more land north of the equator than south of it. For a long time people thought that migration began when the last great Ice Age drove all living creatures southwards from their old homes.

People sometimes think migration means moving north to a good breeding place in the spring and back to a suitable winter home in the autumn. But there are other kinds of migration as well—up mountain ranges like the Himalayas in the spring, and down again in the autumn; in from the sea to cliffs and islands for breeding, and out again at the end of the summer; or from dry to wet regions in the tropics and back again.

We know a certain amount about what starts migration off. The bird gradually gets excited until something—it may just be that the days are getting longer—makes it set off on its long and dangerous journey. Every year people in

Centre left: Eric Hosking. Lower right: Frank Blackburn–
Bruce Coleman. Others: John Markham

The pheasant (top) is cautiously approaching her nest. The osprey (centre left) is a rare bird in Britain though found all over the world. As with many birds of prey, the female is larger than the male. Another bird of prey, more common, is the sparrow hawk (lower right). Its food is chiefly small birds. Curlews (left) build their nests on the ground, among grass and rushes. The eggs in this nest are just hatching.

John Markham

Top left: The nightingale, famous for its colourful song, has dull plumage. So has the tawny owl (right), another wood-land bird. Bottom left: A young cuckoo, bulging from the nest of its adopted parent, a reed warbler. Cuckoos lay up to twelve eggs and place them all in different nests. Bottom right: The green woodpecker feeds its young with insects.

62

John Markham

Four familiar British birds. The wren (top left) is the smallest of the common British birds. The linnet (top right) has a crimson forehead and breast but loses this colour in winter. It nests in a bush or hedge, and here it has chosen a blackcurrant bush. The great tit (bottom left), beautifully marked, is the largest member of the tit family. The song thrush (bottom right) is easily recognized by its speckled breast. The young, as yet, have few feathers.

Top and bottom right: John Markham. Centre and bottom left:
Eric Hosking

The black backed gull (top) is the largest of its family and can be recognized by its dark markings. The avocet (centre left), once very rare, has long legs typical of wading birds and a beak made for catching insects on the water. Terns (bottom left) are smaller than gulls. They are sometimes called "sea swallows" because of their long, graceful lines. The puffin (above) is found round the British coasts, nesting on islands and cliffs in burrows.

Britain can see the winter flocks of redwings and fieldfares become more and more excited, until one night in March or April they disappear altogether. They may leave behind one or two birds who are not ready to go, but they too have usually disappeared a few days later.

In the last few years scientists have found out a lot about the routes followed by migrating birds. They have done this by putting light aluminium rings round the birds' legs in the hope that some of the birds will be picked up, alive or dead, somewhere on their journey. Then they hope that anyone who finds the birds will write to them and tell them about it. A lot has been learned by watching birds at places where they can be seen moving in large numbers. It is probable that long "waves" of birds start off, but that these are broken up into little parties by obstacles like mountain ranges, or else by stopping at places that they like, such as islands and good feeding places. So birds may fly together in the same direction for part of their journey and gather together in good feeding and resting places, but for the rest of the way they spread out over large areas.

Bird Navigation

How birds find their way is much more difficult to discover. Anyone who keeps racing pigeons knows that they are good at "homing", but these birds are carefully trained to find their way home. First of all they are released quite near the pigeon loft and then gradually farther and farther away. But why is it that young wild birds often go thousands of miles to places they do not know by a route they have never travelled before? For although they sometimes travel with older birds, the young ones often seem to be in parties of their own.

Many scientists have tried to answer this question, but we still do not know for sure how birds do navigate. It may be that they use the sun and perhaps the stars and the moon, as sailors do. They seem to have a good memory for landmarks, too, after they have migrated once.

Much the easiest question to answer is where birds migrate to. Bird ringing has shown roughly where migrating birds spend the winter or go to breed. It is also known how long they take to get

there, too; and ringing has also helped people to find out how long different birds live.

Song, Courtship and Territory

When a summer visitor arrives, or when a resident bird feels that spring is in the air, it begins to make preparations for nesting.

The male bird tells other birds where he is by singing his spring song. He is not only singing a welcome to a possible wife, but also warning other male birds in the neighbourhood. Very few females sing, although the European robin is one of the exceptions. So bird song usually means that the male has taken up a "territory". A territory is an area of land, trees, bushes or water which a bird or a pair of birds will defend against their own kind. Some birds, like robins, take up winter territories; the pairs separate after nesting and the female has a territory of her own.

When a male first takes up his territory he does not only chase away birds of his own species. He also chases away other species which are rather like his own. In the end he allows a female to remain and even begins to woo her by singing special songs, flying about or displaying his plumage in a special way.

A territory may be many acres or even square miles in size, as in the case of large birds of prey. On the other hand it may be just a small piece of ground round about a nest in a colony of birds. In this case, however, the bird may have its own little territory round the nest, in which it can reach out and peck, and it may also share in the larger territory belonging to the whole colony.

So you can see that the idea of a territory is not quite as simple as it sounds. It is safest to say that because birds have territories they are spread out more or less evenly over suitable types of country and that this means that there is plenty of food for all.

Nests, Eggs and Young Birds

Suppose that the male has staked out his territory and found a mate. From now on the start of nesting usually depends on the weather. A bad spell may delay the nesting date of small birds by as much as a fortnight, and a fine period

NESTS

Each kind of bird nests in its own way. Even if it does not construct a nest, it chooses a particular place in which to lay its eggs. All British birds except the cuckoo sit on the eggs to hatch them, and most rear the young within the nest.

The guillemot (above) lays its egg on a bare rock ledge but the shape of the egg helps to prevent it rolling off.

The chaffinch, like many other small birds, builds a deep, cup-shaped nest. The eggs are protected by a thick wall of interwoven hair, moss, lichen and feathers.

Nests like these are usually built high out of harm's way in bushes or trees where the leaves hide them from beasts and birds of prey. The young hatched in such a nest are naked and blind at birth so it keeps them safe and warm until they are ready to leave its protection.

The song thrush's nest is not lined with warm feathers but has a hard lining of "plaster" made from rotten wood or dry dung mixed with saliva.

A really snug nest is made by the tiny long-tailed tit, which builds a completely domed and enclosed nest. It may contain 2,000 feathers and its construction of moss and cobwebs allows it to expand with the growing family of up to twelve nestlings.

A ROOKERY

Large birds such as rooks or herons build big untidy nests of twigs and sticks which last through the winter, to be repaired and used the following spring, often by the same birds.

66

HOUSE MARTINS

The swallow and house martin build nests of mud. They collect mud pellets which, mixed with saliva, form a hard setting cement that sticks firmly to a wall or beam.

NUTHATCH

Nuthatches, which are hole nesters, also use mud to reduce the size of tree holes which might otherwise be taken by larger birds such as starlings. They often choose holes originally hollowed out by woodpeckers.

Many species nest on the ground. Birds like the skylark or meadow pipit, with helpless young, build nests similar to the tree nesting song birds but hide them under thick tufts of grass.

SKYLARK

Other birds excavate holes, sand martins in sand pits and quarries and kingfishers in river banks. These tunnels are often very long with a nesting chamber - usually unlined - at the end.

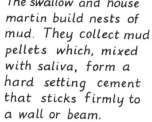

SAND MARTIN

The young of many ground nesting birds are not helpless on hatching but are able to leave the nest within an hour or two.

Wading and game birds, ducks and geese, gulls and nightjars are all examples of ground nesters. Their young are nearly all coloured like their background - camouflaged in fact. Here are some examples.

LAPWING - eggs camouflaged   MALLARD DUCK - well hidden   LITTLE TERN - chick camouflaged   NIGHTJAR - bird camouflaged

Water birds such as grebes are not adapted to life on land and their nests are therefore built on the water. Often these are floating platforms, anchored to overhanging branches or built among reed stems, but where the water is shallow the base of the nest may rest on the bottom. These nests are often quite exposed but look like piles of rotting vegetation. To protect the whitish eggs the bird covers them with nest material before slipping from the nest into the water.

GREAT CRESTED GREBES

(1) The cormorant is a relative of the pelican. It is a marvellous swimmer, pursuing fish at great speed under water.
(2) Largest of the pelicans is the African pelican, sometimes called the rosy pelican. (3) The American white pelican.
(4) The brown pelican found along the southern sea coasts of America.

1

2

3

4

(1) The crowned crane has a tufted crest of wire-like bristles. It is found in Africa and its voice makes a jarring sound. (2) The Stanley or blue crane is found in South Africa. (3) The smallest crane, called the demoiselle, gathers in flocks in winter in southern Europe. It is also found in Asia and Africa. (4) The Sarus crane, found in Asia, often performs dances, flapping its wings and leaping about.

Members of the stork family. (1) The shoebill or whalehead stork from Africa. (2) The marabou stork, a valuable scavenger in Africa. (3) The woolly-necked stork from Africa and Asia. (4) The saddle-billed stork, from tropical Africa. (5) The white stork, found in Europe, Asia and Africa. It often builds its nest on a chimney or in a tree near a house.

(1) The swan goose is a rare bird found in eastern Siberia. (2) The coscoroba of South America is sometimes called the coscoroba swan, although it is not a true swan. (3) The black swan of Australia and Tasmania is slightly smaller than the other swans. (4) The black-necked swan is found in South America.

All the flamingos have red wings with black quills and build cone-shaped nests of clay and vegetable matter. (1) The Chilean flamingo (foreground) lives in temperate South America but is never as brightly coloured as the deep vermilion American flamingos (background) will become. (2) The pinkish-white African flamingo is found in southern Europe, southern Asia and Africa. (3) The American flamingo lives along the Atlantic coast of tropical Africa and is the most colourful member of the flamingo family— the only one of the six species which is mostly red. It can also be found on the Galapagos islands and breeds in the Bahamas, Cuba, southeast Mexico and in the Guianas.

Penguins are flightless birds adapted for life in the water. (1) The king penguin is found in the islands of the southern oceans near the Antarctic. (2) The fairy penguin comes from Australia and New Zealand. (3) The Humboldt penguin lives on the west coast of South America. (4) A Humboldt penguin swimming; the body is streamlined, and the wings are fin-like.

BIRD

The four surviving large flightless land birds. Unlike most flying birds they are strong runners and grow to a great size. (1) Bennett's cassowary is found in New Guinea and northern Queensland. All cassowaries have a horn casque (helmet) on the head but Bennett's cassowary is not as colourful as most. It has a reddish purple neck instead of the blue, red and yellow of its relatives. (2) The ostrich, largest of all birds, lives only in the sandy bushland of Africa. It is the only bird which has two toes. (3) The rhea lives in the pampas of South America. Though smaller than the ostrich it has powerful legs and can run at great speed. (4) The emu, the second largest living bird, is found in remote, open regions of Australia. It is a good swimmer, and, as with the cassowary, each of its feathers is double.

Photo 1, Gjon Mili

These birds, although unlike in appearance, are related. (1) The rhinoceros hornbill is found in Java. Other birds of the same species are found in Malaysia, Sumatra and Borneo. Hornbills have "casques" on top of their large beaks and these growths are spongy in contrast to the heavy bill. When nesting, the female is sealed in a hollow tree and kept there until the single egg has hatched and the young is well grown. (2) The sacred kingfisher is found from Sumatra to Australia. It nests in a hollow branch, a river bank or a termite's nest in a tree. (3) The laughing jackass, or kookaburra, is found in Australia. As its name suggests its cry is wild and jarring. (4) The chestnut headed motmot, like most of its family, has a racket-shaped tail which develops after the two long central feathers have grown. It is found in Guatemala.

(1) The budgerigar comes from Australia. The normal colour in the wild is green but selective breeding has produced blue, yellow and white varieties. (2) The blue and yellow macaw from South America. (3) Leadbeater's cockatoo, sometimes called the pink cockatoo, from Australia. (4) The red and blue macaw of Central and South America.

(1) The swinhoe pheasant is found on the island of Taiwan. It is common in captivity and easily bred, but little is known of its natural habits. (2) The impeyan pheasant, found in the Himalayas, feeds on greens, grains, tubers and insects. (3) The golden pheasant, one of the most beautiful pheasants, is found in western China in rocky regions covered with scrub bamboo. (4) The Landy Amherst pheasant is found in the mountains of Tibet and China.

77

may make it a fortnight early. Big birds, however, seem to be less affected by the weather.

Once it has begun, the building of the nest may take any time from one day to three weeks. The long-tailed tit starts early on a very complicated dome-shaped nest and it may have to stop building during bad weather. The nesting site may be chosen just before building begins or, in the case of a resident pair, it may have been chosen the autumn before. Many birds return to the same site, or very near to it, year after year.

The site may be chosen, and the nest built, by the male or the female, or they may work together. The parts played by the two birds vary a lot and the only certain thing you can say is that the female lays the eggs. With some birds—the phalaropes and the dotterel, for example—the female may leave the territory altogether while the male sits on the eggs and looks after the young. With many ducks and game birds the opposite happens. Usually, however, it is the duller looking partner who does most of the work.

Birds' nests may be found in almost any place —under the ground, on the ground, or high up in trees, rocks or buildings. Some penguins lay their eggs on ice floes and never come to dry land at all. The nests range from the complicated nests of the weaver birds, which are often shared by several pairs, to nothing at all, as in the case of the guillemot.

The eggs may be pure white and nearly circular like those of the owls, or pointed and densely coloured like the waders'. These are laid in the open and designed to match their surroundings so that enemies cannot find them.

Two very interesting subjects are the usual number or "clutch" of eggs a bird lays in a nest, and the time of year it does it. Why should a sea-bird like the fulmar petrel, which seldom lays its single egg until the end of May, be able to increase its numbers as fast as it has done in Great Britain? The tits and game-birds and many others lay up to 12 or even 20 eggs, but the number of actual birds does not grow in the same way. The reason is probably this. Birds lay a clutch to produce a family they can feed without tiring themselves out, and they lay them at the time of year when there is plenty of food. But the number of birds to be found in a country at any particular time depends upon completely different things. These may be changes made by man in the birds' surroundings or perhaps gradual changes in the climate.

Small eggs usually hatch more quickly than large ones. But how long the young stay in the nest depends on how well prepared for life they are when they hatch. Young ducks, game-birds and waders can run or swim a few hours after leaving the egg, but although young nightjars are born on the bare ground, like waders, they are helpless for about a fortnight. Most young birds which hatch out in elaborate nests, or in holes and burrows, are also helpless.

Normally, the smaller the bird the more often its parents feed it. Each young great tit in a brood may be fed 40 times in a day. Young hawks, on the other hand, are stuffed with large meals every few hours. Most of the birds whose young remain in the nest remove their droppings; otherwise the nests would become very dirty.

When the young are due to leave the nest they are not taught to fly by their parents, as some people think. Flying comes by instinct. That is, they fly naturally but they improve with practice. The parents of most small birds watch their family "fledge", or leave the nest. Some sea-birds, such as the shearwaters, leave their young ones to look after themselves, but most birds care for their families for a while after they have fledged. If there is to be a second brood, one parent may remain with the first lot of young, while the other builds the new nest. Some species have three or four broods in a season, and many will have a second. This is most likely to happen if the first clutch is destroyed.

The Scattering of Birds after Breeding

What happens in the breeding season is fairly clear, but it is much harder to find out how birds live at the end of the summer and in the autumn. Their numbers are then at their greatest, and many of them begin to form flocks. In some species, however, the young scatter in all directions. The proper name for this is dispersal.

The moult usually takes place at this time.

The old feathers fall out and new ones grow. Moulting birds are shy of showing themselves, especially when, as in the case of ducks, it means they cannot fly for a while. But in Great Britain the bushes and plants are thickest in late summer, and this helps the birds to hide. It also explains why we know less about what birds do at this time of year.

When at last they have finished moulting it is time for the summer visitors to leave. The autumn migration is more exciting to watch than the spring one, because most birds take part. For that reason you can often see large numbers of travelling birds, particularly at some places on the coast. At the same time as the summer migrants leave Britain, so the winter visitors begin arriving from the Arctic, where they have nested. By November, the bird population is settling down once more to its winter way of life.

The Study of Birds

The correct name for the study of birds is ornithology. The Father of Ornithology is usually reckoned to be William Turner, an English clergyman who lived about 400 years ago. The first man to work out a system of scientific names for all birds and other living things was the Swedish naturalist Carl von Linné. He is known as Linnaeus and he lived in the 18th century. At about the same time lived Gilbert White, who was the curate of Selborne in Hampshire. He wrote a famous book called the *Natural History of Selborne* which was really a diary of all the birds and wild animals he saw. He still believed that when some birds disappeared in the autumn and winter they were hibernating, or sleeping, instead of migrating.

Today, we know a lot about the way birds are spread over the world. Naturalists concentrate now on the problems of migration, the way birds fit into their surroundings and their behaviour. Perhaps the last is the most fascinating of all.

Great Britain is lucky enough to have a number of bird observatories, mostly on the coast, where people can study migration and other problems. There are several field study centres, as they are called, where young naturalists can go for training in how to watch birds. There are also private bird sanctuaries and a law has been passed which sets aside national nature reserves as well.

BIRD OF PARADISE. Because they were once believed to feed on the dew of heaven, a large family of birds in New Guinea, northeastern Australia and the nearby islands are called birds of paradise. They live in the thick forest. Some of them are no larger than a song thrush, while others are as big as crows.

Fully grown cocks, three to five years old, often have strange plumes of scarlet, gold, green and many other colours, as well as brilliant feathers. Some have very long tails; others have long feathers growing from the head, under the tail or wings, or in tufts on the breast. Many show off their wonderful plumes by doing an elaborate kind of dance. First they spread out their wings and tails. Then they make their feathers stand on end and vibrate them until they seem to be covered with a quivering spray of colours.

The females, however, are plain, and this helps them to hide their nests from their enemies.

There are nearly 50 different species and they can usually be told apart by the colouring and arrangement of the cocks' plumes. The king bird of paradise has fiery red wings, back and head, and his middle tail feathers curve out like slender wires, ending in bright green spirals. The twelve-wired bird of paradise gets its name from the six wire-like feathers which spring from each side. The Prince Rupert's, or blue, bird of paradise displays its feathers by hanging by its feet, head downwards. This makes its blue plumes fall over it like a shimmering waterfall.

The greater bird of paradise is one of the most beautiful and best known. It has long, yellowish plumes on its back and lovely, emerald green feathers on its neck, and it is found only in New Guinea and the nearby Aru Islands. When in 1522 Ferdinand Magellan's sailors returned from their voyage round the world, they brought two skins of these birds home with them. The natives had cut off the feet of the birds, and for many years people believed that such strange footless birds existed. There was a story that the female laid her eggs in a hollow on the cock's back and hatched them there. The lesser

The male greater bird of paradise, from New Guinea. This was the first bird of paradise known in Europe.

bird of paradise is rather like the greater, but it is smaller and paler.

The rifleman birds, or rifle birds, are found in Australia and New Guinea. They probably got their name because their green and black colouring looked rather like a uniform which had once been worn by the British rifle regiments.

The manucodes are the ugly ducklings of the family and are almost the only members which look like their distant relatives the crows.

When they are showing off their beautiful plumes in the breeding season, a party of birds of paradise will gather together in a tree. Then they become so excited with their dance that they are easy to kill. This was done for a time, when their feathers were much wanted by women for trimming their hats. Hundreds of thousands of the birds were shot and the greater and lesser birds of paradise were in danger of dying out.

Luckily, however, Britain, the United States and some other countries stopped the feathers being brought into the country, and laws were also passed to protect the birds in their native haunts. In this way they are fairly safe, although many countries still import them.

Birds of paradise generally nest in the branches of trees, but some species nest in holes in the trunk. Usually two eggs are laid, mainly a creamy buff colour streaked and spotted with brown, grey and lavender. They eat almost anything they can find, from fruit to snails and insects. Birds of paradise are closely related to the bower-birds. (See BOWER-BIRD.)

BIRD SANCTUARIES.

A person who has a bird table (and preferably no cat), or a coconut hanging outside the window, has a simple kind of bird sanctuary, for in its simplest form a bird sanctuary is any place where birds may rest and feed undisturbed.

However, the word "sanctuary" can be used for various kinds of refuge for birds. The name may be given to a few square yards of trees and bushes in a garden or in a corner of a town park, or to something much larger like St. James's Park in London. This park attracts a remarkable number of species, or kinds, of birds, among them ducks and gulls which spend the winter on or near the lake before returning to nest in distant parts of Europe.

In Britain some, but by no means all, of the places commonly called bird sanctuaries are officially recognized as such and protected by law. Since 1949 the Nature Conservancy has had the power to set up Nature Reserves and in these all wild life is protected. Nature Reserves are not the same as National Parks (see NATIONAL PARKS), which are great areas of country set aside chiefly for humans to enjoy, though they may contain Nature Reserves within their limits.

The largest Nature Reserve is in the Cairngorm mountains, and there are several other big ones in Scotland, such as the island of Rhum in the Inner Hebrides. Reserves are maintained in woodland areas, coastal marsh and reed beds in East Anglia.

Anyone may apply for his garden to be officially declared a bird sanctuary, but most people prefer to rely on the ordinary laws protecting private property. There are many ways in which a garden can be made more attractive to birds. Bird tables in the winter and nest-boxes in the breeding season are obvious methods. Also, shrubs can be planted to give cover at all times and food in the form of berries in autumn. Sunflowers and other plants with large seeds are also welcomed. A bird bath or a small pond is a great attraction but should not be put too near cover from which a cat may pounce.

Larger gardens and parks can be improved for birds in the same way although any areas of open space must be well protected from interference by animals and humans.

Some land-owners preserve their estates only because they like to shoot game-birds and duck in season. This preservation helps many other birds, though there are still gamekeepers who shoot birds of prey and even owls because of the harm these are said, with little proof, to do to young game-birds.

Sanctuaries for Water Birds

The sporting interest in ducks and geese has led to the provision of great sanctuaries for them all over the world. The Canadian and United States governments, being worried about the vast

Tom Weir

Sea birds on the Farne Islands, a bird sanctuary off the Northumberland coast. The birds on the skyline are guillemots. Most of the gulls are kittiwakes.

E. E. Jackson

Rushy Fen, part of the Wildfowl Trust's refuge at Slimbridge, Gloucestershire. The ducks, geese and other water birds which belong to the Trust's permanent collection are joined every year by thousands of wild birds which spend the winter in the safety of the enclosures.

numbers which have been killed, maintain many sanctuaries for waterfowl; even outside these refuges the hunting of ducks and geese by gun or in any other way, is only allowed for a few weeks each winter. Similar arrangements are made on a smaller scale in Britain.

Some sanctuaries in North America are for particular species, such as the few remaining trumpeter swans and whooping cranes which would probably have died out otherwise. Other birds, such as herons, pelicans, egrets, ibises and spoonbills, which nest in colonies, or groups, and whose breeding places are well-known to their human and other enemies, are also specially protected. There are British reserves for ospreys and snowy owls.

In Great Britain there are several big wild-

fowl refuges in the Humber, between Yorkshire and Lincolnshire, but the best known is the one at Slimbridge beside the River Severn in Gloucestershire. Here thousands of wild geese spend part of the winter on the "dumbles" (an area of grassy salt marsh) or on the fields nearby, while in the enclosures are many kinds of ducks, geese and swans brought from all over the world. These are free to walk or swim but most of them have been "pinioned"; that is, the large outer feathers of their wings have been cut off and they cannot fly. Each winter, however, they are joined by hundreds of wild ducks.

The Wildfowl Trust also has its own Waterfowl Gardens at Peakirk, in Northamptonshire, near the Borough Fen duck decoy. Most of the few remaining duck decoys in Britain are now

☐ Read WHAT TO SEE IN OUR NATURE RESERVES in the blue pages of volume 5

used to catch birds for ringing, a numbered aluminium ring being placed round their legs before they are released.

Bird Observatories

Bird ringing is also the main object of the chain of bird observatories now established round the British coasts. Few of them are bird sanctuaries in the strict sense, but the ordinary law on bird protection covers most of the birds which visit them.

These observatories are usually set up on islands or headlands which are well known to be visited by numbers of small migrating birds on their long journeys northward to breed in spring or south again in autumn. Large funnel-shaped traps of wire netting are put up where there are a few bushes or other cover. These attract the birds, which can then be driven into the mouth of the trap and caught and ringed at the narrow end. If a ringed bird is recovered and the ring is returned to the address marked on it, it gives valuable information about the bird's migration.

The first bird observatory in Great Britain was on Skokholm Island, off the coast of Pembrokeshire. The most famous is on Fair Isle, between the Shetland and Orkney Islands, and here over 300 kinds of birds have been recorded. There are about a dozen coastal observatories around the coasts of England, Scotland, Ireland, Wales and the Channel Islands.

Sea-bird Sanctuaries

Several of the bird observatories are on islands famous for their colonies of sea-birds and many of these are now protected as legal sanctuaries or Nature Reserves. The people who look after the birds' safety, called watchers, live on some of them, such as the Farne Islands off Northumberland, all through the nesting season. To spend a summer on one of these sanctuary islands, among the gulls and terns, the puffins, razorbills and guillemots, the gannets and cormorants, is one of the greatest experiences a bird-watcher can have.

There are similar sanctuaries for sea-birds in many other countries of the world, particularly in North America. Bermuda, in the North Atlantic, has several small sanctuaries for the capped petrel; Hawaii Island in the Pacific has a nature reserve for albatrosses and other sea-birds, while the breeding places of the royal albatross and the yellow-eyed penguin are protected at Taiaroa Head, New Zealand.

BIRD-WATCHING. To watch birds you need a sharp eye and a keen ear. It is also important to have a bird book with coloured pictures, which tells you about all the birds you are likely to see.

That is all you really need to begin with; but you will probably find it also helps to carry a small notebook in your pocket. Then you can make a note on the spot (with the date) of any bird or thing which interests you. The notes you make while you are out bird-watching are called field notes. It is also a good idea to keep a larger notebook at home and copy out these field notes properly, so that you have a permanent record.

Before long, by using your bird book and if possible with the help of someone who knows a lot about birds, you will get to know all the most common birds in the garden and along the hedges. Then you will want to find new kinds, or species, of birds. To do this you must explore farther afield in woods and on commons, and perhaps on hills, marshes, reservoirs and sea cliffs. In this wilder country you may find it difficult to get close to the birds you are watching. So if you can you should bring them "closer" to you by looking at them through binoculars.

Good binoculars are expensive, even second-hand ones, but when you become an expert bird-watcher you will realise that it is better to wait until you can buy a good pair of binoculars than to get a cheap pair on the spur of the moment and then be disappointed because they do not magnify well and give a blurred image or picture. If you use a good pair of 24 mm. × 6 or 32 mm. × 8 prismatic glasses (these figures measure their power) you will find yourself entering an exciting new world in which the most distant bird is brought close to you. Also, glasses like this will show up every detail of a bird's plumage, even in the dim light of a wood or the inside of a bush.

When you can recognize a bird by eye you

have taken the first step in your training as a naturalist. (A naturalist is a person who studies animals and plants.) For identifying birds a good ear is just as important as a keen eye. This is because there are many birds, like some of the warblers, which look so much alike that even an experienced naturalist can only tell them apart by measuring their wings, beak and legs. However, no two species of bird have exactly the same call-note or song, and before you can call yourself a really good naturalist, you should be able to distinguish blindfold all the notes and songs of the most common birds. So long as you have a fairly good ear and a good memory, this is not so difficult as you might think. The important thing is to practise. You can buy records of bird songs by Ludwig Koch which will help you. So really there is no hurry for the binoculars. Begin learning with naked eye and ear on the common birds first.

Secrets of Bird Life

What is the point of watching birds at all? The answer is that if you do not, every time you go for a walk you are missing a great deal. If you do not know what are the birds you see, what they are doing or where their nests are, you might as well be blind and deaf. There is a tremendous amount to find out about birds; in fact you could watch one kind of bird all your life and still not learn everything about it. For that matter, you could watch one pair of birds all through the nesting season, and learn a lot about their habits that no one else has discovered. Oddly enough, some of the commonest British birds, like the house sparrow, are those we know least about.

There are certain secrets of bird life which are especially interesting. The first of these is how a bird spends its time. People have found out a lot about how a bird behaves at the nest, when it is sitting on its eggs or brooding its nestlings; but we do not know much about what a bird does when it is away from the nest or during a winter's day. It is difficult to follow one particular bird, but it is fairly easy to keep in touch with a flock of birds, such as rooks and jackdaws, for several hours at a time.

We know that a bird spends a good deal of its time in feeding or searching for food, but we are not so certain about what food is eaten by different kinds of birds. This is a problem which most farmers would like to solve. For if there were no birds then in a few weeks the insects they feed on would have eaten up every green thing on the earth. However, there are some birds which eat large quantities of grain or seedlings as well as insects. The question is, do these birds which eat up the farmer's grain make up for it by also eating plenty of the insects and grubs which harm the farmer's crops? In the case of the rook, it does.

As well as finding out what a bird does, a bird-watcher usually wants to know where it lives. When you go away for a holiday you may find the birds you know at home living in quite different surroundings. You may discover bull-finches living in pine forests, or starlings on sea cliffs among the gulls and puffins, or sparrows on an island several miles from the mainland. Ornithologists (the name given to people who study birds) would like to know how many of these "foreigners" there are compared with their fellows living in their normal surroundings. They would also like to know whether their habits and food are different. Also, if you have learnt all the songs and call-notes of your home birds, you will find, if you have a good ear, that these may be a little different in other parts of the country.

If you take your holiday at the seaside in the spring or autumn you will be able to watch migration; that is, birds leaving the coast to go to a warmer climate or else arriving in your country from a place which is colder. Seeing great colonies of sea-birds on cliffs and islands, watching wild geese on the marshes, watching huge flocks of wading-birds such as curlew or dunlin in massed flight, observing birds on migration—these are the most exciting part of bird-watching. Remember, you have as good a chance as the expert of seeing on migration some rare wanderer which has only been seen once or twice before, or perhaps never before in the British Isles. Your local natural history society, or field club, will want to hear about your good luck and also about any unusual movement of birds you see, both on the coast and inland.

☐ Read more about BIRD-WATCHING in the blue pages of volume 12

If you want to encourage birds into the garden the first rule is to keep it free of bird-hunting cats. The next important thing is to provide plenty of cover, that is, bushes and trees in which the birds can take refuge when alarmed and in which some will be able to build their nests in the spring. Robins are among the very few garden birds that will nest on the ground and even these prefer a bank. Blackbirds, song thrushes, hedge sparrows and linnets will build in fairly low bushes; but finches and missel thrushes prefer to be higher, goldfinches choosing fruit trees and chaffinches and greenfinches liking evergreens such as cypresses. One or two birds—perhaps even a pair of spotted flycatchers—will nest in a plant climbing the wall of the house. Tits will make use of wooden nest-boxes.

A pool with waterweeds to stand on will appeal to finches in particular, but a small bird bath or bowl will be enough for many birds, particularly if the ice is broken for them in frosty weather. Food is also most needed when the ground is frozen and perhaps snow-covered; it is best to put the food on a one-legged bird table so that rats and mice cannot reach it. Many birds will eat scraps of bread and cake crumbs and even cold potato and porridge. Tits—blue, great, coal and marsh—prefer bacon rind or any other fat, as well as cheese, and will enjoy half a coconut hung on a tree. Finches need mixed seeds such as are sold at pet shops.

BIRMINGHAM in the English midlands is the second largest city in Great Britain, with about 1,013,366 inhabitants. The city is in the geographical county of Warwickshire, but in the reorganization of local government it becomes part of the metropolitan county of the West Midlands.

The people of Birmingham earn their living in a great variety of ways. A large number are metal workers of various kinds, producing everything from motor cars to jewellery, but there are also thousands who make such things as glass, chocolates, rubber and leather goods, brass and chemicals, paints and plastics. Many large manufacturing cities in Great Britain came to rely on one or two main industries but Birmingham has over a thousand trades, so that only part of the population suffers when an industry falls on bad times.

The gun trade was thriving before the end of the 17th century and in the following century a considerable amount of steel was made in Birmingham, for the town was not far from coal and iron mines. The steel industry moved away from Birmingham, but the people who used metal to make their goods remained and were joined by others who started to manufacture cars, cycles, railway rolling stock and many

Central Office of Information

The Rotunda is a landmark in the changing city centre.

other things. Today there is a car firm that can produce 1,000,000 vehicles a year. Here too is the world's largest cocoa and chocolate factory. These are large and famous factories, but there are a great number of smaller and even "one-man" businesses turning out all kinds of products. Many an individual hopes that his efforts will start a large new firm. It was always easy for a new-comer to set up business in Birmingham for he did not find the other manufacturers working against him, as happened in so many towns in the 17th century in particular. (See GUILD.)

This freedom from restrictions encouraged a number of remarkable men whose inventions and discoveries have benefited the whole world.

Those famous partners, Matthew Boulton and James Watt, built an improved steam engine and William Murdock, who worked for them at the famous Soho Manufactory, invented gas-lighting. Other famous men who lived and worked in Birmingham were Joseph Priestley, the chemist who discovered the elements oxygen and nitrogen, and John Baskerville, the printer.

Like other cities which grew rapidly in the 18th and 19th centuries (see INDUSTRIAL REVOLUTION), Birmingham has experienced most of the problems which people meet when they live together in large numbers. The most famous name in the city's history is that of Joseph Chamberlain, who was elected to the Council in 1869; this was a period of rapid development during which the gas and water supplies came under civic control and the first slum clearance scheme was started which, costing £1,500,000, swept away a dense slum area to provide what is now Corporation Street. Much of this area has again been rebuilt.

John Bright, who helped Richard Cobden to get rid of the tax on corn from abroad in the middle of the 19th century, was a member of parliament for Birmingham for many years. So was John Cadbury, who was one of those who urged parliament to stop the use of boys for cleaning chimneys (see CHIMNEY SWEEP); he even provided local chimney sweeps with brushes and insisted that they used them. George and Richard Cadbury had the idea of "a factory in a garden village" and in 1879 they started Bournville.

There are separate articles on many of the men and women mentioned who set out to improve the town and living conditions of the people of Birmingham.

The Sights of the City

Nineteenth-century Birmingham grew up haphazardly, with scarcely any plan, but the city now has well planned roads to cater for the needs of modern traffic. In the city centre is the Bull Ring, an ancient market area which has been turned into a modern air-conditioned shopping centre with facilities of all kinds. An open-air market is held also.

The memory of Joseph Chamberlain is preserved by a 325-foot tower which marks from afar the University of Birmingham at Edgbaston. Another university, that of Aston, was opened in 1966. Some of the stained glass windows in St. Philip's Cathedral were designed by Sir Edward Burne-Jones, a famous painter who was born in Birmingham in 1833. The Oratory of St. Philip Neri was the home of Cardinal John Henry Newman in the 19th century.

The people of Birmingham have also one of the finest art galleries in the country, and an interesting Museum of Science and Industry. Aston Hall is a beautiful 17th-century mansion on the northeast side of the city open to the public. The Repertory Theatre, one of the first and most successful, founded by Sir Barry Jackson, has been re-housed in a new theatre adjoining the civic centre. The city also has a fine symphony orchestra. In Cannon Hill Park the Midlands Art Centre allows young people to enjoy all forms of the arts, including drama, painting and music.

Some at least of the industrial importance of Birmingham is due to its position so near the centre of England. It is served by railways and by roads which fan out in all directions and there is a modern airport at Elmdon. The British Broadcasting Corporation has its regional broadcasting headquarters in Birmingham and Independent Television studios are operated there also. The first television transmitter outside London was built at nearby Sutton Coldfield.

BIRTHSTONE. From very early times people have believed that precious stones have mysterious powers that can bring good luck to their owners. A particular jewel was often thought to be connected with one particular month of the year and so if a person wore that jewel in the right month or if he was born in that month himself, it was specially lucky. These stones connected with the months of the year were therefore called birthstones.

In olden days the jewels for each month were as follows: January—Hyacinth; February—Amethyst; March—Jasper; April—Sapphire; May—Agate; June—Emerald; July—Onyx; August—Cornelian; September—Chrysolite;

Geological Museum

From left to right: garnet, amethyst, bloodstone, aquamarine, diamond, rock crystal, emerald, chrysoprase, moonstone, pearl, ruby, carnelian, peridot, sardonyx, lapis lazuli, sapphire, opal, tourmaline, topaz, zircon, turquoise.

October—Beryl; November—Topaz; December—Ruby.

There are slightly different versions, however, as can be seen in the list below. This is a list of birthstones, their months as they are usually given and the properties the stones are said to have—that is, their powers for good or evil:

Month	Stone	Property
January	Garnet	gives faithfulness
February	Amethyst	stops violent passions
March	Bloodstone	gives courage and wisdom
	Aquamarine	brings new friends
April	Diamond	gives purity and peace
	Rock crystal	
May	Emerald	ensures true love
	Chrysoprase	
June	Moonstone	warns of impending danger
	Pearl	gives wealth
July	Ruby	discovers poison
	Carnelian	
August	Peridot	
	Sardonyx	gives married happiness
September	Sapphire	gives freedom from enchantment
	Lapis lazuli	
October	Opal	brings mental or physical harm
	Tourmaline	causes an accident
November	Topaz	gives friendship and faithfulness
December	Turquoise	gives prosperity in love
	Zircon	safeguards health and wealth

BISCAY, BAY OF. The Atlantic Ocean takes a great bite out of the west coast of Europe to form the Bay of Biscay, which, with the Pyrenees Mountains, cuts off Spain from the rest of the continent. Sailing to or from the English Channel, people are always glad when they have left the bay behind for this part of the voyage is often so rough that only the hardiest of sailors escape sea-sickness.

There are rocky cliffs along most of the southern (Spanish) shore, with the Cantabrian Mountains rising in the background. The curving French shore is generally low and only in Brittany, in the north, are there many natural harbours, although the large estuaries of the Loire and the Gironde have provided suitable places for the great ports of Bordeaux and Nantes. The westerly winds, the heavy waves and the tides, working together, are constantly piling sand and mud from the sea bed on to the French part of the coast. In the Landes district the sand dunes threatened to spread inland and cover the farms until pine trees were planted to help anchor the shifting sand.

Trained in these stormy seas, the fishermen of the Basque ports, in the southeastern corner of

the bay, and of Brittany, in the north, long ago became skilful sailors. For centuries they have visited the fishing grounds of Iceland and Newfoundland in their small sailing ships and these can still be seen beside the modern steamers which carry wine from Bordeaux and iron ore from Bilbao, in Spain.

BISCUIT. The word biscuit is really two French words, *bis cuit*, meaning "twice cooked". Today the only biscuit which is in fact baked twice is a rusk, but the name was first given to a kind of bread which was baked twice so that it would keep for a long time. It was the food of sailors, soldiers on campaigns and travellers on long journeys. "Hard tack", as it was called, was so hard that it had to be broken up with a mallet. A tastier biscuit, however, was being made in France as long ago as the 13th century. For this, light bread was cut up, soaked in wine and then dried.

All biscuits today are baked with a basis of flour mixed with milk or water. The many different kinds of biscuits are made by the addition of all sorts of other ingredients and flavours, such as butter, eggs, sugar, honey, oatmeal, chocolate, almonds, salt, cheese, ginger, cinnamon and all manner of spices. Some biscuits are made to be eaten spread with butter or with cheese, and these are usually unsweetened; among such dry biscuits are cream crackers, thin captain, rusks and Bath Olivers. Wheaten biscuits are fine wafers of the kind once served with a glass of wine at mid-morning.

Most of the biscuits eaten today are sweet biscuits, the most famous of which are probably shortbread (a Scottish speciality), ginger nuts, digestive, Marie and petit beurre. There are all sorts of variations on these plain sweet biscuits. Some have dried fruit in them, like the currant biscuit named after the 19th-century Italian leader Garibaldi but often known to English children as "squashed flies"; some are sandwich biscuits, with fillings of cream or chocolate, like custard creams, wafers and bourbons; some are coated with plain or milk chocolate—one biscuit has marshmallow on a sweet biscuit beneath a covering of chocolate. Chocolate fingers and biscuits with chocolate cuttings are popular.

Every biscuit manufacturer probably makes his own versions of all these, and English biscuits are sent in great quantities all over the world. In modern factories much of the work is done by machines. The biscuits are mixed and cut into shape by machines and sometimes baked in long ovens on moving belts. Machines, too, often do the packing of finished biscuits.

The flavour of manufactured biscuits is never quite the same as that of home-made ones. Some favourite home-made biscuits are shortbread and brandysnaps.

The chief full-bore rifle shooting competition in Great Britain is held at Bisley in July.

BISLEY. The setting up in 1890 of rifle ranges at this little village in Surrey, 29 miles from London, was an important event in the history of firearms. Before that the National Rifle Association used to hold its meetings on Wimbledon Common, London, but small arms had become so effective towards the end of the 19th century that it was necessary to provide longer ranges where there were fewer people.

The ranges were opened on Bisley Common and here the Association organized meetings for their shooting competitions. The annual meeting in July attracts marksmen from all parts of the Commonwealth. The Queen's Prize consists of badges, medals and money prizes valued at about £1,200, which is divided into 300 prizes of between £1 and £250. The value of all the various prizes at the big annual meeting is more than £10,000. (There is a separate article RIFLE SHOOTING.)

BISMARCK, Prince Otto von (1815–1898). Bismarck was a great German statesman who lived in the 19th century, and it was due to him more than to any other man that Germany became a united and powerful country. When he began his public life the German peoples lived in several separate states; Bismarck's aim was to unite them all in one strong nation which would be one of the great powers of Europe. This new Germany was to be led by Prussia, the state to which Bismarck himself belonged. He was hard and ruthless in everything he did—he himself said that he would use methods of "blood and iron" to make the new Germany—and he earned the nickname of "the Iron Chancellor".

Bismarck came from a family of *Junkers*, that is, soldiers and country gentlemen. After he had finished his education, he went into the Prussian civil service, but he did not like having to accept rules and discipline so he gave up the work when he was 25 and went back to live on his father's estates in the country.

He did not live quietly like this for long, however, for in 1847 he was elected a member of the Prussian general assembly, or parliament. At that time people in all the countries of Europe were beginning to want changes in the way they were governed. They wanted to have some say in the government themselves and to be able to choose the men who would guide and govern their countries, instead of having to obey without question the orders of their kings and the noble families who made up the ruling classes. Bismarck hated these new ideas and refused to have anything to do with them; he was extremely conservative—that is, he wanted at all costs to keep the old way of government.

Soon after his election to the general assembly Bismarck began to be very important in German affairs. He held several high positions, including being ambassador to Russia and later, in 1862, to France. At this time the new king of Prussia, William I, had quarrelled with the assembly about whether the king or the assembly should have control over the army. It was then that Bismarck agreed to become prime minister. He lost no time, but straight away dissolved the assembly and claimed that the laws of the country allowed him to run the army without asking the assembly's opinion at all. From then on he determined that he would let nothing stand in the way of the power of the king; he would make Prussia the leader of Germany and Germany the leading nation of all Europe.

The Growth of Germany

Bismarck's first move was to persuade the Austrians to help him in a war against Denmark (1864). As a result the states of Schleswig and Holstein (previously ruled by the king of Denmark) became German and Austrian possessions. In 1866 Bismarck picked a quarrel with Austria which led to a seven weeks' war in which Austria was beaten. This left Prussia in control of the north German states.

Radio Times Hulton Library
Otto von Bismarck.

The next task was to get the south German states under Prussia's control too. To do this Bismarck tried to find a quarrel with France, for he hoped that in such a quarrel Prussia would appear to be the champion and defender of all the Germans. His chance came in 1870 when France demanded that King William, as head of the German royal family called the Hohenzollerns, should give up any claims to the throne of Spain. The king refused and Bismarck very cleverly succeeded in his plan of making the French and German governments quarrel, and as a result war broke out. All the Germans stood by Prussia, France was beaten after a great defeat at Sedan and German troops occupied Paris, all in less than six months.

All Bismarck's dreams of power for Prussia and power for Germany had come true. The king of Prussia became the ruler of the new German Empire, set up in 1871. Bismarck became his chancellor, and was made a prince for all he had done.

Bismarck wanted no more wars, but concentrated on making the new Germany strong and wealthy. He tried to keep peace by arranging a system of alliances, known as the League of the Three Emperors, between Germany, Austria and Russia; he hoped this would prevent France making a war of revenge on Germany, and also keep Austria and Russia from quarrelling. In spite of his efforts, arguments and troubles between the great powers did arise, and gradually, although there was not another war, Russia and the other countries of Europe began to distrust Germany.

At home in Germany, Bismarck managed to uphold the emperor's power by encouraging the political parties to argue among themselves instead of joining together against the royal rule. He tried, too, to give ordinary people advantages which would make them more content—he started a scheme of health insurance so that workers should be paid money when they were ill and had to be away from their work, for instance—but he did not let them have any share at all in the government. He also succeeded in his other aim of making Germany prosperous, for it became rich in trade and industry, with a strong army.

In 1890 Bismarck retired, for the new emperor, or kaiser, William II, did not want his services any longer.

BISON. The so-called American buffalo that used to roam in millions on the North American prairies is actually a bison. The true buffaloes are a rather different group of wild cattle found in the warm regions of Africa and Asia. (See BUFFALO.)

A full-grown bull bison is a large, powerful animal standing nearly 6 feet high and weighing well over 15 hundredweight. It has a big head which is made to look even bigger by the thick fur and beard. Its shoulders are humped and heavy and thickly furred, while the hindquarters slope away and are not so well covered.

The bison provided food, clothing and shelter for the Indians of the American plains and many of the tribes used to follow close behind the herds when they were on the move in search of new grazing, shooting them with their bows and arrows. The bison's meat is delicious and the Indians ate it either fresh or sun-dried. They made the hides into winter clothes, tents, saddles and harness, shields and the coverings for their boats; even the bones, sinews and horns were

Zoological Society of London

Whipsnade Zoo has herds of both European bison (left), and the more heavily built American bison (above). Both these animals are now protected in reserves.

used. However, there were so many bison from central Canada down to Mexico and from near the east coast across to the Rockies that the Indian method of shooting them made little difference to their numbers. It was not until the white man arrived with his rifle that the herds were reduced and the livelihood of the Indians threatened.

By the end of the 18th century the bison had been completely destroyed east of the Mississippi, though even after the middle of the 19th century there were millions of bison on the western plains. When the first railways were built across the continent, whole herds were shot to feed the thousands of men working on the lines. One of the most famous of these hunters was Buffalo Bill, about whom there is an article. There were still such enormous numbers of bison that it seemed impossible for them ever to be wiped out.

However, in 1888 the last herd in the southern states was completely destroyed in Texas and in the following year it was suddenly realized that only a little over 1,000 bison were left in the whole of America, most of them in northern Canada. Funds were raised to save the bison and strict laws were passed to protect them. Today there are about 20,000 of these animals in the United States and Canada, mostly in reserves, and the American bison seems to be quite safe. There are specimens in many British zoos, and a small flourishing herd at Whipsnade.

The American bison's only near relative is the European bison, or wisent. It is higher at the shoulder than its American cousin and also

longer, but it is a much less heavily built animal. In ancient times it used to live in many forested parts of eastern and central Europe but by the end of the 19th century its numbers had been considerably reduced. There was a small herd in the Caucasus Mountains in Russia and another in the Polish forest of Bialowieza, formerly a hunting preserve of the Russian tsars. After World War I there were no wild bison left in Europe and very few even in protected places. New herds were built up, and now there are a few hundred pure-bred wisents in Polish reserves.

BITTERN. This bird is famous for its "boom", which is a most curious sound made by the male bird at the beginning of the nesting season. The bittern makes this sound by puffing out its throat and then letting the air out again with a resounding noise which carries over a great distance. Sometimes the cocks will go on booming at each other for a long time, usually at night.

Both male and female have a golden-brown plumage streaked with black, and long, pointed beaks. This colouring allows them to hide themselves in the reed-beds where they spend most of their time. If a bittern is surprised or frightened, it stands quite still and stretches up its neck and bill, looking just like a reed. When it flies it usually keeps fairly low. It is a heavy bird, about 60 centimetres long, and it moves slowly with its long legs stretched out behind.

The nest is made of reeds, low down, and the female starts to sit as soon as the first egg is laid in April or May, so that the young in the nest are of various ages. They are funny little creatures, with large, greenish eyes and blue bodies covered with long reddish down. A bird-photographer once saw a mother bittern swallow one of her young when she was alarmed—possibly in order to hide it. Like their relative the heron, bitterns eat fish, frogs and water insects.

In the 19th century the bittern was killed in large numbers in Great Britain because it was good to eat and also because people liked to see it stuffed in a glass case. Many of the marshes and fens where it lived were being drained, too,

A bittern with its young. The dark streaks in its plumage make it hard to see when it stands upright among reeds.

and by the end of the century it had ceased to breed in Britain. In 1911, however, a nest was found in Norfolk and was protected with great care. Since then the number of bitterns has steadily increased, but they remain rare birds. They are resident in East Anglia and possibly one or two other parts of Great Britain but are found more widely in winter, especially if it is a severe one.

Bitterns are found in many places in Europe, and in winter a lot of them leave for Africa and Asia. There are species very like the English bittern in Australia, Canada and New Zealand, although the Canadian least bittern is much smaller. The European little bittern occurs occasionally in Great Britain and may have bred there in the past.

BIZET, Georges (1838–1875). The French composer Bizet is most famous for his wonderful opera *Carmen* which tells the exciting and tragic story of a Spanish gypsy girl. Among the men she fascinates is the bull-fighter Escamillo, and it is he who sings of his triumphs in the bull-ring in the well-known Toreador's Song. When the curtain falls on a performance of *Carmen* the audience feels that all the romance and drama, all the colour and gaiety of Spain have been expressed by Bizet's music. Yet at its first performance in Paris the opera seemed a failure and its real popularity did not begin until after it had been brought to London. Since then it has never stopped being popular and many people have thought it the best opera ever written.

Alexandre Bizet (who was later called Georges) was born in Paris, the son of a French singing-master. He learned his musical notes at the same time as his A B C and by the time he was 17 he had written a symphony. He was a student at the Paris Conservatoire (School of Music) where he was taught by a composer named Halévy whose daughter he afterwards married; at 19 he won the musical prize called the *Prix de Rome,* which gave him three years of study in Italy.

He wrote orchestral works and piano pieces including a picturesque set of piano duets called *Jeux d'enfants* ("Children's Games") but he is best known for his operas *The Pearl Fishers, The Fair Maid of Perth* and the famous *Carmen.* He was able to express through the instruments of the orchestra all the moods and feelings of the characters on the stage. Bizet's exciting music was, however, strange to people at the time and it was not appreciated until after his death.

BLACKBERRY. The bramble, or blackberry plant, is rather like its relative the rose in the way it grows and in its thorns and pink or white flowers. Its many seeds have a fleshy covering, however, and are grouped round a thimble-shaped centre.

The blackberry is probably the commonest

wild fruit in countries with mild climates, for it spreads quickly by means of its seeds or by its branches, which bend over and take root where they touch the ground. It is often a troublesome weed, clinging to passers-by with its thorns and choking other plants to death. However, most people enjoy blackberry jam, jelly or pies, and people still go blackberrying in Britain when the autumn comes.

Wild berries can be found in different sizes, and some taste better and have fewer seeds than others. In about 1850 the Americans began to pick out the best kinds for cultivating properly, and 40 years later the "Himalaya Giant" was raised from Indian seed. These plants are immensely vigorous and have to be planted 12 feet apart and trained on wires. The bramble canes bear fruit on their side shoots in their second season and can then be replaced by new suckers which grow up from the root. The thornless "Parsley-leaved" kind is popular in the garden, for its fruit has a good flavour.

When the berries have become juicy, sweet and black it is time for children to go blackberrying.

Mustograph

BLACKBIRD. An old male blackbird is very handsome with jet-black plumage, a brilliant orange bill and a yellow ring round his eye. He is about the size of a song thrush. Young males have brownish wings. The hen is dark brown with a speckled breast, so you should be careful not to mistake it for a thrush, and the young birds are a lighter brown than their mother. Blackbirds like gardens and woods and can often be seen in the centre of large towns where there are bushes and trees.

The blackbird is much noisier than the thrush, and if it is disturbed, there is a low "tchook, tchook" of protest. When it is alarmed it flies off with a shrill, excited, nervous cackle. It has a loud, clear song which is richer than that of the song thrush. Sometimes it imitates other birds.

The blackbird feeds on worms and berries, and in a quiet wood it can often be heard noisily turning over the dead leaves as it looks for spiders and ants. It is also fond of strawberries, cherries and other fruit in season.

The hen bird usually builds her grassy nest a few feet up in hedges and bushes or on banks. Like the thrush, she gives it a mud lining (one bird used old tea leaves) but she also adds an inner layer of moss. She lays three to five bluish-green eggs with red-brown speckles. These can be found at any time from March until July, for there may be two or three broods.

The blackbird is common all the year round in the British Isles and Europe. It also ranges across northern Asia to China, and can be found in North Africa. It is really one of the thrush family, and it has a close relative, the ring ouzel, which has a white crescent on its breast and nests in the mountains of Scotland and Wales and in some hilly districts elsewhere. (See THRUSH.)

In Canada there are several birds called blackbirds, but they belong to quite a different family and are rather smaller. The best known are the yellow-headed and the red-winged

Mustograph
Dinner time: a male blackbird with its young.

blackbirds. Both these birds are black but the first has a yellow head and neck, while the other has a patch of red on the angle of its wing. Both live in the marshes and nest in colonies among the reeds, and in the autumn they gather into large flocks and feed on the stubble, returning to roost in the reed-beds. There are also the grackles or crow blackbirds, the commonest of which is the purple grackle which nests in tree-top colonies. When the male sings, it sounds like a rusty hinge. The cowbird is often called a blackbird, too. It is a shiny black with a brown head, and it makes no nest but, like the cuckoo, lays its eggs in the nests of other birds.

BLACK DEATH. In 1348 a terrible plague which had swept over Europe reached England. This deadly disease was later called the Black Death, and other names for it were bubonic, oriental or Levantine plague. It spread from Asia and the infection was brought by ships from the Black Sea to Mediterranean ports.

The pestilence was so infectious that some villages were completely wiped out, and some reports say that one-third of all the people in England (the population was about 3,000,000 then) died of it in two years. In those days, when

houses were unhealthy and had no proper drainage, plagues happened fairly often, but the Black Death was the worst one ever known. Black rats became infected with the disease and the fleas from these animals bit other rats and human beings, and so the plague quickly spread. A writer of the time said: "The cattle roamed masterless over the countryside, crops rotted in the fields for lack of hands to reap them, and so few priests were alive that our Holy Father the Pope gave permission that laymen should minister to the dying."

For the next 300 hundred years the plague broke out at intervals in England, though never so badly again.

Because of the Black Death there were far fewer men to work for the lords of the manors and for the master craftsmen, and those that were left began to demand higher wages. Their employers were unwilling to pay more and so argument and quarrels began. In 1351 parliament passed a law known as the Statute of Labourers, which tried to keep wages at the same amount as they had been in the plague year (1348) and to stop food prices rising. This law did not after all manage to keep prices down, and it made people angry and discontented. The country men, or villeins, were now no longer willing to work on their lords' land in return for being given land for themselves. They began to want to pay rent for their lands instead, which would leave them more free than the old system of work on the lords' manors. (You can read about this system in the article FEUDALISM.) Gradually new agreements of work came to be made between the lords and their villeins, and the villeins began to pay rent in money for the lands they held. This change was called commutation.

BLACK FORTY-SEVEN or POTATO FAMINE. This was a famine in Ireland in the year 1847. Very many of the poor and country people in Ireland lived almost completely on potatoes, for they were cheap and nourishing and could easily be grown on their tiny farms. This was all very well as long as the potato crop grew well, but in 1845 a blight or disease of potatoes appeared and spread through the country. In 1846 about three-quarters of all the potatoes were ruined by the blight, and the worst time came in the winter of 1846 and in 1847. Thousands of people died of starvation or fever, and thousands left Ireland for America or the British colonies, packed into crowded ships.

The British government did not realize at first quite how terrible the conditions were in Ireland and did not do enough for the starving people. They tried to help by starting all sorts of public works such as making roads, building bridges and draining swamps to provide jobs for those who had none, and a great deal of maize was brought into the country to help people who had nothing to eat. In spite of this, more and more people died because of the famine, and the government at last decided that much more must be done. In 1847 a new scheme of giving out rations of cooked food to those in need was started, and in July of that year over 3,000,000 starving people were being fed every day.

During the years between 1840 and 1850 there were famines in many parts of the world, and the time is still known as the "Hungry Forties". The Irish famine was the worst there has ever been in the British Isles, and Irish people still talk with horror and bitterness of "Black Forty-Seven". The years of famine made a great difference to the country. Over 1,000,000 people out of the population of 8,000,000 died, and stories are still told of how whole families and sometimes even whole villages were wiped out.

BLACK MARKET. If goods are in short supply, people who can afford to are usually prepared to pay more than the fixed price for articles they want. The government may ration the goods in question and state the maximum price at which they can be sold. If a dealer supplies customers with goods, charging above the fixed price, these dealings are said to be on the "black market".

As the black market operates when supplies are short, it happens most often during times of war and disaster, or when there is a disruption in transporting goods from one country to another. A country at war will direct its efforts to producing weapons and fewer people will be producing clothes and food. It may be neces-

sary for certain foods and goods to be rationed.

For example, during World War II Great Britain was very short of all animal feeding stuffs, which it usually imports from other countries. This affected the supply of eggs because the government had to limit the number of chickens that people might keep and also ration the amount of corn to be fed to them. Denmark was occupied by the Germans and so no eggs were imported from there. A black market in eggs grew up and unscrupulous people paid more than the legal price for eggs in order to get more than their ration.

Poorer countries may not be able to pay for goods they need from abroad and if this happens, the shortage can lead to a black market which may damage the country's finances even further. Natural disasters such as earthquakes and floods also lead to shortages in supplies.

A different kind of black market operates when less important commodities, such as tickets for popular events, for example, are restricted in number. People are prepared to pay far more than the face value of the tickets.

BLACKPOOL is a famous holiday resort. It is situated on the Lancashire coast and is one of the most popular seaside resorts in Great Britain. Each year more than 8,000,000 people come to it by road and rail, by sea and even by air—for Blackpool has its own airport. About 151,000 people live there.

H. A. Hallas. Courtesy, Publicity Department, Blackpool

Its entertainments and amusements have made Blackpool one of the most popular seaside resorts in Britain.

Blackpool has 10 kilometres of promenade, built in tiers one above the other where the cliffs are high enough, vast stretches of sand and a good climate. However, the secret of its success lies in the wide variety of entertainment and amenities which the town provides in all kinds of weather.

In the early days hospitality seems to have been concentrated on food, for in 1778 a well-known doctor complained that most visitors ate far too much; but nowadays a great deal of attention is given to the entertainment of visitors. Ten kilometres of flat sandy beaches provide safe sea bathing but there are also three indoor and one open air baths. There are also eleven theatres, three piers, an ice rink, a zoo, an aquarium, four ballrooms, the Pleasure Beach Amusement Park, which is the largest in Europe, and the tower, 158 metres high with a lift to the top.

The autumn illuminations along the seafront have become so celebrated that visitors come from all over Britain and from abroad to see them. Political, trade union and scientific conferences are often held in the town and the delegates find much to amuse them when they are not working.

BLACK SEA.

In many ways the Black Sea is very curious. It is far from the ocean and almost completely surrounded by land, the U.S.S.R. lying to the north and east, Turkey to the south and Bulgaria and Romania to the west. Its only outlet is southwestwards through the narrow straits of the Bosporus and the Dardanelles and the not much wider Sea of Marmara. (See Bosporus and Dardanelles.)

Most of the seas in the atlas look like portions of the ocean partly cut off from it by land barriers. The Black Sea, on the other hand, is more like a vast lake linked to a true sea (the Aegean) by a short river. What also makes it rather like a lake is that it overflows in quite a strong current through the straits to the Aegean and the Mediterranean. While this water is flowing out near the surface, water from the Aegean and Mediterranean is flowing in beneath it, at depths below 20 metres. The layers of water remain separate because the surface water

of the Black Sea is less salt, and therefore less dense, than that of most other seas. The Sea of Azov, its northeastern offshoot, is even less salt. All the rivers of any length which enter the Black Sea do so on its northern side. In this region it receives the waters of some of the

longest European rivers—the Danube, Bug, Dniester, Dnieper and Don—which explains the comparative freshness of its surface waters. All these rivers freeze in winter and so does the Sea of Azov. Though the Black Sea itself is seldom ice-covered beyond a short distance from the land on its northern side, all the Russian ports are troubled in this way every winter.

In area, the Black Sea is about three-quarters the size of the North Sea. Its northern half is shallow and bordered by low marshy coasts where few people live. There are few fish in its waters and so the fishing villages found on most sea coasts are absent. The southern part is very deep, over 2,000 metres in some parts. These deeper waters are scarcely disturbed by any currents and are therefore dark and stagnant, which helps to explain the absence of fish. The dark colour, so different from that of the bright Mediterranean, may account for the name of the sea, but this may have been given to it because of the frequent storms and fogs. The southern shores are either hilly or mountainous and some parts are still covered with dark forests.

Two sections of its shores are more attractive than most. The Crimean peninsula juts out from the north and its southern face falls steeply to the sea, facing the sun. Here the hills provide protection from the fierce winter winds that blow across the steppes, or treeless plains, of Russia and so the climate is mild and sunny. Vines and olives grow, and so do other trees and shrubs of a Mediterranean type, making it look more like a stretch of Italian or southern French coast than a part of Russia. The eastern corner of the Black Sea is sheltered by the Caucasus Mountains and has similar conditions. Both these coastal areas have long been holiday and health resorts for the Russian people.

The Greek sailors knew the Black Sea shores centuries ago and founded colonies at suitable places upon them. They knew the eastern corner well and named it Colchis. This was the fabled land of the Golden Fleece to which Jason and his Argonauts sailed. (See GOLDEN FLEECE.) The Vikings from Scandinavia also came to the Black Sea, sailing down the Dnieper River. When Constantinople was built beside the Bosporus in A.D 330 the inhabitants traded with eastern lands across the Black Sea waters. The chief ports are now Odessa on the northwest, Batum on the southeast (both Russian) and Constanta, Romania.

BLACKSMITH.
No other village craftsman has interested people quite so much as the blacksmith, with his smoky workshop and its extraordinary litter of iron scraps, its smell of burnt horn and its sparking, red-hot forge.

Even in the past when his chief job was shoeing horses there was little that was romantic about a blacksmith's job. It meant hard work, long hours and a great deal of skill. The smith had, for instance, to know something about the workings of horses' bodies and about their ailments, for the health and strength of a horse depended a great deal on the skill and understanding with which it had been shod.

In addition the blacksmith was called upon to do all sorts of other skilled tasks. Indeed, most of the village at one time or another called in the smith's help, to sharpen the labourers' scythes as harvest came round or to make hoes for them in spring, to mend the farmer's tools or to make hinges and hasps and staples for his gates, to repair the housewife's pots and kettles or to make iron rolling hoops for her children. If, after all

this, he found himself with time to spare, he had to make up his stock of horses' shoes.

The centre of his shop, of course, was the hooded fire of fine, slack coal, blown by enormous leather bellows. As for his anvil, the block of iron on which he hammered the hot metal into shape, this was often mounted on an unshaped block of wood, two-thirds of which was usually buried underground, to make sure it was really firm. The comforting glow of the fire and the musical ring of the hammer on the anvil attracted not only children, for the shop was a favourite gathering place for villagers.

Sometimes the blacksmith's shop was situated close to the wheelwright's, for when the wheelwright had made a cart wheel he took it to the blacksmith, who then fitted the iron tyre—an outdoor task calling for good teamwork and nimble handling. Today, however, there is less call for this work and for horse-shoeing, and in fact for almost all of the smith's old craft, for the repairing of farm machinery and farm implements is often done by local garages.

BLACKSTONE, Sir William (1723–1780).
William Blackstone, who became one of England's greatest lawyers, was born after the death of his father, who was a London merchant. His mother died soon afterwards and he was helped in his education by the statesman Sir Robert Walpole. He became a professor of English law at Oxford in 1758 and a member of parliament in 1761. Two years later he was made solicitor-general to Queen Charlotte, the wife of George III, and in 1770 he was appointed a judge of the old Court of Common Pleas.

Blackstone was most famous for his great book *Commentaries on the Laws of England* which was taken from the lectures he gave at Oxford. It was written in a simple and interesting manner and was meant to teach ordinary people about law. These commentaries have been translated into many languages and have had a great effect on the development of law in the United States.

BLACKTHORN.
This tree, sometimes known as the sloe tree, is a member of the family called Rosaceae, which also includes the rose and the plum. It can be found wild in Europe,

British Travel Association

This scene in an Oxfordshire smithy shows how a traditional village industry is adapting to changing conditions. Ornamental work in wrought-iron is now much in demand. The skills of the blacksmith, handed down from father to son, have now to include knowledge of farm machinery, oxyacetylene and arc welding, hydraulics and modern engineering practice. Although the horse no longer has an important place in farming, many more people ride for recreation so the smith has to be a farrier as well. The number of blacksmith's shops is smaller than it used to be, but the help provided by the Council for Small Industries in Rural Areas enables those that survive to be in a stronger position to continue their craft.

Asia and parts of North America, rarely growing more than ten feet high, with a black bark and strong thorns. The flower buds, which are

Blackthorn, as it looks in winter, spring and summer.

formed in the previous summer, open into little white flowers either in March, when the small leaves appear, or else in February, before the leaves, as a welcome reminder that the season is changing. After this few people pay any attention to the blackthorn until late autumn when its fruits, the sloes, are gathered for jellies and for sloe gin. These black berries covered with a bluish bloom, like a fine powder, can only be eaten when fully ripe, if then, for they are very sour.

To take the flowers indoors is said to bring bad luck and even today some people will not have them in their homes. Some of these people will, however, make the flowering trees into the shape of a cross and set it up in a manure heap to keep witches away. In Germany water-diviners prefer to find water with a rod of blackthorn, instead of hazel (see WATER DIVINING), and the Germans also scrape the bark off the tree to make a tea which is supposed to cure some stomach troubles. Blackthorn tea is not unknown in Britain and there, too, the leaves were once dried and smoked by many who could not afford tobacco.

BLAKE, William (1757–1827). William
Blake was a great and very unusual man. He was little known during his life but now he is famous both as an artist and as a poet. His parents, a London shopkeeper and his wife, realized how unusual he was very early in his life. As soon as he was old enough to hold a pencil, William Blake began to draw and his pictures were often of things he imagined, instead of being copied from the real things around him. This imagination of his worried his parents, for they loved truth and when he said that he had seen a tree full of angels they thought he was telling lies. Yet they understood enough about his character to know that he would not mix well with other children and his mother therefore taught him to read and write at home.

When he was ten he was sent to an art school and his father allowed him to spend all his pocket money on prints of the pictures of great painters such as Michelangelo and Raphael, and gave him models of Hercules and other heroes and gods of mythology to copy. His father wanted to send William to study with some great painter but the boy felt that the expense would be unfair to his brothers and sister. He asked instead to be apprenticed to James Basire, who for £50 taught him the craft of engraving—making pictures by cutting drawings in lines on metal plates, which are then used for printing. (There is a separate article ENGRAVING.)

During the time he was learning his chosen trade he was also reading all sorts of books and writing poetry of his own. His verses then were simple, fresh and beautiful; the poems he wrote later were often equally beautiful, but often also full of sadness at the cruelty and evil of life.

After he had finished his apprenticeship William Blake began to earn his living as an engraver, illustrating books. He was very happily married in 1782 to Catherine Boucher who was a perfect wife to him, even learning to draw and paint so as to help him.

He did not become rich and famous despite all his wonderful work, which is now valued very highly. His pictures, now hanging in many art galleries such as the Tate Gallery in London, are not always easy to understand for they are not pictures of the ordinary world most people see about them. From the time when he first showed his imagination as a boy, Blake had always seen visions and, as he grew older, visions came to him very often. In his pictures he drew what he saw in these visions and he also put them into his poems.

Although in looking at Blake's pictures or reading his poems one may not understand the full meaning that he meant them to have, one can understand their beauty and the idea of glory and greatness that they give. Blake's genius as an artist was shown best of all in the illustrations he made for the Book of Job in the Bible and for one of the greatest poems ever written, the *Divine Comedy* by Dante. Some of Blake's most famous

Fitzwilliam Museum
Blake's illustration of the parable of the Wise Virgins.

poems are from two books called *Songs of Innocence* and *Songs of Experience*. One is the poem about the tiger, which begins :

Tiger ! Tiger ! burning bright
In the forests of the night,
What immortal hand or eye
Could frame thy fearful symmetry?

Another of his best known poems is now called "Jerusalem" and often sung as a hymn. The first verse begins :

And did those feet in ancient time
Walk upon England's mountains green?
And was the holy Lamb of God
On England's pleasant pastures seen?

BLARNEY STONE.

An expression often heard in English conversation is "that's a bit of blarney". Most people know what the speaker means by this—an exaggeration, or "a tall story"; also, when someone accuses a person of "blarney" he may mean that the person is trying to get round him by making fine speeches and being specially charming. Not everyone knows, however, where these expressions come from in the first place.

In County Cork in Ireland stands a castle called Blarney. It was built about 1446 by a person named Cormac McCarthy and it has walls as much as 18 feet thick. The castle is famous in Irish history, but it is now best known because in one of its thick walls is the Blarney Stone, which is supposed to give the gift of wonderful speaking to any person who kisses it. It is set far down in the wall and the only way to kiss it is to be tied or held by the heels and lowered backwards over the edge head first.

People often describe a person who tells wonderful tall stories by saying "he's kissed the Blarney Stone".

BLEACHING

is a process for taking the natural colour out of things, either to make them white or to prepare them for being dyed some other colour. Many things can be bleached, but bleaching is used most often in the manufacturing of goods from woven materials. The natural colour of linen, for instance, is greyish brown, so it must be bleached to make it white for tablecloths, sheets and handkerchiefs. Nowadays bleaching is done by chemicals of various kinds but in earlier days the methods people used were simpler, though they took a great deal longer.

The ancient Egyptians used to wrap their dead in snow-white linen. How they bleached it is not known, but perhaps they left the work to nature in one of the ways we *do* know about. In this method, every fine day during spring and summer the cloth was damped and laid out in the sun on the grass of a special bleaching field, where the sun's rays and the moisture gradually destroyed the natural colour.

The Dutch were the people in Europe who first became experts in bleaching, at the time after the Crusades in the 12th century. They found that they could obtain a very fine quality and colour of linen by giving the cloth alternate baths of lye (a strong alkaline liquid) and buttermilk, which is the liquid left after butter has been made from milk. Between baths the cloth was spread out to dry. In early spring the Scottish and English weavers sent to Holland all the cloth they had woven during the winter and the Dutch sent it back bleached in the autumn. Even with this new way it took six months to bleach linen white, but nowadays it can be bleached in a few days and so can cotton.

The discovery that first made the quick modern bleaching processes possible came in 1785, when the French chemist Claude Berthollet found that chlorine gas could be used for whitening materials. Fourteen years later, in Scotland, Charles Tennant produced a solid chemical which would do the same work and was easier to handle. This substance is now known as bleaching powder or chloride of lime. The material to be bleached is soaked in a liquid made by dissolving the bleaching powder in water.

Bleaching powder is still used today, but many bleachers prefer a different method of preparing the bleaching liquid, by mixing liquid chlorine with milk of lime. This makes the same liquid as dissolving chloride of lime in water. Linen, cotton, rayon and other fabrics and paper pulp can all be bleached by a liquid of this kind. Wool and silk and cotton are bleached with hydrogen peroxide. Man-made fibres generally do not need bleaching, though to gain a very high degree of whiteness, nylon can be bleached.

Some of the other things besides fabrics that are often bleached by various chemicals to make them more attractive are wood, fur, feathers, hair, straw and oils.

BLENNIES AND GOBIES are fairly closely related groups of fishes, many of which live in shallow water. Some can be found in rock pools after the tide has gone out, but they are not very easy to catch as they dart quickly to cover when alarmed. Some blennies have interesting names like the Shanny Gunnel and the Butterfly Blenny.

One of the chief distinguishing features in blennies is the position of the pelvic fins. These are often far forward on the lower surface of the body, almost level with the back end of the gill cover; in some forms the fins may be absent. On the head of some blennies are small feelers.

A large blenny, found in deeper water off the coasts of Great Britain, is the wolf-fish which is sometimes found in British fish markets.

Gobies have no tentacles, or feelers, and the pelvic fins are often joined together to form a sucker-like structure. Several kinds of goby are found on the coasts of Britain and they are interesting because of their breeding habits. The

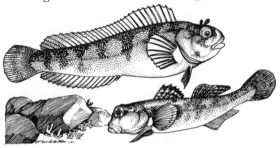

Above: A blenny. Below: A goby standing guard by its nest.

male is usually more highly coloured than the female and often makes a rough kind of nest of seaweed beneath an empty shell or stone, over which he stands guard after the eggs have been laid. Often the males will fight for possession of a female. An unusual kind is the transparent goby, which may be found swimming near the surface of the sea far from shore. It is so small and colourless that it was at one time thought to be the young of some other species, or kind, of fish.

The jumping habit has been highly developed by a tropical goby known as the mud skipper, which spends almost as much time out of water as in it, springing about over mud-flats in mangrove swamps by using the powerful muscles at the base of its pectoral fins. Its eyes, set right on top of the head, can move independently, so that it can lie just below the surface of the water and look all round, as with a periscope, skipping out when it sees an insect worth chasing. It often climbs trees. Among the coral reefs of the tropics live hundreds of other kinds of goby, some of them brilliantly coloured. They include the smallest known animals with backbones, less than half an inch long when fully grown.

BLÉRIOT, Louis (1872–1936). Louis Blériot was one of the great pilots in the early history of flying. He was born at Cambrai, in the north of

France, in 1872. He was trained as an engineer and even as a young man began to take an interest in the new science of aeronautics.

In 1900 Blériot constructed a model aeroplane with flapping wings and managed to make it fly. Pleased with this success, he built a full-sized machine like it, but unfortunately this would not fly. He tried again and built several other unsuccessful aeroplanes. In 1907 he built a monoplane in which he made several short flights, the best about 550 yards. It was one of the first monoplanes, or single-wing aeroplanes.

Blériot's new aircraft had many features which were better than those in most aeroplanes of the time. It had simple ailerons (flaps to give the aircraft balance), a two-wheel undercarriage which was fitted with shock absorbers, and a tail wheel.

During the next two years Blériot built and flew a number of machines, each of them better than the last. He spent thousands of pounds on these aircraft and had many narrow escapes from death. By 1909 he had produced a much better small aeroplane which weighed only 462 pounds and was equipped with a three-cylinder Anzani engine of 22–25 horse-power. It was the first aircraft to be fitted with a single lever with which the pilot could make the aeroplane go in any direction and also higher or lower, as he wished. This was the origin of the modern control-column or "joy-stick".

In 1909, the *Daily Mail* offered a prize of £1,000 to the first person to fly the English Channel. Three Frenchmen determined to try to win the prize—the Comte de Lambert, Hubert Latham and Louis Blériot. De Lambert crashed his plane while testing it. Latham made an attempt but his engine failed in mid-Channel and he was picked up by a French destroyer. A few days later, on July 25, Blériot made his attempt, although he was suffering from burns received in a crash some time before.

Blériot was up at dawn. He found that although there was still a stiff breeze it was not as strong as it had been, so he set off from Les Baraques, a few miles from Calais.

He had no map or compass and when he was out at sea he ran into a fog so that he could only guess where Dover was. Soon his engine became overheated, but luckily a storm of rain cooled it down and also cleared the fog. Blériot recognized Margate below him and so he turned south for Dover. When he saw the castle, he shut off his engine and glided down to land just in front of it. In the strong wind he landed roughly and broke the undercarriage and propeller, but he himself was unhurt. He had made the first crossing of the Channel in an aeroplane—a distance of $24\frac{1}{2}$ miles in 37 minutes.

Blériot was not content with this success. Later in the same year he played an important part in the first international aviation meeting at Reims. He was just beaten in the speed contest by Glenn Curtiss, an American, but afterwards one of his aeroplanes, piloted by Léon Delagrange, recaptured the record with a speed of 50 miles an hour. By this time Blériot had set up an aircraft factory and showed at Reims a passenger-carrying monoplane with a 60-horse-power engine.

The Blériot factory had many triumphs in the next five years. Amongst these were the successes in the Circuit of Eastern France race in 1910 and the Circuit of Europe race in 1911. Also, Adolphe Pégoud's invention of the *loop* and the *half-roll* in 1913 showed how good Blériot's designs were.

When World War I broke out, the factory naturally began making military aeroplanes. One of the most successful of these was the Spad fighter, which gained many air victories.

Radio Times Hulton Picture Library

Louis Blériot was the first man to fly the English Channel. He reached Dover after a flight of 37 minutes.

Blériot never imagined that the use of aircraft in warfare would continue for long. To him aviation was a way of bringing men closer together so that they might better understand each other. With this aim he hoped to open up the long ocean routes to multi-engined aircraft.

As he grew older, ill-health made it impossible for him to take an active part in aviation, but he kept his interest in his aircraft firm until he died in Paris in 1936.

BLINDNESS.

Any person who is unable to do work for which eyesight is essential is classed as blind, as are children who cannot be educated by sighted methods, even though they may be able to see objects distinctly.

There are several causes of blindness. In children the eye may have been affected before birth by an illness in the mother, such as German measles caught before her baby is born, though a German measles vaccine may eliminate this danger. After birth the eye may be damaged by an infecting microbe or accident. Later in life blindness may be due to certain infections, to accidents or war injuries, and in old people to cataract, which means that the lens, the part that lets in light, has become dim with age.

For certain types of blindness there are very delicate and complicated operations which can bring back the sight. One of these is performed by removing the cornea from the eye of a dead person and grafting it on to a living eye. However, many blind people cannot be cured and it is therefore necessary to teach them to live as independently and happily as they can.

Until nearly 200 years ago it was taken for granted in most countries that blind people could not be taught to work or to look after themselves in any way, and many were forced to be beggars. Retreats or homes were built for them in some countries, but it was not until late in the 18th century that efforts were made to educate them.

In 1771 a Frenchman named Valentin Haüy saw a group of blind people being mocked by a crowd at a fair. He went away determined to devote his life to educating the blind and generally improving their condition of life.

Soon afterwards he found a blind boy, François Lesueur, begging and took him home to try to educate him. It was obvious that one of the most important tasks in the education of this boy was to find a way to teach him to read. As blind people have to find their way about by touching objects, they often have very sensitive fingertips. Before Haüy's time there had been only a few attempts to teach reading by touch. These included carving letters on blocks of wood, and making letters in wood and lead so that blind people could recognize their shapes when they touched them and spell out words. However, Valentin Haüy found a better way, almost by accident.

One day when he was writing the blind boy François came to his desk and began to arrange some papers. Among them was a sheet of cardboard with heavy printing on it. As the boy's fingers passed over the dents made by the type he showed interest in them. This gave Haüy the idea of print with raised letters that could be recognized by touch. With the help of his blind pupils he developed a method of printing in this way and published some books in the new print. He also founded the first school for the blind, an institution which is now supported by the French government. Within a few years he proved that blind children could be taught to read, write, play musical instruments and do many useful things. Haüy's work caused him to be known as the "Father and Apostle of the Blind".

Another kind of raised type was invented in 1847 by William Moon, who simplified the letters of the written alphabet, hoping that it would be easier to read than Haüy's print. It was not very suitable for blind children, but

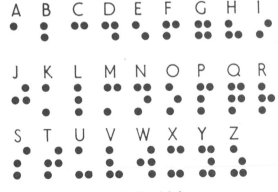

The Braille alphabet.

Left: Essex County Newspapers. Right: Royal National Institute for the Blind
Left: A guide dog will cross only when it sees the road is clear of traffic. Right: A school for blind children.

books in Moon type are still used by people who became blind after they grew up and who are therefore used to the written alphabet.

All kinds of raised printing, however, could be read only slowly and could not be easily written, so it was plain that a new method had to be found. One of Haüy's blind pupils, Louis Braille (see BRAILLE, LOUIS), worked on a system that used raised dots instead of letters, and in 1829 he published what is now known as the Braille alphabet. Certain changes were made to this system and for a while other dot alphabets were also used, but today only the Braille alphabet is taught to children in Great Britain and the United States.

In the Braille alphabet each letter is represented by a group of six or less raised dots arranged in an upright oblong known as the Braille cell. One dot stands for A; two dots one under the other, B; two dots side by side, C; and so on. As six dots can be arranged to form 63 different patterns, the signs left after making the 26 letters of the alphabet are used for punctuation, numbers, musical notes and signs for short words that are frequently used. Instead of writing "for" as three separate patterns of dots, it is simply six dots arranged in an oblong.

Braille is written by making dents on paper so that raised dots appear on the other side.

Braille books are, of course, very large and also expensive to buy. The first Braille Bible, published in the 19th century, was in 39 volumes.

Even Braille has not completely solved the problem of teaching the blind to read, for many blind people find it impossible to read by touch. In order that these people need not go through life ignorant of the books that have been written, many books have been read aloud from beginning to end and recorded on tape. The tapes are played on a machine known as a "talking book". One tape can play for about 12 hours.

Since 1893 it has been the law in Great Britain that blind children must be educated, and the same rule applies in many other countries. The children generally go to special schools in which they are taught the ordinary school subjects in such a way that they can understand them. For instance, geography is taught by means of maps with raised outlines and natural history by means of models and stuffed animals and birds. Most blind children are taught to type, using what is known as the touch typing system, in which even a person with sight does not look at the keyboard.

Some blind people study so well at school that when they leave they can go to one of the universities, where they are provided with special tutors who read to them and help them with their work. In this way they can fit themselves for professions such as law, banking, literature and teaching. All branches of music, from playing an instrument to tuning pianos, provide good careers for blind people as they require clever use of the hands and good hearing. (Often blind people hear very well, as they have to use their ears more than other people do.) Some of the blind earn their living by working at a trade and to do this they go to classes where they are taught such work as weaving or making baskets, cane chairs, brooms and cabinets.

It is very important for blind people to be able to amuse themselves, and they can learn to play games such as chess and dominoes by touch. They can also play cards, using special cards on which Braille markings show the suit and value of the card. They can be taught to swim and dance and they get much pleasure from listening to their radio sets, which they are allowed to have without paying for the licences. Receivers which pick up the sound of television transmissions are also available for the blind.

One of the biggest problems facing the blind is that of finding their way about by themselves without getting lost or having accidents. Some blind people do this with little help other than a stick, with which they can tell if the way is clear in front of them. These sticks, which are white, are often ordinary walking sticks, but there are also various special sticks, some of which fold up.

Others have guide dogs. These dogs are very carefully chosen for their character and intelligence. Alsatians and Labradors are generally found to be the most suitable for the purpose, although many other large, intelligent dogs are used as well.

Each dog is trained for about four months and is then introduced to its blind master or mistress. The two are then trained together for a few more weeks until each understands the other completely. When they set out together the dog, on a special kind of lead, takes its owner safely through crowds and waits until the streets are clear before crossing them.

Although blind people are looked after by the state to a certain extent, there are also many societies for them that are mostly kept up by money given by charitable people. One of these is the Royal National Institute for the Blind, which provides literature, apparatus and games for blind people and provides homes and schools for them. The same kind of society has been set up in many Commonwealth countries.

Another society that has done much good work is St. Dunstan's. This was founded in 1915 by Sir Arthur Pearson, who, having become blind when grown up, determined to help those who had lost their sight in World War I. It has helped great numbers of people blinded in the service of their country ever since.

Some Famous Blind People

Many blind people have, in spite of their great handicap, succeeded in living happy and useful lives and doing work that would be remarkable even if done by people with sight. John Milton, who went blind when he was in his forties, afterwards dictated *Paradise Lost,* which is one of the most splendid, as well as one of the longest, poems in the English language.

Edward Rushton, who lived in the 18th century, became blind from catching ophthalmia, a disease of the eyes, from some Negro slaves whom he was looking after on a slave ship. It was Rushton who showed English people that not only money was needed for the blind when he founded an institution for them at Liverpool.

Probably no blind person has had more difficulty in overcoming loss of sight than Helen Keller, who was born in the United States in 1880. When she was 19 months old she had an illness that made her both blind and deaf, and she later became dumb as well. A special teacher, Anne Sullivan, who had been partly cured of blindness, taught Helen the names of things by spelling them out by means of a sign alphabet on her fingers. Helen first understood a name when the word "water" was spelt out on one of her hands and a stream of water was poured over the other. Gradually Helen learnt to read, write and speak, and because she was found to be remarkably clever she was able to go to college and take a degree. She did a great deal to make things better for the blind, besides learning several languages, writing books and travelling from place to place to give lectures.

BLOEMFONTEIN is the capital of the South African province of the Orange Free State, lying high up in the midst of the plains known as the High Veld. Its geographical position in South Africa (the "Centre City") makes it a favourite place for national meetings and conferences. There are many interesting relics of the period in the second half of the 19th century when the Orange Free State was a republic on its own (see SOUTH AFRICA). There is the Fort, and the Presidency where the presidents of the republic lived, for example, and the Raadsaal, or parliament buildings, where the provincial council now meets. The South African court of appeal, which is the highest court in the land, sits at Bloemfontein and here too is the University of the Orange Free State and the National Museum.

On the outskirts of the city is a small game reserve where may be found elands and springboks (two kinds of antelopes) and zebras. The chief pleasure resort, Mazelspoort on the Modder River, has a big swimming bath. The population of Bloemfontein is about 154,000, nearly half of it European and the rest mostly Africans of the Bechuana and Basuto tribes.

BLONDIN (JEAN FRANÇOIS GRAVELET) (1824–1897). Blondin was one of the most daring tightrope walkers who has ever performed. His circus acts were exciting enough, but he is chiefly remembered now because of his amazing feat in crossing Niagara Falls on a tightrope. The distance from side to side is 1,100 feet and the rope on which he walked was stretched 160 feet above the water.

Blondin was a Frenchman whose real name was Jean François Gravelet. When he was only five years old he began his training as an acrobat and after six months he made his first appearance as "The Little Wonder". He first crossed Niagara Falls in 1859, taking 20 minutes from side to side. One account describes how he stopped in the middle and let down a rope to the crew of the little ship waiting below in case of an accident. They tied a bottle to the end of the rope, which Blondin then hauled up. From it he poured a drink and then, balancing on one leg, raised his glass to drink the health of the terrified

spectators. Blondin crossed Niagara several times after this, always in a different and even more exciting way. Once, for instance, he wheeled a man across in a wheelbarrow, once he

crossed on stilts, once with his feet in a sack.

When he was over 50 Blondin walked a rope stretched between the masts of a ship in a violent storm. He made his last appearance the year before he died, at the age of 72.

BLOOD travels round the body by means of a network of blood vessels known as the circulatory system. It is kept in movement by the heart, which acts as a pump (see HEART), and it reaches all parts of the body except the hair and the nails.

For many centuries, although it was known that the blood moved inside the body, people did not understand that it is the same blood all the time and that it goes round in a circular motion. This was proved by William Harvey, a doctor who was born in 1578 and died in 1657. He wrote a book in which he described the heart and the circulation of the blood and also showed how to study the organs of the body. (The organs are those parts of the body which have specially important tasks to perform in keeping the body alive.)

Blood absorbs food from the digestive system and oxygen from the lungs. While circulating, it carries the food and oxygen to the millions of cells in the body. Every cell takes from the blood exactly the kind and amount of nourishment needed for life and growth and throws back into the blood its waste products, including water and carbon dioxide. These waste products are carried by the blood to the organs that excrete or pass them out of the body. Blood also carries important chemical substances to different parts of the body. It helps to destroy germs and to keep the body at much the same heat all the time.

In the body of an adult there are about 11 pints of blood. It is made up chiefly of a straw-coloured watery liquid known as plasma, and looks red because of the millions of microscopic red cells or corpuscles floating in the plasma. It also contains white corpuscles, which are larger and scarcer than red corpuscles.

The red corpuscles are disc-shaped and thinner in the centre than at the edges. About one-third of each red corpuscle is haemoglobin, which is the substance that actually colours the blood. While the blood is flowing through the capillaries (tiny blood vessels) in the lungs, the haemoglobin takes oxygen from the air in the lungs. The blood continues on its way and the haemoglobin gives out oxygen to all the cells in the body that need it.

Human blood has about 500 red corpuscles to every white one. Both red and white corpuscles are made in the marrow of the bones. The white corpuscles, also known as leucocytes, can change their shape, and instead of merely floating in the plasma all the time like the red corpuscles they are capable of moving independently and can squeeze through the walls of the capillaries and enter the body tissues.

Whenever any bacteria, or germs, such as those that cause lockjaw and scarlet fever, enter the blood, the leucocytes increase in number and crowd round the bacteria to destroy them. This they do by changing their shape, surrounding the bacteria and gradually digesting them. Many of the leucocytes die in their fight with bacteria and form the sticky, yellowish substance known as pus.

The number of corpuscles in the body varies according to age, the time of day, the time of year, how recently food has been eaten and other conditions. Any great increase or decrease in one kind shows that the body is in an unhealthy state. For example, when a person has too many white corpuscles and not enough red ones he is said to be anaemic. Anaemia is not so much a

disease as a sign that something is causing too many red corpuscles to be destroyed or lost.

When a slight wound is made in the skin, blood begins to flow out and substances in the blood set to work to make it clot; that is, prevent it from draining away. These substances include fibrinogen and blood platelets, which are a kind of cell, much smaller than either the red or the white corpuscles. When fibrinogen is exposed to the air it forms sticky little threads which catch blood cells and platelets and thus form a clot.

In some people the substances that clot blood

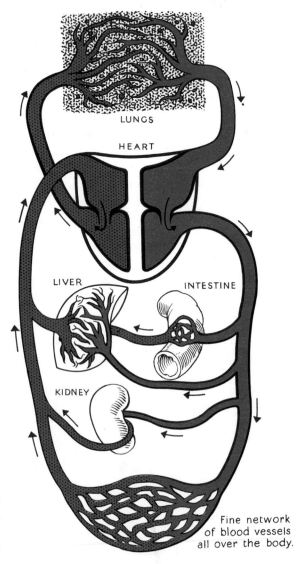

LUNGS

HEART

LIVER

INTESTINE

KIDNEY

Fine network of blood vessels all over the body.

The circulating bloodstream is the transport system which serves all the widely separated organs of the body.

are missing, and this condition is known as haemophilia. It is very dangerous, for such people can bleed to death from a very small cut or from having a tooth taken out. Women never have this trouble, but it is through the women in a family that it is passed on to the children. Thus, a man with haemophilia may marry a woman from a family with normal blood and if they have children, say a boy and a girl, neither of them will have haemophilia. The girl, however, even if she marries a man with normal blood, may pass on haemophilia to her son.

If a normal, healthy person loses a few pints of blood the body will make new blood to take its place, but if more is lost in what is known as a haemorrhage the person may die. Some people frequently lose blood from the veins in the nose. A nose-bleed is seldom serious, but if it shows no sign of stopping after a few minutes, one of the fingers should be pressed to the affected side of the nose so that the blood cannot escape and held there until the flow stops. Sometimes it is necessary to plug the nose with cotton wool to stop the bleeding.

After blood has been shed and has clotted it leaves a liquid that contains no cells and is called serum. It has been found that when toxins, which are poisons made by bacteria and causing diseases, are injected into the blood, antitoxins, which fight the disease, appear. Blood, generally that of horses, is treated in this way and serum is made from it. The serum is injected into a person suffering from the same disease as the one caused by the original toxin. Serums are most successful when used in the treatment of diphtheria and for poisoning caused by the bite of a snake.

BLOOD TRANSFUSION.
The process of putting blood into the veins of patients to replace a loss is known as blood transfusion. Blood for this purpose is obtained from human beings described as blood donors, and the person receiving the blood is called the recipient.

The idea of blood transfusion first appeared during the 17th century and the first experimental transfusion between dogs was made in England by the scientist Richard Lower in 1665. The earliest transfusions to humans used animal blood but it was clear that this was harmful to man and it was not until 1818 that a London doctor took human blood from one person and transfused it to another.

In transfusion the problem is that the blood from one person may damage the blood cells of the other. When this happens, the blood samples are said to be "incompatible". The reason for this was discovered early in the 20th century by an Austrian scientist, Karl Landsteiner, who showed that different people have different types of blood. He discovered that there are four main types or groups and described them as O, A, B and AB. In 1940 the rhesus factor was discovered; human blood may be classed as either "rhesus positive" or "rhesus negative". There are other rarer blood groups. These discoveries made it possible to "cross-match" blood from different people, and thus made blood transfusion a safe procedure, as it made sure that the transfused blood would not damage the recipient's own cells.

Developments in blood transfusion have taken place chiefly during wars in the 20th century. Transfusions were available in World War I and the idea of storing blood in "banks" was started at this time.

Serious blood loss for which the patient requires a transfusion is most commonly the result of accidents when arteries may be damaged and bones broken. It can also occur during major operations such as long heart operations when perhaps as many as 11 litres may be needed. Transfusions may also be necessary for people suffering from anaemia. Very rarely, a baby is born with a blood condition which requires its blood to be completely replaced soon after birth.

The supply of blood depends on donors who, in Britain, are volunteers. They must be healthy so that their blood will not spread disease to the recipients. After the blood has been taken into bottles, it is tested for its blood group and then stored in refrigerators in a "blood bank" until it is needed. Clotting is prevented by adding small amounts of chemicals. Extracts of blood are prepared for use in various blood diseases. Plasma is blood from which the red cells have been removed (see BLOOD). Plasma "freeze dried" into powder can be stored much longer than blood. When it is needed, sterile water is added. As it has no corpuscles, plasma can usually be given to anyone, whatever his blood group.

When a patient requires a blood transfusion his own blood is tested for its group, a bottle of the correct blood drawn from the "blood bank" and the two bloods are cross-matched to ensure they are compatible. Blood flows through a tube connecting the bottle to a needle inserted into a vein.

BLOODY ASSIZE.
This was a court of law held in various towns in the west country of England during the reign of James II. (Assize courts are explained in the article ASSIZE.) The King sent the Chief Justice of England, George Jeffreys, and four other judges to try all the people who had been accused of taking part in a rebellion against the King led by the Duke of Monmouth in 1685. Monmouth's army had already been defeated at Sedgemoor, but it was the King's policy so to frighten people that they would not repeat the attempt at rebellion. So many people were condemned to death or sold into slavery during these trials that the court came to be called the Bloody Assize.

Judge Jeffreys shouted and raged at the prisoners, refused to let them speak and bullied the witnesses. He ordered 320 people to be executed for high treason, about 800 others were sold into slavery on West Indian plantations, and

Blowpipe.

The judge raged savagely at both prisoners and witnesses.

much of the profits went to people in favour at Court.

Judge Jeffreys was promoted to be Lord Chancellor as a reward for the way he had carried out the trials.

BLOWPIPE.
The blowpipe, or blowgun, is one of the weapons used by peoples of Malaysia, Indonesia, Guiana and the basin of the Amazon River in South America. It is a pole about seven feet long, the middle of which has been hollowed out by a sharp iron rod. The hole is about one third of an inch across.

The darts, which are blown through this tube, are splinters of palm wood, eight to ten inches long, fixed to the end of a piece of soft wood, or pith. These fit exactly into the tube. The darts have notches on them so that the poisoned end will stick in the victim's body when the pith portion breaks off.

In 1938 it was discovered that curare, which is one of the poisons used by South American Indians, is a valuable drug for use in medicine. It is used in surgical operations to relax the patient's muscles, or sometimes to stop him moving.

BLUEBELL
is the name given to several wild flowers. Probably the best known is the wood hyacinth, which carpets the English woods with blue flowers in May and belongs to the Liliaceae or lily family. These bluebells, which are found in many places in western Europe, are seen at their best in Kew Gardens, London, where they make a sea of colour beneath the beech and silver birch trees. They are perhaps at their worst after they have been picked, for however carefully they are cut the juice runs out of the stems and they droop sadly and soon die.

These bluebells have bulbs and the young plants generally come up from new bulbs that are formed between the scales of the mother bulb. (See BULB.) They can also, however, spread by means of seeds, but these are small and have less power to push new growth up through the shade of the surrounding plants into the light. Bluebells in the woods grow as high as 18 inches in their search for light, but they are much shorter when they grow in the sun. Occasionally a white bluebell is found among the others.

The little bells, often a dozen together, hang on short stalks down one side of the main stem. As they bend to the wind the floor of the wood changes from dark to light blue and back again, just like blue velvet being smoothed down and then ruffled up once more.

Sir Harry Lauder, a well-loved comedian who died in 1950, used to sing "I love a lassie, a bonnie Hieland lassie, . . . Mary, ma Scotch bluebell." "The bluebells of Scotland" are really harebells, however, sometimes called witches' thimbles. They have wiry stems up to a foot high; the leaves low down are round and crinkly, but higher up they are long and narrow. The flowers, which appear in July, are usually a

Left: Harebell.
Right: Bluebell.

light mauvish blue but sometimes white, and they tremble on stalks as thin as hairs. The harebell is found on heaths and pastures throughout Great Britain, in Canada and elsewhere. It is a member of the true bell-flower family, to which campanulas like the Canterbury bell belong.

BLUEBOTTLE. Sometimes known as blowflies, bluebottles and greenbottles of one kind or another are found all over the world. When blue-

bottles appear in buzzing swarms it is usually a sign that rotting animal matter is lying about, for the females generally lay their eggs in bad meat or fish or other animal refuse. Cooked meat is also an attraction to them and they may work their way into openings in a joint and lay their eggs there in clusters. The eggs hatch out into white maggots which are called "gentles" and are often used as bait for fish.

Many of the green-bottles are not content with dead meat, but choose living animals on which to breed. They lay their eggs on the wool of sheep, for example. When the grubs hatch out they burrow through the skin and into the flesh of the sheep, sometimes killing them and in any case making their skins less valuable.

G. E. Hyde
Above: A female bluebottle on a meat bone. Below: Bluebottle maggots, or "gentles".

Two troublesome flies of this kind, whose maggots even attack human beings, are found in Africa. The Tumbu fly lays its eggs on the earth floor of native huts and, since many of the people sleep on the floor, the grubs often burrow through their skins in the night. They then make their homes under the skin, feeding on the flesh and causing painful itching and swelling. The Congo floor maggot just has one meal, however, and goes away again.

BLUE MOUNTAINS. From many points near Sydney Cove in New South Wales, Australia, the early settlers could see, 30 miles to the west, highlands usually shrouded in blue haze. These they called the Blue Mountains. They soon found that the highlands formed an almost impassable barrier, but in May 1813 Gregory Blaxland decided to attempt a climb in a part immediately west of the Nepean River where the forested slopes rise steeply and rivers emerge in deep, rocky gorges. His route is now followed by a road and a railway.

The Blue Mountains are really part of the

Eastern Highlands (see the separate article EASTERN HIGHLANDS) and their limits are not very definite. Nowadays the name is usually applied only to a plateau, or tableland, between 3,000 and 4,000 feet high, made of hard sandstone, and this is more correctly called the Blue Plateau.

This plateau, with its slopes covered with gum forests, its fern gullies, gorges and waterfalls, is fine country to explore. Rivers, such as the Grose, have cut so deeply into it that their valley sides are like cliffs, perhaps 2,000 feet high. Near Katoomba is Echo Point where a man, facing westwards, finds that it takes two minutes before he hears the echo of his voice reflected from the slopes of the Narrow Neck Plateau.

BLUEPRINT. The craftsmen who work together in building a house, an aircraft or a machine need what are called working drawings to guide them. These are drawn accurately to scale so that the size of parts can be found by measuring the drawing. Many copies of the working drawings are needed, and they are often called blueprints because they used to be copied by a process which reproduced them as white drawings on a blue ground.

Blueprinting was invented in 1840 by Sir John Herschel, a British astronomer and chemist. The original drawing was done in black ink on tracing paper or translucent tracing cloth. This was then placed over white paper which had been prepared with chemicals sensitive to light. Strong light was allowed to shine through the drawing, causing a blue substance to form on the copy paper wherever it was not screened by the ink lines of the drawing.

Nowadays drawings are more often copied by the whiteprint or diazo process. This gives a copy showing black lines on a white ground, as in the original drawing. Light-sensitive copy paper is used, and the image is developed either by a dry method using ammonia fumes or by a semi-moist method using a thin coating of developer. Some photocopying machines make use of heat-sensitive paper.

Xerox copies are made by a different process which uses magnetism instead of chemicals. The copy paper is charged positively and picks up a pattern of negatively charged powder which is heated to form a permanent image.

BLUESTOCKING. "Bluestocking" is the nickname for a very learned woman, and it was first given to the followers of Mrs. Elizabeth Montagu (1720–1800). In about 1750 she began to hold assemblies of men and women for discussions on literature and other serious subjects; her idea was to make social life more intellectual and stop so much time being spent in gossip and cardplaying. Her followers dressed very plainly and one of them, Benjamin Stillingfleet, wore blue stockings below his knee-breeches. Perhaps it was this that gave Mrs. Montagu's friends the nickname of the *Bluestocking Society*, or Mrs. Montagu may herself have chosen blue stockings as an emblem.

Although at first either men or women could be called bluestockings, the word soon came to be used only of women.

BOA CONSTRICTOR. Blood-curdling tales have often been told about this snake, but it is neither so huge nor so powerful as the storytellers suggest and some of them have probably confused it with its larger relations the anaconda

Paul Popper
The boa constrictor's jaws are so elastic that it can swallow animals larger in diameter than its own head.

and the python. The boa constrictor is seldom longer than 3.5 metres and it cannot swallow any animal larger than a lamb.

There are many different kinds of boas, but most of them are found in Central and South America. All of them have traces of hind legs which are little more than useless claws. The

A Roman historian tells how Queen Boadicea in her war chariot led her people into battle against the Romans.

female hatches her eggs inside her body, so that the young are born alive. Boas have very large families; a boa from Paraguay once gave birth to 42 young snakes at the London Zoo.

The boa constrictor is found from northern Mexico to central Argentina and in the West Indies. Its colour is ruddy brown, turning to deep red at the tail, with large oval patches of tan turning to cream. It spends most of its time coiled round the branches of trees where it is in a good position to strike at its unsuspecting victims. It feeds on small mammals and birds, seizing them with its long curved teeth and then wrapping them in its coils (constricting them) until they are suffocated.

People sometimes say that it crushes its prey to a pulp before eating it, but this is not true; nor does it have to hold on to a branch with its tail before it can constrict its prey. On the other hand, it is true that it can swallow an animal which is bigger across than its own head, for it has such elastic jaws.

BOADICEA, or Boudicca, was queen of a British tribe called the Iceni during the time when the Romans were masters of Britain. The Iceni lived in the east of England, in what is now called Norfolk. Their ruler King Prasutagus, Boadicea's husband, was very wealthy and the Romans allowed him to keep his kingdom provided that he obeyed Roman commands. Prasutagus had no son and when he died in about the year A.D. 60 he left his property to be shared between the Roman emperor Nero and his own two daughters. However, the Romans, taking no notice of his will, seized everything and also ill-treated his widow and his daughters.

The Iceni were furious. Led by the warlike Boadicea, they rebelled against the Romans and half Britain rose with them. The Roman governor, Suetonius Paulinus, and his army were away in the north of Wales. The Britons captured and destroyed the Roman strongholds of Camulodunum (Colchester) and Verulamium (St. Albans) and several others; more than 70,000 Romans and Britons who had made friends with the Romans were slaughtered. A legion marching south to the rescue from Lincoln was cut to pieces. Paulinus hurried back to Londinium (London) ahead of his army, but at first could do nothing against the victorious Britons.

Boadicea's triumph did not last long, however. Paulinus, having rejoined his army, prepared for battle in a valley, probably near Fenny Stratford in Buckinghamshire. Boadicea drove her chariot along the British battle lines, urging her soldiers on to revenge, but the Romans were too strong and they inflicted a terrible defeat on the Britons. Boadicea despaired when she realized that all was lost, and took poison.

BOAR. This name is given both to a male wild pig and to the male of the ordinary domestic pig which is descended from it. (See PIG.) The wild boar is a large, powerful beast, with a heavy black-bristled body, short legs and sharp, up-curved tusks. It can move very fast and, when attacked, will resist fiercely. It lives in forests and marshy woodland districts, where there is plenty of cover, and prowls mostly at night, feeding on roots, nuts, birds' eggs and any small animals that it can catch or dig up. It is still found in parts of Europe including France, Spain, Austria, Germany and the U.S.S.R., as well as in central and northern Asia and in North Africa. Wild boars were once common in the British Isles but the last one was killed in Windsor Park early in the 17th century.

Because of its fierceness and speed, hunting the wild boar has always been an exciting and dangerous sport. In England in the middle ages wild boar, like deer, were preserved in the royal forests and boar hunts were often held by the king in honour of important visitors to the court.

Radio Times Hulton Picture Library
The wild boar is the fiercest animal hunted in Europe.

When an animal was killed its head was cut off, soaked in wine, roasted and then eaten at the banquet held after the hunt. In India, where the sport is called pig-sticking, a slightly smaller but just as fierce kind of wild boar is still hunted on horseback with spears.

BOAT RACE, THE. The day of the Boat Race between Oxford and Cambridge Universities is one of the most exciting sporting occasions

of the year in Great Britain. A commentary of the race is broadcast on radio and television, though many people watch from the water's edge along the course, which is the stretch of the River Thames between Putney and Mortlake. Other observers follow the teams at a distance in their own boats. The race is nowadays rowed on a Saturday in late March or early April, and for it the river is cleared of all other traffic. Course positions are decided by the toss of a coin.

The first Oxford and Cambridge Boat Race in 1829 was not rowed on this course, but at Henley-on-Thames, where the world's most famous rowing regatta, or meeting, now takes place. Seven years later the second race took place, this time from Westminster to Putney. The Oxford crew were wearing white jerseys striped with dark blue and before the race a Cambridge supporter tied a piece of light blue ribbon to the Cambridge boat for luck. From then on the Oxford colour has been dark blue and the Cambridge light blue. The first race on the present course from Putney to Mortlake took place in 1845.

This course is about four and a quarter miles long and the race over it is said to be one of the hardest there is, so it is not surprising that the result is not usually very close. Only once, in 1877, has there been a dead heat. Cambridge has won the Boat Race on more occasions than has Oxford. Apart from the very hard physical task of rowing at full strength over such a distance, the crews sometimes come up against other difficulties as well. In the old days, for example, the crews were sometimes held up by·other craft on the course, and one crew might even try to foul the other deliberately. The weather cannot always be depended on at Boat Race time either: several times one boat has sunk in rough water—Oxford sank near the beginning of the race in 1951, for instance, and the race had to be re-rowed during the following week—and in 1912 both boats sank. In 1952 the race was rowed in a blizzard.

BOATS. Roughly speaking boats are small (less than 45 feet long) and ships are large, but there are a lot of exceptions to that rule. (See SHIPS.) Cross-channel steamers are sometimes called packet boats; quite sizeable naval vessels are called motor torpedo boats; and some tugboats are as big as trawlers.

The first man to use a boat was the primitive hunter who ferried himself over a river by lying on a tree trunk or large piece of floating driftwood, using his hands as paddles. From that beginning boats have grown up in two distinct ways. One group of men learnt to hollow out a tree-trunk, partly by burning and partly with stone tools; this kind of boat is usually known as a dug-out. Another group learnt to tie several tree-trunks together and make a raft. Sooner or later both groups began to improve their craft by building up the sides with planks to keep out the water and prevent themselves—and more important their cargo—from getting wet. Those who started with a dug-out built eventually a boat that must have been rather like a heavy, clumsy rowing boat of the present day; and those who began with a raft ended up with a flat-bottomed boat rather like a punt. All early boats must have been paddled or poled along with the boatmen facing in the direction in which they were going. This method was, and still is, the easiest to arrange and had the advantage that the boatmen could pick their way over unknown water and look out for game or enemies ahead of them. In such conditions there are great disadvantages in facing the stern and rowing a boat along with oars, although

this method enables the oarsman to make better use of his weight in propelling the boat.

Nowadays the design of boats varies greatly in different parts of the world and according to the many purposes for which boats are used. Many of the early designs of boats are in use today because they still have practical advantages. In Wales coracles are still used by fishermen on some rivers; the coracles are built of canvas stretched over a wicker frame and are similar to some of the earliest boats built by man. They have the obvious advantage of being so light that a fisherman can pick his boat up and carry it about on his shoulders. In the same way nobody has been able to improve on the design of the North American Indian canoe, a wonderfully efficient boat of such shallow draught (that is to say needing little water to float it) that it can be safely navigated down rock-filled rivers. At the same time, although a canoe will carry three men, or two men and a load, it is so light that one man can carry it on his back from lake to lake, or along the bank of a river where there is a waterfall or a rapid too dangerous for navigation. (See the article CANOEING.)

Rafts are little used in the modern world except as a means of getting logs down a river, but in 1947 a small group of adventurous men sailed westwards across the Pacific on a raft called the "Kon-Tiki". The raft was made of balsa wood, in the same way as those used by the early inhabitants of Peru. The object of the expedition was to prove that the Pacific Islands could have been peopled from South America.

Rowing boats range from heavy, strongly built boats used at sea (and these themselves vary considerably in design according to whether they are to be used in and out of harbours or to be hauled up over a beach) down to light, fast, delicate boats designed for racing. Sailing boats show similar differences in design. The more solidly built type of boat consists of a keel and ribs on to which are fixed planks, often called strakes. If the planks are overlapped the boat is said to be clinker-built; if they are placed together to present a smooth surface to the water the boat is carvel-built. Sailing boats require a deeper keel than rowing boats, partly (if the keel is heavy or weighted at the bottom) to prevent

BOATS

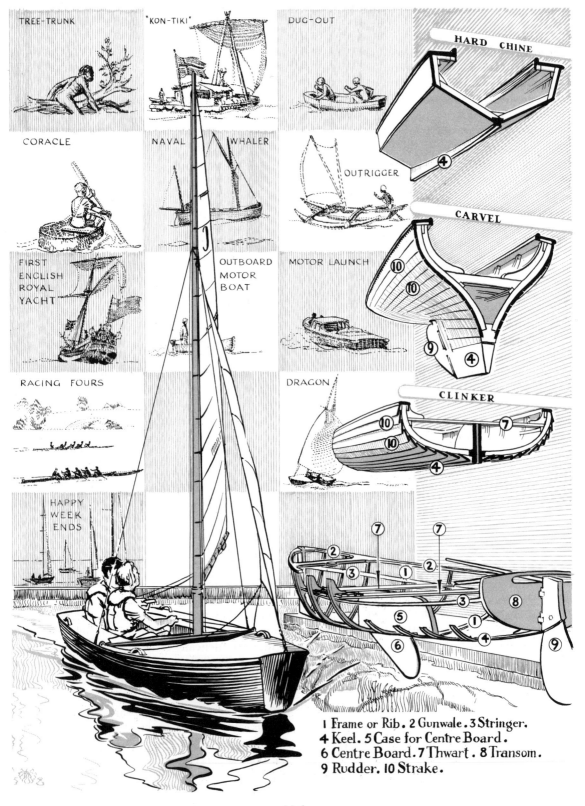

TREE-TRUNK

"KON-TIKI"

DUG-OUT

HARD CHINE

CORACLE

NAVAL WHALER

OUTRIGGER

CARVEL

FIRST ENGLISH ROYAL YACHT

OUTBOARD MOTOR BOAT

MOTOR LAUNCH

CLINKER

RACING FOURS

DRAGON

HAPPY WEEK ENDS

1 Frame or Rib . 2 Gunwale . 3 Stringer.
4 Keel . 5 Case for Centre Board .
6 Centre Board . 7 Thwart . 8 Transom.
9 Rudder . 10 Strake.

them from being overturned by the pressure of the wind on the sails and partly to stop the whole boat from being blown sideways over the water. Sailing boats that have to be used in and out of shallow water have a small keel which can be hauled up within a box in the centre of the boat and which is known as a centre board or centre plate. The fast sailing boats called catamarans have twin hulls connected by a deck that is clear of the water. Trimarans have one hull, with a float on each side. (See CATAMARAN.)

Rowing boats used for racing on lakes or rivers are built of thin sheets of wood bent round a light frame. They are so narrow that they can only be balanced by the oars or sculls. (A scull is a smaller type of oar.) If a crew sat in the boat without oars the boat would roll over. Racing rowing boats are nowadays not built to carry more than eight oarsmen and a coxswain, or cox, who steers. Boats for four oarsmen may be designed either to carry a cox or to be rowed without a cox. A coxswainless four is steered by one of the oarsmen, usually the one nearest the bow of the boat, who has the rudder lines fixed to the toe of one of his shoes; he has to glance over his shoulder as he rows. Racing boats to carry two may be designed to carry either two oarsmen, each using one oar, or two scullers each using two sculls. Modern racing boats have sliding seats and each oar usually moves in a metal U-shaped support called a rowlock, which is free to swivel or turn. Very little change has been made in the design of racing rowing boats since about 1900. (See BOAT RACE, THE; ROWING.)

In the construction of light sailing boats many new materials are now used; for example, moulded plywood, fibre-glass and light metal such as aluminium alloy. Carvel building with wood is still popular for larger yachts.

Motor boats range in size from fully decked vessels, capable of going to sea, to small open boats driven by an outboard motor; that is, a motor fitted over the outside of the stern. An outboard motor is generally noisier than an inboard motor, but it has the advantage that it can be taken off one boat very easily and fixed on to another or carried from place to place. Also, because it is outside the boat there is no need to have a propeller shaft through the woodwork, and so there is no problem of keeping the water from getting up the shaft into the boat. (See MOTOR BOAT.)

The life-boats carried by ships are sturdy craft able to keep afloat in rough seas. The bigger ones (those carrying 100 people or more) are motor boats fitted with radio and searchlights. All ships' life-boats have masts with orange-coloured sails that can be seen easily by rescuing ships, and carry torches for signalling, flares and distress signals. Many of the smaller life-boats are propelled not by oars but by a screw propeller driven by handles worked with a push-and-pull action, so that trained seamen are not needed for rowing. Ships also carry rubber life-saving rafts which are launched from chutes and automatically inflated (blown out) by gas to make them float. These rafts take up little space and are easier to launch than boats. The life-boats stationed around the coast for rescue work are described in the article LIFE-BOAT.

Houseboats are designed for living in when moored to the bank of a river or lake. They have no engines. In far eastern countries many people live permanently in houseboats, but in Europe and the United States they are more often used for summer holidays.

BOER WAR. In this war in South Africa, which began in 1899 and ended in 1902, Britain, which controlled the two colonies of Natal and Cape Colony, fought against the people of the two independent republics of Transvaal and the Orange Free State, which were the northern neighbours of these colonies. These people were the Boers, the descendants of early Dutch settlers. (You can read about the history of South Africa, and about the reasons why the war began, in the article SOUTH AFRICA.)

During the first part of the war the Boers were successful nearly everywhere. As soon as it started they seized the diamond fields at Kimberley and surrounded the town. They quickly managed to besiege the important towns of Mafeking and Ladysmith, which were British strongholds.

The Boers were strong and brave and very unusual soldiers. Many of them had come straight from their farms to fight. They had no proper uniforms and they chose their own officers. Their generals, such men as Christiaan de Wet, J. H. de la Rey, Louis Botha and later Jan Smuts, were to prove themselves cunning and skilful fighters. The British general Sir Redvers Buller tried twice to drive the Boers away from Ladysmith, but twice he was defeated. In the "Black Week" in December 1899 the British forces suffered three serious defeats.

These defeats made the people of Britain realize that they were fighting a determined and skilful enemy. The country made a great effort and sent out many more soldiers, some of whom were volunteers and not soldiers by profession. Lord Roberts became Commander-in-Chief of the British forces, with Lord Kitchener as his Chief-of-Staff.

From this point the fortunes of the war changed and the British began to be victorious. First the Boers were driven from their position surrounding the town of Kimberley, and then one of the Boer generals surrendered with 4,000 men, in February 1900. The Boers retreated from the town of Ladysmith and soon Lord Roberts' forces captured Bloemfontein, the capital of the Orange Free State. Mafeking was relieved (this word means that the armies who were besieging the town were driven away) in May, and there was great rejoicing when the news got through to England. (Colonel Robert Baden-Powell had commanded the British soldiers inside Mafeking.) More victories followed and finally in November 1900 the aged President of the Transvaal, Paul Kruger, who had himself gone into the field with his fighting men, left South Africa in a Dutch warship to try to get help in Europe, where he was later to die without seeing his country again. Meanwhile the Boer republics were declared to be British colonies and the war seemed to be over.

It was not over, however, for the Boers would not give in. For nearly two years they carried on a guerilla war against the British—that is, a war fought not with organized armies, but with small groups called commandos, determined to damage their enemies as much as possible in every way. The Boers made lightning raids on British posts, and captured ammunition and

supplies, and disappeared into the spaces of the *veld* (the grass country of South Africa) as fast as they had come. Every farmhouse helped them, giving them food and information about their enemies.

The British began to burn and destroy the farms that helped the commandos. Thousands of people were made homeless and the women, children and native servants were gathered together to live in concentration camps. At first there was not enough food and medicine in the camps. Disease broke out and more than 20,000 Boer women and children perished.

In spite of all this distress the Boers went on fighting, but their leaders gradually realized that their struggle was hopeless and that it would be better to give in before their nation was quite worn out. After many discussions between the leaders of the Boers and the British, peace was made in May 1902. The Boers finally had to agree to become subjects of King Edward VII, while Britain promised that they should govern themselves as soon as possible. The British government granted £3,000,000 to help with rebuilding the farms which had been destroyed.

BOG is the name given to an area of soft, spongy, waterlogged ground which often has many pools. Plants such as mosses, reeds and heather grow there and when these die they cannot decay completely, partly because the soil is so acid, and so peat is formed beneath the surface. (See PEAT.) It is dangerous to walk on bogs if one does not know where to find the patches of firm ground and sometimes, after heavy rain, there is a danger of a "bog-burst" or "bog-slide" in which the contents of the bog may spread over cultivated land near by.

BOGOTA is the capital of Colombia, a country in the northwestern corner of South America (See COLOMBIA.) The city lies near the centre of the republic on a sloping plateau, or high plain, in the Andes. Above it tower the mountains Guadalupe and Monserrate and through it a stream runs to join other streams in the Bogota River, which plunges over the edge of the plateau 20 miles from the city in a beautiful vertical waterfall of nearly 500 feet. Bogota is not far north of the equator but, because it is so high in the mountains, the climate is moist and cool.

The city was founded by Jimenez de Quesada in 1538. Having come from the warm land of Andalusia in Spain, many of his men built their houses with courtyards in the middle, like those they had known at home, and their sons copied the style. In the ancient parts of Bogota one can still see these houses, their heavy doors studded with nails and their windows barred with grilles or balconies. There are old churches, too, which Roman Catholic monks and priests built quite simply, although they decorated them inside with elaborate carvings, gold leaf and paintings of saints, together with sacred images gorgeously arrayed in velvets, pearls and emeralds.

For centuries Bogota has been a gathering place for writers, artists, musicians, scientists and philosophers. The Dominican friars started a university here in the 16th century and the present university grew out of this. Bogota is also a busy industrial city and its factories make cloth, cement, foods, beer, soft drinks, fats and oils. The plains outside the city are good pasture land for sheep and cattle.

Some railways lead out of the capital but many people who want to travel from Bogota to other parts of Colombia still go by road or else by boat on the Magdalena and other rivers. However, aeroplanes are being used more and more to bring people and goods to and from this mountain city with a population of about 1,662,000.

BOHEMIA is now a part of the republic of Czechoslovakia but once it was a separate country and a powerful kingdom. Czechoslovakia contains people of several races, among them, as the name of the country shows, the Czechs and the Slovaks. The Czech people have had their home in Bohemia for 1,500 years, and today it is one of the most important parts of Czechoslovakia.

Bohemia is shaped like a diamond, closed in on all sides by mountains or high hills which are covered with forests and also contain many other riches. In the middle ages their silver mines were the richest in Europe—the word dollar comes from *thaler,* the silver coin coming from Joachimsthal in Bohemia—and today there are

many industries of all kinds. In the open rolling country in the centre of Bohemia, where all sorts of crops are grown, there are many orchards and every road is lined with apple or cherry trees. Flocks of geese and herds of swine roam under the trees.

The forefathers of the Czech people came to settle in Bohemia and in a land just to the east of it called Moravia during the first few centuries after Christ. Bohemia's chief enemies from the beginning were the Germans, and later the Austrians. After many struggles against the Germans, the Bohemian prince Ottakar became a king in 1198, and the kingdom of Bohemia and Moravia grew powerful and wealthy. One of its greatest rulers was Charles IV, who founded a university in his favourite city of Prague. After his reign, however, the history of Bohemia became very troubled. The people of Bohemia belonged to the Roman Catholic Church, but in the 14th century a man named John Huss founded a Protestant church, and many people in Bohemia and Moravia joined it. (This church, which still exists, is described in the article MORAVIANS.) In 1415 Huss was burnt at the stake as a heretic, and bitter religious wars broke out in Bohemia. (A heretic is a person who teaches beliefs which do not agree with those of the church.)

In 1526 Bohemia and Moravia became part of the Austrian Empire (see AUSTRIAN EMPIRE) and for nearly 400 years they were ruled by the Austrians. The spirit of the Czech people of Bohemia was never quite crushed, but it was not until the 18th century that they began the long struggle against their rulers and against the large numbers of Germans who had their homes in Bohemia. At the end of World War I, Bohemia and Moravia at last became independent and joined with other countries to form the new state of Czechoslovakia. You can read about this part of Bohemia's history in the article CZECHOSLOVAKIA.

BOILER. Anything in which a substance is boiled is, strictly speaking, a boiler, but in industry the word generally refers to large tanks in which liquids are heated and more especially to those in which water is changed into steam. The latter are often called steam boilers although, in fact, they boil water.

If a closed container is partly filled with water and its temperature is raised continuously, in due course the water will boil and steam will begin to form. As the steam is formed it escapes from the water into the space above the water level in the container and tries to occupy a very much greater volume than it did as water. If it were allowed to escape freely, the steam would occupy a volume nearly 1,700 times as great as it did as water. However, the closed container does not permit this expansion. The effect is the same as pumping air into a bicycle tyre; as more air is pushed in, the pressure in the tyre rises. Similarly, as more steam is formed it pushes into the space above the water and so the pressure in the boiler rises. As the pressure rises, the temperature of the water has to be higher before it will boil. The pressure must not be allowed to become more than the strength of the boiler can safely stand. All boilers must have safety valves fitted to allow steam to escape if the pressure exceeds the safe limit.

In early boilers the pressure was rarely greater than 0·7 bar above atmospheric pressure. (Boiler pressures are generally stated as "gauge pressure", which is the difference between the pressure of the steam and the pressure of the atmosphere. The pressure of the atmosphere is roughly 1 bar.) James Watt, the pioneer of the steam engine, realized the advantage of using higher pressures and tried to make a boiler for 4 bars pressure, but up to about 1860 the pres-

sures were seldom above 3 bars. By 1900 pressures had risen to 20 bars in certain types of boilers. The boiler pressure of one of the first Cunard liners, "Britannia" (1840), was only 0·6 bar but that of the "Queen Elizabeth 2" is 59 bars. Pressures of over 10 bars have been used in boilers other than those on ships, although pressures of 40 to 50 bars are more common.

If steam is taken from the boiler and heated still more, away from the water from which it was formed, its temperature rises and it is called superheated steam. Most engines use superheated high-pressure steam.

A boiler consists of two main parts—the furnace and the water tank. The hot gases pass through flues or flame tubes which are surrounded by water, or round the outside of drums and tubes which are filled with water. The first type, used for lower pressures, is known as a shell boiler since the water is contained in a large shell; the second, used for higher pressures, is called a water-tube boiler as the water flows through tubes. In the shell type of boiler the quantity of water is large and the time taken to raise steam from starting is much longer than in the water-tube boiler, where there is much less water and the tubes may be only about 5 centimetres in diameter.

A flash boiler has almost no water capacity in the boiler itself; instead a pump feeds water directly into the boiler tubes when steam is being drawn off.

Various fuels are used for supplying the necessary energy, but the commonest in Great Britain

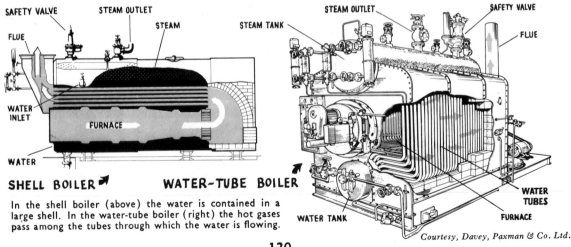

SHELL BOILER

WATER-TUBE BOILER

In the shell boiler (above) the water is contained in a large shell. In the water-tube boiler (right) the hot gases pass among the tubes through which the water is flowing.

Courtesy, Davey, Paxman & Co. Ltd.

are coal, oil fuel and natural gas. In the large power stations the coal may be carried on some form of mechanical stoker which feeds it on to the moving grate as it enters the furnace. It burns as it passes through, and by the time it reaches the back of the furnace is completely burnt and falls as ash into a pit. It is usual practice to reduce the coal to a powder which is then blown into the furnace with a blast of air. When oil fuel is used it is sprayed into the furnace mixed with air and so readily catches fire.

Steam can be used both as a source of power through driving turbines and as a means of transferring energy by heat, so industry uses boilers in many situations. Heat from industrial processes is sometimes used to generate steam in what is called a waste heat boiler.

The article NUCLEAR ENERGY explains how steam is produced in nuclear power stations.

BOILS are small abscesses which form in the tissues of the body just beneath the skin. They are also called furuncles and are caused by a germ known as *Staphylococcus pyogenes*.

These germs (staphylococci) are always present on the skin of a healthy person, particularly near the nose, eyes and ears, and do no harm. However, when a person is constantly feeling tired or is recovering from a long illness the staphylococci often become active and harmful. They work their way under the skin, usually entering where a hair is growing, and increase in numbers very quickly. A hot red swelling comes up. White corpuscles in the blood battle with the staphylococci and pus is formed. (See BLOOD.) A white or yellow head appears in the centre of the red swelling and some days later the boil usually bursts and the pus escapes. Afterwards complete healing slowly takes place.

Boils are often brought about by part of the skin being constantly rubbed so that the hair growing there is irritated. For example, boils frequently appear on the backs of the necks of people who wear hard collars that rub the skin.

Whatever the cause, it is important to get rid of a boil as quickly as possible, or else the infection will spread and more boils will be produced. A boil that does not burst should be opened by a doctor. Hot, antiseptic cloths may be applied in order to make the pus come out. A boil should not be touched or interfered with by anyone except a doctor. He may order some special drug, such as penicillin, which attacks the microbes.

BOLIVAR, Simon (1783–1830). When the Spanish colonists in South America revolted against Spain early in the 19th century, their success was largely due to the genius and patriotism of Simon Bolivar, the Liberator. The countries of Bolivia, Colombia, Ecuador, Panama, Peru and Venezuela all owe their independence largely to him.

Bolivar was born in Caracas, Venezuela. His family was wealthy and his father, who was a Spanish nobleman, owned much land and many slaves. Both his father and mother died when he was a boy and his uncle and guardian sent him to Madrid in Spain to be educated. There, at the age of 18, he married a young girl whose family were neighbours of his in Caracas, but within a year of their return to Venezuela she died of yellow fever.

Bolivar, who now had no family ties, returned to Europe in 1804. He went to France where Napoleon was just reaching the height of his power. He also visited Italy and in Rome his old tutor urged him to go back so that he could help the colonists to free themselves from the rule of Spain. The young man gave a promise that he never broke and devoted the rest of his life to the cause of freedom. In Madrid he had seen how the Spaniards had quarrelled among themselves and greatly weakened their country after the Napoleonic wars. He believed the time had come when his own country, Venezuela, could become independent and remain so.

The Struggle for Freedom

In 1810 the Venezuelans drove out the Spanish governor and set up the first local government in South America. The new state was not strong enough to resist the Spanish troops, however, and when they reconquered it in the following year Bolivar fled to New Granada, now Colombia, where he continued the struggle against the Spaniards for several years. Then he appealed to the Negroes in Hispaniola (Haiti) for help, promising in return that he would free the Negro slaves in Venezuela; this promise he kept some years later. He landed in Venezuela in 1819 with 2,500 soldiers and, after various battles, marched over the hot, rain-drenched Orinoco basin and then across the snow-covered Andes to the tropical grassland of New Granada—one of the most terrible forced marches in the history of warfare. A few days later, without giving his troops time to rest, he defeated an army twice as large as his at Boyaca and so New Granada was freed from Spain. The Liberator then united it with Venezuela as the Republic of Colombia and was elected its first president.

In 1822 the province of Quito, now Ecuador, was freed from Spain and the next year Bolivar turned to Peru where the Spaniards were again completely defeated and he was made dictator. As soon as the new government was well estab-lished he resigned, refusing a gift of money worth about £200,000. Meanwhile Upper Peru had become a separate republic and had been named Bolivia in his honour.

During Bolivar's absence a civil war had broken out in Colombia. When he returned he was unable to restore peace, so he resigned his office as president and went to the coast, intend-ing to sail for Europe, but he found that he had not enough money to pay for his passage. Saddened by news of the murder of his friend General Antonio de Sucre in Venezuela and weakened by tuberculosis, he fell ill and died near Santa Marta, Colombia, at the age of 47.

BOLIVIA is one of the only two South Ameri-can republics that do not touch the coast, the other being Paraguay which lies to the southeast. Bolivia's northeastern neighbour is Brazil, while Peru and Chile form the western frontier and Argentina lies to the south.

Three-fifths of the country is lowland, with great plains stretching from the Brazilian frontier to the Andes. (See ANDES MOUNTAINS.) In the west, about 3,700 metres up between two lofty mountain ranges, lies the Bolivian *altiplano*, or highland plain.

Bolivia is within the tropics but it has every kind of climate from the moist heat of the eastern lowlands to the bitter cold of the mountains. The plant life ranges from the luxuriant tropical forests of the east to the scanty vegetation of the high mountains, but most of the *altiplano* is covered with coarse, dry grass.

The animals in Bolivia include pumas, jaguars, tapirs, sloths and many kinds of monkey in the lowland forests, the alligator-like caymans

Simon Bolivar the Liberator stormed across South America, freeing countries from Spanish rule.

Mansell Collection

of the rivers in the northeast, armadillos, opossums and skunks, and giant snakes like the anaconda. Some of the forests of the warm valleys and plains are filled with beautiful but harsh-voiced parrots, macaws and toucans. On the lakes on the Bolivian *altiplano* there are many geese, ducks, grebes, flamingoes and other water birds. In the mountains live great eagles and condors, while vultures are found all over the country.

The Bolivian *altiplano* is one of the highest inhabited regions in the world and about three-quarters of the people of Bolivia live there. The total population of the country is small, however. More than half are full-blooded Indians, the descendants of people originally ruled by the Incas. (See INCAS.) Nearly one-third of the population is a mixture of Indians and white people, while about one-eighth are pure white. These white people are mostly the descendants of the Spaniards who conquered the country in the 16th century, although some of them have come from other European countries and the United States.

It is the white people who often have important positions in government and industry, while the people of mixed blood are usually skilled workers, shopkeepers or have minor jobs in the government.

When the Spanish invaders conquered the Inca rulers they took the subject Indian peoples under their control and made them Roman Catholics. They also introduced the Spanish language to some extent, although most of the Indians still speak one or other of their own languages. The chief Indian languages are Aymara and Quechua.

The Indians in the mountains live much as their ancestors did before the Spanish conquest. Their main occupation is farming and they

work together in communities. The men plough with metal-shod sticks exactly like those their ancestors used and the women follow behind breaking up the clods of earth. In this way they produce their two chief foods—*quinoa*, which is a grain crop, and potatoes, which originally came to Europe and the rest of the world from the Andes—but the crops are often too small to provide the Indians with enough to eat.

Almost as important to them as their food are *chicha*, a drink made from maize, and coca leaves, which they chew to deaden the pains of hunger and cold.

The Indians make their own household utensils, including pots of baked clay, and they weave most of their clothing on primitive hand looms. The women wear gay skirts and shawls and the men have brilliantly coloured ponchos, which are like cloaks. The woman wear hats which look rather like bowlers.

The Indians are good craftsmen but produce less artistic work than their forefathers who made beautiful cloth and pottery. Their homes are thatched huts built of dried-mud bricks or of stone, with earthen floors. These huts are some-

---

FACTS ABOUT BOLIVIA

AREA: 1,098,581 square kilometres.
POPULATION: 5,062,500.
KIND OF COUNTRY: Independent republic.
CAPITAL: Sucre, but La Paz is the place where the government meets and is Bolivia's biggest city.
GEOGRAPHICAL FEATURES: One of the highest inhabited areas of the world. There is no sea coast.
CHIEF PRODUCTS: Tin, copper, lead, zinc and petroleum; agriculture is backward and foodstuffs have to be imported.
IMPORTANT TOWNS: Sucre, La Paz, Cochabamba, Oruro, Potosi, Santa Cruz.
EDUCATION: Children must attend school between the ages of 6 and 14, but this law cannot be enforced in the country districts. Less than half the population can read and write.

times grouped on the outskirts of the cities and sometimes in little villages by themselves.

Mining, Farming and Transport

It was gold and silver which attracted the Spaniards to Bolivia, then called Upper Peru, and the mountain of Potosi, in particular, contained a vast amount of silver. Mining is Bolivia's leading industry and many Indians are employed in the mines. Gold and silver are still produced but tin has become by far the most important metal. It makes up two-thirds of all the products Bolivia sends abroad (most of it goes to Great Britain and the United States) and the country is normally the world's third largest tin producer. Other mineral products are petroleum, copper, lead, antimony and zinc. The Santa-Cruz area has petroleum and natural gas deposits.

The eastern slopes of the Andes are warm and well-watered and in the valleys are grown grain crops, coffee, tobacco, sugar, cotton and semi-tropical fruits like pineapples and bananas. Cattle are raised on the eastern plains and sheep in the mountains.

Some valuable trees—ebony, mahogany, rosewood and others—are found in the tropical forests. When the trees are felled the logs are floated down the rivers that flow through the jungles, for there are almost no real roads. Railways are few and are mostly on the western plateau. Two lines connect the city of Santa Cruz with towns on the frontiers of Argentina and Brazil. Air transport is very important because the surface communications are so inadequate.

Supplies are taken to the cities high up in the mountains by Indian porters who carry their burdens many kilometres over twisting trails. The heavier loads are carried by mules, donkeys or llamas. The llama can travel great distances on very little food or water and it is extremely sure-footed, as a large animal must be in such mountainous areas. The Indians weave its wool into coarse, warm fabrics, but finer wool comes from its relatives the vicuna and the alpaca. All three animals are extremely useful to the Indians, who may have made their home in the highlands because the beasts thrive there.

On the border between Bolivia and Peru lies Lake Titicaca, the largest lake in South America. It is the highest lake in the world that is navigable—3,809 metres above sea level—and its waters are icy cold. Passengers and goods are carried across it by steamers which had to be

Left: Picturepoint. Above: Paul Popper

Above: Two Indians lead their donkeys in one of the high, barren regions of Bolivia. Behind them is Illimani, a mountain 6,880 metres high.

Left: The cathedral of San Francesco in La Paz, the world's highest big city, 3,655 metres above sea level.

Paul Popper

Reed boats on Lake Titicaca, which is 180 kilometres long. It is swept by strong winds and the water is always cold.

brought over the mountain in parts and put together on the shores of the lake. The Indians still use boats called *balsas*, however, as their people have done since the days of the Incas. These boats, shaped rather like large rounded canoes and woven of heavy reeds, with reed sails, can carry both passengers and livestock.

Towns and Places of Interest

Beside Lake Titicaca, at Copacabana, is the shrine of the Virgin of the Light, which is the most famous modern shrine in South America. In August, which in Bolivia is the early spring, Indians from neighbouring countries gather to ask the blessing of the Virgin Mary on their herds and crops. Towards La Paz is Tiahuanaco, where there are strange stone monuments carved long before the days of the Incas.

La Paz, 3,650 metres above sea level, is the largest and most important city in the country, with modern office buildings, banks, breweries, candle and match factories, and spinning and weaving mills. The houses are plaster covered or of stone, with red-tiled roofs, but there are modern concrete buildings in the central district. Although most of its 490,000 inhabitants are Indians, nearly all the foreigners to be found in Bolivia live in La Paz.

The city lies in a shallow, sun-baked valley beneath one of the highest peaks of the Andes, not far from Lake Titicaca. The region all round is barren and food is scarce. On Saturdays mule trains and llama caravans wind into the city bringing potatoes and barley from the highlands and fresh vegetables and fruits from the eastern valleys of the Andes. On Sundays these goods are offered for sale by the Indians, who have booths in the market place or squat beside their goods on the pavement.

The government is at La Paz and this is where the president lives and the parliament meets, but the official capital of Bolivia is Sucre. The university of Sucre, founded in 1624, is one of the oldest on the whole American continent, but there is a great shortage of schools and trained teachers in the country and more than half the people cannot even read or write.

Wars and Revolutions

In 1809 a Bolivian, Pedro Domingo Murillo, was the first to declare independence from Spanish rule in South America, but Bolivia was not freed until 1825. The new state was named Bolivia after Simon Bolivar, who led one of the armies that drove out the Spaniards and who became the first president. (See BOLIVAR, SIMON.)

Since then, however, Bolivia has suffered many disturbances. There have been more than 170 revolutions (not all of them successful) and 70 presidents, and the country has had 11 constitutions laying down the kind of government it is to have. While many of the presidents gained office by bloodshed, most of them were soon turned out by force and six were assassinated.

The Bolivians have had many quarrels with their neighbours too. The most serious of these were with Chile and Paraguay. From 1879 to 1883 Bolivia and Peru fought a war with Chile, as a result of which Bolivia lost the little sea coast it then had, though it later gained access to the port of Arica. In 1930 a bitter war began between Bolivia and Paraguay, again because of a boundary dispute. It was called the Chaco War, for it was fought in the Chaco jungle. After that war ended in 1935, the boundary line was settled. A number of political groups grew up after the war and many attempts were made to improve the way of life of ordinary people and to develop remote parts of the country. Since then the political situation has been unstable and guerrillas, including Ernesto "Che" Guevara, have attempted revolution.

BOMB. One of the earliest kinds of bomb was a hollow metal ball filled with gunpowder and exploded by means of a slow-burning match. Such bombs were first used in the 16th century and were thrown into the enemy's defences by hand or by a kind of gun called a mortar.

From the beginning of World War I airmen on both sides dropped bombs on enemy soldiers and camps. These bombs were generally light, being not more than about 20 pounds in weight. At first they were dropped by hand but later they were carried on racks underneath the wings of the aeroplane and released by means of a cable which the pilot operated from his seat.

They had an iron case and were filled with explosive. When they hit the ground, a pin was driven into a detonator filled with a small quantity of an explosive which went off easily; this in turn set off the main explosive filling which shattered the iron case, and it was the pieces of iron that did the damage as they scattered in all directions.

It is by no means easy to hit a target with an object dropped several thousand feet from an aeroplane which, even in those early days, was travelling at 60 miles an hour or more. Quite apart from the difficulty of aiming, which requires some kind of bomb-sight, the bomb itself has to be streamlined so that it can travel as fast as possible through the air.

Bigger and Bigger Bombs

As World War I went on, each side produced bigger and bigger bombs and, before the end, a bomb weighing 3,000 pounds had been made. It was never used, however, because bomb-sights were not accurate enough for an airman to carry only one bomb on his plane, as there was a good chance that he would miss his target.

After the war bombs of various kinds were developed. For the time being their size was usually kept below 1,000 pounds, but more violent explosives were used, the most common being amatol. Special kinds were designed for piercing the armour of fortifications, sinking

Imperial War Museum
Bombs of World War I seem small beside the 12,000-pounders of World War II.

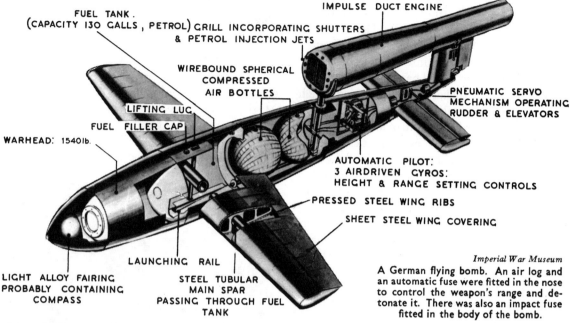

FUEL TANK.
(CAPACITY 130 GALLS, PETROL) GRILL INCORPORATING SHUTTERS
& PETROL INJECTION JETS

IMPULSE DUCT ENGINE

WIREBOUND SPHERICAL
COMPRESSED
AIR BOTTLES

LIFTING LUG

FUEL FILLER CAP

WARHEAD: 1540lb.

PNEUMATIC SERVO
MECHANISM OPERATING
RUDDER & ELEVATORS

AUTOMATIC PILOT:
3 AIRDRIVEN GYROS:
HEIGHT & RANGE SETTING CONTROLS

PRESSED STEEL WING RIBS

SHEET STEEL WING COVERING

LAUNCHING RAIL

LIGHT ALLOY FAIRING
PROBABLY CONTAINING
COMPASS

STEEL TUBULAR
MAIN SPAR
PASSING THROUGH FUEL
TANK

Imperial War Museum
A German flying bomb. An air log and
an automatic fuse were fitted in the nose
to control the weapon's range and de-
tonate it. There was also an impact fuse
fitted in the body of the bomb.

ships, killing people and so on. Bomb-sights were also made more accurate.

In World War II much larger bombs were often used, weighing 4,000, 8,000 and 12,000 pounds. To destroy factories and buildings the biggest possible blast was needed, so bombs were made with thin cases filled with as much explosive as possible. Thus the 4,000-pound bomb produced a damaging blast of air over about 5 acres, the 8,000-pound bomb over 10 acres. When the Germans protected their U-boats and other targets with heavy concrete shelters, the Allies fighting against them improved their armour-piercing bombs so that some of them, weighing as much as 22,000 pounds, would penetrate deeply into concrete before they exploded.

For some targets on the surface, however, bombs did the greatest damage when they exploded above the ground. A great deal of work went into the development of bomb-fuses that would make the bomb explode at the moment when it would do most damage. One of these fuses worked by radio, sending out a signal as the bomb was falling and receiving back an "echo" from the ground on the same wavelength. It was so arranged that the action of these two signals on each other made the bomb

explode at the desired height above the target.

Another type of bomb was the incendiary or fire-bomb. London suffered heavily in 1940 and 1941 from bombs which had not only a filling that burned very readily, but also a magnesium case which itself melted and flared fiercely. Oil and phosphorus bombs were also developed, and many of these were dropped on German cities in the later stages of the war.

V1 and V2

There were other kinds of projectile which can be classed as bombs, although they were very different from the normal type. One was the pilotless aircraft known as the V1, which had an explosive nose, and another was the giant rocket, usually called the V2. With these two "secret weapons" the Germans hoped to win the war, and it was fortunate that the Royal Air Force was able to delay their use by bombing the factories where they were made and the sites from which the Germans intended to launch them. Had this not been done, the effects might have been much more serious.

The V1, or flying bomb, was the first to come into operation. It consisted of a small aircraft with an automatic pilot (a device for steering the plane on a steady course) and a simple form of jet engine, with just enough fuel to take it as far as its target. When the fuel was used up, the V1 fell to earth and exploded. The Germans launched more than 8,000 V1s against London and nearly as many against targets on the continent of Europe in Allied hands.

The V2 was a rocket 16 feet long and weighing 12 tons. Propelled by alcohol and liquid oxygen, it reached a height of 60 miles and a speed of 3,000 miles an hour. Great efforts were made to develop missiles which could be guided all the way to the target. The simplest of such missiles was the Japanese *kamikaze*, or suicide plane, which was filled with explosives and guided towards an enemy ship by the pilot, who blew himself up with the aircraft. After the war both the United States and the U.S.S.R. began developing long-range inter-continental ballistic missiles (I.C.B.M.s), carrying explosive warheads. (See GUIDED WEAPONS.)

Nuclear Bombs

Towards the end of World War II, American, British and Canadian scientists working in great secrecy in the United States produced a weapon more terribly destructive than anything the world had known before. The first atomic bomb was exploded on July 16, 1945 at Alamogordo in New Mexico. This test was successful, and in the next month two atomic bombs were dropped on Japanese cities. The first was on Hiroshima, on August 6, when four square miles of the centre of the city were destroyed and about 75,000 people were killed. The second was on Nagasaki, on August 9, when about 39,000 people were killed. The Japanese surrendered next day.

After World War II, the United States tested more powerful atomic bombs in the South Pacific and Nevada, and by 1952 had tested the even more destructive hydrogen bomb. The article NUCLEAR ENERGY describes how an atomic bomb gets its enormous explosive force from the splitting, or *fission*, of uranium and plutonium atoms. A hydrogen bomb gets its explosive force from the joining, or *fusion*, of hydrogen atoms to form helium atoms; this is called a thermonuclear reaction.

By 1949 the U.S.S.R. had made an atomic bomb and in 1953 it exploded its first hydrogen

bomb. Britain exploded its first atomic bomb in 1952 and its first hydrogen bomb in 1957. In 1960 France exploded its first atomic weapons, followed in 1964 by China. At first bombers were used to carry nuclear weapons, but guided missiles designed to be launched from underground or from submarines replaced aircraft. Missiles were developed which could carry several hydrogen bombs in independently-targeted warheads.

The blast and heat produced by a nuclear explosion would destroy everything within a radius

Crown copyright

A mushroom cloud billowing up after the testing of a British atomic bomb. The bomb was dropped from an aircraft and exploded high above Christmas Island, in the Pacific.

of several miles while the radiation given off would destroy or damage all living things and remain in the atmosphere for a long time. Radioactive dust (see RADIOACTIVITY) would be carried on the wind and descend as "fall-out", causing sickness and death.

In 1963 the United States, the U.S.S.R. and Great Britain signed a treaty to stop the testing of nuclear bombs in the atmosphere. Other proposals have been made to stop the spread of nuclear weapons and end the expensive and dangerous "arms race". (See DISARMAMENT.)

BOMBAY is the largest city in the Republic of India and the capital of the state of Maharashtra. It is the chief seaport on the west coast. Bombay was ruled by the Hindus from the 9th century until 1348, when it became part of the sultanate of Gujarat. In 1534 the sultan handed over the city to the Portuguese, and they gave it to the British in 1661 as part of the dowry of Catherine of Braganza when she married Charles II. In 1668 the British government leased it to the East India Company and they moved their headquarters there in 1672.

Bombay Island, as the city was called for many years, used to consist of seven islands covered with coconut palms and separated from one another and the mainland by creeks which became unhealthy swamps at low tide. The city's real founder was Gerald Aungier who, in the 17th century, drained the swamps, built a hospital, set up law courts and fortified the city. Above all, he allowed the people to practise whatever religion they chose and this tolerance attracted the Armenians, Parsees and Hindu Banias, well-known trading peoples. The Parsees in particular contributed very greatly to Bombay's development. They extended the docks and built the first shipyard. In 1838 a regular steamship service between Bombay and England was begun, and in 1869 the opening of the Suez Canal shortened the journey by 15 days.

The Parsees also built the cotton mills which brought such prosperity to the city in the 19th century. Bombay became "the first city of India". Large parts of the seafront were built up and covered with shops and houses. Railways were built over causeways to the mainland and Bombay became the shipping and trading centre for most of western India. Its natural harbour covers nearly 180 square kilometres. The Gateway of India, a huge arch, was built to commemorate the visit of King George V in 1911.

The best view of this lovely island city and the bay in which it lies is from Malabar Hill. The long arc of shining lights along Marine Drive is often called the "necklace" of the city. Besides being the chief port for goods brought into India, Bombay is the centre of the cotton and textile industry. Other important industries are leather, wool, chemicals, oil and engineering. Nuclear research is carried on in the suburb of Trombay, where a large atomic reactor has been

W. Suschitzky

The Gateway of India faces the Arabian Sea.

built. The city and its suburbs cover an area of 480 square kilometres and have a population of nearly 5,000,000. The Marathi language is spoken by nearly half the people of the city, but more than 50 other languages are spoken there. Bombay (Santa Cruz) airport is one of the important international air traffic centres.

Bombay city was the capital of the Presidency of Bombay until India achieved independence in 1947. It was then the capital of Bombay State until 1960, when the states were reorganized and Bombay State became Gujarat (with Ahmedabad as its capital) and Maharashtra. The state of Maharashtra stretches far into the heart of India, beyond the city of Nagpur and the fertile plain of Berar, where excellent cotton crops are grown. It has a source of hydroelectric power in the northern section of the Western Ghats, a mountain range inland from Bombay and running from north to south. Two important cities are Poona and Sholapur.

One of the foods for which the Bombay coast is famous is the Bombay Duck. This is not a bird but a dried and salted small fish which is eaten in curried dishes.

BONE forms the framework, or skeleton, of man and of all other vertebrates (animals with

as
ody
one is
nes are
, though
to the type
rom the tiny
lephant bones
ds and the huge
ters.

BONE

white substance of
whic... s inorganic (mineral)
matter, ... e of lime, which gives
hardness. ... ining third is organic
(animal) matter ... h gives the bone toughness
and helps it not to break.

Some bones are hollow and filled with a substance called marrow. In the long bones of adults the marrow is yellow and fatty. In other bones

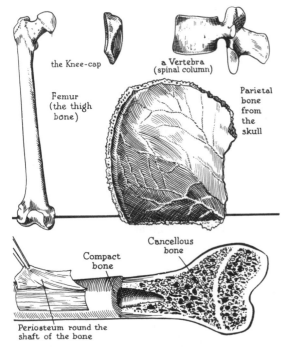

the Knee-cap

a Vertebra
(spinal column)

Femur
(the thigh
bone)

Parietal
bone
from
the
skull

Cancellous
bone

Compact
bone

Periosteum round the
shaft of the bone

the marrow is red and in it are made the red and white corpuscles of the blood. (In young children most of the bone marrow is red.) There are also some tiny passages in compact bone which carry blood, lymph (a watery fluid) and nerves through the bone.

Bones contain a small amount of water, which seems to dry out as the body grows older. This drying, with a decrease of mineral matter, makes the bones of elderly people more breakable and slower to knit, or heal, than those of young people.

Bones can be described as compact (dense and smooth) or cancellous (resembling sponge inside). There are four different shapes: long bones, which are found in the limbs and are compact; short, cancellous bones, such as those in the wrists and the ankles; flat bones, which make up the skull; and irregular bones, such as those of the spine.

All bones have names of their own. The ribs are the cage-like framework of bones which enclose the organs of the chest (the heart and the lungs). The humerus is the long bone in the upper part of the arm, and the femur, which is the strongest bone in the body, is the bone of the thigh.

Every bone is enclosed in a thin sheath known as the periosteum, which contains many blood vessels and nerves; during the growth of the bone the periosteum produces layers of new bone which increase the thickness. The periosteum helps to mend the bone after injury and also forms a base to which muscles are attached.

Fractures

A bone may be broken by a severe accident, such as a fall or a motor crash. This injury is called a fracture. Fractures can be of several kinds, the two main types being simple and compound. A compound fracture is one where the tissues of the body are torn and the bone is exposed to the open air. This is a very serious injury, as blood is lost and there is danger of infection. A simple fracture is one where the bone is broken but there is no wound.

When a fracture occurs the bone must be set; that is, the broken ends are placed together so as to get the bone into its normal position, then a sling or a splint is applied (see BANDAGE) and the bone is left to knit. During the knitting process tiny cells known as osteoblasts produce a substance that makes the bones hard and firm again. These cells also help in natural growth. Other cells called osteoclasts tear down old bone tissue. This double process of building up and tearing down is going on in the bones all the time.

some uses of bone in industry

fertilizer   gelatine   poultryfood

soap   glue

Uses for Animals' Bones

When bones are burned the animal substance is consumed and the mineral, which is extremely brittle, is left. The burned bone may remain perfect in shape and outline but if touched it will crumble into powder. On the other hand, when bones are treated with certain acids the mineral elements dissolve, leaving only the tough animal substance. In this case the bone may be left so supple, or flexible, that is can be tied in a knot. Thus by different chemical treatments bones can be prepared for the making of different products. Among these products are fertilizer (artificial manure), gelatine, glue and bone ash.

"Degreasing" is the name given to the process by which the different parts of bones are separated from each other. The ends of thigh and leg bones are sawn off and the bones are soaked in weak brine to get rid of the blood and fibre inside the marrows. They are then boiled for six hours and the marrow fat is removed. The bones themselves are then cooled, scrubbed clean, dried and sold to be made into articles such as knife-handles and buttons.

Gelatine, which is used in cooking to make jellies and creams, is made from cancellous bones. After the phosphate of lime has been removed by acid, the remainder of the bones is steamed until a fatty liquid is produced. In turn the liquid is evaporated and the remainder is left as gelatine. Glue is made in much the same way.

Bones that have been ground and treated with acids to remove the fat are valuable as artificial manure, owing to the phosphate, and bone ground to a fine powder forms part of some poultry foods. The fat obtained from bone marrow is used in soaps. The animal charcoal or bone black left after bones are burned is used in black varnishes, as a deodorizer to take away smells, and to whiten and purify sugar. Bone ash, also obtained by burning fresh bones, can be treated with acids to make it into a substitute for cream of tartar in baking powder.

BONIFACE, Saint (c. 672–754).

St. Boniface's real name was Wynfrith and he was born in Crediton, Devon. He became a monk and was a distinguished scholar and preacher. In 716, however, he followed the example of other Saxon monks and left England on a missionary journey to Frisia (now the northern part of the Netherlands).

Boniface was unsuccessful and returned to his monastery in Hampshire for about a year. He then went to Rome to obtain permission from Pope Gregory II to preach the gospel to the heathens. Gregory sent him to Germany, where he converted and baptized many of the heathen people. After being made a bishop at Rome in 722 he returned to Germany. Charles Martel, King of the Franks, a warlike people who lived in western Europe, protected Boniface, who went far into Germany, founding churches and monasteries, overturning idols and even cutting down with his own hands the oak of Geismar which was sacred to the pagan god Thor.

In 732 Boniface was made an archbishop. He organized the Bavarian and Frankish churches under the direct control of Rome and sent for monks from England to be bishops. At the same time he founded the abbey of Fulda which afterwards became the great centre for religious learning in Germany.

When in 754 he felt that he had finished his work in Germany, Boniface resigned as archbishop and again took up his earlier plan of converting the heathens of Frisia. However, later that year, on June 5, which is now celebrated as his festival, he and his companions were slain by the heathens near Dokkum in Frisia. His remains were afterwards taken to the abbey at Fulda.

Courtesy, German Embassy, London
This modern building in Bonn is the meeting place of the *Bundestag*, or West German Federal Parliament. The other side of the building looks out over the wide Rhine River.

BONN, the capital of western Germany, or the German Federal Republic as it is called officially, stands on the Rhine River about 15 miles south of Cologne. It was chosen as the capital in 1949 in preference to one of the larger German cities because, although it had been damaged by bombing in World War II, it was easy to reach from either the north or south. The Federal Parliament, now called the *Bundestag*, meets in a modern building where teachers used to be trained. The President and the Chancellor of the Federal Republic have their residences near the *Bundeshaus* (the building where the *Bundestag* meets). About 145,000 people live in Bonn.

Before the war Bonn was just a pleasant university town. It had never played much part in the history of Germany, although the electors, or rulers, of Cologne, had lived there from the 13th to the 18th century. The great composer Ludwig van Beethoven was born in Bonn. Its most beautiful building is the university which was originally the palace of the electors of Cologne. The university was founded in 1786 by the archbishops of Cologne. A botanic garden, an observatory and a zoological museum are connected with it.

Bonn originally began, not long after the death of Christ, as a settlement for Roman soldiers. So its history goes back much further than Berlin, which was the old capital of the German Empire up to the end of World War II.

BONNIE PRINCE CHARLIE (CHARLES EDWARD STUART, "THE YOUNG PRETENDER"; 1720–1788). The best known part of the story of Bonnie Prince Charlie begins with his coming to Scotland to proclaim his father, James Stuart, King of England and Scotland; it ends with his wanderings in the Highlands, a hunted man in danger of his life, helped by only a few loyal friends. The tale of his journey from the island of Benbecula to the Isle of Skye disguised as the maidservant of Flora Macdonald is famous.

The Prince was brought up abroad, where his father was in exile waiting for a chance to seize the crown of England again for the royal family of Stuarts. (See the article JACOBITES.) Charles and his father decided that the time had come in 1745, and Charles set sail for Scotland, even though his friends there thought there was no chance of success. He gathered an army of about 2,000 men and began his march southwards. He took Edinburgh without a battle and on September 18 proclaimed his father King James VIII of Scotland. At the battle of Prestonpans his army defeated a force loyal to King George II.

At the beginning of November Charles left Edinburgh to invade England, hoping that the

Scottish National Portrait Gallery
Prince Charles Edward Stuart, by an unknown artist.

French would send an army to help as they had secretly promised him. Five thousand men marched south behind him, but as they went many of the Highlanders deserted to go back to their homes. In spite of this Charles continued victoriously as far as Derby. By now, however, two English armies were marching against him and his friends advised him to turn back. He did so with a heavy heart, for the end of the years of exile had begun to seem near. Several times Charles's men managed to win small victories in Scotland, but the end came at Culloden in the spring of 1746. There Charles's little army, starving and worn out by long marches, was completely beaten by the English, and the rebellion was over.

For five months Charles was hunted by English troops and spies of the government, but at last, after being helped by Flora Macdonald, he escaped in a French ship. For the rest of his life he lived abroad, making plots to return to England which could never succeed. The gallant young hero of the 1745 rebellion died a bitter, disappointed and drunken old man.

BOOKBINDING. A good way to start learning how to bind books by hand is to make and bind a notebook. You will need a very large sheet of drawing paper which measures about 30 inches by 22 inches, but if you cannot get the exact size any really large sheet will do.

Fold the sheet of paper across and carefully tear it or cut it at the fold. Fold each of these pieces in the same way and tear them. Do the same to the four pieces, making eight in all. Now fold each of the eight pieces as before, but do not cut them. Place them one inside the other so as to form what is called a "section". This section is the inside of the notebook.

Take some coloured paper or card (manilla card is the best) and cut out a piece to the same size as one of your paper sheets; fold it in the same way. Put the section inside this folded card, so that the card makes a cover, and then open the "book" at the middle. Make a hole in the centre of the fold and one on either side two inches from the centre. Then sew the pages to the cover with strong thread as in diagram 1.

This of course is only a beginner's job. Next

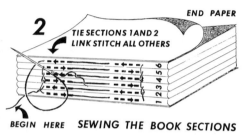

1 START HERE — END HERE — TIE ENDS OVER HERE

SINGLE SECTION NOTEBOOK

2 TIE SECTIONS 1 AND 2 LINK STITCH ALL OTHERS — END PAPER — BEGIN HERE — 1 2 3 4 5 6

SEWING THE BOOK SECTIONS

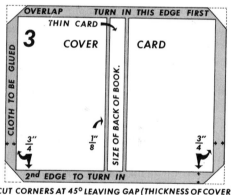

3 OVERLAP — TURN IN THIS EDGE FIRST — THIN CARD — COVER — CARD — CLOTH TO BE GLUED — SIZE OF BACK OF BOOK. — 3/4" — 1/8" — 3/4" — 2nd EDGE TO TURN IN

CUT CORNERS AT 45° LEAVING GAP (THICKNESS OF COVER)

SETTING OUT COVER

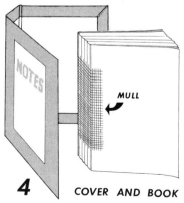

NOTES — MULL

4 COVER AND BOOK

try making up a thicker notebook and binding it properly. If you look at any well-bound book you will see that it is made up in sections and that the "end" papers, those next to the covers, are of a different kind of paper from the pages.

Prepare as many sections as you wish, and also cut and fold some tinted or patterned paper to make end papers. These should be pasted on, one at the beginning and one at the end of the book. Bore four holes in each section, then sew all the sections together as shown in diagram 2.

The cover is made from two pieces of stout card (or strawboard), each cut to the same width as the pages of the book, but a quarter of an inch more in length. A strip of stiff paper or thin card, exactly the same size as the back, is also needed. The covering material (leather-cloth, plastic or linen) is set out as shown in diagram 3. Mark out on the back of the cloth the positions of the pieces of card, paste or glue the cloth all over, and having pressed the cards into place turn in the overlap. Use a clean rag to rub down the folds.

To make the book hold together more firmly, cut a piece of stiff muslin, or mull, about one inch shorter than the length of the back and two inches wider than its width. Glue this to the back of the book so that the two sides overlap on to the end papers by one inch.

Lay the book on the table and fit it exactly into the cover. Raise the cover carefully so as not to disturb anything and paste the back of the end paper. (A piece of scrap paper under it will protect the rest of the book.) Turn the book over, paste down the other end paper and put it to dry under a pile of books or some other weight.

This is one of many methods of making a book and is known as Case Binding.

BOOK-LOUSE. This tiny insect, which is not really a louse, is sometimes to be found running about quickly among old books and papers and in collections of all kinds of objects, such as boxes of dried insect specimens, especially if these are a little damp. It seems to like nothing better as a food than the very minute moulds or fungous growths that grow in such places, and it also eats the paste of book bindings.

More than 200 years ago an English clergyman kept some book-lice which, he said, made a ticking noise. They seemed to do this by tapping on a piece of paper with their heads. It is curious that since then no one has been able to repeat this experiment.

Besides these wingless species there are also many relatives of the book-louse which live out of doors under the bark of trees and in similar places. They feed on the lichens and fungi that grow on trees and may also be found among straw and chaff. They have wings, but as a rule they are very slow to use them. They are found all over the world, but even the biggest, which live in South America, measure barely an inch from wing-tip to wing-tip.

BOOK OF THE DEAD. This was a book written and used by the priests of ancient Egypt. In it were prayers for the soul of a person after it had left the body, and magic spells to help the soul in its life after death. In some of the writings the dead person was made to proclaim his innocence by statements such as "I have not caused any to hunger" and "I have not taken milk from the mouths of babes." (You can find more about the ancient Egyptian ideas on the life of the soul in the articles EGYPT: ANCIENT and FUNERAL RITES.)

The Book was written on papyrus, a kind of paper made from reeds, with the sheets pasted together in a strip which was rolled up to form a scroll. (See PAPYRUS.) The scribes who wrote it used reed pens and inks of various colours, in the kind of writing called hieroglyphics. (See HIEROGLYPHIC.) Many copies were illustrated, some with beautiful water-colour pictures, often recording happenings at the temple.

BOOKS are the greatest of all the discoveries and inventions made by man. Everything we know, and all the ideas and thoughts that have come to mankind through the ages, may be found in books. The teaching of the religious leaders from earliest days, the wisdom of great thinkers, the stories and poetry and plays of the great writers are all alive and as fresh for us in books today as when they were written.

Books are important not only because of all the pleasure and satisfaction that reading them gives, but also because they teach the things that people need to know. In schools there are books about most of the subjects that are studied; young men and women who are training to be scientists or lawyers or doctors must all read books; and if there is no one to tell you how to mend a bicycle, or build a model aeroplane, or make a dress, you can find out how to do any of these things by reading a book about it.

More and more is found out every year about different subjects, and most of this new knowledge is written down and printed in books. For instance, the scientists who discover new medicines, or new machines, or new ways to use the power of the atom to make steam and electricity without coal, explain in books how they have done these things, and through books like these people all over the world can then learn how to use the scientists' discoveries: how to cure diseases which could not be cured before, how to make new sorts of engines, or how to make plants grow for food where they would not grow before. When the men and women who have new ideas die, most of their thoughts and inventions would die and be forgotten too if there were no books; but books never die for they can be printed again time after time, and so can keep alive all the knowledge and wisdom in the world.

The earliest books we know were made by the Egyptians about 2500 B.C. They were written on a sort of paper made from a reed called papyrus, and were in long strips which were rolled up round a stick when not being read. The Romans were the first to make books which look like those we know today, but all their books were written by hand on parchment, which is a kind of paper made from the skin of animals. For hundreds of years every book had to be hand-written, and it was not until printing was invented in the middle of the 15th century that more than one copy of a book could be made at a time.

How a Book Begins its Life

When a man writes a book, whether it is a novel or a book of poems or a history or any other sort of book, he sends it to a publisher. You will see the name of the publisher at the bottom of the back of a book when it is in the

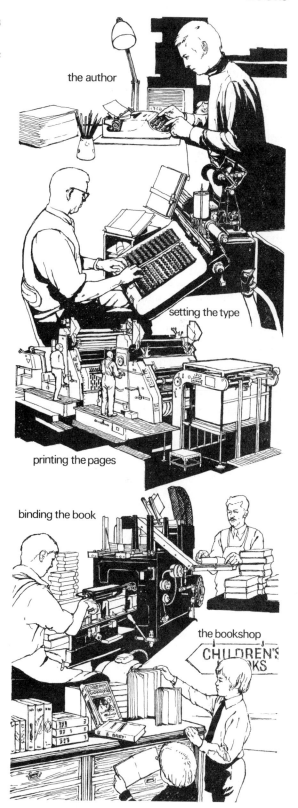

the author

setting the type

printing the pages

binding the book

the bookshop

CHILDREN'S
BOOKS

bookshelf. The publisher's name is also printed on the title-page, usually the third page of a book, beneath the title of the book and the name of the author.

The publisher is the man who decides whether a book shall be printed and sold in the bookshops. If he thinks it is not good enough, or that not many people will buy it, he sends it back to the author. Then the author sends it to another publisher, perhaps to several more before one of them decides to have it printed. Very often no publisher will accept it, or the author gets tired of trying, and then the book he has written is never read by anyone else. Almost all stories and novels, poems and plays are written without the author's being sure that they will ever be published, unless he is already famous or very well known. But a great many of the other books—those which are used in school, or which describe some country or subject or a man's life, or explain how to make or do something—most of these are not written until their authors have talked about them to a publisher and are sure that he will publish them. A book is often written because the publisher believes that it is wanted, and he finds an author who knows about the subject and asks him to write a book.

When the publisher has a typewritten copy, or typescript, of a book he is going to publish, he first of all reads it very carefully, or asks someone else in his office to read it, to make sure that the author has made no mistakes, and to see whether there are any ways in which it can be made better. Then he sends it to a printer, telling him what size and shape he wants the book to be, what size of type it is to be printed in, and how many copies are to be printed. (The little blocks with letters on which are used in printing are known as type, and the printed letters themselves are also often called type.) The printer works out the number of pages the book will make, and how much it will cost the publisher to have it printed.

While the book is being set up in type ready for printing (the article PRINTING explains more about this) the publisher buys from a papermaker enough paper, of the right size and thickness, for the number of copies he has decided to have printed. After it is made the paper goes to the printer, who has meanwhile been busy printing roughly a very few first copies of the book, which are called "proofs". The proofs go to the publisher, who sends two or three of them to the author with his typescript, so that the author can read the proofs carefully and correct any mistakes which the printer has made. Sometimes, when the author sees these first printed proofs of his book, he makes a large number of alterations and improvements in what he first wrote. When this happens, the publisher sends the corrected proofs back to the printer, who has to print a few more copies of the altered proofs to show that he has made all the author's changes properly. When at last the author and the publisher are both satisfied that the book is as good as they can make it, and that there are no mistakes in it, the printer is told to print the whole number of copies which the publisher believes the booksellers can sell.

The large flat sheets of printed paper, on each of which are usually 32 pages of the book, are sent by the printer to a bookbinder. The binder folds the sheets to the size of the book, sews them together and glues them into cloth covers the colour the publisher has chosen. On most books except school textbooks the binder then puts the coloured wrappers or jackets which protect them from dust and dirt and make them look attractive in the shops.

Now the books are ready to be sold. They go from the binder to the publisher's warehouse, and then they are sent out to all the bookshops that have ordered them from the publisher's salesmen, whose job is to travel all over the country telling booksellers about new books that are being published. The bookseller buys as many copies of a book as he thinks he can sell, and he shows as many sorts of book as he can in his shop, to interest all the different people who come in to look at them. A good bookseller will always be glad to see boys and girls in his shop and to let them look at as many of his books as they like, even if they are going to buy only one.

BOOKS FOR CHILDREN. A boy or girl who goes into a good bookshop today can find plenty of books of all kinds to choose from. Picture books, adventure stories, fairy tales and legends, myths and fables, tales of history, stories of famous people, nature books, books of poems, books of information about almost anything under the sun—there are dozens of them crowding the shelves. In fact there are so many that it is sometimes hard for a person to decide what he wants from among them all.

More children read books now and enjoy reading than ever before. Even anyone who has not much money can still get plenty to read. In towns the public libraries have children's departments or children's corners where books can be borrowed and taken home free of charge and country children in some places can borrow books from mobile libraries, where the books are taken round the countryside in vans. More and more schools have their own libraries, run either by the local public library or by the school itself. (See LIBRARIES.)

It has not always been easy to find books to read. If you started talking about books to a child who lived only a little more than 100 years ago, you would find that though you could talk about authors and books for a long time, he would have very few to tell you about; and a child who lived still earlier would probably know hardly any books and not want to talk about them at all. He would think of them as lesson books full of instructions about good behaviour. It is only quite recently that authors have written books to be interesting and exciting and amusing for children, instead of to teach them something.

The rest of this article describes some of the books children read in the past, the way children's books have changed since the first ones were written and some of the kinds of books that are favourites today. At the end of the article is a list of children's books of all kinds, with their authors; there may be many that you know and like already, but there are probably some new ones too. Magazines are described in a separate article, MAGAZINES FOR CHILDREN.

Early Literature

At first there were no story books for anyone, adults or children. Instead of reading, people listened to stories told by minstrels, stories of the deeds of heroes and the glory of great battles, of kings and queens, giants and fairies and strange talking beasts. These tales of wonder and enchantment were told over and over before they were ever printed, or even written down.

There were a few story books for grown-ups later, in the middle ages. The most popular was *Gesta Romanorum*, a collection of tales in Latin. As adventure stories people also read Marco Polo's account of his journeys in Eastern countries, and the fantastic travel tales, full of strange adventures, that Sir John Mandeville wrote in the 14th century.

All these were later used by William Caxton, the first man to print books in England, when he started looking round for manuscripts to translate and publish. He never thought of printing story books especially for children, though many of the ones he published contained stories that the younger members of the family would enjoy as much as their elders. Probably parents (the ones who could read, that is, for not everyone in those days was able to) read them aloud or told them to their children. Caxton published many romances, including Sir Thomas Malory's *Noble History of King Arthur* and his own *History of Troy*; he also translated *Aesop's Fables* and the *History of Reynard the Fox*.

All this time, however, in the early days of printing and before, there were some books that were specially meant for children. The first ones were lesson books, written about 800 years ago by the monks. They were written out by hand on sheets of vellum (fine parchment) and were far too precious for the pupils to handle themselves. They were usually written in the form of imaginary conversations in Latin to help the children learn this language, but the monks did sometimes put in stories of fabulous beasts and miraculous descriptions of heaven and earth to make them more interesting.

Then came the printed books. They were not exciting adventures or fairy tales, but were supposed to improve the boys and girls who read them—either lesson books or books telling the reader how to behave. For instance, there was the *Babee Book*, written about 1475, which gives advice of this sort :

"If any speak to you, look straight at them and listen well until they have finished; do not chatter or let your eyes wander about the house."

Another one, *The Lytlle Childrenes Lytil Boke*, written about 1480, tells them to see that their hands and nails are clean, not to eat until grace is said, and not to sit down until they are told to do so. All these books show that the birch rod was used to teach good manners if the advice given in books had failed to do so, for parents did not hesitate to beat their naughty children then.

For many years after this children's books became more and more improving and serious. They were full of the dreadful punishments that would come upon bad and disobedient children, and warnings of hell fire and everlasting damnation. A boy or girl reading one of them today would find it deadly dull and hard to understand, and probably the children living in those times cannot really have liked them either. They must have been read, however, because very many copies of some of them were sold, and they were often reprinted.

Here is a quotation to show what they were like. It comes from a book written by Abraham Chear in the 17th century, which had a great success. It was called *A Looking glass for Children: being a narrative of God's gracious dealings with some little Children: together with sundry seasonable lessons and instructions to youth, calling them early to remember their creator.* Girls often had to recite these lines to keep them from being vain.

> "When by Spectators I am told
> What Beauty doth adorn me :
> Or in a Glass, when I behold
> How sweetly God did form me;
> Hath God such comliness displayed
> And on me made to dwell?
> 'Tis pitty such a pretty maid
> As I, should go to Hell."

The children who read these books probably did not think them quite as terrible as children would today. They were living at a time when life in England was disturbed by civil wars and bitter quarrels about religion, and they would often hear their parents talk about a terrifying God and about the nearness of death and punishment. These children had never known stories like *Treasure Island* or *Alice in Wonderland* or *The Wind in the Willows* and they probably never thought of books as things to enjoy.

Adventure and Fairy Stories

One of the earliest children's favourites to survive to our own day is *The Pilgrim's Progress*, a great religious book, but also a tale of exciting adventure told in such an easy simple way that it has been loved and enjoyed by people of all kinds ever since. John Bunyan who wrote it was a simple man who was imprisoned for his faith, and his book was inspired in its style by the chap books which were the popular reading of his time. (These were small penny books of adventure tales, carried round by the pedlars who roamed the countryside with their wares.) A little later came two other great story books, Daniel Defoe's *Robinson Crusoe* in 1719, and Jonathan Swift's *Gulliver's Travels* in 1728. These were the first two of a long line of adventure stories and they are still readable because they are both exciting and original. None of these books was written specially for children and *Gulliver* was intended to show up the foolish customs and opinions of the day, but they are now enjoyed for the story alone, and as much by children as by grown-ups.

About this time, though, a new kind of story intended for children did appear—the fairy story. Fairy stories first came from France, where a man named Charles Perrault published a book of them in 1698. The French titles have long since been forgotten in England : to us they are *Cinderella, Little Red Riding Hood, The Sleeping Beauty, Hop o' my Thumb* and *Puss in Boots*, and there are many others. Soon *The Arabian Nights* was translated into English too.

One man during the 18th century did realize that books should be things children could enjoy and love to keep. His name was John Newbery and the fairy stories he published, though they were still full of morals and good advice, were attractively printed and had pictures. They were meant to amuse children as well as to improve their minds.

Tales for 19th-Century Children

The children of about 150 years ago did at last have stories written specially for them. More fairy stories were published (though even some of these were not written for children in the first place): Grimm's fairy tales were translated into English in 1823 and later Hans Andersen's stories were put into English too. Even in the 19th century, however, authors still could not get away from the idea that when children read a book they must learn something from it. The stories these authors wrote were often good, but

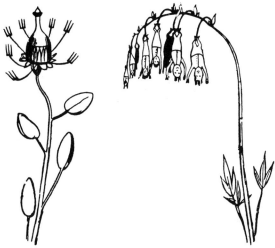

"*Bottlephorkia spoonifolia* and *Manypeeplia upsidownia*," from Edward Lear's *Nonsense Botany*. Like the others on the next five pages, this is the author's own illustration.

there was always a moral behind them. Wonderful things happened to a good child and terrible things happened to a bad one.

The best writer of this type of story was Maria Edgeworth. Her stories of what happened to Lazy Lawrence and Simple Susan were still rather pious and she gave her book the depressing title of *The Parent's Assistant*: but the stories were much more interesting than anything that had been written before for children, and they can still be read with enjoyment today.

Other children's authors of the time were Thomas Day, who wrote *Sandford and Merton*, the first novel for children, and Mrs. M. M. Sherwood, who wrote *The History of the Fairchild Family*. This book was popular for many years. In time Maria Edgeworth's example led to some lively stories by such authors as Mrs. J. H. Ewing and Mrs. M. L. Molesworth. Many children today read and like Mrs. Ewing's *Jan of the Windmill* and Mrs. Molesworth's *The Cuckoo Clock*. *The Water-Babies*, Charles Kingsley's story of Tom, who was first a badly

treated chimney-sweep and later lived under the sea, is still a favourite.

One writer who did not believe in giving his stories a moral was Lewis Carroll, who in 1866 wrote what is still the most famous of all children's books, *Alice's Adventures in Wonderland*. No other book like *Alice* had ever appeared before and there has been nothing like it since, though many have tried to imitate it. The world that Alice enters down the rabbit-hole is a strange dream world, but soon the reader stops being surprised at even the craziest things that happen. The people and animals in it have become so well-known that they are a part of everyday speech.

Alice in Wonderland and *Through the Looking-Glass* were almost the first books for young people written just to entertain, not to improve, and from that time better books for children began to be written. Authors no longer tried always to show a moral; instead they wrote stories about ordinary children, not too good and not too wicked, tales of adventure, school stories, stories about animals, books of make-believe— in fact, all the kinds of books there are in libraries and bookshops today. Some of these old books are so good that children still read them, and probably always will; for instance, *Black Beauty* by Anna Sewell is one of the best animal stories that has ever been written. This book was first published in 1877 but children today know it as well as their parents and grandparents did.

Adventures of Ordinary Families

One of the first of the new kind of books that described things that happened to ordinary children—real, natural children who might live next door—was *Holiday House* by Catherine Sinclair. Later, E. Nesbit wrote sometimes about adventures that could really happen, sometimes about imaginary ones. The best known of her realistic books are the ones about the Bastable family: *The Story of the Treasure-Seekers*, *The Would-be-Goods* and *The New Treasure-Seekers*. They have fun and excitement, mystery and adventure and the children are real children like yourselves.

Just before World War I broke out, Frances Hodgson Burnett wrote the loveliest and most lasting of her books, *The Secret Garden*. In it Mary and Colin, two spoilt and bad-tempered children, become friends and in the secret garden they grow into happy and healthy human beings. The garden is very real, but in some ways it is an enchanted one too.

Among the good writers of books about real children today are Noel Streatfeild, who writes about children in pantomime, ballet and circus; Kitty Barne, whose family stories are sincere and full of kindly humour; Eve Garnett, whose *The Family From One End Street* is a series of delightful and sympathetic stories about a dustman's poor but contented family; and Honoré Morrow, whose book *The Splendid Journey* is a true story about a family of children who travelled along the Oregon Trail in America in the pioneering days of the 19th century. In the terrible hardships of the journey they lost both their parents but 13-year-old John, facing starvation, illness and every kind of peril, struggled bravely on with his young brothers and sisters to the end of the long trail.

Perhaps the best families of all, however, are the Walkers and the Blacketts of Arthur Ransome's books. There is something special about his stories, as everyone who has read them knows, and they are quite different from anyone else's. From the first page of the first book, *Swallows and Amazons*, on which Roger runs across the field with a message, in long tacks (he is pretending to be a sailing boat) because the wind is against him, the reader knows he is in wonderful company. There are 12 books in the series and the children grow older from book to book. They are so real that hundreds of British children have written to the Blacketts and Walkers for advice about their own problems—usually to do with sailing, for nearly all the books are about boats and sailing. Arthur Ransome was an expert, and had a great gift for explaining about boats and exactly how things are done in them. His books are full of exciting adventures, yet one feels they could all really happen, even when the Swallows and Amazons are sailing far away in the China Seas. There is no doubt that Arthur Ransome was one of the greatest modern writers of books for children.

Other good writers about ordinary children and their families are William Mayne, whose stories of fantastic treasure-hunts, such as *The Thumbstick*, have a firm background of family life; Elizabeth Stucley, whose *Magnolia Buildings* is a lively picture of a working-class family; and John Rowe Townsend, who in *Gumble's Yard* and *Widdershin's Crescent* has realistically portrayed life in tough, slum areas.

One characteristic of recent books of this type is that they are no longer about children who go to boarding schools and whose families take long holidays by the sea. They are about ordinary children going to grammar schools or secondary modern schools, and living in semi-detached houses in large cities.

Another new kind of book is the "career" story, which tells in story form the adventures of someone beginning adult life. Examples are Monica Edwards' *Joan Goes Farming* and Bernard Farmer's *Tom Ward, Policeman*.

Adventures Far Away and Long Ago

Perhaps the largest number of books for children are tales of the kind of adventures—full of dangers, excitements and hardships—that do not usually happen in ordinary life and to ordinary people at all. Sometimes they take place in far-off countries, or in other times when daily life was more dangerous than it is now; sometimes they are strange and perilous adventures set in the world of today.

The first modern writer to understand that boys wanted a downright tale of adventure and not just a story book was R. M. Ballantyne. His first attempt at this kind of book was *The Young Fur Traders*, published in 1855; his most famous were *The Coral Island* and perhaps *The Dog Crusoe* and *Martin Rattler*.

Then came W. H. G. Kingston with his realistic sea-adventure stories, and G. A. Henty and others. The adventures in these books were thrilling ones in romantic places, sometimes on the Spanish Main, sometimes in the jungles and mountains of some long lost land. The dangers were real and frightful, the heroes brave and upright young men ready to die for their country. Some of the best of these books are the ones written by Robert Louis Stevenson, including *Treasure Island*, and Rider Haggard's novels

Courtesy, Jonathan Cape Ltd.
"Tom came sailing home." An illustration from *Coot Club*, Arthur Ransome's story about sailing, bird-watching and other out-of-door adventures on the Norfolk Broads.

King Solomon's Mines and *Allan Quatermain*.

An author whose books were mostly for grown-ups but who wrote fine books for children too was Rudyard Kipling. *The Jungle Book* describes the life of the boy Mowgli among the wild beasts of the jungle, and *Kim*, which gives a wonderful picture of India, tells how an orphan boy travels with a lama carrying secret messages.

Arthur Conan Doyle wrote chiefly for grown-ups too, but his books are very popular with boys. His hero Sherlock Holmes is perhaps the best known of all characters in fiction; in fact it is difficult to realize that this great detective never really existed. Conan Doyle had just the right sort of clear, careful mind for writing detective stories and could produce stories which are accurate and interesting down to the smallest detail. He also wrote *The Lost World,* which tells how Professor Challenger and three companions discover a lost plateau in South America. They have some frightening experiences with weird prehistoric animals, one of which they manage to bring home with them. Another fine adventure story writer for older children is John Buchan. *Prester John* tells of a young Scotsman's adventures in Africa with

diamond smugglers, while *The Thirty-Nine Steps* and its sequels *Mr. Standfast* and *Greenmantle* are exciting stories of the British Intelligence Service.

Among the best of adventure stories are historical novels, and again Conan Doyle wrote some of the finest of these with books such as *The White Company* and *The Adventures of Brigadier Gerard.* Two good modern authors are Rosemary Sutcliff, who wrote *The Shield Ring,* about the Vikings, and Ronald Welch, who wrote a fine book about the Crusades, *Knight Crusader.* Geoffrey Trease has also written many historical novels full of action with real characters.

The thrilling Biggles books of W. E. Johns are popular modern adventure stories describing hair-raising events in the career of a daring British pilot. Some space stories have too many scientific details, but Paul Berna's *Threshold of the Stars* and *Continent in the Sky* have interesting characters and a feeling of the poetic excitement of space. Other writers of science fiction are Angus McVicar, Arthur C. Clarke and Isaac Asimov. (See SCIENCE FICTION.)

School Stories

The first school stories were about real schools and often about things that had actually happened, perhaps to the author himself while he was a pupil. This gave them a vivid and realistic atmosphere quite different from some of those written today, when the school is often an impossible place full of sliding panels and secret passages and midnight feasts in the dormitories.

One of the most famous of the old stories was *Tom Brown's Schooldays,* written by Thomas Hughes about Rugby; another, which is still very readable, was *The Fifth Form at St. Dominic's* by Talbot Baines Reed. Rudyard Kipling's *Stalky and Co.,* published in 1899, was read and enjoyed not only by boys but by their fathers too, and so was *The Hill,* a story about Harrow by H. A. Vachell. Not quite so well-known are E. F. Benson's two stories *David Blaize* and *David of King's,* the latter telling of early days at University.

There are not very many school stories being published today, since family and adventure stories seem more popular, but Antony Buckeridge's Jennings and his friend Darbishire talk lively slang, and William Mayne's three books about life in a cathedral choir-school are exciting school stories with a difference. Antonia Forest has brought new life to the girls' boarding-school story, while E. W. Hildick sends his hero, Jim Starling, to Cement Street Secondary Modern.

Make-Believe and Magic

Many books of make-believe are for young children but even grown-ups can go on enjoying the best ones and remembering characters like Peter Rabbit and Winnie-the-Pooh all their lives.

One book like this that is often well-remembered is Kipling's *Just So Stories*: "How the Whale Got his Throat", "How the Leopard Got his Spots", "The Elephant's Child" and so on. They were written for "best beloved", Kipling's four-year-old daughter.

The Tale of Peter Rabbit was first written to amuse a little lame boy. Beatrix Potter wrote it in the form of letters in her own handwriting, with funny drawings to illustrate it. Later she made a book of the story which was so successful that others soon followed. Before long Squirrel Nutkin, Mrs. Tittlemouse, Jemima Puddleduck and other famous characters were born.

Kenneth Grahame did not write many books —he was a banker for most of his life—but throughout the whole realm of children's books there are few as good or as famous as *The Wind in the Willows*. It has romance, adventure, fun and a touch of poetry too. The little world of the river bank is a delightful land, and no one who reads about them can ever forget the humble Mole, the practical Water Rat or the boastful, irresponsible but lovable Toad who gets them all into such difficulties and adventures.

Another favourite character of make-believe is Peter Pan. James Barrie's play *Peter Pan* was first acted in 1904 and, except during wartime, it has been put on in London during the Christmas holidays ever since. It has appeared in story form, too. Children for over 50 years have not tired of reading of the flight of Wendy, John and Michael in the company of Peter Pan to the Never-Never-Land, of their adventures with the Indians and their fights with Captain Hook and the pirates.

Magic comes into some of the books of E. Nesbit too; some of the children in her stories experiment with magic and find that it works. One of the best is *The Phoenix and the Carpet*, in which the children buy a magic carpet to go travelling on and make friends with a conceited phoenix (a legendary bird).

There are delightful modern fairy tales in the four *Mary Poppins* books of P. L. Travers.

Courtesy, William Heinemann Ltd.
One of the delightful illustrations by Helen Oxenbury for *The Hunting of the Snark*, the poem by Lewis Carroll.

Mary Poppins blew in with the east wind to be nurse to a family of children and blew out again a year later when the wind changed. She had some unusual accomplishments, one of which was sliding *up* banisters. Patricia Lynch, the Irish writer, also succeeds in mixing magic with ordinary everyday happenings so cleverly that one hardly notices which is reality and which is not. *The Turf-Cutter's Donkey* is an enchanting tale of the Irish countryside, with fairs and tinkers and leprechauns.

Another wonderful character is Dr. Dolittle. The author of the Dr. Dolittle books, Hugh Lofting, imagined the life of a country doctor who was so fond of pets that he gave up his own

Courtesy, Oxford University Press

"Pat-a-cake, pat-a-cake baker's man", an original drawing by Brian Wildsmith from *Mother Goose*, a book for younger children.

practice to look after animals and took them on his travels. They included Dab-Dab the duck, Polynesia the parrot and the never-to-be-forgotten Pushmipullyu, who had a head at each end and could therefore talk while he was eating without being rude. These animals are almost as well known as Toad and Mole and Peter Rabbit.

The famous Christopher Robin books were written for Christopher Robin by his father, A. A. Milne. Nearly everybody has heard of Winnie-the-Pooh, the Bear of Little Brain who was enormously fond of honey, and Eeyore, Kanga, Tigger and Piglet are just as familiar. When Christopher Robin grew older A. A. Milne gave up writing for children.

C. S. Lewis has written a magical series of adventure stories about the kingdom of Narnia. They are fairy tales full of excitement and suspense with a great and moving climax. A most original book, *The Borrowers*, by Mary Norton, explains where all the lost hairpins, and similar things that aren't there when they should be, go to. For younger children, Alison Uttley's books about Sam Pig and Little Grey Rabbit follow the example of the Beatrix Potter books.

Some of the most exciting and original fantasies for older children are those by Alan Garner. His stories such as *The Weirdstone of Brisinga-*

men bubble over with strange and wonderful happenings, touching everyday life with supernatural magic.

Poems

There are several good books of poems for children, some serious and some not so serious. Among the not-so-serious ones are the verses and limericks of Edward Lear in his *Book of Nonsense*; in the limericks all sorts of people find themselves in peculiar and uncomfortable situations, and Lear's pages are full of the adventures of strange and wonderful creatures. There are also Lewis Carroll's *The Hunting of the Snark* and Hilaire Belloc's *Cautionary Tales for Children*. A. A. Milne wrote poems for young children as well as his collections of stories, and many children have enjoyed and laughed at *When We Were Very Young* and *Now We Are Six*. Eleanor Farjeon has written some gay rhymes too, some of which are based on counting-songs and singing-games, and they are fresh and musical. There are also witty and interesting stories in verse by Ian Serraillier, based on old tales.

By far the finest poet for children in modern times—perhaps the greatest children's poet who has ever lived—was Walter de la Mare, whose *Peacock Pie, Songs of Childhood* and other books are full of poems of delight and magic, and fun and laughter too.

Real People and Real Things

Books that tell children about the lives of real people, or about real things in the world, are nowadays not at all dull and not at all like lesson books. One of the best of the life stories of famous people is *Radium Woman*, by Eleanor Doorly, the story of Madame Curie. Other similar books are James Kendall's *Humphry Davy*, John Rowland's *The Penicillin Man* and Nora Langley's *Dr. Schweitzer*.

Things to know about and things to be enjoyed are described in the "Young Traveller" books, which help British children to find out about life in other countries, and in the "Excursions" series, which shows how to enjoy all sorts of things that children may come across when they are taken out, such as concerts or paintings.

The "Land and the People" books are another similar series, with many titles.

There are few subjects which do not have at least one book on them which is full of information and readable as well. On history H. W. Van Loon's book *The Story of Mankind* with its many pictures makes history really exciting, and *The Home of Mankind* does the same for geography. A Russian book on the story of printing called *Black on White*, by M. Ilin, has become well known. Agnes Allen's *The Story of Painting* and *The Story of Your Home* make difficult subjects clear and interesting with diagrams and drawings.

There are also books to help in doing things better, whether games and sports or handicrafts and arts. There is a whole series on improving your games, sponsored by the M.C.C., the Football Association and other sporting associations. There are the "How to Draw" series and

Courtesy, Macmillan and Co., Ltd.

"This is the picture of the Cat that Walked by Himself, walking by his wild lone through the Wet Wild Woods and waving his wild tail." From Kipling's *Just So Stories*.

the "Instruction" series, of which one is Elizabeth Craig's *Instructions to Young Cooks*. All these books are by experts who not only know the subject but also know how to explain it.

Pictures in Children's Books

The earliest books for children had simple woodcut illustrations (see WOODCUTS), often crude and badly drawn. Thomas Bewick's wood-engravings of the late 18th century (see ENGRAVING) showed that children's books could be beautiful as well as entertaining, and soon other artists followed. George Cruikshank drew the pictures for the first English edition of Grimms' fairy tales and Sir John Tenniel, the *Punch* cartoonist, made the drawings that now seem so much a part of the "Alice" books.

When in the late 19th century printing in colours became common, the books illustrated by Walter Crane, Randolph Caldecott and Kate Greenaway were full of life, humour and charm. By the 20th century pictures were an important part of children's books. The work of artists such as Beatrix Potter (see POTTER, BEATRIX), Arthur Rackham, C. E. Brock and H. R. Millar became known and loved. Rudyard Kipling drew the pictures for his *Just-So Stories* and Hugh Lofting illustrated his "Dr. Dolittle" books with funny and friendly drawings.

Artists today have a wide choice of styles and methods. Lithography has made it possible to produce brilliantly coloured and lavishly illustrated picture books. An important prize, the Kate Greenaway Medal, is awarded yearly to an outstanding British illustrator. It has been won by Antony Maitland, Brian Wildsmith, Victor Ambrus, C. Walter Hodges and Charles Keeping. Other fine illustrators include E. H. Shepard, Helen Bannerman, Edward Ardizzone, Clarke Hutton, Joan Hassall, William Stobbs and John Burningham.

There are all sorts of styles and methods of doing illustrations: drawings in black and white, woodcuts, water colours, wash drawings (a kind of water colour), scraperboard drawings and—often the most attractive of all—coloured lithographs. Some of the best modern picture-books have been produced in this way; an outstanding example is the series of Puffin Picture Books.

Nursery Rhymes and Stories for Little Children

Ardizzone, Edward. *Tim and Lucy go to Sea* and others by the same author

Awdry, W. *Tank Engine Thomas* and others by the same author

Bannerman, Helen. *The Story of Little Black Sambo* and others in the series

Berg, Leila. *Little Pete Stories; Lollipops*

Bone, Stephen, and Adshead, M. *The Little Boy and His House*

Brisley, Joyce L. *Milly-Molly-Mandy* books

Brooke, Leslie. *Johnny Crow's Garden* and others in the the series

Bruna, Dick. *Tilly and Tessa* and others by the same author

Brunhoff, Jean de. *The Story of Babar* and others in the series

Buck, Percy (Compiler). *The Oxford Nursery Song Book*

Burningham, John (Illustrator). *ABC* and others by the same artist

Caldecott, Randolph. *Caldecott's Collection of Pictures and Songs*

Coe, Richard, *Crocodile*

Gag, Wanda. *Millions of Cats*

Greenaway, Kate. *Mother Goose; Under the Window*

Hale, Kathleen. *Orlando, the Marmalade Cat* and others in the series

Heward, Constance. *Ameliaranne and the Green Umbrella*

Hillyard, M. D. *Minikin's Visit* and others in the series

Hughes, Shirley. *Lucy and Tom's Day*

Leaf, Munro. *The Story of Ferdinand*

Lefevre, Felicite. *The Cock, the Mouse and the Little Red Hen*

John Burningham's drawing of Simp from his book *Cannonball Simp*.

Lines, Kathleen (Editor). *Lavender's Blue*

Opie, Iona and Peter. *The Oxford Nursery Rhyme Book*

Potter, Beatrix. *The Tale of Peter Rabbit* and others in the series

Reid, Alastair. *I Will Tell You of a Town*

Ross, Diana. *Nursery Tales; The Story of the Little Red Engine* series

Stobbs, William (Illustrator). *Jack and the Beanstalk; The Story of Three Little Pigs*

Uttley, Alison. *The Adventures of Sam Pig;* the *Little Grey Rabbit* series

Wildsmith, Brian (Illustrator). *ABC; Mother Goose*

Stories for Younger Children

Baker, Margaret J. *Hannibal and the Bears; Tip and Run*

Barrie, J. M. *Peter Pan*

"B.B." *The Little Grey Men; Down the Bright Stream; The Forest of Boland Light Railway*

Berg, Leila. *A Box for Benny*

Bianco, Margery Williams. *Poor Cecco*

Bond, Michael. *A Bear Called Paddington* and others in the series

Brand, Christianna. *Nurse Matilda*

Bretherton, J. B. *The Story of Small Pig*

Brown, Palmer. *Beyond the Pawpaw Trees; The Silver Nutmeg*

Clare, Helen. *Five Dolls in a House*

A Story to Tell is written and illustrated by Dick Bruna.

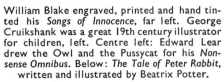

William Blake engraved, printed and hand tinted his *Songs of Innocence*, far left. George Cruikshank was a great 19th century illustrator for children, left. Centre left: Edward Lear drew the Owl and the Pussycat for his *Nonsense Omnibus*. Below: *The Tale of Peter Rabbit*, written and illustrated by Beatrix Potter.

Leslie Brooke's illustrations for *Ring O'Roses*, centre right, and, bottom right, Kate Greenaway's for *Under the Window*, are among the most successful for children. Bottom left: Randolph Caldecott's illustrations for *The Diverting History of John Gilpin* were some of the first printed in colour.

Right: *The World of Pooh* contains a map of A. A. Milne's make-believe world drawn by E. H. Shepard. The book contains *Winnie-the-Pooh* (1926) and *The House at Pooh Corner* (1928). Centre left: One of Mary Shepard's illustrations for P. L. Travers' *Mary Poppins*.

Courtesy, (top, centre right, bottom left) Methuen & Co. Ltd.; (centre left) Collins; (bottom right) André Deutsch

Centre right: *The Story of Babar*, written and illustrated by Jean de Brunhoff. Bottom left: Maurice Sendak wrote and illustrated *Where the Wild Things Are*. Bottom right: Illustration for *Madeline's Rescue* by Ludwig Beme'mans.

One of Garth Williams' illustrations from *Charlotte's Web* by E. B. White.

Collodi, Carlo. *Pinocchio*
DeJong, Meindert. *The Cat that Walked a Week; The Wheel on the School*
Dunn, Mary. *Mossy Green Theatre*
Farjeon, Eleanor. *The Old Nurse's Stocking Basket; Martin Pippin in the Apple Orchard; Martin Pippin in the Daisy-Field*
Field, Rachel. *Hitty*
Gag, Wanda. *Gone is Gone*
Godden, Rumer. *The Dolls' House*
Guillot, René. *Pascal and the Lioness*
Hope-Simpson, Jacynth. *The Edge of the World*
Hough, Charlotte. *The Hampshire Pig*
Judah, Aaron. *The Fabulous Haircut*
Kaeser, H. J. *Mimff* and others in the series
Lilius, I. S. *The Unicorn*
Mayne, William. *The Fishing Party; No More School*
Milne, A. A. *Winnie-the-Pooh; The House at Pooh Corner; When We Were Very Young; Now We Are Six*
Nesbit, E. *The Story of the Treasure Seekers; The Wouldbegoods*
Norton, Juster. *The Phantom Tolbooth*
Pearce, Philippa. *A Dog So Small*
Proysen, Alf. *Little Old Mrs. Pepperpot; Mrs. Pepperpot Again*

An illustration by the author from *Moominsummer Madness* by Tove Jansson.

Rongen, Bjorn. *Anna of the Bears*
Sendak, Maurice. *Where the Wilds Things Are*
Spyri, Johanna. *Heidi*
Todd, Barbara Euphan. *Worzel Gummidge* and others in the series
Tozer, K. *Here Comes Mumfie*
Travers, P. L. *Mary Poppins* and others in the series

One of E. H. Shepard's drawings from *Winnie-the-Pooh* by A. A. Milne.

Uttley, Alison. *The Sam Pig Storybook; Magic in My Pocket*
Vallance, Rosalind. *Tittymouse and Tattymouse* and others in the series
White, E. B. *Charlotte's Web; Stuart Little*
Williams, Ursula Moray. *The Adventures of the Little Wooden Horse; Gobbolino the Witch's Cat*

An illustration from *Three Little Funny Ones* written and illustrated by Charlotte Hough.

Fiction for Nine and Upwards

Avery, Gillian. *The Warden's Niece; Trespassers at Charlecote*
Barne, Kitty. *She Shall Have Music*
Brown, Pamela. *The Swish of the Curtain* and others in the Blue Door series; *Harlequin Corner*
Burnett, Frances Hodgson. *A Little Princess; The Secret Garden*
Burton, Hester. *The Great Gale; Time of Trial; Thomas*
Coolidge, Susan. *What Katy Did; What Katy Did at School; What Katy Did Next*
Cresswell, Helen. *The Night-Watchman; The Signposters*
Crompton, Frances E. *The Gentle Heritage*

Mayne, William. *The Thumbstick; The Rolling Season; Sand* and others

Pearce, Philippa. *Minnow on the Say*

Porter, Sheena. *Nordy Bank*

Ransome, Arthur. *Swallows and Amazons; Winter Holiday; Pigeon Post; We Didn't Mean To Go To Sea* and others by the same author

Sawyer, Ruth. *Roller Skates*

Spring, Howard. *Sampson's Circus; Tumbledown Dick*

Stafford, Ann. *Five Proud Riders*

Streatfeild, Noel. *Ballet Shoes; The Circus is Coming; White Boots; Wintle's Wonders; A Vicarage Family*

Stucley, Elizabeth. *Magnolia Buildings*

Symons, Geraldine. *The Workhouse Child*

Townsend, John Rowe. *Gumble's Yard; Widdershins Crescent; The Intruder*

Treadgold, Mary. *We Couldn't Leave Dinah; No Ponies*

Turner, Philip. *Colonel Sheperton's Clock; The Grange at High Force*

Twain, Mark. *The Adventures of Tom Sawyer; The Adventures of Huckleberry Finn*

Vipont, Elfrida. *The Lark in the Morn; The Lark on the Wing*

Fairy Tales, Folklore and Myths

Almedingen, E. M. *The Knights of the Golden Table; The Treasure of Siegfried*

Andersen, Hans. *Fairy Tales*

A drawing by Annette Macarthur-Onslowe from *Nordy Bank* by Sheena Porter.
Courtesy, Oxford University Press

Courtesy, Oxford University Press
One of Victor Ambrus' illustrations from *The Changeling* by William Mayne.

DeJong, Meindert. *Far Out on the Long Canal; The House of Sixty Fathers; Shadrach; The Tower by the Sea*

Durrell, Gerald. *The Donkey Rustlers*

Edwards, Monica. *Wish for a Pony; No Mistaking Corker; Punchbowl Midnight* and others by the same author

Enright, Elizabeth. *Thimble Summer; The Sea is All Around; The Saturdays*

Fleischman, Sid. *By the Great Horn Spoon!*

Freeman, Barbara C. *The Name on the Glass*

Garnett, Eve. *The Family From One End Street; Further Adventures of the Family From One End Street*

Hildick, E. W. *Louie's Lot*

Hull, Katherine, and Whitlock, Pamela. *The Far-Distant Oxus; Crowns*

Jones, Cordelia. *Nobody's Garden*

An illustration by E. H. Shepard from The Silver Curlew by Eleanor Farjeon.

Browne, Frances. *Granny's Wonderful Chair*
Coatsworth, Elizabeth. *The Cat Who Went To Heaven*
Crossley-Holland, Kevin. *King Horn; Havelok the Dane*
de la Mare, Walter. *The Three Royal Monkeys; Collected Stories for Children*
Dixon, Charlotte (translator and editor). *The Arabian Nights*
Ewing, Juliana Horatia. *The Brownies and Other Stories*
Farjeon, Eleanor. *The Silver Curlew; The Glass Slipper*
Green, Roger Lancelyn. *Adventures of Robin Hood; Heroes of Greece and Troy; Myths of the Norsemen; Modern Fairy Stories*
Grimm, Jacob and W. K. *Fairy Tales*
Guillot, René. *The Elephants of Sargabal; The Children of the Wind*
Harris, Joel Chandler. *Uncle Remus*
Hawthorne, Nathaniel. *Tanglewood Tales*
Hope-Simpson, Jacynth. *The Hamish Hamilton Book of Myths and Legends*
Ingelow, Jean. *Mopsa the Fairy*
Kingsley, Charles. *The Heroes*
Kipling, Rudyard. *Puck of Pook's Hill; Rewards and Fairies*
La Fontaine. *Fables*
Lang, Andrew. *The Blue Fairy Book* and others in the series
Lynch, Patricia. *The Turf-Cutter's Donkey; The Grey Goose of Kilnevin*
MacAlpine, Margaret. *The Hand in the Bag*
Macdonald, George. *At the Back of the North Wind; The Princess and the Goblin; The Princess and Curdie*
Manning-Sanders, Ruth. *Peter and the Piskies; A Book of Dragons* and others in the series; *The Red King and the Witch*

Molesworth, Mrs. M. L. *Fairy Stories*
Morgan, Mary de. *On a Pincushion; The Necklace of Princess Fiorimonde; The Windfairies*
O'Faolain, Eileen. *Children of the Salmon*
Perrault, Charles. *Fairy Tales*
Picard, Barbara Leonie. *The Mermaid and the Simpleton; The Faun and the Woodcutter's Daughter; Celtic Tales*
Reeves, James. *English Fables and Fairy Stories*
Ridley, M. R. *The Story of Sir Gawain and the Green Knight*
Ross, Diana. *The Wild Cherry; The Bridal Gown; The Enormous Apple Pie*
Sawyer, Ruth. *The Long Christmas*
Simpson, Helen. *Mumbudget*
Sleigh, Barbara. *North of Nowhere*
Sutcliff, Rosemary. *Beowulf; Dragon Slayer; The Hound of Ulster*
Thackeray, William. *The Rose and the Ring*
Tolkien, J. R. R. *The Hobbit; The Lord of the Rings*
Untermeyer, Louis. *Aesop's Fables*
White, T. H. *The Sword in the Stone*
Williams-Ellis, Amabel. *Fairy Tales from the British Isles*

Novels and Tales of Fantasy and Magic

Aiken, Joan. *Night Birds on Nantucket; Black Hearts in Battersea; The Wolves of Willoughby Chase; The Whispering Mountain*
Alexander, Lloyd. *The Castle of Llyr* and others
Baum, Frank. *The Wonderful Wizard of Oz*
Bosco, Henri, *Barboche*
Boston, Lucy M. *The Children of Green Knowe*
Carroll, Lewis. *Alice's Adventures in Wonderland; Through the Looking Glass*
Christopher, John. *The White Mountains; The Guardians*
Cooper, Susan. *Over Sea, Under Stone*

The drawing of the Little Tailor and the Unicorn is one of Fritz Wegner's illustrations from *Grimms' Fairy Tales* retold by Amabel Williams-Ellis.

Courtesy, Jonathan Cape

The title-page drawing by Pat Marriott from *The Whispering Mountain* by Joan Aiken.

Coppard, A. E. *Pink Furniture*
Crowder, Dorothy E. *The Hounds of Black Magay*
Garner, Alan. *The Weirdstone of Brisingamen; The Moon of Gomrath; Elidor; The Owl Service*
Goudge, Elizabeth. *Linnets and Valerians*
Gray, Nicholas Stuart. *Mainly in Moonlight*
Haldane, J. B S. *My Friend Mr. Leakey*
Hughes, Richard. *The Spider's Palace*
Hunter, Mollie. *The Kelpie's Pearls; The Ferlie*
Hunter, Norman. *The Incredible Adventures of Professor Branestawm*
King, Clive. *Stig of the Dump*
Kingsley, Charles. *The Water Babies*
Krüss, James. *My Great-Grandfather and I*
Lagerlof, Selma. *The Wonderful Adventures of Nils*
Lewis, C. S. *The Lion, the Witch and the Wardrobe* and others in the series
Lewis, Hilda. *The Ship That Flew*
Lindsay, Norman. *The Magic Pudding*
Linklater, Eric. *The Pirates in the Deep Green Sea; The Wind on the Moon*
Lofting, Hugh. *The Story of Dr. Dolittle* and others in the series
Lyon, Elinor. *The Day That Got Lost*
McNeill, Janet. *My Friend Specs McCann; Specs Fortissimo*
Martin, J. P. *Uncle; Uncle Cleans Up*
Masefield, John. *The Midnight Folk; The Box of Delights*
Maurois, André. *Fattypuffs and Thinifers*
Mayne, William. *A Grass Rope; Earthfasts; Over the Hills and Far Away*
Molesworth, Mrs. M. L. *The Cuckoo Clock*
Nesbit, E. *Five Children and It; The Story of the Amulet; The Phoenix and the Carpet; Wet Magic*
North, Joan. *The Cloud Forest; The Whirling Shapes*
Norton, Mary. *Bedknob and Broomstick; The Borrowers* and others in the series
Pearce, Philippa. *Tom's Midnight Garden*
Sleigh, Barbara. *Carbonel; Snowball*

Storr, Catherine. *Marianne Dreams*
Strong, L. A. G. *The Fifth of November*
Uttley, Alison. *A Traveller in Time*
Welch, Ronald. *The Gauntlet*
Whistler, Theresa. *The River Boy*
Wood, Lorna. *The People in the Garden; Rescue by Broomstick*

Adventure Stories

Armstrong, Richard. *Sea Change; The Lost Ship; The Big Sea*
Balfour, Andrew. *The Golden Kingdom*
Ballantyne, R. M. *The Coral Island*
Berna, Paul. *Threshold of the Stars; Continent in the Sky*
Blackmore, R. D. *Lorna Doone*
Boldrewood, Rolf. *Robbery Under Arms*
Brand, Max. *Destry Rides Again*
Buchan, John. *The Three Hostages; Prester John; The Thirty-Nine Steps*
Craigie, David. *The Voyage of the Luna 1*
Defoe, Daniel. *Robinson Crusoe*
Dillon, Eilis. *The San Sebastian; The Lost Island*
Fuller, Roy. *Savage Gold*
Haggard, H. Rider. *King Solomon's Mines; Allan Quatermain*
Household, Geoffrey. *The Spanish Cave*
Knight, Captain F. *The Golden Monkey; Voyage to Bengal; Clippers to China*
Kullman, Harry. *Pony Express*
Marryat, Captain F. *Mr. Midshipman Easy*
Masefield, John. *Dead Ned; Live and Kicking Ned; The Bird of Dawning*

One of Pauline Baynes' illustrations from *The Horse and his Boy* by C. S. Lewis.

Courtesy, Bles

The illustration by Anne Mieke van Ogtrop on the title-page of *The Donkey Rustlers* by Gerald Durrell.

Muhlenweg, Fritz. *Big Tiger and Christian*
O'Brian, Patrick. *The Road to Samarcand*
Post, Laurens van der. *Flamingo Feather*
Robb, John. *Sioux Arrow; Ten Guns for Shelby*
Schaefer, Jack. *Shane; The Big Range*
Sperry, Armstrong. *The Boy Who Was Afraid; Danger to Windward*
Stevenson, R. L. *The Black Arrow; Kidnapped; Treasure Island*
Suddaby, Donald. *Prisoners of Saturn*
Verne, Jules. *Around the World in 80 Days; Twenty-Thousand Leagues Under the Sea*

Animal Stories and the Outdoor World

Batten, H. Mortimer. *The Singing Forest*
"B.B." *Brendon Chase*
Durrell, Gerald. *Encounters with Animals; A Zoo in my Luggage*
Fisher, James. *The Migration of Birds*
Fortescue, Hon. J. W. *The Story of a Red-deer*
Grahame, Kenneth. *The Wind in the Willows*
Grigson, Geoffrey. *The Shell Country Book*
Guillot, René. *Kpo the Leopard; Oworo; Sama; Sirga* and others
Jefferies, Richard. *Bevis*
Kipling, Rudyard. *The Jungle Book; The Second Jungle Book; Kim*
Knight, Eric. *Lassie Come Home*
Masefield, John. *A Book of Discoveries*
Matthews, Gillian. *Sea Shore Life*
Montgomery, Rutherford. *Carcajou; Mister Jim*
Observer's Pocket Series. *Birds; Butterflies; Trees and Shrubs; Horses and Ponies; Pond Life* and many others

Patchett, Mary. *The Brumby; Tiger in the Dark*
Rawlings, Marjorie Kinnan. *The Yearling*
Salten, Felix. *Bambi: The Story of a Forest Deer*
Scott, Peter. *My Favourite Stories of Wild Life*
Seton, Ernest Thompson. *The Best of Ernest Thompson Seton*
Sewell, Anna. *Black Beauty*
Stephen, David. *String Lug the Fox; The Red Stranger*
Williamson, H. *Salar the Salmon; Tarka the Otter*
Wilson, Erle. *Coorinna*
Young Specialist Looks at series. *Birds; Animals (mammals); Marine Life; Weather; Wild Flowers* and others

History in Fact and Fiction

Allen, Agnes. *The Story of Your Home* and others by the same author
Broster, D. K. *The Flight of the Heron; The Gleam in the North*
"Bryher." *The Fourteenth of October*
Clarke, Pauline. *The Boy with the Erpingham Hood*
Collins, Norman. *Black Ivory*
Cottrell, Leonard. *The Bull of Minos; Enemy of Rome*
Daniell, David Scott. *Hunt Royal; Polly and Oliver* series
Denny, Norman, and Filmer-Sankey, Josephine. *The Bayeux Tapestry*
Doorly, Eleanor. *The Story of France*
Fabricius, Johan. *Java Ho!*
Forbes, Esther. *Johnny Tremain*
Forester, C. S. *Mr. Midshipman Hornblower* and others in the series
Fyson, J. G. *The Three Brothers of Ur*

An illustration by Brian Wildsmith from *A Hundred for Sicily* by Geoffrey Trease, a story of the period of Garibaldi's uprising.

Courtesy, Penguin Books

An illustration by G. Walter Hodges from his book *The Namesake.*

Garfield, Leon. *Jack Holborn; Devil-in-the-Fog; Smith; Black Jack; The Drummer Boy; The God Beneath the Sea*

Gray, Elizabeth Janet. *Adam of the Road; I will Adventure*

Grice, Frederick. *Aidan and the Strollers*

Guillot, René. *Riders of the Wind*

Harnett, Cynthia. *The Wool-Pack; Monasteries and Monks*

Hodges, C. Walter. *Columbus Sails; The Namesake; Shakespeare's Theatre*

Hunter, Mollie. *The Spanish Letters; A Pistol in Greenyards*

Jackdaw series. *Joan of Arc; Cardinal Wolsey; Sir Thomas More; The Tower of London* and others

Lewis, Hilda. *Here Comes Harry*

Manning-Sanders, Ruth. *Circus Boy*

Marryat, Captain Frederick. *The Children of the New Forest*

Masefield, John. *Jim Davis; Martin Hyde*

Meynell, Laurence. *The Hunted King*

Mitchison, Naomi. *The Land the Ravens Found; The Hostages*

Moorehead, Alan. *The Blue Nile* (children's edition)

Mott, Michael. *Master Entrick*

O'Brian, Patrick. *The Golden Ocean*

Oliver, Jane. *The Eagle and the Angry Dove; Watch for the Morning*

Picard, Barbara Leonie. *One is One*

Plowman, Stephanie. *The Road to Sardis*

Quennell, Marjorie, and Quennell, C. H. B. *A History of Everyday Things*

Reade, Charles. *The Cloister and the Hearth*

Reason, Joyce. *The Secret Fortress*

Renault, Mary. *The Lion in the Gateway*

Rugoff, Milton. *Marco Polo's Adventures in China* and others in the "Caravel" series published by Cassell

Rush, Philip. *Queen's Treason; A Cage of Falcons; King of the Castle*

Sperry, Armstrong. *Wagons Westward*

Strong, L. A. G. *King Richard's Land; Mr. Sheridan's Umbrella*

Sutcliff, Rosemary. *The Eagle of the Ninth; The Shield Ring; Warrior Scarlet; The Lantern Bearers; Knight's Fee; The Mark of the Horse Lord*

Trease, Geoffrey. *Cue for Treason; The Hills of Varna* and others

Treece, Henry. *Men of the Hills; The Bombard; The Last of the Vikings; The Bronze Sword* and others by the same author

An illustration by Antony Maitland from *Smith* by Leon Garfield.

Courtesy, Longmans Young Books

Courtesy, Oxford University Press
An illustration by Charles Keeping from *The Lantern Bearers* by Rosemary Sutcliff.

Twain, Mark. *The Prince and the Pauper*
Uden, Grant. *The Dictionary of Chivalry*
Ulyatt, Kenneth. *North Against the Sioux*
Van Loon, H. W. *The Story of Mankind*
Welch, Ronald. *Knight Crusader*
Wilder, Laura Ingalls. *Little House in the Big Woods; Little House on the Prairie; On the Banks of Plum Creek; By the Shores of Silver Lake*
Wilson, Barbara Ker. *Path-Through-the-Woods; The Lovely Summer; Beloved of the Gods*

Mysteries and Detective Stories

Berna, Paul. *A Hundred Million Francs; The Street Musician; The Mystery of the Cross-Eyed Man*
Dillon, Eilis. *The Island of Horses* and others
Forest, Antonia. *The Marlows and the Traitor*
Hildick, E. W. *The Boy at the Window*
Kastner, Erich. *Emil and the Detectives; Emil and the Three Twins*
Kyle, Elisabeth. *The House of the Pelican; Caroline House; The Seven Sapphires; Run to Earth*
Lewis, C. Day. *The Otterbury Incident*
McLean, Allan. *The Hill of the Red Fox*
Newby, P. H. *The Loot Runners*
Treece, Henry, *Ask for King Billy; Hunter Hunted; Don't Expect Any Mercy*
Warner, Rex. *The Kite*
Wilson, Anthony. *Norman and Henry Bones, the Boy Detectives* series

School Stories

Buckeridge, Anthony. *Jennings Goes To School* and others in the series
Forest, Antonia. *Autumn Term; End of Term*
Harris, Mary K. *Seraphina; The Bus Girls*
Hildick, E. W. *Jim Starling* and others in the series
Hughes, Thomas. *Tom Brown's Schooldays*
Kipling, Rudyard. *Stalky and Co.*
Lunt, Alice. *Secret Stepmother; Jeanette's First Term*
Mayne, William. *A Swarm in May; Chorister's Cake; Cathedral Wednesday*
Reed, Talbot Baines. *The Fifth Form at St. Dominic's; The Willoughby Captains*

Fiction for Teenagers

Alcott, Louisa M. *Little Women; Good Wives; Little Men; Jo's Boys*
Austen, Jane. *Pride and Prejudice*
Bagnold, Enid. *National Velvet*
Bowen, Marjorie. *Dickon; The Viper of Milan*
Brontë, Charlotte. *Jane Eyre*
Cary, Joyce. *Charlie is my Darling*
Chesterton, G. K. *The Innocence of Father Brown* and others in the series
Conrad, Joseph. *Lord Jim; Typhoon*
Craik, Mrs. *John Halifax, Gentleman*
Dickens, Charles. *A Christmas Carol; David Copperfield; Oliver Twist*
Dickinson, Peter. *Heartsease*
Doyle, Sir Arthur Conan. *The Memoirs of Sherlock Holmes* and others
Duggan, Alfred. *Knight With Armour; Leopards and Lilies*
Du Maurier, Daphne. *Frenchman's Creek; Jamaica Inn; Rebecca*
Eliot, George. *The Mill on the Floss*
Goudge, Elizabeth. *Towers in the Mist*
Graves, Robert. *Antigua, Penny, Puce; Wife to Mr. Milton*
Grossmith, George and Weedon. *The Diary of a Nobody*
Guareschi, Giovanni. *The Little World of Don Camillo* and others
Hartley, L. P. *The Shrimp and the Anemone*

Courtesy, Oxford University Press
One of Trevor Ridley's illustrations from *The Oak and the Ash* by Frederick Grice.

Heyer, Georgette. *The Tollgate*
Household, Geoffrey. *Rogue Male*
Irwin, Margaret. *Young Bess; Royal Flush; Still She Wished for Company*
James, M. R. *Ghost Stories of an Antiquary*
Jerome, Jerome K. *Three Men in a Boat*
Leacock, Stephen. *Nonsense Novels*
Lewis, C. S. *Out of the Silent Planet; Perelandra; That Hideous Strength*
London, Jack. *The Call of the Wild*
Mason, A. E. W. *Fire Over England*
Moore, George. *Evelyn Innes*
Orwell, George. *Animal Farm; 1984*
Paton Walsh, Jill. *Fireweed*
Peyton, K. M. *Thunder in the Sky; Flambards; The Edge of the Cloud; Flambards in Summer*
Priestley, J. B. *The Good Companions*
Streatfeild, Noel. *The Fearless Treasure*
Sutcliff, Rosemary. *Sword at Sunset*
Swift, Jonathan. *Gulliver's Travels*
Trevor, Meriol. *The Rose Round*
Walpole, Hugh. *Jeremy; Jeremy and Hamlet*
Wells, H. G. *The First Men in the Moon; The War of the Worlds*
White, T. H. *Mistress Masham's Repose*

Poetry and Verse

Belloc, Hilaire. *The Bad Child's Book of Beasts; Cautionary Tales for Children*
Blake, William. *A Grain of Sand*
Blishen, Edward (Compiler). *The Oxford Book of Poetry for Children*
Blunden, Edmund. *The Midnight Skaters*
Britton, James (Compiler). *The Oxford Book of Junior Poetry*
Clark, Leonard (Compiler). *Here and There Poems for Children*
Cole, William (Compiler). *D. H. Lawrence Poems selected for Young People; Oh! What Nonsense*
Carroll, Lewis. *The Hunting of the Snark; Jabberwocky and other poems*
de la Mare, Walter. *Collected Rhymes and Verses*
de la Mare, Walter (Compiler). *Come Hither*
Eliot, T. S. *Old Possum's Book of Practical Cats*
Farjeon, Eleanor. *Cherrystones*
Frost, Robert *You Come Too*
Herrick, Robert. *The Music of a Feast*
Holbrook, David (Compiler). *Iron, Honey, Gold*
Lear, Edward. *Nonsense Omnibus*
Marquis, Don. *Archy and Mehitabel*
Meynell, Sir Francis (Compiler). *By Heart*
Reeves, James. *The Blackbird in the Lilac*
Reeves, James (Compiler). *The Merry-Go-Round*
Serraillier, Ian. *Happily Ever After*
Smith, John (Compiler). *My Kind of Verse*
Stevenson, R. L. *A Child's Garden of Verses*
Summerfield, Geoffrey (Compiler). *Voices* (3 vols.)
Thomas, Edward. *The Green Roads*

Famous Men and Women

Barbary, James. *The Young Lord Byron*
Barne, Kitty. *Elizabeth Fry*
Chissell, Joan. *Chopin*
Cottrell, Leonard. *Enemy of Rome* (Hannibal)
Doorly, Eleanor. *The Insect Man* (Fabre); *The Microbe Man* (Pasteur); *The Radium Woman* (Madame Curie)
Green, Roger Lancelyn. *The Story of Lewis Carroll; Tellers of Tales*
Lindsay, Jack. *Nine Days Hero: Wat Tyler*
Rolt, L. T. C. *The Story of Brunel*
Smyth, A. M. *A Book of Famous Pirates*
Trease, Geoffrey. *Fortune, my Foe. The Story of Sir Walter Raleigh*
Vipont, Elfrida. *Sparks among the Stubble*

Hobbies and Interests

Allen, Agnes. *The Story of Painting*
Blishen, Edward. *The Junior Pears Leisure Book*
Britten, Benjamin, and Holst, Imogen. *The Wonderful World of Music*
Challand, Dr. Helen, and Brandt, Elizabeth. *375 Things to do*
Croome, Angela. *Know About Wrecks*
Darling, Lois and Louis. *The Science of Life*
de Vries, Leonard. *The Third Book of Experiments* and others by the same author
Edwards, Monica. *Joan Goes Farming; Rennie Goes Riding*
Folsom, Franklin. *The Wonderful Story of Language*
Fry, Jane and Maxwell. *Architecture for Children*
Gray, Dulcie, and Denison, Michael *The Actor and his World*
Grigson, Geoffrey and Jane. *Shapes and Adventures*
Haskell, Arnold. *Going to the Ballet*
Hazelwood, Rex, and Thurman, John. *The Peacock Camping Book*
Laffin, John. *Codes and Ciphers*
McWhirter, Norris and Ross. *The Guinness Book of Records*
Meynell, Laurence. *Animal Doctor; Policeman in the Family*
Salter, Lionel. *Going to the Opera*
Shaw, Margaret, and Fisher, James. *Animals as Friends and How to Keep Them*
Wainwright, David. *The Volunteers. A study of the Voluntary Service Overseas organization.*

Religion

Brisley, Joyce. *My Bible Book*
Canton, William. *A Child's Book of Saints*
de la Mare, Walter. *Stories from the Bible*
Kamm, Josephine. *A New Look at the Old Testament*
Lagerlof, Selma. *Christ Legends*
Turner, Philip, and Wildsmith, Brian. *The Bible Story*

BOOMERANG. This is one of the oldest and most peculiar weapons used by men. It is made of wood and curved in shape, as you see from the diagram. When it is thrown in the air, it moves in a very unexpected way. It flies round in a circle, for instance, or after travelling straight for a certain distance, turns in the air and comes back to the thrower. It is used in Australia by the Australian aborigines, in northeast Africa and southern India, and by the Hopi Indians of Arizona in the United States.

There are two kinds of boomerang : the kind that returns to the thrower and the kind that does not. The non-return boomerang is the heavier; it is nearly straight, and is a deadly weapon in hunting and in war. Aborigines can cut a small animal almost in two with it. The return boomerang is the one most people know about, but the aborigines think of it as a toy, not as a serious weapon. It is made of hard wood, and bent at an angle of between 90 degrees (like the two sides of a square) and 120 degrees (wider apart). One side is flat and the other has a rounded surface. When it is thrown, the air presses on the bulge of the rounded side, and this and the slight twist of the two arms are what make the boomerang circle and return.

The Australian aborigines can throw a boomerang so that it will travel straight for 30 yards, then go round in a circle 50 yards across, and then return to the thrower; or they can make it hit the ground, circle in the air, and then return.

You can make simple boomerangs of your own that will return to you when thrown. The diagrams will help you.

(1) Get a piece of plywood at least $13\frac{1}{2}$ inches long and 8 inches wide, with a thickness of $\frac{3}{8}$ inch.

(2) The tools required are a saw to cut out the shape of the boomerang, a spokeshave to shave down the blades, a small rasp to round off the edges and sandpaper to make the finished job smooth all over.

(3) With the saw, cut out the boomerang in the shape and size shown in the diagram.

(4) Shape the edges flat at first and make sure that the boomerang balances evenly on point A.

(5) Next shave off the back ; the shaded area must be flat and the amount shaved off must increase gradually from nothing to about $\frac{3}{32}$ inch at the extreme edge of the blade. Both blades should be done identically.

(6) Next shave off the front of the blades a lesser amount, ranging from nothing to $\frac{1}{16}$ inch at the edges.

(7) Lastly, round off the front edges evenly and sandpaper the whole boomerang smooth all over.

It is important to remember that the boomerang will not return properly if too much or too little is shaved off, and some experimenting may be necessary to find just the right amount.

How to Throw a Boomerang

Hold one end of the boomerang in the right hand with the other end pointing upwards and away from you, flat side to the right. You should be facing into the wind and about 10 degrees to the right of it, and the boomerang itself should be tilted slightly to the right. Direct the boomerang carefully at a spot about

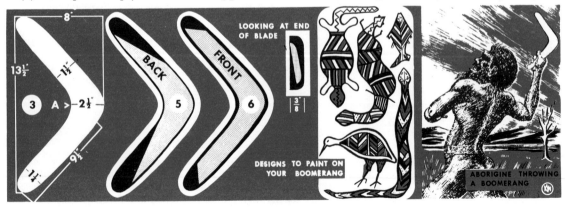

LOOKING AT END OF BLADE

DESIGNS TO PAINT ON YOUR BOOMERANG

ABORIGINE THROWING A BOOMERANG

Each time the Red Indians swept down upon the fort, Daniel's family fought beside him at the stockade.

15 feet from the ground and about 25 yards distant. As the boomerang is thrown the wrist and fingers must "flick" and give it a good spin. It will start straight, spinning as it goes, then turning to the left in a circle, still vertically spinning and climbing. Then, when it is about 40 feet above the ground, it flattens out and spins back towards the thrower. Finally it should drop gently, still spinning, until it lands on its flat side.

Although they seem harmless, these weapons can injure a person very seriously if they hit him. When you practise, therefore, you should do so only in open fields where there is nobody to be hurt. In time you should be able to hit objects about 100 feet away.

BOONE, Daniel (1734–1820), was the most famous of the American pioneers and backwoodsmen who developed the country in the 18th and early 19th centuries. His father was a blacksmith and Daniel was born in Pennsylvania, which was then on the frontier which the Americans were pushing westwards. As a boy he had hardly any schooling, but he learnt about the life of the forest and the ways of Red Indians. From the age of 12 he carried a rifle of his own. At 21 he took part in an expedition against Indians and soon afterwards he married.

After a few years in North Carolina, he became interested in the stories told by people who had explored Kentucky. He went there and roamed through the forests for two years, mostly on his own because his companions were soon killed or captured by the Indians. He helped to buy great areas of land from the Cherokee tribe, some of it for himself and his family, but he lost it all because he made no proper claim to it.

He built a fort where the town of Boonesborough now stands, and here he and his family were twice attacked by many Indians in 1777. They beat them off, but the following year he led an expedition to obtain a supply of salt from the Lower Blue Licks and was captured by a band of Indians. Eventually, however, they adopted him and gave him so much freedom that he was able to escape in time to defend the fort against another attack.

In his old age, Boone moved to Missouri, which was then a wilderness belonging to Spain. Again, when the United States bought this territory in 1803, he lost his claim to his land. This time, however, the American Congress (parliament) came to his rescue and gave him some land as a reward for all his work as a pioneer. For 50 years he had never slept without first filling his food pouch and laying his gun and moccasins by his side. (Moccasins are a type of very flexible shoe made from doeskin or other soft leather.)

BOOTH FAMILY. The Salvation Army was created by William Booth and for years all its national commanders belonged to his family. (See SALVATION ARMY.)

William Booth (1829–1912) was born at Nottingham in England. He became a Methodist minister but left the church with a group of people later known as the Methodist New Connection, among whom was Catherine Mumford.

William Booth became the minister of the Methodist New Connection in 1852 and married Catherine three years later. In 1861 William broke away from his church and began to preach independently among poor people. Catherine was also a preacher and did much good work at Gateshead in Durham. The Booths organized a mission band which worked among convicts, and by 1878 this had become the Salvation Army.

Salvation Army
William Booth.

William Booth was the first general of the Salvation Army. He gave help to many poor and lonely people and worked to relieve unhappiness and to prevent crime. For a time General Booth and his workers were laughed at. The government looked upon the Salvation Army as a nuisance and sometimes its members were fined and imprisoned for causing disturbances. He kept on with his work, however, and gradually the public came to respect the Army, which grew and spread to Europe and to America.

When William Booth died in 1912 his son Bramwell (1856–1929) succeded him as general. Under Bramwell Booth, Salvation Army organizations did much social work, particularly for women in distress. Another of William's sons, Ballington (1859–1940), was in charge of the Army in the United States and was succeeded by Frederick Booth-Tucker, the husband of William Booth's daughter Emma. In 1934 Evangeline Booth, the seventh child of William, became the first woman to be general of the entire Salvation Army. She retired in 1939 and died in 1950.

BORDEAUX. The French city of Bordeaux lies on the Garonne River, 60 miles inland from the Bay of Biscay. It is a flourishing port and a centre for the wine trade. As one stands on the bridge of Bordeaux and looks westwards, the river curls to the right in a great arc and along it are the city's quays and public buildings. The centre of the town is the square called the Place des Quinconces. The main streets run into the neighbouring Place de la Comédie. The city is built in the spacious style of the 18th century, with broad avenues and open squares. Some interesting old buildings include the remains of a Roman amphitheatre, in which the spectators sat in a semi-circle, the 13th-century cathedral of St. André, the university (founded in 1441) and the bell tower of the Church of St. Michel.

Bordeaux was a city of the people called Celts until the Romans came and made it a commercial centre and the capital of a province. It is still the capital of the French *département* (rather like a county) of the Gironde. By the marriage of Henry II of England to Eleanor of Aquitaine, Bordeaux passed into English hands in 1154 and was not regained by France until 1453. Not quite three and a half centuries later it was the headquarters of the Girondists, the chief political party of the French Revolution. In 1870, after the Germans had captured Paris in the Franco-Prussian War, Bordeaux became the temporary capital of France. Again, in 1914, at the beginning of World War I, the French government moved to it for a time when Paris was threatened by German armies and in World War II, after the fall of Paris in June 1940, several million Frenchmen fled to the Bordeaux region for safety.

The city has a population of over 250,000, many of whom are engaged in the wine business or in trades connected with it such as coopering —that is, the making of barrels. Others work in the shipyards and railway engineering workshops, while each year a large fishing fleet sets out to catch cod off Newfoundland and Iceland.

BORE, TIDAL. This looks like a wall of water that rushes up a narrow river, but actually it is a steep wave caused by a high tide from the sea meeting the water coming down the river. The higher the tide, the higher the bore. Near Bristol, the tide sometimes rises 18 feet in 90 minutes as the water is pushed into the narrowing funnel of the Severn estuary. This produces the famous Severn bore, which is often three or four feet high in the river. There are also tidal bores,

Radio Times Hulton Picture Library
The bore that sweeps up the tidal part of the River Severn is a steep wave that may be three or four feet in height.

which are sometimes called eagres, in the Humber and the Trent. The Amazon bore is sometimes as high as 16 feet.

BORGIA FAMILY. The Borgias became a powerful family in Italy during the Renaissance. Originally they were noblemen from Valencia in Spain, where the name was spelt Borja.

Alfonso de Borja (1378–1458) came to Italy in 1443 and became pope as Calixtus III in 1455. He was a good and learned man but showered favours on his nephew Rodrigo Borgia (1431–1503). Rodrigo also entered the church, but nevertheless managed to be the father of at least eight illegitimate children. He was frivolous, worldly, crafty and ambitious, and was elected pope in 1492 through the bribes and promises he gave to his rivals. As Alexander VI he was probably the wickedest pope ever to rule. He too did all he could to advance the power and riches of the family, especially those of his son Cesare Borgia (1476–1507) and daughter Lucrezia Borgia (1480–1519).

Cesare through his father's influence became an archibishop and a cardinal in his teens, but in 1498 he left the church with Alexander's approval. Next year he married a French bride, obtained a French dukedom and gained French support for his plan to become the master of central Italy. By 1502 he succeeded in this.

Alexander and Cesare stopped at nothing to gain their ends. If rivals could not be tricked or bribed, they were killed, Father and son became experts in murder. One way was to stab the victim with an ice dagger so that no weapon remained as a clue. Or, the victim might be asked to share an apple. The Borgia would cut it in two and eat one half himself. Seeing this, the victim would readily eat the other half; but he would soon die in agony because the Borgia had smeared poison on one side of the knife-blade. Indeed, Cesare probably killed his father with poisoned wine, though he had intended that someone else should drink it.

On Alexander's death Cesare's power soon crumbled. He died fighting in an unimportant battle in Spain. His sister Lucrezia was a beauty with blue eyes and golden hair. Alexander and Cesare arranged three marriages for her one after the other so as to win powerful alliances for themselves, getting rid of the first two husbands when they had served their purpose. In later life Lucrezia was devoted to her children, good works and the encouragement of the arts.

One of Alexander's great-grandsons was Francisco de Borja (1510–1572). Born and educated in Spain, he held important posts there but on his wife's death entered the Society of Jesus (see JESUITS). He was ordained priest in 1551 and for the rest of his life was engaged in missionary work and in strengthening the Jesuits, whose General, or head, he became in 1565. He was canonized—that is, proclaimed a saint—in 1671, and is usually known as St. Francis Borgia.

BORNEO. Among the great number of islands rising from the sea between Asia and Australia are New Guinea and Borneo, the largest and second largest islands in the world, if Australia and Greenland are not included. Borneo lies astride the equator, southeast of the Malay peninsula. Its area is about five times that of England and Wales together. Borneo is roughly kidney-shaped, very mountainous and covered with dense rain forest. The rich vegetation includes marketable timber such as ironwood. Wild life includes the orang-utan, honey bear, clouded leopard, deer, wild ox, elephant and the near-extinct rhinoceros. Insects abound, particularly butterflies, moths and beetles. In many areas communications depend on navigable rivers

and northern Borneo was until recently one of the least-known parts of the world. The island is thinly populated by Asian standards, the population consisting of Dayaks, Malays and Chinese, with other races such as Javanese, Buginese (from the island of Celebes), and Indians.

The British and Dutch came to Borneo to trade with the local sultans in the early 17th century. Trading stations and bases were set up and measures taken to suppress piracy which was a constant menace to trade. The southern two-thirds of the island are now part of Indonesia (see KALIMANTAN) and in the north are three states: Sabah and Sarawak, which in 1963 joined the Malaysian federation; and Brunei, which is a British-protected sultanate. (See BRUNEI; SABAH; SARAWAK.)

BOROUGH. A borough is a town possessing a mayor and symbols of authority such as a mace and coat of arms. Some boroughs have been honoured with the title of city and a few of these have a lord mayor rather than a mayor.

When the Domesday Book was made in 1086 there were 90 boroughs, and more towns became boroughs as time went on. From the days of Henry III they sent representatives to parliament. In 1835 boroughs were given councils elected by the ratepayers and they were also given a definite part to play in local government.

Until 1974, boroughs in England and Wales outside London are either municipal boroughs or county boroughs. Municipal borough councils look after certain local government services, such as housing, while other services are looked after by the county council. County borough councils look after all local government services. In 1974 (as explained in LOCAL GOVERNMENT), district councils will take the place of borough councils. Nevertheless, the traditions of many of the larger towns and cities will be continued because the districts will be able to apply for a royal charter making them boroughs, with any special titles enjoyed by the old authorities. Smaller boroughs—many of them country towns dating from the middle ages—will be able to keep their mayors and other dignitaries but will cease to be local authorities.

Local government in London was reorganized in 1965. London boroughs have different responsibilities according to whether they are inner or outer London boroughs (see LONDON).

In Scotland's present system of local government, royal and parliamentary burghs correspond to the county boroughs of England and Wales. Police burghs correspond to municipal boroughs. The title provost is used instead of mayor.

BORSTAL. A borstal is a place where young people between the ages of 15 and 21 who have broken the law can be sent to be trained to be better citizens in the future. It is not a prison, and many borstals today are in open camps or country houses with no locks, bolts or bars.

In the past, young people under 21, and even children, who broke the law were sent to ordinary prisons in large numbers without any account being taken of their age. It was found that because of this system (which meant that young people who had perhaps committed some small offence were imprisoned with hardened criminals) many young people took to a regular life of crime after they were released.

The new treatment of young offenders began from 1894 when a committee appointed to look into the English prison system suggested that in future young people should be kept in separate prisons away from older prisoners and should not be treated as criminals. They would be punished for doing wrong, but they would also be taught and encouraged to do right.

Sir Evelyn Ruggles-Brise, the chairman of the prison commissioners for England and Wales, decided to follow this advice. He brought a number of young men with long sentences of imprisonment to the old prison at a village in Kent called Borstal, where he thought out ways of treating them as the committee had recommended. His experiment, which became well-known as "the Borstal system", was so successful that in 1908 parliament adopted it as a new method of treating young people between 16 and 21 who had committed offences and needed long periods of training. Special institutions were set up for this purpose which were not prisons, and as no better name could be found, they were called borstal institutions.

Young People in Borstals Today

In England and Wales in 1970 there were 24 borstals in which boys and girls were being trained to lead good and useful lives. There are also borstals in Scotland and Northern Ireland and the system has been copied in many countries. It has worked well, for it has saved many of these young offenders from becoming criminals afterwards.

In recent years borstals have become even less like prisons and more like schools. Even in some of the stricter institutions, which are called "closed" borstals, the young people work, go for walks and play games outside.

Borstal life is vigorous and discipline is strict. There is hard work all day at useful trades and educational classes on most evenings. However, time is allowed both for indoor and outdoor recreation and there are many interesting social activities such as young farmers' clubs and social clubs which help the boys and girls to fit into ordinary life later on. The whole system tries to develop all that is best in them and to teach them to be responsible and to think for themselves so that they will know how to choose what is good and right after they have left the borstal.

How long they stay there depends on how well they get on. The legal maximum is two years; some may leave in less than a year but a minimum period of six months is usual. Then, for two years, they are supervised by a probation officer who helps them to find work, settle down and keep out of trouble.

BOSPORUS. The narrow strait which links the Sea of Marmara, Turkey, with the Black Sea is called the Bosporus. The name means "ox ford" and comes from the Greek story of Io who was changed into a heifer by Zeus and swam across the strait to escape the jealous anger of Hera, the wife of Zeus.

The beautiful strait, 719 metres wide at its narrowest, divides Europe from Asia. It is spanned by a great suspension bridge now, but has always been an important crossing place. It was here that the Ottoman Turks crossed westwards to capture Constantinople (now known as Istanbul) from the Greeks in 1453, later extending their empire to the gates of Vienna and the

Courtesy, Turkish Information Bureau
Istanbul and the inlet known as the Golden Horn. The Bosporus itself can be seen at the right of the picture.

borders of Poland. Istanbul was built on the shores of the Golden Horn, a deep inlet on the European side of the strait which makes a fine harbour, well protected from the strong current that flows from the Black Sea through the Bosporus to the Sea of Marmara and eventually out to the Aegean. Istanbul's position is therefore a magnificent one for a trading city, for it stands at the cross-roads of two great natural highways—the land route across the strait from Europe to Asia, and the strait itself, through which passes the trade between southern Russia and the Mediterranean.

Whichever country controls the land on either side of the Bosporus can command all the shipping passing through it. Turkey has been in this position for five centuries. For a long time Russia has wished to obtain control of the strait but the countries of western Europe have always been against this. At present merchant ships of any nation can pass through freely, but warships only with the permission of the Turkish government. The same applies to the Dardanelles, the strait linking the Sea of Marmara to the Aegean Sea. (See DARDANELLES.)

BOSWELL, James (1740–1795). James Boswell was the author of the most famous biography that has ever been written, *The Life of Samuel Johnson*. He was born at Edinburgh on October 29, 1740, the son of a Scottish judge. He studied law at Edinburgh University and in 1766 began to practise as a lawyer at Edinburgh, although he was not very successful at this, for he cared more about literature than he did about law. His chief aims in life were to become a great author and to know many famous people. He described himself in a letter to one of his friends in a verse which began:

> Boswell is pleasant and gay,
> For frolic by nature designed.

It was a good description for, although vain, he was always enthusiastic and energetic and loved to spend his days surrounded by witty and merry company.

The most important day in Boswell's life was the day, on one of his visits to London, when he first met the celebrated author Dr. Samuel Johnson, whom he admired very much. (See JOHNSON, SAMUEL.) Boswell was then only 23, and very anxious to make a good impression on so famous a literary man. He was drinking tea with a London bookseller named Tom Davies and his wife when Johnson called, according to Boswell's description in an early chapter of the *Life*. Boswell was very agitated when introduced,

and remembering how much Johnson was supposed to dislike Scotsmen he said quickly to Tom Davies, "Don't tell where I come from."

Davies, however, cried mischievously, "From Scotland!"

"Mr. Johnson", said Boswell quickly, "I do indeed come from Scotland, but I cannot help it", upon which came Johnson's crushing reply,

"That, Sir, I find, is what a very great number of your countrymen cannot help."

After this embarrassing beginning for Boswell, however, the two soon became close friends, and Boswell decided to write Johnson's biography. He took down in a notebook everything he heard Johnson say and described all that went on among Johnson's circle of friends. Hundreds of simple happenings that other people might not have noticed or might have thought unimportant were put down, and when they were gathered together they made up a wonderful portrait of Dr. Johnson.

Boswell also wrote a *Journal of a Tour to the Hebrides*, describing a visit that he and Johnson made together. This was published in 1785 and the *Life* followed in 1791. Both were best-sellers.

Boswell had married in 1769 and there were five children. In later years his love of pleasure eventually led him into debt, and gradually he lost his cheerfulness. He died in 1795.

Between 1927 and 1946 many manuscripts by Boswell were discovered in Ireland and Scotland. The papers now belong to Yale University in the United States and are being edited by distinguished scholars: several volumes of them have been published, including *Boswell's London Journal*.

BOTANY is the natural science that deals with plants. Although there is an enormous variety in the shapes and sizes of plants, they can nevertheless be put into groups according to their structure (the way they are made) and form (the shapes of their parts) and their life histories. In many cases the study of a group has a special name: for example, algology is the study of algae, pteridology is the study of ferns, mycology is concerned only with fungi and bryology deals with liverworts and mosses.

As well as these studies, which are concerned

with different types of plants, there are seven main branches of botany dealing with the various aspects of plant life. These seven branches are listed below with a short description of each one.

1. *Plant anatomy*. This is the study of the way plants are made—how the roots, stems, leaves and other parts are built up.

2. *Plant cytology*. This is the study of the cells of plants. Every part of a plant is made up of cells and these cells vary in shape, size, thickness of their walls and other things in different parts, such as a root or leaf. They also vary inside the root, leaf, or other part.

3. *Plant morphology*. This is the study of the forms or shapes of plants and of their parts; for example, the shapes of leaves and flowers and how these are folded in the buds. Classification, or the arranging of plants in classes, orders and so forth, is based on morphology.

4. *Plant physiology*. This is the study of how the plant grows, breathes, makes its food and so on; for example, the way the roots take up water from the soil and how the water moves along to the leaves where it is used in the manufacture of food.

5. *Plant pathology*. This is the study of diseases affecting plants and their growth.

6. *Plant taxonomy*. This is the naming of plants and groups of plants.

7. *Plant ecology*. This is the study of the plant in its habitat, or surroundings, and its relation to its habitat. The plant ecologist studies the effect on a plant of soil, moisture, temperature, light, other plants, animals and so on. He also studies what are called plant communities, such as woodlands, tropical forests, marshes, bogs, moorlands, salt and fresh water, sand dunes, deserts, mountains and all the others.

Botany is a necessary study for the three practical sciences of agriculture (farming), horticulture (flower cultivation) and silviculture (forestry).

The article BIOLOGY tells how botany developed into a science at the same time as the study of animals (zoology).

BOTHA, Louis (1862–1919).

One of the greatest men South Africa has produced was Louis Botha, the first Prime Minister of the Union of South Africa after it was formed in 1910. He was born on a farm in Natal, one of a family of 13, and as a boy lived a rough and adventurous life. Later he helped to found the "New Republic"—the Vryheid district of Zululand—which was afterwards made part of the

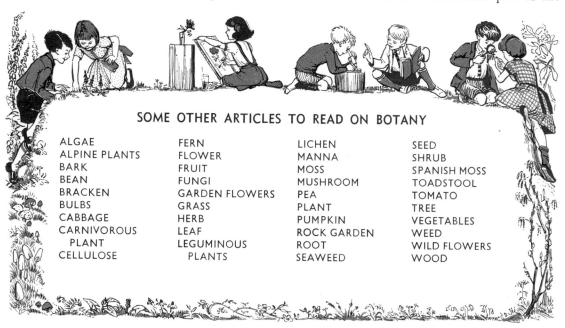

SOME OTHER ARTICLES TO READ ON BOTANY

ALGAE	FERN	LICHEN	SEED
ALPINE PLANTS	FLOWER	MANNA	SHRUB
BARK	FRUIT	MOSS	SPANISH MOSS
BEAN	FUNGI	MUSHROOM	TOADSTOOL
BRACKEN	GARDEN FLOWERS	PEA	TOMATO
BULBS	GRASS	PLANT	TREE
CABBAGE	HERB	PUMPKIN	VEGETABLES
CARNIVOROUS	LEAF	ROCK GARDEN	WEED
PLANT	LEGUMINOUS	ROOT	WILD FLOWERS
CELLULOSE	PLANTS	SEAWEED	WOOD

Transvaal. Thus Botha became a citizen of the Transvaal, then an independent country.

When the Boer War broke out in 1899 between the British and those people of Dutch descent, called Boers, who lived in the two republics of the Transvaal and the Orange Free State, he showed such skill in warfare and was such an outstanding leader that before the war was over he was put in command of the Transvaal army. When he realized that the defeat of the Boers was certain, he did his best to get honourable peace terms from the British. (See BOER WAR.)

Botha and his friend Jan Christiaan Smuts persuaded their countrymen to accept the terms, which meant that the two Boer republics became British colonies. Then they persuaded the British government to allow these colonies to govern themselves. When this was granted in 1907, Botha became Prime Minister of the Transvaal. Afterwards he joined with statesmen of the neighbouring colonies in the work of uniting them as the Union of South Africa. (This is explained more fully in the article SOUTH AFRICA.) In 1910, when the Union was formed, Botha became its Prime Minister. Soon afterwards came World War I and Botha and his government gave South Africa's full support to Great Britain. Many of his countrymen rose in rebellion, however, in the hope of restoring their lost independence. (South Africa did not become fully independent until 1931.) Botha put down the rebellion and conquered German South West Africa. He attended the Versailles peace conference in 1919, but died just after his return home.

BOTSWANA is a republic in southern Africa. It is a large but sparsely populated country, over 500 kilometres inland from the Atlantic and Indian oceans. It has a very short frontier with Zambia and otherwise is surrounded by Rhodesia, South Africa and South West Africa.

There is some fine hill scenery in the eastern part of Botswana with many trees and shrubs as well as excellent grass for grazing cattle. Through this part runs a single-track railway which links the South African town of Mafeking with Bulawayo in Rhodesia. Much of the region called Ngamiland in the northwest consists of papyrus swamps (papyrus is a reed) which lie between the Okavango and Chobe rivers. The Chobe (or Kwando) runs into the Zambezi west of the Victoria Falls and has some beautiful river scenery; here the people do much of their travelling in canoes hollowed out from the trunks of trees.

The rest of the country is part of the dry area known as the Kalahari Desert, about which there is a separate article. In this region people often obtain their water from wells, and in parts

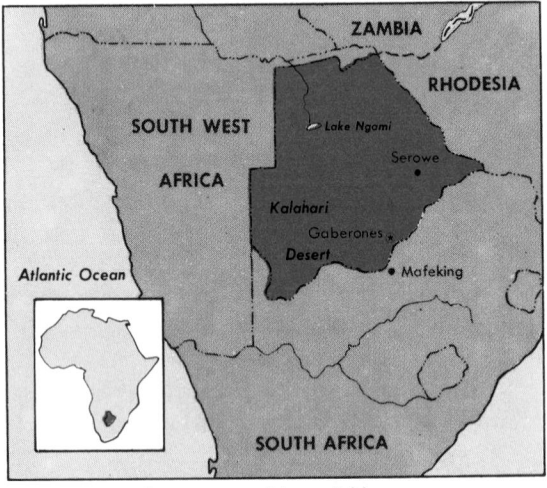

Botswana and its neighbours.

of it the camel is used for transport. Botswana teems with wild life—elephants, giraffes, buffaloes, zebras, lions, ostriches and poisonous snakes. Animals are specially protected in the Chobe game reserve. The climate is warm on the whole, but less so as one travels higher above sea level or further south from the equator. Most of the rain falls between December and the end of April in short, heavy, showers.

The People and their Lives

In some of the more remote parts of Botswana there are still some survivors of the little Bushmen, a fast-disappearing people who speak a strange language, full of clicking sounds, and who make a bare living by hunting animals with bow and poisoned arrow. (See BUSHMEN AND HOTTENTOTS; RACES AND PEOPLES.)

The Bechuana people form most of the population, however, and the majority of them live in large villages, some of which have more than 10,000 inhabitants. There are eight main tribal groups in Botswana, each with its own chief and territory. Seven of these territories are in the eastern part of the country and one, that of the Batawana tribe, is in Ngamiland. In two cases they are bigger than Wales.

Very important to the Bechuana people are their herds of cattle, which form their most valuable export to other countries. They are tended by boys and young men at places where there is water and good pasture, often far from the villages. During the summer the villages are almost deserted, except for elderly people and schoolchildren, because the others go off to their cultivated land which, like the cattle posts, is quite often a long way from the main settlement. The people stay away for several months tilling the ground and raising crops of maize, millet, beans and pumpkins, which are among their main foods. Every year thousands of Bechuana men go to South Africa where they work in the factories and mines.

Thanks to the work of the missionaries (David Livingstone, the great Scottish missionary and explorer once lived here), every village has a building that can be used either as a school or as a church. Some of the towns—such as Serowe in the territory of the Bamangwato tribe—have several schools with some thousands of pupils between them. There are teacher training colleges at Lobatsi and Serowe, and some students attend the University of Lesotho, Botswana and Swaziland which is at Roma, near Maseru, in Lesotho.

Picturepoint

Cattle herds in Botswana are tended by boys.

There are not many Europeans in Botswana. Most of them live in the south or to the east of the railway line or at Ghanzi, near the border of South West Africa. They are mainly traders, missionaries, farmers or railway workers, but in the Tati area in the northeast some are engaged in mining gold. Diamonds have been found at Orapa in central Botswana.

Government of Botswana

In 1885, with the agreement of the chiefs, Sir Charles Warren proclaimed the country a British protectorate. For many years it was governed by a British commissioner who lived at Mafeking, in South Africa, where the government of Bechuanaland had its headquarters.

However, by the middle of the 20th century, the people of the country were taking a greater part in its government and on September 30, 1966, they became an independent nation. At the same time the country was turned into a republic—with Sir Seretse Khama as president—and its name was changed to Botswana. The new capital is the small town of Gaborone (in the southeast and on the Mafeking–Bulawayo railway). The Botswana parliament, which consists of the House of Chiefs and the National Assembly, and the various government depart-

FACTS ABOUT BOTSWANA

AREA: 600,375 square kilometres.
POPULATION: 667,000.
KIND OF COUNTRY: Independent republic within the Commonwealth of Nations.
CAPITAL: Gaborone (Gaberones).
GEOGRAPHICAL FEATURES: Hills and wooded grasslands in the east; swamps and rivers in the northwest; dry plains to the west.
CHIEF PRODUCTS: Cattle, maize, millet, vegetables, skins. Some gold, asbestos, manganese and kyanite is mined. (Kyanite is used in insulators of sparking plugs.)
IMPORTANT TOWNS: Serowe, Kanye, Molepolole, Lobatsi, Francistown.
EDUCATION: School attendance is not compulsory.

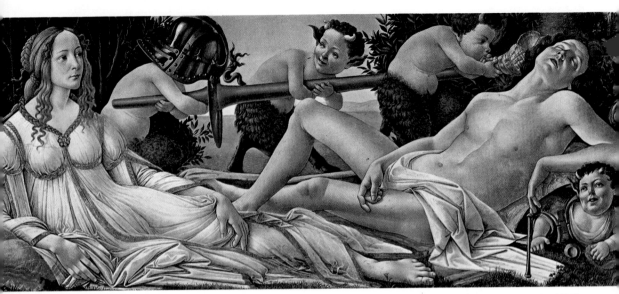

"Mars and Venus" painted in about 1485 by Botticelli. While the god of war sleeps, fauns play with his armour.

ments are situated there.

Botswana is a member of the Commonwealth of Nations.

BOTTICELLI, Sandro (1444–1510), was

one of the most famous of Italian painters. Botticelli was not his real name, for he was christened Alessandro di Mariano dei Filipepi, but was a nickname meaning "Little Barrel". He lived with his elder brother in Florence, and because the brother was called Botticelli, the young Sandro was known by this name too. His father was a tanner, but Sandro was at first an apprentice to another of his brothers who was a goldsmith. However, he soon gave this up and became apprenticed instead to one of the greatest painters of the day, a friar called Fra Filippo Lippi. From him Botticelli learnt how to paint in fresco and tempera. Frescoes are paintings done in a special way on the walls or ceilings of buildings. Tempera painting is done by mixing powder colours with egg yolk, which makes the permanent colours light and delicate.

When Fra Filippo died, Botticelli was only 22, but he was already well known. He was employed by a powerful and wealthy family called the Medicis who ruled Florence and who employed all the greatest artists of the time.

(There is a separate article on the Medici family.) It was for one of the Medicis that Botticelli painted one of his most lovely pictures, called "Primavera" (Spring). In 1481 he was summoned to Rome with some other artists of Florence to paint frescoes on the walls of the Sistine Chapel. After two years he came back to Florence, where he lived for the rest of his life. During the next ten years, he painted some of his greatest pictures. One of these is the "Birth of Venus", which shows the goddess rising out of the sea; another, "Mars and Venus", is in the National Gallery in London.

Towards the end of his life Botticelli's paintings became less gay and bright, because he took to heart the teaching of a monk named Savonarola, who preached against the evils of the court of the Medicis. The later paintings are more mystical and serious.

Like most painters of his time, Botticelli chose religious subjects for many of his pictures; but the subject of "Primavera" and "The Birth of Venus" and some other paintings came from the myths, or stories, of classical times. His paintings are full of light and delicate colour, and the graceful figures in them have real life and movement. His best pictures are as fresh and alive today as they were when he first painted them.

BOTTLING AND CANNING. A good kitchen store cupboard today nearly always contains some bottled or tinned foods, which means that all kinds of fruit and vegetables can be eaten all the year round and not just at the time when they are in season. The first bottling was done about 150 years ago. When, in 1795, the armies of Napoleon were occupying much of Europe, the French government offered a prize of 12,000 francs (that is, about £9,500 today) to anyone who could discover a way of preserving food, so as to ease the problem of feeding soldiers far away from stocks of fresh food. The prize was won 15 years later by François Appert, a Paris confectioner, who discovered that food would keep if put carefully in sealed jars, the jars being then boiled for several hours.

A few years later an Englishman, Peter Durand, discovered that unbreakable metal containers were cheaper and more practical than glass, and so canning, or tinning, food began. Canning methods improved steadily during the 19th century. In 1824 an Arctic explorer, Sir Edward Parry, took tinned food with him on an expedition. Some of these tins were later brought back to England but were not opened until 1911 —87 years later, when the contents were found to be still perfectly eatable. In 1957 Peter Scott opened some of the tins of food left in the Antarctic by his father, Captain Scott, over 40 years before, and this time, too, the food was in good condition. By 1820 the first canned food appeared in the shops and in 1855 soldiers in the Crimea were issued with the first "iron rations", as they were called.

About this time the work of the great French scientist Louis Pasteur, which American scientists later continued, showed that the preserving of canned and bottled food was made possible by the absence of the invisible bacteria or "germs" that normally make food go bad. These bacteria are killed by the heat in the bottling or canning process.

How to Bottle Fruit

It is quite easy to preserve food at home and bottling is the simplest method. Fruit is more often preserved than vegetables and is also the safest, for fruit contains acid which helps to kill the bacteria. Vegetables must be cooked at a very high temperature to kill the bacteria. Several kinds of preserving jars or bottles are used but they all have a lid (often made of glass), a rubber ring to make the lid airtight and a metal clip or screwband to go on over the lid.

Here is one of the easiest ways of bottling fruit. When you have washed the jars, pack the fruit, which should be firm and clean, tightly into them. Then put them into a moderate oven (about 350 degrees Fahrenheit), covering them with lids to prevent the fruit from being discoloured. The jars must be placed on asbestos, cardboard or several layers of newspaper to keep them from touching the oven shelf, for if they did so they would crack with the heat. The fruit should be cooked for three-quarters of an hour or an hour. While it is cooking put the rubber rings and the jar lids into a pan of cold water and boil them for 15 minutes to sterilize them; that is, to make them clean and free of germs.

When the fruit is cooked take the jars out of the oven one at a time and fill them to overflowing with boiling water or syrup. (The syrup is made by dissolving two to eight ounces of sugar in each pint of water and boiling the liquid for a few minutes.) Some soft fruits such as raspberries shrink during the cooking and it is a good plan to prepare an extra bottle of fruit so that you can fill up the other bottles. Fit the rubber ring, hot, on to the jar, put the lid on and fasten down the metal screwbands or clips. As the jars cool, you may have to tighten the screwbands. After the jars have stood for 24 hours remove the screwband or clip and lift each jar a little (not more, or you may have an accident) by the lid. If the jar is properly airtight, the lid will not come off. If the lid does come off, the fruit must be sterilized again—or else it must be eaten.

There is another method of preserving which needs a pan deep enough for the jars to stand covered with water. The jars must not touch each other or the bottom or sides of the pan, because they might crack if they did so. A false bottom can be made with layers of newspaper, straw or folded cloth.

Wash the jars and pack in the fruit. Soak the rubber rings in cold water. Then fill the jars to overflowing with cold water or syrup. Put on the

| Prepare the fruit & pack into washed jars | Stand jars in preserving pan on folded newspapers | Pour in water to cover Simmer for about 15 minutes | Remove some water to uncover jars | Test for airtightness |

rubber rings, lids and screwbands or clips and tighten the bands nearly as tightly as they will go, but not quite. Then stand the jars in the pan, cover them with cold water and heat slowly to simmering point (almost 185 degrees Fahrenheit). This should take at least an hour and a half. Keep them simmering for 15 minutes, or rather more for some fruits such as pears. When they are ready, take some of the water out of the pan with a cup or jar until the necks of the jars are uncovered. Lift them out one at a time and tighten the screwband. After that follow the same instructions as in the oven method.

Canning in the Factory

Canning can also be done in the home but for this a can-sealing machine is required. The same type of can and methods of sealing are used at home as in a factory. Food canning has become a major industry. Canning factories are usually built near the place where the foods to be canned come from, for it is essential that they should be fresh. The food is inspected, washed and sorted into different sizes and qualities. Next it is peeled, shelled, boned, blended or whatever is necessary for the kind of food being used.

Then comes the cooking process. Some foods shrink when they are cooked, so they are cooked before they are put into cans, to ensure that the can will be completely filled. After the cans have been filled machines suck out the air and seal up the cans. Next they are heated in boiling water or in steam under pressure and finally they are stored and labelled. In factories most of the necessary processes are performed by machines so that the food is touched by hand as little as possible. Automation or doing the work by machines also speeds up the process enormously.

Courtesy, Smedley's Ltd.

The machine on the right measures peas into the cans. The lids are then fixed tightly before sterilization.

BOUGAINVILLE, Louis Antoine de

(1729–1811). The French explorer Bougainville began his career in the army, and in the Seven Years' War distinguished himself against the British in Canada. In 1764 he led an expedition to settle the Falkland Islands as a French colony, but France soon gave it up. Bougainville was chosen to make a voyage of discovery round the world in the frigate "La Boudeuse". Passing through Magellan Strait he crossed the Pacific in 1768, touching at Tahiti and Samoa, but made few important discoveries until he reached the western part of the ocean. There he gave the first firm report of Malekula in the New Hebrides and discovered several of the Solomon Islands, including Bougainville, the largest of them. He returned to France after a voyage lasting more than two years.

In 1782 Bougainville commanded a squadron in the Battle of the Saints against the British fleet under Admiral Sir George Rodney. The French were severely defeated and Bougainville was banished from court. He became a vice-admiral in 1791 and was awarded high honours by Napoleon I. Although resourceful and bold, Bougainville was overshadowed as an explorer by the Englishman James Cook. The showy climbing plant bougainvillea, sometimes seen in greenhouses, is named after him.

"BOUNTY", MUTINY OF THE.

The story of the mutiny—that is, the rebellion of the crew against their captain—that happened on the British ship "Bounty" as it was sailing through the Pacific Ocean in 1789 is a famous one. The ship was commanded by William Bligh, whose nickname was "Breadfruit Bligh". He got this name because he led an expedition to take some breadfruit plants from the island of Tahiti in the south Pacific to St. Vincent in the British West Indies, where no breadfruit had been grown before.

The "Bounty" sailed to Tahiti, and Lieutenant Bligh and his crew spent five or six months there. The crew became used to living comfortably in the soft, lazy climate of Tahiti, and many of them longed to settle there and not go back to the hard life of sailing. Many, too, hated their captain, for he was a hot-tempered man and a bully.

and his rule was harsh. When it was time for the "Bounty" to set sail again the crew grew rebellious, and on April 28 they mutinied, led by Fletcher Christian, the master's mate.

The hated Bligh and 18 members of the crew who had remained loyal to him were set adrift in an open boat about 25 feet long; they were given no chart and very little food and drink. In this little boat they sailed for nearly three months and for a distance of nearly 4,000 miles. Some of them died, but the rest managed to keep alive

on breadfruit and shellfish which they obtained from small islands, and at last they reached Timor, an island near Java. Bligh at once sailed for England and his companions followed.

Meanwhile, the mutineers had sailed back to Tahiti and then sought a refuge. They were the first Europeans to visit Rarotonga in the Cook Islands but settled on Pitcairn Island, where people descended from them still live. Some of the ringleaders of the mutiny were later captured and brought back to Portsmouth, where three of them were executed.

William Bligh had a successful career and later became a vice-admiral, though his character did not change. He was once governor of New South Wales, in Australia, and was so unpopular that in another mutiny against him, the mutineers kept him prisoner for two years.

BOURNEMOUTH

is a well-known seaside resort in Hampshire, England. The town is a modern one and the first house was built in 1810. In the middle of the 19th century Bournemouth was just a village, but, with the development of the railways which made travel

Bournemouth's sandy beach attracts many holidaymakers.

easier, its sheltered position and pleasant climate were already beginning to attract holiday-makers. A wooden pier was built in 1861, the railway reached the town in 1870 and ten years later a second pier was built. By then the population had started to increase rapidly and the houses were spreading inland and along the shore in both directions. The town grew very fast after World War I and steps had to be taken to protect the pine trees which were being cut down to make way for building.

Today there are about 153,000 people living in Bournemouth, many of whom have moved to the town after reaching retirement age. The only industry is that of catering for hundreds of thousands of holidaymakers and for the many conferences which are held in the town. The chief attraction for visitors is the sandy bathing beach, 10 kilometres long, lying below picturesque sandstone cliffs which are broken by wooded gullies, known locally as chines. There are 8 kilometres of promenades both along the top of the cliffs and at the foot, together with lovely public parks and pleasure gardens. Entertainments include a fine pavilion providing plays, ballet and opera, an ice skating rink, an indoor swimming pool and a concert hall which is the home of the Bournemouth Symphony Orchestra. There are also three theatres, a fine shopping centre, an art gallery and a museum, so that Bournemouth is a pleasant place in winter as well as in summer.

From the main pier there are trips by pleasure steamers in the summer to the Isle of Wight and to points on the Dorset coast, such as Swanage and Lulworth Cove. From the smaller jetty motor boats make trips in the bay or round Poole Harbour and its islands, lying just to the west of Bournemouth.

BOW AND ARROW. One of the first weapons of early man was the bow and arrow. He used it for hunting and for killing his enemies. If you are very lucky you may still find in Great Britain a stone arrowhead, a relic of the Stone Age.

In Europe men used to have an ordinary short bow which they held upright and pulled to their chest. Then during the Crusades most of them used instead the crossbow, which was held across the body and had a metal groove for the arrow and a trigger to let it off. Later it was proved that the crossbow was not the best weapon for a skilled archer. The longbow was probably first used by the Welsh. As tall as a man, the longbow was drawn to the right ear and shot an arrow a yard long. Edward I discovered the value of the longbow during his Welsh campaigns and his

The English longbow with its long arrow could shoot faster and pierce armour better than the complicated crossbows which shot metal bolts, or "quarrels"

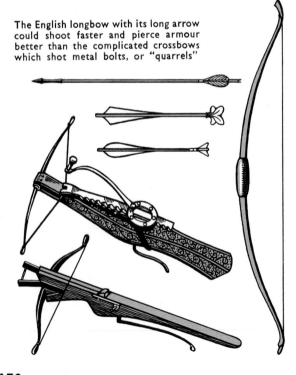

armies and those of Edward III had many archers. The great English victories at the battles of Crécy, Poitiers and Agincourt were won largely by the English and Welsh archers.

The "bowyers" who made the bows from Spanish yew, and the "fletchers" who tipped the arrows with iron, found their trade was out of date in Queen Elizabeth I's time, but archery is still a popular sport today and you can read about it in a separate article. You may know *Sir Nigel* and *The White Company* by Conan Doyle. These two books describe England in the times when the bow was the chief weapon of defence, and they are well worth reading.

How to make a Bow and Arrow

If you want to make a bow for yourself, you must find a straight stave without any branches. Yew or bamboo is the best wood to use, and it should be four or five feet long. Cut a notch at each end, then take a thin piece of cord and rub wax on it to stop it fraying. Tie one end of the cord to one of the notches and make a loop at the other end, so that it is a little shorter than the stave. Put the end of the stave against the inside of your foot, bend it (but not too much) and hook the loop over the outer notch. To make the bow-string last, you can wind waxed thread round the part in the middle which is rubbed by the arrows. You can also put a leather band round the wood where you hold it.

To make an arrow, you need a thin, straight stick about two feet long and free of knots or bumps. Sharpen one end, and harden it in the fire if you like. At the other end, cut a small notch to fit the bowstring; then stick three feathers, or stiff, triangular pieces of paper, as near as possible to the notched end.

Now your bow and arrow are ready to use, but you should remember to unhook the bow-string when you are not using it, and to take care *how* you use your bow and arrow, or you may injure someone. An archery club will teach you how to use a bow properly.

BOWER-BIRD. These birds make little bowers, or leafy nooks, where they perform their courtship. The bowers are beautifully built by the cock, of sticks and twigs, lined with grass.

They have nothing to do with the saucer-shaped nests, which are built by the hens in bushes or trees and may be placed some distance away from the bower.

Bower-birds are found only in Australia and New Guinea. There are many different species, each of which makes its bower in a different way with a different shape. The best known is the satin bower-bird, found in many parts of Australia and more often seen in zoos than any of the others. The male is glossy blue-black while the general colour of the female is greyish-green. The male does not get its final plumage for several years. The eyes of both male and female

A female satin bower-bird waits near the bower.

are brilliant. For its bower the bird first makes a little platform of twigs and then places upright twigs at each side which bend over a little at the top so that they almost form an arch. It decorates the floor with stones, bones, feathers or any brightly coloured objects it can find, particularly anything blue.

The regent bower-bird, which is found in eastern Australia, makes a similar but less elaborate bower; the twigs at the side are longer and more upright. The floor is covered with shells of various colours and with freshly picked leaves. The male bird is brilliantly coloured with the most beautiful orange and velvety-black plumage; the hen is mottled brown.

The brown gardener bower-bird of New

Guinea constructs a wonderful bower like a little hut about two feet high. It uses the trunk of a tree as a central pillar and makes slanting walls of orchid stems round it. One side is left open and in front of this is placed a bed of moss, thickly covered with brightly coloured flowers and berries. When the flowers wither, the bird replaces them with fresh blooms—perhaps this is why it was given the name of "gardener".

Cock bower-birds spend a lot of time in their bowers, running in and out and round them, rearranging the twigs and bringing fresh decorations. In the breeding season the cocks "dance" and entice the hens into the bowers.

BOWLS. The game of bowls is played on a bowling green of smooth green turf and the object of the game is to roll the wood, the proper name for the bowl, as near as possible to a small white ball or target known as the "jack" or

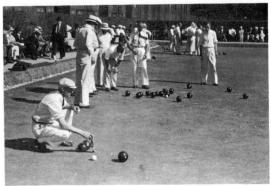

Radio Times Hulton Picture Library
In bowls the white ball, or jack, is the target and the players roll their woods as close to it as they can.

"kitty". The jack is first rolled on to the green at least 20 yards away from the players.

The wood may be made of *lignum vitae*, a hard wood which comes from the West Indies, or of some artificial substances. When it is bowled from the mat on which the player stands it rolls in a curve to its destination. The reason for this is that the wood is specially made with a "bias". The bias (which means something that is not straight, in other words lop-sided) was produced in olden times by putting a piece of lead into one side of the bowl. Nowadays it is done in the maker's shaping, or turning, of the

wood, which ensures that one side is a little rounder than the other. As a result the bowl is not perfectly round; if you can imagine half an orange and half a lemon stuck together, it would look rather like the two sides of a bowl, although of course in a very exaggerated way.

The player (or side) whose wood is nearest to the jack at the conclusion of a round, or "end", scores. If he has one wood nearer than his opponent, he scores one; if two woods are nearer he scores two, and so on. If the game is between two players only, the first one to score 21 points wins. If it is between two pairs of players, or two sides of four players each, the game finishes when 21 ends or rounds have been played. These sides of four players are called "rinks", and each member of the rink uses two woods. When the game is between two players only or between two pairs, each player has four woods.

There are two kinds of bowls, the level-green game and the crown-green game. A crown green has a "crown" or hump in the middle which makes it more difficult to judge the curve and direction of the wood's course. The crown-green game is played mostly in the north of England.

Bowls is one of the oldest of English sports and was certainly being played 700 years ago. It was so popular in the middle ages that laws were passed forbidding people to play it, as well as other games, because they were neglecting their archery—a skill needed in times of war. The game, too, will always have its place in history because of its connection with Sir Francis Drake. According to the well-known story, Drake was playing bowls with his sea captains on Plymouth Hoe when news was brought that the Spanish Armada had been sighted. Turning to his fellow players, he calmly suggested that they should finish the game first and beat the Spaniards afterwards.

BOW STREET RUNNERS. The Bow Street Runners were a small group of men who were paid to go into the streets and try to prevent crimes and riots. This group was started in 1750 by the novelist Henry Fielding, who was a magistrate at Bow Street Court, London. On this idea our present police force was founded.

They wore red waistcoats and because of this

were often called Robin Redbreasts. When Fielding died, they became a dishonest group of policemen. They mixed with criminals and when there was a theft or burglary they soon found out who had committed the crime. Then, promising not to arrest or charge the thieves, the Runners arranged with them to return some of the stolen goods. In this way they received payment from the owners of the stolen property and also from the thieves. Some of the Runners were found to be very rich when they died. They were never more than about eight or ten in number.

BOXING is the art of fighting with gloved fists according to a set of fixed rules. It is a sport in which skill is even more important than strength. The boxer learns to control and use his strength well and to keep his temper while hitting as hard as he can—a bad-tempered person or a bully is unlikely to make a good boxer. The sport, especially international amateur boxing, demands a high level of fitness and other merits including strength, speed, stamina, mobility and a high degree of skill.

Good boxing depends on four main points, which the beginner must master completely, so that he can put them into practice during a bout without having to think deliberately about them at all. These four points are.

1. Knowledge of the rules.
2. A well-balanced stance or position, combined with purposeful footwork.
3. Correct punching.
4. Active defence.

It may seem obvious that a boxer should know the rules, but many do not. The beginner must know what he is boxing for, and what he may or may not do. Generally, he is boxing for points. Each round of boxing usually lasts two or three minutes and the maximum number of points (20) is awarded to the boxer who wins the round; that is, who lands the greater number of scoring blows in it. The loser of the round is awarded a lesser number of points according to his merits. When both boxers are judged to be equal in a round, they are each given maximum points. If at the end of the bout both boxers have the same number of points, the judges should give the decision to the boxer who has done the most "leading off". If equal in this respect, the winner is to be the best stylist. If they are still equal in both "leading off" and in style the decision goes to the boxer who has shown the best defence. In professional boxing the verdict of a draw is allowed.

Points are gained by clean blows delivered with the knuckle part of the closed glove of either hand on the front or sides of the opponent's face and on his body above the belt. (The line of this so-called belt is important—it is reckoned to be at the level of the navel.) When a boxer is knocked down and does not get up within ten seconds, counted by the referee, he loses the contest and he can also be counted out if he is hanging or leaning helpless on the ropes of the ring. This is popularly known as a knock-out. (A boxer is considered down when any part of his body other than his feet is touching the floor.) If a boxer is obviously much better than his opponent, the referee may stop the bout.

Certain blows are forbidden in boxing and are fouls. Hitting with the open glove—for example, with the palm of the hand—is not allowed, neither are punches over the kidneys nor on the back of the neck nor backhanded blows. Naturally a punch below the belt or hitting a man when he is down is a foul.

The stance the boxer takes up is most important, for the power and speed of his attack and defence depend on his balance and readiness to move. It is essential to remember that footwork must be purposeful: that is, every movement of the feet must have a purpose. The boxer should move only to get into a better position to deliver a blow, or to avoid the opponent's attack, or to deceive the opponent about what he is going to do by "feint", or pretence, moves. Good footwork means that the boxer is always near enough to deliver a punch yet just far enough away to be able to draw back and avoid a blow in return.

In order to achieve this, the boxer's stance

should be relaxed. The right foot should be off-set to the right with the left foot a little forward. The toes of both feet should be pointing slightly to the right, so as to present the left side of the body to the opponent. The boxer should "feel" the floor with the balls of his feet. His left arm should be up and forward, with the fist loosely clenched about on a level with the chin. The right arm should also be up, guarding the body, with the fist even more loosely clenched, again about chin level and about six inches from it. Both elbows should be kept in, to guard the body better, and the chin should be tucked down into the left shoulder. To make it easier to draw back from an opponent's blow without loss of balance, the boxer should lean slightly forward from the waist. He should move like an alert and stealthy cat. This is known as the "English" or orthodox style. A boxer whose stance is exactly the reverse—that is, with his right foot forward—has what is known as a "southpaw" stance.

Correct punching is essential. The boxer's fist must be clenched firmly in the glove when delivering a blow. The fingers should be closed and

the thumb should be across the joints of the first two or three fingers.

There are two main kinds of punches in boxing—"straights" and "hooks". A "jab" is a short straight punch and an "uppercut" is an upward hook. In delivering a "swing", a boxer should turn his wrist to make sure the blow is made with the knuckle part of the glove.

Naturally a good defence is extremely important. To defend himself, a boxer tries to prevent his opponent's blows from being effective and he does this by guarding his own body, turning or keeping off the blows with his hands and arms, or making them miss by ducking or, moving out of range. "Active defence" is the thing to aim at—this means that the defensive action should leave the boxer all set for a counter punch. That is the way to return the attack and control the bout.

The Spirit of the Contest

The young boxer will one day find himself in the ring, waiting for his first round of competitive boxing, with his second there to encourage and support him. A boxer's second may give him advice between rounds and give him any attention needed at the same time, such as a mouth wash of water. An assistant second may also act, but he may not advise or coach the boxer or enter the ring. No advice or coaching is allowed during the actual boxing. Also to encourage him he has the knowledge of the traditions of boxing, his sound basic skill and a well-trained body and sturdy spirit. He is probably a little nervous, but this merely means that he is really keyed up for the contest. He must shake hands with his opponent before the contest begins and again after the winner has been announced. He must retire to a neutral corner if his opponent is down and must not start boxing again until told to do so by the referee. He should never take unfair advantage of his opponent. He should be a modest winner and a generous loser.

The ancient Greeks and Romans practised a kind of fist fighting as a sport, but it was in London that boxing really began. In 1719 James Figg, a wandering fairground showman, proclaimed himself champion and set up an arena in the Tottenham Court Road, where he gave

Courtesy, B. T. Batsford Ltd.
By the end of the 18th century, boxers were using skill as well as weight and hitting power. This illustration, from an old engraving, shows the final fight between Daniel Mendoza (shown on the left) and Richard Humphries in London in 1790. Mendoza won after 72 rounds.

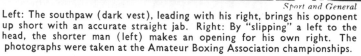

Left: The southpaw (dark vest), leading with his right, brings his opponent up short with an accurate straight jab. Right: By "slipping" a left to the head, the shorter man (left) makes an opening for his own right. The photographs were taken at the Amateur Boxing Association championships.

Sport and General

lessons, challenged all comers to fight him and showed a rough type of boxing with bare fists. For this sort of prize-fighting, as it was called, there were at first no rules—biting, kicking and throwing an opponent to the ground were not forbidden. One of Figg's pupils, however, a man named Jack Broughton, drew up written rules, invented boxing gloves, originally known as "mufflers", and introduced the art of guarding blows and of throwing a man skilfully in the wrestling which was allowed in the fight. Until about 1864, however, gloves were only used for exhibitions and practice and boxing matches were fought with bare fists. These fights were often very hard on the contestants and sometimes they went on for hours. For instance, one lasted for 276 rounds, and the longest on record took 6 hours and 15 minutes. Each round came to an end only when one of the boxers was knocked down or thrown; he was allowed half a minute to get up and carry on with the fight.

Prize-fighting—the prize was money—was very popular between 1795 and 1825 with all classes of people from the highest to the lowest in the land. The most popular teacher of the art was "Gentleman Jackson", who was champion from 1795 to 1800. Some of the richest and most distinguished men in England crowded into his rooms, among them the poet Lord Byron. After these years, however, prize-fighting became less and less respectable, partly because of the ruffianly crowds who followed it, partly because of the gambling that took place and partly

because some of the fights were very brutal.

In 1866 the Amateur Athletic Club was formed. Through its chief supporters, John Chambers and the 8th Marquess of Queensberry, rules were drawn up for matches with boxing gloves. All modern boxing is based on those rules.

Boxers today are put in classes according to their weight and a boxer usually competes only against a man in the same class as himself. The maximum weights of the amateur classes are:

Light Fly-weight	7 stone 7 pounds
Fly-weight	8 stone
Bantam-weight	8 stone 7 pounds
Feather-weight	9 stone
Light-weight	9 stone 7 pounds
Light Welter-weight	10 stone
Welter-weight	10 stone 8 pounds
Light Middle-weight	11 stone 2 pounds
Middle-weight	11 stone 11 pounds
Light Heavy-weight	12 stone 10 pounds
Heavy-weight	Any weight

These weights apply to senior boxers (over 17 years old). For schoolboys and juniors the weight classes are different, and such boxers may not be matched if there is more than five pounds difference in weight or 12 months difference in age between them. For the rules of boxing see Volume 8.

Nowadays, the most exciting professional boxing matches are the ones between the champions of different countries and the matches for the world championships of each weight. Among the most famous modern boxers have been the

American heavyweight champions Jack Johnson, who held the title from 1908 to 1915, Jack Dempsey (1919–1926) and Joe Louis (1937–1950; see Louis, Joe). Other world heavyweight champions included Rocky Marciano (1952–1955); Floyd Patterson (1956–1958 and 1960–1961); Ingemar Johansson (1959); Charles Liston (1962–1963); Cassius Clay, later named Muhammad Ali (1964–1967); and Joe Frazier (1970–   ).

BOX TREE. This is an evergreen shrub or small tree that grows wild in parts of Europe, Asia Minor, North Africa and Central America. One of the 30 or so different kinds of box is found on a few of the chalk lands in southern

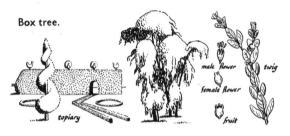

Box tree.

male flower twig

female flower

topiary fruit

England where it is thought to be wild. The most famous collection of English box trees is on Box Hill in Surrey where the trees grow to about 20 feet in height. There is another box wood at Boxwell in the Cotswold Hills and there was once one at Boxley in Kent, as the names suggest.

The leaves, which are small, dark green and shiny, grow opposite each other in pairs at frequent intervals along the branches so that the tree or bush looks very thick. For this reason box trees are often cut into all sorts of shapes when they are grown in gardens. The art of cutting trees—generally box or yew—into shapes such as peacocks and other birds and animals is called topiary. The box is sometimes grown as a tiny hedge, about six inches high, along garden paths or round flower beds.

The box flowers do not show much because they have no petals. The male and female flowers are separate but they grow together in little clusters and when they die papery pods can be seen in which the black and shiny seeds are packed.

The box tree is a very slow-growing plant, its diameter (thickness) increasing by not more than two inches in 20 years. Therefore the rings in its trunk are close together (see Tree), forming a hard, dense, yellowish timber with a fine, regular grain. For these reasons boxwood is valued for making flutes, mathematical instruments, wood blocks for engraving and the handles of tools. Most of that used is called Turkey boxwood and is grown in Asia Minor. It comes from a species (kind) of box tree much larger than the common box of southern England.

BOY-BISHOPS. A custom of the middle ages which seems strange to people now was the election of a boy-bishop in cathedral cities every year at the time of the Festival of the Holy Innocents. In England he was elected on December 6, the Feast of St. Nicholas, patron saint of children, and remained "bishop" until December 28, Holy Innocents' Day. Once chosen, the boy was dressed in bishop's robes and walked round the city, blessing the people. The "bishop" with his boy companions, dressed as priests, took possession of the cathedral and performed all services except Mass.

The custom spread from cathedral cities to many parishes. In England it was stopped in the 16th century by Queen Elizabeth I, but it remained popular in Europe, even though the church had forbidden it, and continued at Meiningen in Germany until 1799.

BOYCOTT, Charles Cunningham (1832–1897). Captain Boycott was not a very important person himself, but because of something that happened to him his name gave a new word to English and to some other languages.

Captain Boycott was an Englishman who retired from the army to become land agent for the Earl of Erne; that is, he looked after the affairs of the earl's estates in County Mayo in Ireland. In 1880 the tenants demanded to be allowed to decide for themselves what rent to pay for their farms, but Captain Boycott refused to allow this. The whole neighbourhood was on the tenants' side, and so to make Captain Boycott take notice of the demands, everyone joined together to "send him to Coventry". No one would serve him—not the shops, the laundry, the blacksmith or the post-office—and not a soul would help to gather in his harvest.

Captain Boycott hired workers from Northern Ireland to do the harvesting, but the tenants by then were so angry that it took a force of 900 soldiers to protect the hired workers from them while they brought in the crops. The harvest was gathered, but it was a defeat for Captain Boycott and a victory for the tenants, for they left him "in Coventry" and he had to give up his post and leave the district.

The word "boycott" soon began to be used everywhere for this particular kind of "sending to Coventry", a refusal to have any dealings at all, in trade or in any other way, with a person, or with a country or business. One country may "boycott" another country's goods, for instance, if it disapproves of its actions.

BOYLE, Robert (1627–1691). Robert Boyle lived at a time when many brilliant men in England were becoming interested in science and in making scientific experiments, and he himself was a pioneer in chemistry. His life was spent in

Robert Boyle's assistants at work in his laboratory.

study and scientific research and he made a number of important discoveries. He was one of a group of learned men who often met together to discuss new developments and discoveries in science; this "invisible college", as it was called, became the Royal Society in 1660.

Boyle, the son of the first Earl of Cork, was born at Castle Lismore in Ireland. When he was only eight years old he went to school at Eton and three years later he set off to travel in Europe with his French tutor. While he was in Italy he studied the work of the great scientist Galileo.

When he came home he began his own experiments. He and his assistant made an air-pump which enabled him to perform experiments with air and to discover, for example, that air is made up of several elements, or parts, and that only one part of the air—oxygen—is necessary for breathing and to allow burning.

In one of the books he wrote he stated the law (since known as Boyle's law) that the volume of a gas (that is, the space taken up by it) becomes smaller in proportion to the amount of pressure applied to it. He was the first man in Britain to make a sealed mercury barometer, and was also the first to realize the difference in chemistry between a mixture and a compound. (See CHEMISTRY.)

BOYS' AND GIRLS' CLUBS. The Industrial Revolution of the 18th and 19th centuries compelled many people to live in towns near their work. (See INDUSTRIAL REVOLUTION.) Usually they had to live in cramped back-to-back houses without gardens and with nowhere for children to play. To meet the needs of the children, voluntary organizations set up centres where young people could make good use of their leisure time, and arranged outings to places of interest and to the country.

There is still need for these youth centres and boys' and girls' clubs. Nowadays many people live in blocks of flats. Boisterous games and activities such as carpentry create a good deal of noise which disturbs the neighbours, and often the keeping of domestic pets such as dogs and rabbits is forbidden. So the children tend to let off steam by playing in the streets or by trespassing in empty houses or derelict buildings. Their need is for somewhere to meet each other outside their homes; school does not satisfy this need because it is too big and too official. Some children find it difficult to express themselves fully within their home surroundings, and the boys' or girls' club, with its different atmosphere, offers them scope to develop and to enjoy personal interests.

The keynote of a good club is involvement, which means that each member not only takes part in the activities but feels that he or she has a distinct place in them. If you visit a good club you will notice that it is not the grown-up club leader or warden who suggests all the activities but that these are planned by the members, possibly as a group or sometimes through a members' committee. The club leader therefore has a rewarding but difficult job. He or she must be ready with ideas and guidance but must not become a sort of official who is continually driving the children and saying "don't".

By making their own programme, boys and girls develop self-reliance and enterprise which will help them all through their lives to use their leisure time creatively. Again the keynote should be involvement—anything but waiting passively to be amused. The club can organize its own teams for games such as football and cricket. Table tennis is always popular, and there are many indoor games suitable for clubs. (See INDOOR AND OUTDOOR GAMES.) Handicrafts such as woodwork, leatherwork, pottery making, basket work, model making, needlework and dressmaking always attract some members, though it is not always easy to find an instructor, and the same applies to art, singing and drama. If possible, the club should make provision for members who want to use it merely for reading or studying. Members with a problem will usually find club leaders willing to advise.

From the age of about 12 young people begin to feel the need of adventurous outdoor pursuits such as camping, climbing and caving. Often the club organizes these activities and prepares members for entry for the Duke of Edinburgh's Award (see DUKE OF EDINBURGH'S AWARD). When children are developing they are working out their own adjustment to the world around them. They have emotional problems and crises which, sometimes without their recognizing it, can be overcome by playing or talking with others and by taking part in a club's activities.

Most boys' and girls' clubs are still run by voluntary organizations. Others, called Junior Clubs, are run by some local education authorities as a kind of carry-on from school life. These offer a social atmosphere and creative activities on school premises.

BOYS' BRIGADE. The Boys' Brigade was the first uniformed organization for boys to be set

Courtesy, The Boys' Brigade

The Boys' Brigade badge and initials are an important part of the organization's smart, simple uniform.

up in Great Britain as a whole. It began in Glasgow in 1883 as a company of 30 boys formed by Sir William A. Smith, its purpose being: "The Advancement of Christ's Kingdom among Boys, and the promotion [encouragement] of habits of Obedience, Reverence, Discipline, Self Respect and all that tends [leads] towards a true Christian Manliness." From that one small company the Brigade has grown into a worldwide organization with a total membership of more than 255,000 boys and officers in some 60 countries. Its patron is the Queen.

The largest unit in the Brigade is the district, and this is split into battalions and companies. A company is part of the youth work of a church or other Christian organization, and it may be made up of one, two or three sections—called Junior, Company, and Senior. Between them they have members ranging from 8 to 19 years of age. The simplest uniform consists of a cap, belt and white haversack worn with ordinary clothes but full dark blue uniform may be worn.

Each company has a chaplain, from the organization to which it belongs, a captain and lieutenants as well as other more junior officers.

Every company works in its own way, but almost all have a Bible class on Sunday and a weekly parade for activities, including drill. Football, cricket, athletics, physical training and gymnastics, arts and crafts, seamanship, swimming, life-saving, first aid and instrumental bands are other activities. Badges and awards are given for regular attendance and for skill in the various activities, the highest award being the Queen's Badge. An important event each year is the summer camp, when many thousands of boys have a happy and healthy holiday out of doors, sleeping in tents.

BRACKEN is one of the commonest types of fern and grows in almost every part of the world, from the equator to the Arctic, from America to New Zealand.

The plant may grow to a height of 2 metres or more when it is well established. The fronds (leaves) have the shape which is typical of ferns but they are not nearly so delicate as those of the smaller varieties. When the fronds die in the autumn, they become dry and crisp and their golden brown colour is beautiful in the sun.

Unlike most ferns, bracken can grow in dry places such as the heathlands of southern England, where it may cover large areas. Its success is due to the very long and deep-growing underground shoots. In some parts, particularly in the mountain pastures of Wales and Scotland, it is a serious pest because sheep and cattle hardly ever eat it and it shades out the grasses and kills them. Land covered with bracken is useless, but it is a difficult weed to get rid of. The usual way is either to plough it up in winter, so that it dies of frost, or else to keep mowing down the young fronds as they appear in the spring.

Although it is of little use as fodder, bracken can be used as bedding for cattle and was sometimes used for thatching buildings.

BRADFORD. Anyone who looks from the moors down to Bradford in the West Riding of Yorkshire must marvel at the number of people —nearly 300,000—and the amount of industry that is concentrated there. The city is still one of the world's greatest centres of wool and worsted making (there are more wool-combing machines here than in all the rest of England) but in recent times more and more of its people have been working in engineering factories.

The centre of Bradford lies in a deep valley formed by a tributary of the River Aire whose waters, after draining over the peaty soil of the moors, are so soft that they are especially suited to wool washing and other manufacturing processes. Water of the necessary softness is now brought from reservoirs in Nidderdale, but when cloth was first made in Bradford, possibly as long ago as 1311, it was the river which worked the mills and in which the wool was washed. By the end of the reign of Henry VIII woollen manufacturing was an important industry. In the 16th and 17th centuries worsted manufacture took over. The first steam-powered mill in Bradford was built in 1798.

From Bradford come women's dresses, suits for men, velvet, plush and alpaca, but above all it is the centre of the wool textile industry. Its Conditioning House is equipped with laboratories and machinery by means of which it is able to examine samples of materials with such exactness that its certificates are accepted as evidence in courts of law. Its Exchange has long been one of the world's greatest wool buying centres and it has been far-sighted enough to encourage sheep raising in distant countries.

The city is mostly built of stone which quickly turns black, but some of the public buildings are notable. The tower of the town hall is copied from a part of the Palazzo Vecchio, a palace in Florence, Italy. St. George's Hall and the public library are other fine buildings. The parish church of St. Peter became the cathedral in 1919. The Cartwright Memorial Hall, commemorating the inventor of the power loom (see CARTWRIGHT, EDMUND), is an art gallery and museum. Another museum is Bolling Hall. Among Bradford's citizens have been the composer Delius and Margaret McMillan, who started the first open air nursery school in 1914.

BRADMAN, Sir Donald George (born 1908).

The figure who dominated cricket between the years 1927 and 1948, in a way that no other cricketer except W. G. Grace has ever done, was Don Bradman. Of his 21 cricketing years, six were lost through World War II and, because of the limited number of matches played in Australia, he played only 338 innings in important cricket. Yet he scored 117 centuries—a century in every third innings—and is the only Australian player to score 100 centuries. His

Sport & General
Godfrey Evans looks on in admiration as Don Bradman pulls Compton for four in an innings of 173 not out.

batting average for his entire career was 95·14 and his highest score, 452 not out, for New South Wales against Queensland in 1929–30. In his 80 test innings he averaged 99·94 runs, with 29 centuries, and his highest Test score was 334 against England in 1930.

Bradman was a country cricketer who taught himself to play. He captained South Australia and Australia with much success. He was slightly shorter than average in height, with good shoulders, and he was always in training. He was a fine fieldsman and a fair bowler but his greatest success was as a batsman—and this was chiefly due to his immense powers of concentration. He had, too, a magnificent eye for the ball and superb timing of his strokes and was very fast on his feet. Above all, he was an attacking batsman, making his big scores far faster than any other batsman in the same class as he was. He retired from first-class cricket in 1948, after he had captained the winning Australian team in England, and was knighted in 1949.

BRAHE, Tycho (1546–1601).

Brahe, who is usually called by his first name, Tycho, was a Danish nobleman who became famous as an astronomer. In 1571 he built an observatory in his uncle's house and from there, in 1572, discovered a nova, or new star (see STAR). In 1576, King Frederick II of Denmark helped Tycho to build the fine observatory of Uranienborg on the island of Hven near Copenhagen. There Tycho worked for more than 20 years and made most of his important discoveries. However, Frederick's successor, Christian IV, did not like him, so in 1597 Tycho left Hven. In 1599 he went to Prague, where Emperor Rudolf II made him Imperial Mathematician.

Tycho was a brilliant mechanic, and his astronomical instruments were the best that had so far been made. His measurements of the positions of the Sun, Moon, stars and planets were very careful and exact although he had to do everything by naked eye, without the help of magnifying glass lenses, because the telescope had not yet been invented. Indeed, Tycho's measurements were so accurate that Johann Kepler, who became his assistant in 1600, was able to work out from them the laws of motion of the planets; that is, he was able to discover from them certain facts that are always true about the movement of the planets. These laws of motion have come to be known as "Kepler's laws" (see ASTRONOMY and KEPLER, JOHANN). After Tycho's death Kepler arranged for the publication of his work in a book called, after the Emperor Rudolf, the *Rudolfine Tables*.

Tycho lost his nose in a duel when he was 20 years old and afterwards always wore an artificial nose made of copper alloy.

BRAHMA AND BRAHMANISM. Hindu

people are divided into what are known as castes, and the highest caste is that of the priests (see CASTE and HINDUS). The priests are called Brahmans or Brahmins and therefore the Hindu religion is sometimes referred to as Brahmanism. The word Brahmans means "men learned in Brahman". Brahman is the divine spirit which, Hindus believe, fills the whole universe.

The divine spirit is hard to understand, and Hindus worship the three gods, or trinity, who represent different aspects of it. Brahma himself is the father god of the trinity, the supreme God who created the universe. The other two members of the trinity are Vishnu the preserver and

Siva the destroyer, who are constantly warring against each other. Brahma, Vishnu and Siva therefore stand for the three processes of creation, preservation and destruction that are continually going on in the universe.

The Hindu religion is founded on the Vedas, or holy books. A central belief of Brahmanism is that the Vedas were inspired by the divine spirit. The oldest and most important of the Vedas is the Rig-Veda, which is a collection of

religious poems. Vedic writings also include the Brahmana, which describe the religious practices of Hindus.

Brahmans are not allowed to marry people of lower castes or even to eat with them. Not only the priests but also the scholars of Hindu society are Brahmans. They were ministers and advisers to the kings in ancient days and today many are found in the learned professions; that is, they are lawyers, doctors, teachers and so on.

There are four stages in the life of a strict Brahman. When young, he is a student and lives with a teacher in a forest hermitage, undergoing a very thorough training in his religion. He then takes up his duties as a priest and also marries. Later he returns to the hermitage and becomes a teacher. Finally he leaves society altogether and devotes himself to prayer and meditation (thinking about God) until his death.

BRAHMAPUTRA. This great river, which

reaches the Bay of Bengal through the Ganges delta, enters East Pakistan from the Indian state of Assam, south of the Himalayas. For a long while the Indians wondered where it came from, and also whether it was fed by the Tsangpo River which rose north of the mountains, passed near the city of Lhasa, capital of Tibet, and then flowed into a part of Asia which was quite unknown to Europeans.

Many people argued that the Tsangpo, which ran eastwards, could not be the same as the Brahmaputra, for much of this flowed in almost the opposite direction. Besides, they asked, how could the Tsangpo cross the mighty Himalayas? Even if it did so, they said, it might join any one of a number of great rivers which flowed from the hidden region of Asia.

Slowly, explorers made it possible to cross off the names one by one from the list of rivers which might be fed by the Tsangpo, but it was not until 1913 that they were certain that it really joined the Brahmaputra, making it 1,800 miles altogether—longer than the Ganges itself.

North of the Himalayas, this is one of the most remarkable inland water routes in the world, for boats go up and down a stretch of about 400 miles at a height 12,000 feet or more above sea level. The boats are usually simple coracles, made of hide stretched over wooden frame-works, or large ferry boats shaped like oblong boxes. There are hanging bridges made of bamboos and, in a few cases, heavy chains. After flowing east, the river turns northeastwards, rushes through a series of immense forested gorges and then curves suddenly round to the south into the valley of Assam. It rolls majestically down the valley, round many islands, sometimes flooding its banks until it looks like an inland sea, and then flows over the Bengal plains to join the Ganges. This southern stretch is the main highway of trade between Assam and Bengal.

BRAHMS, Johannes (1833–1897).

Radio Times Hulton Library
Johannes Brahms.

The name of the great German composer Johannes Brahms is known by all people who love music, for his waltzes for the piano, his songs, his "Hungarian Dances", for four great symphonies and many other works. Unlike many composers he did not have to suffer the bitterness of poverty and failure before winning success and admiration. From the very beginning people realized that he was a man of great gifts, although it was some time before his work became as well known as it is now.

Music was considered important in Brahms's family, for his father, who was a double-bass player of Hamburg in Germany, had twice run away from home when he was a boy to devote himself to music. By the time Johannes was ten he had already shown such promise that a famous music teacher named Marxsen realized that the boy had greatness and prophesied that one day he would be more famous than Mendelssohn. (There is an article about this composer.)

Brahms was a wonderful pianist and when he was 20 he went on a concert tour as accompanist to a Hungarian violinist named Remenyi. Just before one concert Brahms discovered that the piano he was to play was tuned too low, and so he had to put the whole of the piece of music up to a higher key as he went along ; to be able to do this without making a single mistake was quite astonishing. On this tour Brahms met Joseph Joachim, the well-known violinist, who was so impressed by his playing that he gave the young musician letters of introduction to the composers Franz Liszt and Robert Schumann. (There is a separate article on each of these composers.) Brahms himself was already composing and soon after their meeting Schumann wrote an article in which he named Brahms as the great composer of the future. After Schumann's unhappy death, Schumann's widow Clara played Brahms's first piano concerto in public for the first time, and throughout her life she continued to play his works.

From this time there were few exciting happenings in Brahms's life to disturb his composing. He held posts in Hamburg, in Zürich in Switzerland and in the Austrian capital Vienna, where he settled permanently in 1872. Here he finished his first symphony, which was at once a great success and which resulted in Brahms being hailed as a successor to Beethoven. Although he became rich and famous, however, he remained the same kind of person as he had always been—honest, sincere and plain-spoken, a little rough in his manner sometimes and with simple tastes.

As well as his three other symphonies Brahms's well-known compositions include the "German Requiem", the beautiful violin concerto, played today by all the great violinists of the world, two piano concertos and much chamber music. In much of his music, as in the Hungarian dances, he used the folk tunes (simple tunes sung by the people) that he loved. Brahms did not compose music to tell a particular story but rather to be beautiful and satisfying for its own sake.

BRAILLE, Louis (1809–1852).

The inventor of the raised-dot reading system used by the blind all over the world was Louis Braille. The son of a saddler, he was born at Coupvray, near Paris. At the age of three he blinded himself accidentally while playing with a tool called an awl taken from his father's workbench. He went to school at the institution for young blind people in Paris where he learnt to read books in large, raised capital letters. He also made baskets and played the piano, violin and organ. Later he became a master at the school and was also appointed as organist in two Paris churches.

From boyhood he was keenly interested in the problems of reading by touch and he dreamed of replacing the capital-letter system by dots which could be used for writing as well as reading. In 1819 Charles Barbier, an artillery officer, invented what he called "night writing", a system which used different combinations, or arrangements, of 12 raised dots to represent each letter of the alphabet. This could easily be written with a simple instrument and Braille seized upon the idea and experimented with it until by 1834 he had worked out his own six-dot system. The authorities frowned on it, however, and it was not until 1854 that the school adopted his system. Louis Braille had not lived long enough to enjoy his triumph, having died of tuberculosis in 1852. He was buried in Coupvray. (For the Braille alphabet, see the article BLINDNESS.)

BRAIN. A boy was once said to have begun an essay on the brain with these words : "The brain is a solid lump of nerve cells, with hair on top, an ear on each side, and ME underneath."

He made several mistakes in writing this, and one of them, although not the most obvious, was in calling the brain solid. Human beings and other animals with well-developed brains—monkeys, cats and dogs, cows and sheep, rabbits, rats and mice, for example—have hollow brains.

Before it is born, the baby animal's brain is formed from a tube of skin down its back ; the same tube forms its spinal cord, which is really part of the brain and nervous system. As the little animal grows, this tube gets thicker and knobs bulge out at the top, inside the head, and thus make the brain. This explains how there comes to be a tiny passage all the way up the inside of the spinal cord, opening out into much bigger holes inside the brain.

These holes inside the brain, of which there are four main ones, are called the ventricles and are all connected with each other. They are filled with a colourless, watery liquid called the cerebrospinal fluid. About one drop of new fluid is made every second by little tufts of blood vessels in the ventricles ; they make it simply by letting the watery part of the blood escape through their walls. When it comes to the fourth ventricle the fluid oozes out through a hole in its roof. This was discovered in the 19th century by a Frenchman named François Magendie and the hole was therefore called the *foramen* (Latin for opening) of Magendie.

The fluid surrounds the brain, the spinal cord and many of the nerves. It thus forms a kind of watery cushion which protects the nerve centres from shock and also acts as a support. Finally the fluid is drained back into the blood, mainly by a large vein just inside the skull.

Protection is also given to the brain by linings inside the skull. The one that actually covers the brain surface is called the pia mater and contains the blood vessels that supply the brain with blood.

As the brain is the organ that controls the nervous system, it is mostly made up of nerve fibres and nerve cells. The nerve fibres are what is known as white matter and the nerve cells form grey matter. This explains why "having no grey matter" means "being stupid".

It is partly true, therefore, to describe the brain as a lump of nerve cells, although it is soft rather than solid. The brain of a grown-up man weighs about 1·4 kilograms and there are something like 15,000,000,000 cells in it—about four times the number of people in the whole world. Other organs of the body—the liver and the lungs, for instance—also have a vast number of cells, but the brain cells are the only ones that are never all working at the same time, for each brain cell has its own job.

In human beings and other animals with well-developed brains most of the nerve cells of the brain are spread out over the outside like the rind of an orange, so this layer of cells is called the *cortex*, which is Latin for rind or bark. Each cell has tiny branches sticking out in all directions, like minute whiskers. These never touch the branches of other cells, but they come close enough for a bunch of cells to work together when necessary.

BRAIN

The brain is divided into three main parts—the *cerebrum*, the *cerebellum* and the *medulla oblongata*. The largest part is the cerebrum, or great brain, which consists of two parts or hemispheres. If the grey outer surface of the cerebrum were spread out flat, it would cover quite a large area, but it looks as though it had been gathered together by the finger and thumb into folds.

The cerebrum is made up of many areas containing cells which control the various parts of the body. For example, one area makes it possible for the head to be turned, another deals with the movements of the arms and another controls the expressions—smiles, frowns, etc.—of the face. Sight, hearing and speech are all brought about by this part of the brain. The cerebrum is also the centre of intelligence, and by means of it human beings think, learn, remember and experience those changes of mood and feeling that are known as emotions.

Below the cerebrum is the cerebellum, or lesser brain, which is much smaller than the cerebrum. It is the part of the brain that makes it possible to balance and to co-ordinate the movements, that is, make the limbs work properly with each other.

The medulla is very small. It connects the brain with the spinal cord and is very rich in nerves. The beating of the heart and the breathing movements of the lungs go on all the time from birth until death because of the medulla.

The nerve fibres of the brain run in bundles like telephone cables, carrying messages to or from all parts of the body and linking the different parts of the brain itself. The longest fibres carry messages to the muscles of the arms and legs and bring messages in from the skin, the muscles or the stomach. Other fibres carry messages from the eyes, ears and nose.

These messages have to be sorted out by the brain itself. All that a nerve fibre can carry is something like a Morse code message, made up of dots and dashes of different lengths, with different gaps between them. Dots and dashes from the eyes come in at great speed, but those from the ears or skin are slower. Of course, the messages vary and it is often necessary for the brain cells to act very quickly. For instance, the head sometimes needs to be jerked aside in less than a second when something harmful comes flying towards it. This is a strong message and a specially large number of fibres carries it.

Strangely enough, the movements on the right side of the body are controlled by the left hemisphere of the cerebrum and those on the left side by the right hemisphere. This is because the nerves leading down from the cerebrum cross from one side to the other in the medulla. (See NERVOUS SYSTEM.)

Everything that happens to a person is con-

The brain's soft tissues are easily injured and are protected by the skull and membranes. Beneath are the three main parts of the organ, the cerebrum, the cerebellum and the brain stem (medulla oblongata).

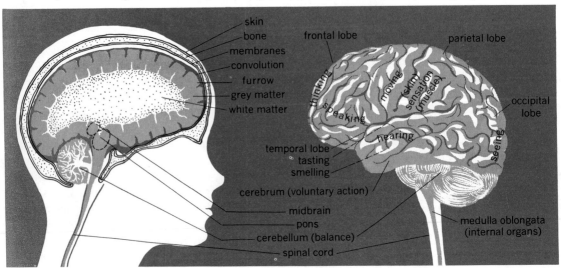

skin
bone
membranes
convolution
furrow
grey matter
white matter
frontal lobe
parietal lobe
thinking
moving
skin sensation (muscle)
speaking
occipital lobe
hearing
seeing
temporal lobe
tasting
smelling
cerebrum (voluntary action)
midbrain
pons
cerebellum (balance)
spinal cord
medulla oblongata (internal organs)

trolled by the brain. By means of it the breathing and the heartbeats continue without effort; it is possible to sit, stand or walk; the eyes can read print and the ears listen to tunes. Also, thoughts are continually going on there and memories are being stored up to be used when needed.

The human brain is probably the most wonderful object in creation. Those of even the great apes, which are the animals most like man, are so inferior that they cannot be compared with it. Generally speaking, the less intelligent the

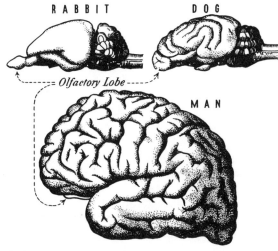

RABBIT   DOG

Olfactory Lobe

MAN

Brains vary in size, smoothness and development of regions like the olfactory lobe which controls the sense of smell.

animal, the smaller and smoother its brain is, for the actual area of the brain has a great deal to do with intelligence.

Invertebrates, or creatures without backbones, such as earthworms, spiders and flies, also have brains but these are simple and small. They also have at least one, sometimes two, spinal cords, down the front of their bodies. The brains of worms are in two lumps, above and below the mouth, joined at the sides to make a ring.

BRAKES. When speeds were low, brakes did not have to act quickly. One of the simplest and earliest types of brake was that used to stop a horse-drawn wagon. A hard wood block was applied to the iron tyre of a cartwheel by a hand lever operated from the driver's seat. The lever resulted in a greater force being exerted at the block than at the handle. Then the hand-

wheel and screw were substituted for the hand lever. The same method of braking continued for years on tramcars and railway trains. This type of brake has two metal blocks, called shoes, pressing on opposite sides of the wheel so that the force from each shoe will cancel the other and the wheel will not move. On trains today this type of brake is applied by air pressure force.

The coming of the bicycle brought the stirrup type of brake, with blocks pressed against the rim of the wheel. Modern bicycle brakes may be applied to small drums at the hub of the wheel or to the side of the wheel rims by hinged arms, or calipers, which are closed in by the pull on the brake cable.

Motor Vehicle Brakes

Motor vehicle brakes have reached a high standard of efficiency. Generally two shoes are pressed outward against the inside rim of a metal drum attached to the axle. The two shoes cover nearly the whole circumference of this rim and thus a considerable slowing-down force can be applied to each wheel. The brakes operate on all four wheels. The brakes must apply equal force on each side of the car or it will turn to the side on which the strongest force is applied. The total force on the front and back wheels must also be balanced so that the back wheels will not slide on the road with the front wheels still turning. If this happens, the car will turn right round.

Motor vehicle brakes can be operated through a system of levers and rods or cables. An alternative method of working the brakes is to use special hydraulic fluid under pressure. A small-bore pipe, filled with oil, is connected to each brake. As the brake pedal is pressed it causes the fluid pressure in a master cylinder to rise. The pressure is sent throughout the system and at each brake it enters a cylinder containing a piston or pistons which press the shoes against the drum. The shoes are "lined" with heat resisting friction material on the face which touches the drum. Brakes on road vehicles are also sometimes worked by air pressure.

In recent years developments have taken place in the design of disc brakes for motor cars. In these, a metal disc attached to the axle takes the place of the drum. Operation of the brake pedal

Above, left: Wagon brake with wooden shoe. Centre: Tramcar brake. Right: Caliper bicycle brake worked by a cable. Below, left: Motor vehicle drum brake (in the "on" position). Centre: Disc brake for a fast car. Right: Band brake.

causes the two faces of the disc to be squeezed between two friction plates. (See FRICTION.) Heat from disc brakes does not distort the disc's shape until it no longer fits the friction material of the pads. This is an advantage as lack of fit between the shoe and the drum is the main problem with the design of drum brakes.

Air Brakes on Trains

Until recently, many goods trains in Britain had brakes on the engine and guard's van only, so they needed a long stopping distance and therefore could not be allowed to go fast. But for effective braking there should be brakes on each goods wagon or passenger coach (this is called "continuous braking"), all the brakes throughout the train should operate at the same time and the driver should be able to operate them from his cab. An air-operated mechanical brake that had all these advantages was invented by the American George Westinghouse in 1869.

In the Westinghouse system an air-compressor—a form of pump—is carried in the locomotive. This supplies compressed air to an air reservoir. The compressor is automatically con-

trolled so that the pressure in this reservoir is maintained at about 90 pounds a square inch. The reservoir is connected to a pipe underneath the coaches called the train pipe, while each coach is connected to the next one by what is known as a hose pipe. Under each coach there is an air tank connected to the train pipe through a special valve which is also connected to the brake cylinder. Compressed air flows from the locomotive reservoir through the train pipe to the coach tank where the pressure is about 70 pounds a square inch. When the driver applies the brakes the operating valve in his cabin allows air to escape from the train pipe, thus reducing the pressure in it. The air pressing back from the coach tank operates the valve under the coach, allowing this compressed air to enter the brake cylinder. There it moves a piston to which is attached a rod. This in turn operates the levers which press the brake shoes against the wheels.

An alternative method often employed is known as the vacuum brake system. In this type of brake the air is withdrawn from the train pipe, thus creating a vacuum in it. By moving the brake lever in his cab the driver allows air to pass into the train pipe. It then enters the brake cylinder where it forces a piston upward and thus operates the brake-shoe links.

In both these systems, if any of the coaches become detached from the main part of the train the connecting hose pipe will break and, either by the escape of compressed air or by the breaking of the vacuum, the brakes will be applied automatically and the train will be stopped. The pulling of a communication cord has the same effect.

The vacuum brake system is sometimes used on road vehicles to add to the force that the driver applies to the brake pedal.

Other Uses of Brakes

Besides their use on vehicles, brakes are a very important part of many different machines. One method of braking on a crane, for example, is to fit a metal band, faced with friction material, around a drum. One end of the band is fixed and the other end is attached indirectly to a lever. In a free position the band is slack, but when the lever is pulled "on" the band is tightened on the drum.

The invention of materials which cause friction has played a major part in increasing braking efficiency. When a brake is applied, the brake and the drum become hot. A wooden brake block was quite suitable for carts which moved very slowly, but for anything moving at high speeds it would char and so be ruined very quickly. The friction materials now employed usually consist of asbestos mixed with a small amount of cotton and interwoven with fine wire or cemented together. Brake shoes or bands are usually faced with this material so that the worn fabric may be replaced instead of the whole brake.

BRASILIA is the capital of Brazil. It is a completely new city which was built on a plateau, or tableland, about 1,070 metres above sea level in the inland state of Goias. It lies 933 kilometres northwest of Rio de Janeiro, the former capital (see RIO DE JANEIRO) and more than 800 kilometres from the sea.

Brasilia was built not only to serve as the central capital of a huge country but also to en-

Syndication International

The Chamber of Deputies in Brasilia.

courage development of the rich but backward interior. Plans to move the capital inland were proposed in 1822 but no progress was made until 1956, when the government chose the site. Air photographs and ground surveys were used to study an area of over 50,000 square kilometres before the decision was taken. Climate, soil, water and power supply, transport and scenery were some of the factors considered.

In 1957 a competition for the design of the city was held among Brazilians. The winning design by Lucio Costa was in the shape of a cross or like the plan view of an aeroplane. Along the fuselage, or body of the "aeroplane" Costa planned government buildings, banks, theatres, cinemas and broadcasting stations, with blocks of flats, hotels, churches and embassies on the "wings". The design of the chief buildings was entrusted to the Brazilian architect Oscar Niemeyer. He designed the Presidential Palace, the Plaza of the Three Powers (government offices), the cathedral, the National Congress (parliament) building, the Foreign Office and the Brasilia Hotel.

Building went ahead swiftly—the stones for the Presidential Palace were brought by air— and Brasilia officially became the capital in 1960, although the first ministry, or government department, did not move there until 1968.

Syndication International

Brasilia is a city of wide open spaces. The High Street bears little resemblance to that of any other city.

Until the rail link with Sao Paulo and Rio de Janeiro was completed most passengers travelled by air, but Brasilia is planned to become the centre of the country's road network. Already a road 2,170 kilometres long joins it with the port of Belem in the north.

The population of Brasilia, which in 1956 did not exist, is more than 450,000. Many people live in satellite towns on the outskirts developed as part of the plan for the region.

BRASS. Long ago, when the alchemists were trying to manufacture precious metals, they produced a yellow material they thought was gold. They had in fact melted together copper and zinc and obtained the alloy brass. (See articles ALCHEMY and ALLOY.)

Many kinds of brass are made now. Some contain copper and zinc only; in others there are proportions of other materials, such as tin or lead. For example:

Yellow brass: copper 30 kg, zinc 20 kg, lead 5 kg
Naval brass: copper 30 kg, zinc 15 kg, tin 0.5 kg

Red brass, gilding metal and Muntz metal are other varieties, each having its special uses. Brass founders often decide the proportions of metals in the alloy after considering the particular purpose for which the brass is intended.

Brass does not rust and it resists wear. Consequently it is particularly useful for bearings and for pumps and machine parts constantly exposed to moisture. It is easily drawn out into rods, wire and tubes, or rolled into sheets. Other important uses are for gears, propellers and scientific instruments. Brass costs more than steel but is cheaper than copper while possessing many of its advantages. It tarnishes, however, and for this reason is often plated if it is to be used in exposed or open places. Household brassware is sometimes lacquered but this spoils the natural shine of the metal. Brass is generally made in electric furnaces when the copper is melted first and the zinc, which melts quickly, is added in lump form.

Brass was not used until shortly before the time of Jesus Christ although copper and bronze had been used for thousands of years.

Courtesy, Victoria and Albert Museum
A Flemish lion-shaped brass pitcher (13th century).

Paul Popper
Gleaming brassware is a common sight in Indian bazaars. Here a young shopkeeper in Bhopal waits for customers.

The Romans may have been the first people in Europe to make brass, using zinc from the ore called calamine. The brass referred to in the Old Testament was probably bronze, an alloy of copper and tin, because tin ore was then more likely to be obtainable than zinc. In the middle ages brass became very popular for church ornaments like altar candlesticks and lecterns. Queen Elizabeth I granted a patent for the making of brass by the battery or hammering process. Rolling mills made this method obsolete (outdated).

Some Asian and African people are highly skilled in the working of brass, and few people who go to India or Morocco come away without an example of the brasswork sold in the bazaars.

BRASS RUBBING. If you put a piece of paper on top of a penny, and then scribble over it, a picture of the penny will appear on the paper, and you have then done some simple brass rubbing. Many people make brass rubbing a hobby; they make pictures not of pennies, but of the plates of brass carved with figures that are found in many English churches.

These brass plates are called brasses and they are fixed either into the wall or into the floor, in the aisles or near the altar. They are a kind of gravestone, in memory of some important person. Often the picture of a knight in armour is engraved (carved) on the brass together with that of his wife; sometimes there are other smaller figures who are the rest of the family. There are also brasses of priests and bishops, of judges and rich merchants, all wearing the sort of clothes that were fashionable when they died.

The oldest monumental brass, as these plates are called, is in Stoke d'Abernon church in Surrey; it was made in 1277. Brasses were put in churches up to the 18th century, but the best and most interesting ones are those made in the middle ages of a type of brass called "latten", which is not made nowadays. It was so hard that armour was made from it, so it must have been very difficult to engrave on it. The art of making monumental brasses began in Flanders and Germany and sometimes brass sheets were sent from abroad, chiefly from Cologne, and were then engraved by English artists. The engravers must have been very skilful, as a study of the detail in a brass will show. It may also be possible to see traces of the colour which sometimes added further decoration.

How to Make a Brass Rubbing

All you need to make a rubbing is a roll of white shelf paper; a cake of heel ball (this is a hard black wax which shoe menders use); an old *soft* shaving brush or clothes brush; and four weights or stones.

When you have found your brass and (this is very important) asked permission to make a rubbing you can begin. First, dust the brass carefully with the soft brush so that you remove all the grit from the engraved lines. Then spread the paper over it and fasten it down firmly at the four corners with the weights. Feel with your fingertips where the brass ends, and rub the heel ball lightly along the edge until the main shape begins to show on the paper. Go on rubbing over the whole plate, but be very careful where there are fine details in the engraving, such as in the joints of armour, so that they come out clearly. If you do this, you should get a perfect likeness.

Crown Copyright

Brasses like these vividly portray knights and ladies of the middle ages.

There are about 4,000 monumental brasses which still remain in English churches and rubbings made from them can be very attractive. It is easy to make them, and you need no artistic skill; nor do you need to buy expensive tools.

BRAZIL, which is the fifth largest country in the world and almost as big as the whole of Europe, occupies nearly half of South America. Lying mostly south of the equator, it touches all the other South American countries except Ecuador and Chile, and has a long sea coast where the land juts out into the Atlantic Ocean. Passengers who travel by air over north Brazil see almost nothing but forest and jungle beneath them all day long. Most Brazilians live along the coast and large parts of the interior of the country have not even been explored.

In such a vast territory there are naturally great differences in the climate. In the Amazon valley is the world's largest tropical rain forest. (See RAIN FOREST.) Here and in the northern coastal belt it is damp and tropical with temperatures of 26°C on average. Farther south, on

Brazil's great plateau, which makes up over half the area of the country, the days are hot but the nights are usually cool. Towards the Atlantic the plateau ends in mountains which slope down to the narrow, fertile coastal plains where again it is very hot and damp. South of Rio de Janeiro it becomes cooler.

The southern plateaus and the coastal regions are the heart and soul of Brazil, for there, on less than a third of the land, live nine-tenths of the people. There, too, are most of the chief cities, roads and railways which are described later on in the article.

Wild Life and Vegetation

Very few large animals are found in Brazil, but there are many of the smaller mammals and also a huge variety of birds and insects. The butterflies alone are said to number over 30,000 different species, or kinds, some of which measure 22 centimetres from wing-tip to wing-tip. The great valley of the Amazon is the richest in wild life. Here are monkeys, red deer, tapirs, jaguars, pumas, ocelots, sloths, anteaters and armadillos (most of these animals have articles to themselves). Morning and evening the parrots and macaws, in brilliant procession, fly to their feeding grounds, and humming birds are also common. Giant leeches fasten on to the unwary traveller to suck his blood, and bats by the million, some of which are also bloodsuckers, fan the night air with their wings.

The number of species of fish in the River Amazon alone has been estimated at about 2,000, though not many of these are good to eat. Many fish are found off the Atlantic coast, too, and sharks, swordfish, crabs, shrimps, lobsters and anchovies are caught in large quantities.

The Amazon basin, again, is probably the richest area of plant life in the world. Sprays of orchids hang from trees, begonias are common and masses of fallen flowers in brilliant shades of red, orange, yellow and pink cover the earth.

In the forests, which spread over about half the country, there is a wonderful variety of timber, both soft and hard. In the Amazon forest there are woods from which fine furniture is made, together with the cinchona tree from which quinine is produced, and timbo from

which an insecticide, or powder for killing insects, can be made.

Other trees and shrubs provide nuts, oils, wax and many kinds of drugs for medicines. Yerba maté, a plant which South Americans use for making tea, grows wild in the forest but is also cultivated. The rubber produced in the state of Para, in the north, is among the best in the world.

Farming, Mines and Factories

At the end of the 19th century and the begin-ning of the 20th century rubber was the chief product exported (sold to other countries). Brazil's rubber industry suffered greatly when seeds were taken from Para to the Far East, where efficiently organized rubber plantations grew up, and also when countries began to make synthetic (artificial) rubber. The principal export has for a long while been coffee, of which Brazil is the world's largest producer. Other exports are cotton, cocoa, timber, iron ore, manganese, hides and skins, rice, maize and sugar.

191

Paul Popper

Sturdy Brahma cattle are a popular breed in Brazil because they can withstand heat, cold, dampness and insect pests.

Although only a small fraction of the land is cultivated, Brazil is an agricultural rather than an industrial country. More than half of its people get their living from the raising of crops or livestock. In one part or another of such a huge country practically every crop known to man can be grown in large quantities. The coffee and cotton are grown on great plantations in the south, where also are huge pasture lands on which large numbers of cattle, sheep and pigs are raised. Crops in the south include maize and wheat. Sugar and cotton are grown in the north and south. Basic food crops include black beans and manioc (cassava). Other crops which

---

FACTS ABOUT BRAZIL

AREA: 8,511,965 square kilometres.
POPULATION: 93,204,379.
KIND OF COUNTRY: Self-governing republic.
CAPITAL: Brasilia.
FEATURES OF INTEREST: Brazil is the largest of the Latin-American republics and has a common frontier with all South American countries except Ecuador and Chile. It is a country of great rivers, such as the Amazon, the Parana, the Paraguay and the Sao Francisco.
CHIEF EXPORTS: Coffee, raw cotton, cocoa beans, iron ore, manganese, timber, hides and skins, rice, maize and sugar.
IMPORTANT TOWNS: Rio de Janeiro, Sao Paulo, Recife, Salvador or Bahia, Porto Alegre, Belo Horizonte, Fortaleza, Belem, Santos.
EDUCATION: The law requires children to attend school but it is not enforced everywhere.

---

are grown in the north and the east include cigar tobacco as well as vanilla, cacao (the tree whose seed yields cocoa and chocolate), oranges, bananas and other fruits. Rice is grown in the coastal plains. In the north-eastern part of Brazil and in other parts further to the south there are more cattle pastures.

Brazil is rich in mineral resources. The reserves of iron ore in the east (mostly in a single mountain range) are estimated to be about one quarter of the available world supply and there are enormous deposits of manganese near the Amazon mouth. (Manganese is a metal used for hardening steel.) There is not enough coal and petroleum but there are valuable deposits of bauxite (a mineral ore containing aluminium), chromium and tungsten (two more metals used in steel), tin, lead, zinc and mercury, together with supplies of asbestos, mica and a rare quartz used for electrical purposes.

Gold, platinum and silver, diamonds, topaz and other precious or semi-precious stones are found. Diamonds have been mined in Brazil for over 200 years and some of the largest gems in the world have been found there.

Besides the mineral and metal industries, which include the manufacture of pig iron and steel, other industries have been growing rapidly, helped by almost unlimited water-power for producing electricity, and most articles of everyday use in the country are now supplied by Brazilian factories, chiefly situated in the southeast especially around Sao Paulo and Rio de Janeiro. In fact Brazil probably has more factories than any other South American country. Their products include vehicles, ships, furniture, clothing, radio and television sets, paper and cement. Most of the raw materials used in the factories are produced in Brazil, but much of the coal and petroleum has to be imported from other countries, besides machinery and tools needed to equip the factories and farms. Other imports are chemicals, fertilizers and wheat.

Transport has always been Brazil's main problem. Except in the north and extreme south, the interior is cut off from the coast and the seaports by steep mountains. Because of this, roads have been built rather than railways, which are mostly in the coastal districts.

The distances to be covered are tremendous, however, and the Brazilians are among the most air-minded people in the world. Regular air services are maintained between the principal towns, overcoming the obstacles of mountain, forest and jungle.

Two of the greatest rivers of the world, the Amazon and the Parana (which is a great tributary of the Rio de la Plata), cut across the country. (See AMAZON and also PARANA, PARAGUAY AND PLATA SYSTEM.) With their many branches these rivers provide 43,000 kilometres of waterways. There is a regular service of river craft along more than half of these waterways.

The People of Brazil

The Portuguese, who discovered and colonized Brazil, gave the country its language and much else in the way of arts and sciences. Brazil is the only country in the American continent whose language is Portuguese.

The early settlers found a scattered population of South American Indians already in Brazil but they also brought in hundreds of thousands of Negro slaves from Africa. Few Portuguese women travelled to Brazil in the early days so the men married Indian and Negro women. This has brought about a considerable mixture of Indian and Negro blood in the population. Since the ending of slavery, however, the immigrants (people coming from abroad) have been almost entirely white. It is probable that about half the Brazilian population is now white, while nearly two-fifths is a mixture of white and Negro or white and Indian blood and the remainder mostly pure Negroes and Indians. Among the white people there are many Italians, Germans, Spaniards and Poles. There are also Japanese settlements.

Many of the people cannot read and write, but elementary education is now being developed, especially in the towns. The secondary school course lasts for five years, with an additional period of two years for those wishing to enter one of the universities. The country has no official religion but most of the people are Roman Catholics.

The jungle cannot be conquered and cultivated until ways have been found of making it possible for civilized people to live there. The terrible malaria and yellow fever plagues which used to afflict many of the cities are now prevented but, in spite of efforts by the government, slower progress has been made in fighting disease

Paul Popper

When coffee is harvested, the beans are thrown into the air to winnow out dust and leaves. They are then carted to the "terreiro", where they are washed and spread out to dry on a concrete floor. Girls sort the beans into different grades.

Barnaby's Picture Library

Children of many races filing out of their new school in Brasilia. This city was made the capital of Brazil in 1960.

in the country districts and in the interior. Because of the high birth rate and high death rate in Brazil, over one-half of the population is under 18.

The literature and art of Brazil is rich and varied. One of the greatest sculptors was Aleijadhino whose carvings can be seen in 18th-century churches. There have been a number of outstanding authors, poets and artists during the 19th and 20th centuries. In 1816 the Portuguese King John VI brought a group of French painters to Brazil to teach their art. In recent years Brazilian music has become popular abroad, mainly through the works of Villa-Lobos and the Brazilian dances, such as the samba. This started as a local folk-dance, becoming known to the rest of the world through the annual street carnival in Rio de Janeiro.

The Chief Cities

The city of Brasilia, which lies in the centre of Brazil, replaced Rio de Janeiro as the capital in 1960. (See BRASILIA; RIO DE JANEIRO.) Rio de Janeiro is a city which has a position of almost unequalled beauty among bays, islands and strange rounded hills that look like camel humps, while its modern architecture is one of the most elegant and imposing sights of the western hemisphere.

The city of Sao Paulo, standing 700 metres above sea level, lies to the southwest of Rio de Janeiro. It is not only the principal industrial centre in Brazil but also the most go ahead city in the country. (See SAO PAULO.)

Santos is the leading coffee port in the world; it is also the port for Sao Paulo, which is reached by road and by one of the world's steepest railways.

Farther to the north, Salvador (also known as Bahia) was founded in 1549 and was the capital of Brazil until 1763. It is now one of the best ports in South America, a centre of the cocoa trade and famous for its cigars and cigarettes.

Porto Alegre is the capital of the most southerly state of Brazil, Rio Grande do Sul. It is situated on the Lagoa dos Patos, a huge lagoon, or lake connected with the sea. It is a port for sea-going ships and a trading centre.

Recife (also known as Pernambuco) is the most important city in northern Brazil and is usually the first South American port of call for steamers from Europe. It is built in three parts—on a peninsula, an island and the mainland—connected by bridges and it is rapidly becoming the industrial centre of the north. The Portuguese named the city Recife, or reef, because of the coral reef on which the original buildings were erected.

Manaus is the only northern inland city of importance. It is situated in the jungle 1,450 kilometres up the Amazon, and many of its buildings were put up during the Brazilian rubber boom of the early 1900s.

Discovery and History

After the discovery of America, Spain and Portugal agreed to draw a line on the map to divide their possessions, Portugal taking all the territory east of the line and Spain claiming the rest. The only part of South America that lay east of the line was the "bulge" of land which is now the main part of Brazil. That is why the Portuguese established themselves in this region.

In 1500 Pedro Alvares Cabral, a Portuguese captain, sailed for the East Indies, intending to travel by way of South Africa. On this voyage, however, Cabral went so far to the west that he sighted the mainland of South America. He took possession of it for the Portuguese King and called it the Island of the True Cross. Soon the name was changed to Brazil, after the red *brasil* wood which was found there in such abundance and later used for making a red dye, or colouring matter. In 1501 Portugal sent a second expedition to the new land. In this fleet was Amerigo Vespucci, an Italian from Florence, whose name was given to the whole continent (America). From then on, Portuguese trading expeditions were fairly frequent.

The Portuguese did not start an actual colony until 1533 and gradually Brazil became a great producer of sugar, gold and diamonds. Meanwhile the Portuguese pushed westwards and extended their territorial claims as far as the Andes Mountains.

Then came the Napoleonic wars in Europe. The Portuguese royal family was driven out of Portugal by the French and fled to Brazil, escorted by British warships, arriving there in 1808. Rio de Janeiro now took the place of Lisbon as the Portuguese capital and the ports of Brazil were thrown open to the trade of the world. After the final defeat of Napoleon in 1815 the colony was raised to the rank of a kingdom, equal with Portugal. The crown could not remain permanently in exile, however, so in 1821 the King returned home, leaving his son Pedro as regent in Brazil, that is, to rule in his absence. In 1822, angered by orders sent from Lisbon, Dom Pedro proclaimed Brazil an independent country, of which he was crowned emperor. Through the efforts of Great Britain, Portugal recognized the independence of Brazil in 1825. Thus, unlike the Spanish-speaking countries of South America, Brazil secured its freedom almost without bloodshed.

Dom Pedro soon lost his popularity and in 1831 he was forced to abdicate, or give up the throne, in favour of his five-year-old son. When this boy was 15 he was crowned emperor as Dom Pedro II. He was a wise and scholarly ruler, interested in the development of his country and the welfare of his people. However, various things, among them the abolition of slavery, led

A. Costa

Salvador (or Bahia) was the capital of Brazil until 1763.

195

B.O.A.C.
The "Sugar Loaf" that overlooks the city of Rio de Janeiro.

to unrest and dissatisfaction and in 1889 Dom Pedro II, like his father before him, had to abdicate. This time the Brazilians decided to do without an emperor and made their country into a republic.

Politically, Brazil is organized in much the same way as the United States and the official title of the republic is *Republica Federativa do Brasil* (Federative Republic of Brazil). There is a congress with a chamber of deputies, representing the people themselves, and a senate which consists of representatives from each state. The president of the republic is elected for a period of four years.

President Getulio Vargas ruled as a dictator from 1930 to 1945, when he was overthrown by the army in a bloodless revolution. Brazil then returned to a more democratic system of government in which the people had some control over their leaders. In 1950 Vargas was democratically re-elected as president but committed suicide in 1954 as a result of strong criticism by senior army officers. He was followed by three more elected presidents, but the leaders of the armed forces took control in 1964.

BREAD. All peoples in all ages of the world have eaten bread in one form or another. When early man first learned to cook his food, he probably began also to make a simple kind of bread

from acorns, ground up and baked on the hot stones round the fire. Later when people began to cultivate grain crops they made flour for bread by grinding the grains of barley, millet, oats and wheat.

For countless centuries the meal or flour was obtained by crushing the grain between two stones, and in Palestine and Egypt the ancient millstones, worked by oxen, are still used by the Arabs. In Europe windmills still stand as reminders of the old method of grinding flour from all parts of the grain except the husk. (See WINDMILL.) Flour from wheat made a light-brown bread and rye flour made the black bread which came to be known as the staff of life.

In the 19th century roller mills were invented which could separate the outer covering of the grain, called the bran, from the starch inside and the "germ" which contains the vitamins. Flour made in this way produced a very white loaf which immediately became popular, though loaves of this kind do not contain all the substances from the grain which make bread such a good food. Many bakers nowadays make what is called an enriched loaf, containing extra vitamins and fats. There are also special breads made from different types of flour, such as whole meal flour, germ flour or starch free flour.

Bread at first was made in flat cakes, and contained nothing to make it rise and become light

Radio Times Hulton Picture Library
Dough being kneaded by hand before it is baked.

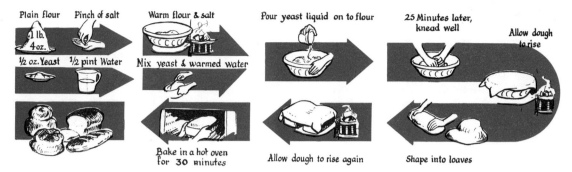

Plain flour — Pinch of salt — Warm flour & salt — Pour yeast liquid on to flour — 25 Minutes later, knead well — Allow dough to rise

1 lb. 4 oz.

½ oz. Yeast — ½ pint Water — Mix yeast & warmed water

Bake in a hot oven for 30 minutes — Allow dough to rise again — Shape into loaves

and tender like the bread of today. Any substances put in bread to make it rise are called "leaven" or "leavening", and the leaven used in most of the bread people eat now is yeast. (It is described in a separate article.) The ancient Egyptians were the first people to discover how to make bread raised with yeast. Another "raising-agent" or leaven used in some kinds of baking is baking powder.

Bread-Making at Home

To make bread using yeast needs some practice, but if the following directions are followed it should not be too difficult. It is important that the kitchen, and the bowl and tins you use, should all be warm.

To make two small loaves, or one large loaf, take the following ingredients :

1 lb. 4 oz. plain flour.	½ oz. yeast.
Pinch of salt (¼ oz.).	About half pint water.

Put the flour and salt into a warm bowl and stand in a warm place so that the flour warms a little too. Dissolve the yeast in the water, which should first be heated till it is lukewarm. Make a well in the middle of the flour and pour the yeast liquid in. Sprinkle a little flour over the top, then cover the bowl with a cloth and leave it to stand in the warm for 20–30 minutes.

Then mix the yeast and flour together with your hands to form a firm dough and knead it well until it is smooth. In kneading, fold the dough from the edge of the bowl into the centre, and keep on repeating this action, turning the bowl round a little each time. When the kneading is finished, cover the bowl again and put it in a warm place until the dough rises and becomes double the size.

Knead the dough well again, and it is then ready for shaping into loaves. For beginners a long loaf is the easiest to make. Roll out the dough into an oblong piece about ¼ inch thick, making the width equal to the length you want the loaf to be. (Use only enough flour on your board and rolling-pin to keep the dough from sticking ; a lot of extra flour spoils the bread.)

Roll up the piece of dough like a Swiss roll and put it into a warmed, greased baking tin, or on to a baking sheet, ready for the oven. It should then be left to rise a second time, covered with a warm, damp cloth.

When the dough has again doubled its size, remove the cloth and put the bread into a hot oven (450 degrees Fahrenheit) for 35 minutes. If it seems to be getting too brown, leave the oven door open a little for the last ten minutes.

When you have taken the loaf out of the oven, put it on a sieve or wire rack to cool ; if it is left in its tin the steam will make the bread wet and heavy as it cools.

BREADFRUIT. In the 17th century, explorers in the South Seas brought home to England tales of a strange melon which grew on trees and was eaten by the natives in place of bread. The Englishmen called it breadfruit and said that its soft pulp tasted like potato meal.

Natives of the Pacific Islands still depend on the breadfruit for their food, and they have many other uses for the tree. The inner bark can be made into a strong cloth, and they use the wood for furniture and for canoes, caulking (filling in) the cracks in these with a gum made from its sap.

The trees, which grow from 40 to 60 feet tall, are usually without branches for half their height. The leaves are large and glossy, with several lobes, or long and projecting tongues. The male flower is like a banana in shape and colour, while the roundish female flower head turns into a fruit between 10 to 20 centimetres across. There are two or three crops every year.

The fruit has a fairly rough rind and is at first green in colour, changing to brown and then to yellow. It is gathered before it is fully ripe and is usually baked whole and eaten as a vege-table. One method of cooking is to put heat-ed stones in a hole dug in the ground, cover them with leaves and put the breadfruit on top; after being covered over for about half an hour they are ready to eat. Cooked like this the fruit can be kept for

female flower · male flower

fruit · leaf

Breadfruit.

weeks, and it is very nourishing. Sometimes the fruit is sliced raw, dried in the sun and ground into flour to be used for bread and puddings.

The breadfruit tree has been introduced into some of the West Indian islands. (Captain Bligh was making the first attempt to take it there when the crew of his ship the "Bounty" mutinied, as described in the article BOUNTY, MUTINY OF THE.) It has spread to the mainland of America and is also found in parts of tropical Africa, but the fruit is rarely seen in Europe.

BREAKSPEAR, Nicholas (c. 1100–1159).
The only English Pope was Nicholas Break-spear. He was born at Abbots Langley in Hert-fordshire (the year is unknown) and his father became a monk in the monastery of St. Albans. Nicholas found his way to Paris and became an Augustinian friar. He was made a cardinal in 1146 and sent to Scandinavia to attend to the churches there. He returned in 1154 and was elected Pope under the name of Adrian IV.

Adrian was Pope during the time of the Holy Roman Empire when there were quarrels be-tween the Popes and the emperors as to which should have the greater power. (See HOLY

ROMAN EMPIRE.) Adrian's reign was taken up with struggles against the Emperor Frederick Barbarossa, who wished to extend his power over Italy, declaring that God and not the Pope had given him the right to rule the empire.

Adrian is remembered in his own country chiefly because he gave Henry II permission to conquer Ireland, which was still partly heathen. By order of Adrian, all parts of Ireland that became Christian were to belong to the Pope.

BREAM.
A freshwater fish of the great carp family (see CARP), the bream is found chiefly in the eastern and southern parts of Britain, but is common also in Europe. It swims in shoals and is a favourite fish with anglers. It grows large, sometimes weighing more than 6 kilograms, and can be recognized by its rather deep body on which the anal fin is much longer than the one on the back. A smaller form, the white or silver bream, which is common on the continent of Europe, is also found in parts of England.

The sea-breams belong to quite a different family, being rather like perch, with a number of sharp spines in the front part of the back fin. They have curious teeth, the front ones being pointed for biting and cutting and the back ones rounded for crushing, arranged in several rows. The red bream is the commonest British species, while the black bream visits the southern coast of England about June each year.

The sea-bream (top) has spines like a perch. The fresh-water bream (below) belongs to a quite different family.

BREATHING. Human beings, as well as all other living animals and plants, have to breathe all the time in order to stay alive. About one-fifth of the air is oxygen and four-fifths is nitrogen, and it is the oxygen that is absolutely necessary to animal life. Animals' bodies include a system, known as the respiratory or breathing system, which does the job of obtaining oxygen from the air and absorbing it into the blood. (For the breathing of plants, see PLANT.)

In man and in most of the other mammals (examples are horses, cows, dogs, cats, rabbits) the respiratory system is designed in much the same way. Air is regularly breathed in and out. When breathed out, the air contains less oxygen and more of another gas, called carbon dioxide, and water. On a frosty day the breath appears in the air like smoke. This is because the water vapour in the breathed-out air forms into tiny drops when it meets the cooler air around. There are really two kinds of breathing or respiration : external and internal.

External breathing is divided into inspiration and expiration. Inspiration means taking in air through the mouth, the nose, or both. Expiration means breathing out air which has had about one-fifth of its oxygen exchanged for an equal amount of carbon dioxide. When people use the word "breathing" in conversation they mean external breathing.

Internal breathing is what happens when the air reaches the lungs. These are two large, hollow organs and their walls are specially designed to carry oxygen to the blood and take away carbon dioxide. Once in the blood, the oxygen is taken to all the tissues of the body, where it takes part in chemical changes in connection with growth and health. When these are finished, water and carbon dioxide are brought to the lungs by the blood (which, among its many tasks, includes that of removing waste products) and finally are got rid of by being breathed out.

The External Breathing System

Air is generally taken into the body through the nose. The mouth may also be used if the nose is blocked up, as happens, for instance, during a heavy cold. The nose, however, is a better organ for this job as it warms the air and re-

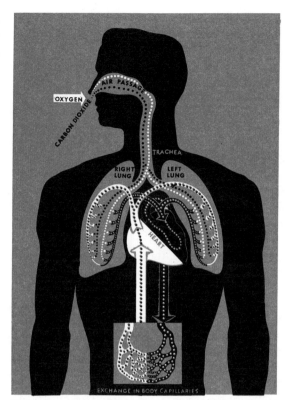

White dots show the path of oxygen into the body. Black dots show how carbon dioxide is breathed out. The exchange happens in capillary blood vessels all over the body.

moves pieces of dust or dirt that may be floating in it.

This is done by tiny hairs which catch the dirt inside the nose and by mucus, which is the slippery material made by tiny glands inside the nose. This mucus has certain germ-killing powers. At intervals the mucus increases and is got rid of in a handkerchief, that is, the nose is blown, and in this way it is kept clean inside. People who have to live or work in smoky cities collect a good deal of dirt in their noses, and at the end of a foggy winter's day their handkerchiefs may be blackened almost all over. People such as coal miners who work constantly in dust frequently get it into their lungs, as the nose cannot keep out such a large amount. (See NOSE.) This may produce chronic irritation and sometimes causes "scarring" of the delicate lining of the lungs. Different dusts produce different sorts of diseases in the lungs and the general name for all these is pneumonoconiosis. This may interfere with efficient breathing.

Air breathed through the mouth, however, is not cleaned or filtered so well, nor is it warmed. Further, breathing through the nose is quiet and when the person is asleep he does not make the loud and irritating noise that is known as snoring, caused by breathing through the mouth.

The Internal Breathing System

Having passed through the nose or mouth the cleaned and warmed air enters the pharynx, which is a passage in the neck down which both food and air pass. Just below the level of the lower jaw the pharynx divides and forms two passages, one of which carries food to the stomach while the other lets the air through to the lungs. The top of the air passage is called the larynx and it has a purpose of its own, which will be explained later. In order to prevent food from entering the lungs, a tiny flap called the epiglottis closes down like a trap-door and covers the larynx so that the food is compelled to go down its proper passage. Thus breathing stops for a second or two while food is being swallowed.

It sometimes happens that, in spite of the way the breathing system is separated from the feeding system, or alimentary canal, objects are swallowed the "wrong way" and enter air passages, even going as far as the lungs. This often happens when young children put small, hard things such as pennies or buttons in their mouths. The exact position of these objects may be found by X-rays; then tiny tubes lighted by electricity are passed down through the mouth into the breathing passages where pincerlike instruments inside the tubes make it possible for the objects to be grasped and removed. One instrument can close an open safety-pin which has been swallowed and then remove it.

The trachea, which extends into the chest, is a muscular tube along which are semicircles of cartilage, a kind of bone. The trachea is lined with a special kind of mucus and has little hairs inside it. After a chest illness such as whooping cough it can become extremely sensitive.

The trachea divides into two bronchi, or branches, each of which enters a lung. The bronchi are divided again and again into further tiny branches, the smallest of all being covered with microscopic balloons called "alveoli". These balloons and tubes, with blood vessels and a network of tissue, form the walls of the lungs.

The pulmonary artery, one of the great blood vessels from the heart, divides into two branches, each of which goes to one of the lungs. Here they divide again and again until they become the very tiny blood vessels that are known as capillaries. The oxygen breathed into the alveoli passes through their fragile walls and enters the capillaries. It is also through those walls that the carbon dioxide and water pass when the blood brings them to the capillaries. They are very light and a little like a honeycomb in appearance. Much surface space is necessary for passing oxygen and carbon dioxide through the walls, and the inner linings of the lungs, if spread out, would cover an area as large as half a tennis court.

The lungs are shaped like two cones set upright. They are situated within the ribs (the cagelike arrangement of the bones of the chest) and they fill most of the space inside the chest. In front of the left lung is the heart.

Each lung is divided into what are known as lobes. The right lung is made up of three lobes and the left of only two, since the heart takes up the space which would otherwise be occupied by a third lobe. Each lobe is covered with a skin, or membrane, called the pleura, and the entire lung is also covered with pleura. Between these two layers of pleura is a space filled with a small amount of fluid, which allows the two surfaces of pleura to slide along each other as the lungs expand and contract during breathing.

How the Lungs Work

When air is taken in, or inhaled, the lungs expand and when it is breathed out, or exhaled, they shrink or contract. They are able to do this by the movements of the diaphragm, a sheet of muscle which forms the floor of the space inside the chest. As air is inhaled the diaphragm descends, pressing down the organs beneath it. The muscles of the chest, including those between the ribs, expand and therefore the chest space is increased. The lungs are thus able to fill and take up this increased space.

When air is exhaled exactly the opposite happens. The diaphragm moves up to its original position and the space inside the chest decreases. The muscles contract, or shrink, and thus pressure is brought to bear on the expanded lungs, which send out their air.

Before a child is born it gets its oxygen from the blood of its mother and its lungs are folded up without any air inside them. With the first breath the child draws in when it is born the tissues of the lungs expand and turn red as the blood rushes in. The breathing continues steadily from that time until death, when it stops altogether. The absence of breathing is one of the first signs by which it can be known if a person is dead or not.

The action of the lungs and diaphragm can be seen by making an experiment. A large glass jar, called a bell-jar, has a piece of rubber sheeting fastened across the opening. It is then turned upside down and a tube is pushed down through a hole in the top. To this tube is fastened a small rubber balloon. The space inside the jar represents the space inside the chest ; the rubber sheeting is the diaphragm; the tube is the trachea ; and the balloon is the lungs. If part of the sheet is taken between the finger and thumb and pulled downwards, the air space is increased and the balloon fills with air. When the sheet is released the balloon collapses.

It is a mistake to imagine that the lungs are emptied completely every time air is exhaled and then filled again with new air. When a person is keeping still and breathing quietly, he exhales about one pint of air and about nine pints stay in his lungs. About a pint is taken in when he next inhales. The air given out in this way is called the "tidal" air. By taking as deep a breath as possible or by breathing out as hard as possible, five or six more pints are added. Even then the lungs would not collapse after breathing out, as about three more pints of air will still remain. This is known as the "residual" air.

By using an instrument called a spirometer, the largest amount of air that it is possible to breathe out can be measured. This is known as the "vital capacity" and it varies according to the age and size of different people. In a child the vital capacity is little over four pints. Most women have a vital capacity of about five pints and most men one of six or seven pints.

The amount of exercise taken by a person or animal makes a great difference to the breathing. For example, when an athlete is running he is using up far more energy than usual and his blood increases its speed. Therefore he needs to take in a much larger amount of oxygen. He begins by breathing more deeply at first and then, as this is not enough, more rapidly as well, until, if he runs hard enough and long enough, he ends the race with his mouth wide open, gasping and trying to take in more oxygen.

The same kind of thing happens when a person is climbing a high mountain, but for a different reason. About a mile above the earth the air begins to grow thin and contains less oxygen (see ATMOSPHERE). Therefore, even after slight exercise the climber finds himself panting and breathing hard as his body tries to take in as much oxygen as it needs.

A good example of the same process in the case of animals can be seen by watching the elephants at a circus. When they are working hard in the performance of their tricks, they have their mouths open. When they are standing at rest in a row, however, their mouths are closed.

The number of times inspiration occurs each minute also makes a difference to the amount of oxygen taken in by the lungs. Normally a newborn baby breathes about once a second. Soon this is reduced to 40 times a minute, and a youth of 15 years old will breathe from 15 to 20 times a minute, or about once every four or five seconds. The elephant breathes about ten times a minute when standing and awake and four or five times a minute when lying down. The horse does about the same. The dog's rate is 15 to 25 times a minute, the cat's 20 to 30, a sparrow's about 90 and a rat's about 100 to 200. It can be seen, therefore, that a large animal breathes slowly and a small one draws in many quick, short breaths in a minute.

During sleep, when the body is still and no energy is being used, the breathing becomes slower and more regular, and this was taken into account in submarines during World Wars I and II. The crews were encouraged to sleep a good deal in order to use as little air as possible.

Depending on the exertions he makes, a man needs between 2 and 3 pounds of oxygen daily.

He breathes out rather more than that amount of carbon dioxide. The headachey feeling you get in a stuffy room arises from too much carbon dioxide, which in cramped surroundings such as those in spacecraft must be removed from the air by chemicals.

Breath Control and Speech

Breathing is usually unconscious; that is, the air is exhaled and inhaled without the person's being aware of it. This is made possible by part of the brain called the medulla, which makes sure that breathing goes on all the time during life. (See BRAIN.) It is, however, possible for a person to stop, or hold, his breath when he pleases and also to change the rate of breathing to a certain extent. A speaker or singer learns to control his breathing in order to get just the right amount of air for making certain sounds. Certain Hindus in India practise breath control in connection with their religion, gaining this control by long practice of special exercises.

It has been found that an athlete soon learns how to manage with less oxygen than he needed at first. Thus a runner or footballer may need more oxygen when he is learning how to run or when he is getting himself trained at the beginning of a new season. Once he is in training he can get along just as well with rather less oxygen and with much less panting and gasping.

Besides the all-important purpose of keeping life in the body by adding oxygen to the blood and removing carbon dioxide, man also uses his breath to make certain sounds to form speech.

The mouth takes only a secondary or minor part in the action of breathing, being used when the nose is blocked or when an extra amount of oxygen is needed. In speech, however, it is extremely important. The entrance to the mouth is formed by the lips which, with the tongue, do most of the actual shaping of words. People who are deaf often learn to understand what is said to them by watching the movements of the speaker's lips, although they cannot hear what is being said.

Inside the lips the mouth is lined with mucous membrane. This is true of all the breathing organs, though the membrane varies in different places for special purposes. The teeth in the upper and lower jaw help with speech as well as with preparing food for swallowing. The tongue, which is a muscular organ with many blood vessels and nerves, does several things, being used in talking, in mixing food with the juices of the mouth and pushing it backwards for swallowing and as the organ of taste.

The roof of the mouth, which comes between the mouth and the nose, is mostly thin bone, covered with membrane. This part is known as

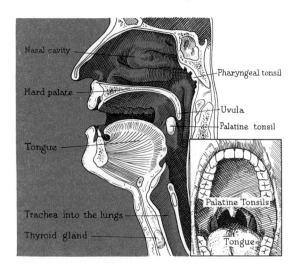

the hard palate. At the back of the mouth the bone stops and the membrane, which is moveable, becomes the soft palate. Part of the soft palate hangs down and this part is called the uvula. At the back of the mouth, just where it joins the throat, are the tonsils. All this can be seen by standing in front of a mirror, pressing the tongue down with the handle of a spoon, opening the mouth wide and saying Ah-h-h-h.

Just below the epiglottis and above the trachea is the larynx or voice box. Part of the larynx forms the small, hard lump in the front of the neck that is known as the Adam's apple. Behind the Adam's apple is a hollow, in the centre of which are two narrow shiny bands like elastic, which are called the vocal cords. Air coming up the trachea is sent between these cords, which are stretched, loosened and made to quiver, or vibrate, in different ways. Various sounds are thus formed, and in this way human beings are able to speak or sing. Animals use their vocal cords to make barks, roars and other sounds.

Diseases of the Respiratory System

Certain diseases attack the breathing organs. Usually they are infections of some kind; that is, they are caused by germs. The most common infection is of course a cold, which has the effect of blocking up the nose and forcing the patient to breathe through his mouth.

More serious infections include sinusitis, which is the inflammation of the air sinuses, or hollows, in the skull. These are found in the forehead, in the cheeks, and above and behind the nose, and they help to keep the skull light and strong. Sinusitis is caused by the infection of a cold spreading into the lining of the sinuses from the nose, and it can be very painful.

Tonsilitis is infection of the tonsils and laryngitis is any trouble that affects the larynx. (The ending "itis" means inflammation, which is of course always found in infections.) Bronchitis attacks the bronchial tubes leading to the lungs. It is usually caused by inhaling cold, damp air and if it reaches right into the lungs and affects their linings, bronchitis may become very dangerous.

Pleurisy, or pleuritis as it is sometimes called, means the infection of the pleura covering the lungs; it has several forms, one including an increase of fluid on the lungs. Another severe infection of the lungs that has several different forms is pneumonia.

One of the most serious diseases that may attack the respiratory system is tuberculosis, which at one time caused many deaths when it attacked the lungs but now, fortunately, it is possible to cure it, and it can often be checked if it is discovered early enough.

Sensible clothing has a good deal to do with breathing properly and therefore keeping the lungs in a healthy condition. At one time women wore such tight clothing that they could not breathe as freely as men. Clothing that allows full freedom of the muscles of the chest and below the chest is always best.

Breathing of the Lower Animals

It can be seen that the human respiratory system takes up very little room and several of the organs are used for other purposes as well. For instance, the nose draws in, cleans and warms the air and also contains the nerves that provide the sense of smell. However, in the case of many of the lower animals, the breathing system is much larger by comparison and may be spread all over the body.

The amoeba, which is little more than a tiny piece of jelly, has no breathing organs at all but simply soaks in dissolved oxygen from the water where it lives and gives out dissolved carbon dioxide to the water. Jellyfish and some kinds of worms breathe in and out in the same way.

The earthworm, which is a more complicated creature, has its own special kind of blood and part of the work of this blood is to carry oxygen from the skin to the internal organs and bring carbon dioxide out. The frog can breathe in a similar way with its skin, but has lungs too.

Instead of lungs, fish have fringes of blood vessels called gills on either side of the head. Water is taken in at the mouth and passes backwards over the gills, which take oxygen from the water. The blood of a fish is pumped round its body by its heart, and therefore carries the oxygen from the gills with it. The skin of the gills is so delicate that oxygen and carbon dioxide pass through both ways. The gills of fish and lobsters are well protected by lids or pouches.

In insects and spiders (whose bodies are small) breathing takes place in a most unusual and interesting manner. If these creatures are examined closely, especially on the abdomen, or belly, a large number of little openings or pores can be seen. Each of these pores is the entrance to a branching tube called a trachea. Such a system of breathing is excellent for a small creature, but in man so many tubes would be needed that there would be no room for other organs.

See also the articles on COLD, COMMON; DIAPHRAGM; HEART; IRON LUNG; LARYNX; PNEUMONIA; SINUS; SPEECH; and WHOOPING COUGH.

BRECKNOCKSHIRE or Breconshire, a county in south Wales, will join with Montgomeryshire and Radnorshire to form the new county of Powys when local government in Wales is re-organized. Brecknockshire is a mountainous county with many rivers. The highest mountains are the Brecon Beacons, which rise to 885 metres above sea-level and extend in a great wall across the southern part of the county into Carmarthenshire. In the north and north-west are mountains which join up with the Plynlimon range and those of central Wales. Between these and the Brecon Beacons there is a group of smaller hills called Mynydd Epynt. Along the eastern boundary another range, the Black Mountains, rises to a height of 810 metres.

The River Usk, which is the principal river of the county, flows from west to east in a broad valley between the Brecon Beacons and Mynydd Epynt, and then southeast towards the sea at Newport in Monmouthshire. The River Wye forms the county boundary in the northeast, while there are many other smaller rivers.

The valleys in which the main rivers flow are all fertile and fairly well wooded, with good pastures for cattle, while on the hills many sheep are bred. Near Brecon there is a fine natural lake, known as Llyn Syfaddan or Llangorse Lake, where a great many wild birds can be seen.

Much of Brecknockshire's soil is red because glaciers in the Ice Age wore away the land surface and exposed the red sandstone beneath the mountains. In the south and southwest of the county there are some exciting caves; they were caused by water flowing through the limestone rocks forming some of the mountains in this area. The limestone gorges and waterfalls in the Mellte, Hepste and Nedd valleys are very attractive.

The county is mainly agricultural except in the south, where some people in the towns of Brynmawr, Cefn Coed and Ystradgynlais work in factories, quarries and coal mines. Most of the factories make clothing, clocks and plastics. From the quarries come limestone, used for the steel industry, farming and roadmaking, and silica rock for furnace bricks. There are no coal mines in Brecknockshire now, but in the south-west at Ystradgynlais a hard coal called anthracite is still extracted by open cast methods. Small manufacturing industries have grown in the rural towns of Brecon, Builth Wells, Hay on Wye and Talgarth and employ many people who formerly worked in agriculture.

Brecon is the county town, with a large market

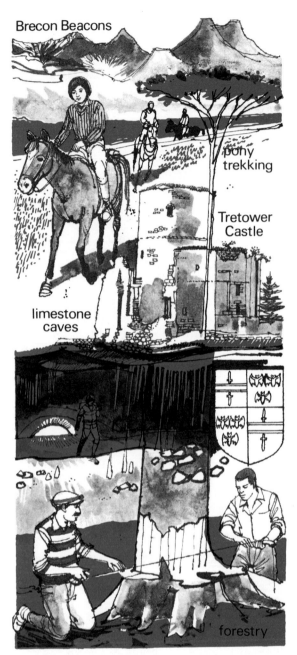

Brecon Beacons

pony trekking

Tretower Castle

limestone caves

forestry

where cattle, sheep and pigs are sold; ponies too are bred in Brecknockshire. Other market towns are Hay-on-Wye and Builth Wells. Large reservoirs (see RESERVOIR) constructed in the north and south of the county provide water for Birmingham, Cardiff, Newport, Swansea and other towns. A number of large forests have been planted by the Forestry Commission and provide pit-props for the coal mines in south Wales. In time these forests will provide large quantities of timber for manufacturing.

Because of its fine scenery, one half of the county is within the Brecon Beacons National Park and many tourists visit the area for fishing, pony trekking, boating and other pastimes. (There is an article NATIONAL PARKS.)

The museum at Brecon has many exhibits which tell something of the county's history. There is a dug-out canoe, probably dating from the 9th century, which was found at Llangorse Lake. There are stone axes, flint knives, mill-stones and beakers which belonged to those ancient people who lived in the county before the Romans came to Great Britain. Many of their graves, barrows, or tumuli as they are called, of which some are nearly 4,000 years old, can be seen in the county. There are also many camps and forts from which these ancient people defended themselves against their enemies. Near Brecon there is a famous Roman fort called "The Gaer" which Sir Mortimer Wheeler excavated in 1925–1926.

Brecknockshire was named after the Welsh Prince Brychan Brycheiniog, who lived about the time when the Romans left Britain. (Its Welsh name is *Sir Frycheiniog*.) The last Welsh prince of Wales, Llewellyn, was killed by an English soldier near Builth in 1282. Many Norman castles can still be seen and the oldest is probably the one at Tretower. Near by is one of the finest examples of a fortified manor house in the whole of Great Britain; this is called Tretower Court and its oldest parts date from about 1400. Two interesting buildings at Brecon are the cathedral, which dates from Norman times, and Newton Farm, which was built in the 14th, 15th and 16th centuries.

Famous people who were born in Brecknockshire include Dr. Hugh Price, who founded Jesus College, Oxford; Sir George Everest, after whom the world's highest mountain was named; Henry Vaughan, the poet; and the actress Sarah Siddons.

BRENDAN, Saint.

The life of Brendan the Voyager, also known as Brandon or Brandan, is more legend than history. The accounts of his voyage across the Atlantic to the "Promised Land of the Saints" were well known in Europe during the middle ages; he is said to have reached America. Charles Kingsley in *The Water-Babies* tells the tale of "St. Brandan's fairy isle".

Brendan was born at Tralee in Kerry, Ireland, probably in A.D. 484, and was educated by Irish and Welsh saints. He visited Brittany in France as a missionary between 520 and 530. He founded many monasteries, of which the most famous was Clonfert in Ireland, formed in 553, and laid down very strict rules for his monks. In his old age he visited the great missionary Columba, and he died some time about 578 when he was over 90. Brendan, who is one of the most important saints in Ireland, is regarded there as the patron saint of sailors and travellers.

BRER RABBIT

is one of the animal characters in the Uncle Remus stories. These stories are old folk tales of the American Negroes which an American author, Joel Chandler Harris, collected and wrote down, and in his books they are

Radio Times Hulton Picture Library
"Mr. Fox goes a-hunting, but Mr. Rabbit bags the game."

told by the kindly old Negro slave Uncle Remus.

Most of Uncle Remus' tales are about the doings of animals such as Brer Rabbit (Brer means Brother), Brer Fox, Brer Wolf and "all de yuther creetures". They spend all their time playing tricks on one another, and Brer Rabbit, being even more crafty and clever than Brer

Fox, nearly always comes off best. One story, for example, tells how Brer Fox plans to catch Brer Rabbit at last and make a meal of him. He spreads the rumour that he is lying at home, dead. Brer Rabbit goes round to see and finds him stretched out on his bed. Is he really dead? Says the wily Brer Rabbit loud enough for Brer Fox to hear:

"Mighty funny. Brer Fox looks like dead, but yet he doesn't look like a dead person. Dead folks lift their hind legs and hollas 'wahoo' when a man's come to see them."

Sure enough, Brer Fox lifted up his foot and holla'd "wahoo".

Then Brer Rabbit, he tore out of the house.

Many times Brer Rabbit outwits the other animals, but he meets his match at last in the race with Brer Tarrypin. Brer Tarrypin—a terrapin is a kind of tortoise—manages to be first at the winning-post by a trick as clever as any of Brer Rabbit's.

BRICK. Good bricks are the most lasting of man-made building materials; they are not much affected by the weather and if a building catches fire, brickwork resists the effects of fire longer than any other normal construction.

Bricks made from clay have been used for building for over 5,000 years. It is that time since Sumerian and Chaldean peoples used bricks for their cities in Mesopotamia and probably even longer since they were used in the Indus valley in India. A wall painting in an Egyptian tomb shows scenes in a brickyard that existed more than 3,000 years ago. In this picture, some of the workmen carry the clay and the water while others have armfuls of straw. Men mix the straw and mud by trampling it with bare feet. Next they shape the mixture in rectangular moulds

Part of a glazed brick wall built in the reign of Nebuchadnezzar of Babylon, who died more than 2,500 years ago.
The Oriental Institute, University of Chicago

and finally they carry the bricks to the drying grounds to be baked by the sun.

This was the method of brick-making which was followed by the people of Israel during their bondage in Egypt about 1500 B.C. Straw was a necessary part of sun-baked bricks for without it they would not hold together. Later, like the Babylonians and Assyrians, the Egyptians discovered that burning the clay with fire instead of baking it in the sun made the bricks so much harder and better able to withstand dampness that straw could be left out of them.

The early Chinese, Greeks and Romans knew the art of brickmaking and the Romans introduced it into England when they came in A.D. 43. Bricks ceased to be made in Britain about the end of the 4th century, and brickmaking did not begin again until the 14th century. Until the Great Fire of London in 1666 buildings with wooden frameworks were common, but after the fire London buildings were usually built with walls of brick or stone. After 1918 building in stone became costly and for almost the whole of Great Britain brick became the normal material for walls.

Moulding the Clay

The clay from which bricks are made has been formed from the natural rocks which make up the earth's crust. Earthquakes, glaciers, heat, water and frost cause these rocks to crumble slowly to form gravel, sand and clay. The clay consists of the very smallest, dust-like particles and when water is added it becomes plastic and can be moulded to shape. Clay suitable for brickmaking is found near the earth's surface in many of the lower lying parts of Great Britain and so there are brickworks to be found in many districts. In some parts a rock called shale is used. This is formed from clay subjected to great pressure underground and if ground up and mixed with water it may be suitable for brick-making.

Originally all bricks were moulded by hand from clay which had been made quite soft, and this method is still used for certain types of bricks which are consequently called *hand-mades*. Nowadays, however, bricks may be more cheaply produced by mechanical methods. Some machines press the clay in rectangular moulds producing *pressed bricks*. Another method is to squeeze a rectangular ribbon of clay from a mixing machine. Lengths are cut from it by wires in order to form the separate bricks. Bricks formed in this way are known as *wire-cuts*.

Firing

After moulding, the bricks are dried for a short time and then baked in large ovens known as kilns. Originally each kiln was a separate building and after the bricks had been stacked inside it was closed and the fires lit. The kiln gradually warmed up until the necessary heat was reached and after about two days at this heat the fire was allowed to die down and the kiln became cool enough for the bricks to be carried out. A few kilns of this type are still used, but nowadays most bricks are fired more economically in kilns consisting of several compartments connected together. The air to make the fire burn is first warmed by being passed through compartments where bricks are cooling down. After it has been through the fire it is taken into further compartments in which bricks are being warmed up. The Hoffmann kiln is the best-known kiln of this type and may have 16 to 36 separate compartments.

Another method of firing bricks which is still used to some extent in the south of England consists in building the unburned bricks into large stacks or *clamps* out of doors, the bricks being left a little apart to allow air and heat to flow through the stack. Layers of small coal and coke are included and when the stack is complete it is set burning. The fire works its way right through the stack and the bricks are fired.

The colour of bricks depends to some extent on chemicals present in the clay and also on the supply of air during burning. Iron in the clay will usually produce either blues or reds in the finished bricks. Yellows and browns are produced by lime and magnesia. Colours may also be produced by dusting the surface with various chemical substances before the bricks are fired. Surfaces of bricks may also be glazed with a white or coloured finish for use where clean, bright surfaces are required.

Large hollow building blocks, clay roofing tiles, flooring tiles, glazed tiles for walls and pipes for drainage purposes may also be made from clay by processes like those used for bricks.

Bricks are also made from a mixture of lime and fine sand. These *sand-lime* bricks are hardened in steam at a high pressure; this causes some chemical action between the lime and sand which binds the brick together. They are normally white or grey in colour.

BRICKLAYING. When a wall is built of bricks, the bricks are set in mortar. Mortar usually consists of a mixture of sand and either lime or Portland cement or a mixture of the two. Enough water is used in mixing the mortar to produce a pasty substance in which the bricks can be firmly bedded. The bricks must be carefully arranged, or bonded as it is called, in the wall in order to produce a structure of good strength and appearance, the pattern of the brickwork depending on the bond which is used.

Above: Cavity wall cut away to show the wall ties. Right: Four "bonds" used in bricklaying—English, Flemish Garden Wall (above), Flemish and Stretching (below).

The "pointing" of mortar joints to give them the colour and finish required is also given careful attention since it affects the finished appearance.

Each layer of bricks is called a course and the bricklayer has to be very skilful to keep his courses exactly level and the thickness of mortar the same throughout the length and thickness of the wall and between each course of bricks. He must also take great care to see that the corners of the walls are quite upright, or plumb.

Nowadays the outer walls of buildings are often built in two separate layers with a space of about 5 centimetres between them, the two layers being held together at intervals by small metal ties. These cavity walls, as they are called, keep out dampness better than solid walls.

When bricks are built in curves, as in arches or curved walls, the bricklayer has to shape the bricks in order to fit them together. Sometimes quite soft bricks are used; these can be rubbed on a hard stone in order to shape them accurately so that they can be built with very thin joints. Curved brickwork demands great skill.

Care must be taken to prevent the face of the

Radio Times Hulton Picture Library

The bricklayer takes care to set his bricks squarely in the mortar. Otherwise the wall will be weak and ugly.

bricks from becoming splashed with mortar; the cleanness and regularity of good brickwork do as much to make it look attractive as the colour of the bricks themselves.

BRIDGES. In spite of their great variety in appearance there are really only three different types of bridges—girders, arches and suspension bridges. We do not know which kind was made first but records exist of bridges built before 2,000 years B.C. The three types can be combined in many ways and although bridges may be made of wood, stone, bricks or iron, the materials most commonly used nowadays are concrete and steel. (See CONCRETE.)

The first beam or girder bridge was probably made by felling a tree trunk across a stream or by laying a flat stone across a narrow brook. Experience with girder bridges showed that, for a given span, a girder had to be of a certain minimum depth to make a satisfactory bridge. If this depth is greater than the size of the materials available, the girder can be made from smaller pieces called struts and ties, joined togther in a framework called a truss.

The ends of girder bridges rest on abutments, the foundations at each end, and loads on the bridge only push the abutments straight down into the ground. Loads on arch bridges tend to flatten the arch and this can become dangerous if the ends of the arch move apart. Therefore an arch bridge must have abutments at each end which cannot move apart.

The simplest kind of suspension bridges consist of twisted creepers hung across a stream and tied to tree trunks on either side of it. The creepers *pull* on the trees and in this way a suspension bridge is the opposite of an arch which, as we have seen, *pushes* on its supports.

The kind of bridge to be built at any site depends mainly on whether the ground is hard or soft, on the width and depth of the river or valley to be bridged and on the weight to be carried.

Hard ground is needed to resist the thrust of an arch or the pull of a suspension bridge and that is why these types are frequently found spanning rocky gorges; for example, the Rainbow Arch at Niagara or the famous Clifton Suspension Bridge spanning the gorge of the River Avon at

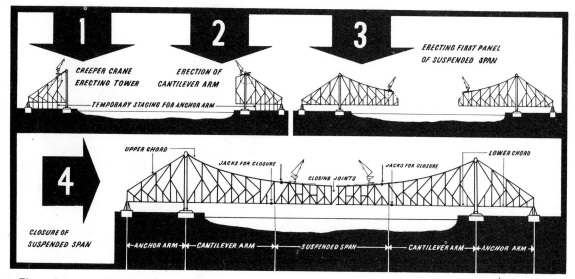

1 CREEPER CRANE ERECTING TOWER
2 ERECTION OF CANTILEVER ARM
— TEMPORARY STAGING FOR ANCHOR ARM —
3 ERECTING FIRST PANEL OF SUSPENDED SPAN
4 CLOSURE OF SUSPENDED SPAN
UPPER CHORD — JACKS FOR CLOSURE — CLOSING JOINTS — JACKS FOR CLOSURE — LOWER CHORD
←ANCHOR ARM→←CANTILEVER ARM—→←—SUSPENDED SPAN—→←—CANTILEVER ARM→←ANCHOR ARM→

The main stages of the building of the Howrah cantilever bridge at Calcutta. Its steel towers are 80 metres high.

Bristol. On very soft ground it is wiser to build a simple girder bridge, as the builders do not then rely on the ground to do anything more than support the weight of the bridge and the traffic on it. In bridges a *span* is the length between one pier, or support, and the next, and a bridge of several spans can be used across a wide river that is not too deep. If the river is very deep or the bridge has to clear the masts of ships, then a long-span high-level bridge may be needed.

Arch and girder bridges are stiffer and more rigid than suspension bridges and are better able to bear the weight of railway trains.

Foundations

The earliest wooden bridges were no doubt supported on trestles of timber *piles*, which may well have followed on the use of piles to support the buildings in primitive lake villages. Caesar's famous bridge which he built over the River Rhine in ten days in 55 B.C. was supported on timber trestles. The tops of the piles stuck up well above the water and were cut off level and capped with cross timbers which carried the logs forming the roadway.

For masonry (stone) arches other types of foundations were required and some of the oldest surviving arches were built spanning between outcrops of rock on either side of the river. When there was no rock, or when masonry piers had to

be built in mid-stream, the work could be done inside a "cofferdam". This is a timber box open at the top and bottom, made by driving piles touching each other side by side, so that they enclose the site in the river where the pier is to be built. The earliest engineers to build coffer-dams on a considerable scale were the Romans. Stones and cement mortar could then be put inside the box through the water in the hope that they would set hard to form a concrete pier. The next development was to make the cofferdam watertight and to bale or pump out the water so that the soft ground near the surface could be excavated (dug up) and the pier built in the dry. Cofferdams are still widely used but nowadays the walls are made of strong, steel sheet piling that can be driven to a depth of 25 metres.

Cofferdams have their disadvantages, however, because the piles cannot be driven very deep nor into rock or hard ground. For deep foundations under these conditions cylinders or wells have to be used. Most of the great bridges built by British engineers in India are founded on brick wells which were sunk into the sand of the river beds in the dry season. As the sand was dug or dredged out of the middle of the well the brick walls were built up above ground and the well sank under its own weight. When it had reached a satisfactory foundation, deep enough to be safe against undermining by the river, the

Top: Scottish Tourist Board. Centre: A. H. J. van der Poll. Bottom left: British Tourist Authority. Right: Ian Berry—Magnum

The Forth Road Bridge (top) was opened in 1964. Built to carry heavy traffic, it links Edinburgh with the north of Scotland. Centre: The East Scheldt Bridge crosses a span of fresh water between reclaimed land in the Netherlands delta project. Shropshire's Iron Bridge (left), built in 1779, was the first iron bridge in the world. Ponte Vecchio (above), Florence's oldest bridge, still has shops on either side of the roadway.

well was plugged at the bottom with concrete and the brick pier shaft was built on top to support the bridge.

Modern bridge cylinders are made of reinforced concrete or steel; if necessary, they have working chambers constructed at the bottom of them and are then known as caissons. (See Caisson.) Compressed air is laid on to the working chamber to prevent water from entering it and arrangements are made so that men can enter the working chamber and dig out the ground so as to sink the caisson.

Girder Bridges

One of the most famous of the early timber bridges, which was roofed-in as they used to be in those days, was the Schaffhausen Bridge over the Rhine (1755–1758), built by two village carpenters, Ulrich and Johannes Grubenmann. It had spans of 59 and 53 metres. In 1832 the first wrought-iron girder bridge was built in Scotland and some 20 years later Robert Stephenson and Sir William Fairbairn built the Britannia Tubular Bridge across the Menai Straits between Anglesey and the mainland of Wales. The trains ran through a pair of wrought-iron tubes, rectangular in section, with two spans of 70 metres and two of 140 metres. The girders of this bridge were floated out on pontoons and then lifted up bodily into place on the piers by means of huge hydraulic machines. It represented an amazing advance in bridge construction and was the forerunner of the tens of thousands of iron and steel plate girder bridges to be seen on the railways today. The trains continued to run through the tubes of this bridge until it was damaged by fire in 1970. On the reconstructed bridge the track is laid at a higher level.

The type of girder bridge suitable for long spans is known as a *cantilever* bridge. The first of the great steel cantilever bridges was the Forth railway bridge in Scotland, which was completed in 1890. It was designed by Sir Benjamin Baker, a few years after the Tay Bridge disaster (1879) when the 13 high spans, which made up more than 800 metres of the Tay Bridge, were blown down in a great gale, and more than 70 persons lost their lives. The huge balanced spans of the Forth Bridge, each 521 metres long, were de-

CANTILEVER   Forth Bridge

STONE ARCH   Wye Bridge Hereford

STEEL ARCH   Sydney Harbour Bridge

SUSPENSION   Washington Bridge, New York

LIFT BRIDGE   Newport Bridge, Middlesbrough

SWING BRIDGE   Newcastle upon Tyne

signed to withstand the fiercest storms and the bridge has an appearance of great strength.

At the beginning of the present century a new material, reinforced concrete, came into use for bridge building. Waterloo Bridge (1942) in London is a fine example of modern reinforced concrete construction; although it looks as though the bridge consists of five arches, they are really continuous cantilever spans. Grave shortages of materials during World War II led to the design of "pre-stressed" concrete bridges which require the least possible amount of steel and concrete. The longest reinforced-concrete girder span is 208 metres in the motorway bridge across the Rhine River at Bendorf, Germany. The 2,285 metre Tay road bridge opened in 1966 is a girder bridge carried on numerous piers.

Arch Bridges

In a desolate part of Spain near the Portuguese border stands a magnificent Roman arch bridge, the Alcantara Bridge over the River Tagus. Built for the Emperor Trajan, the bridge has withstood the ravages of time and floods for nearly 2,000 years. The arches are semicircular, as were all the Roman arches, and the stones of the arch ring, some of which weigh as much as six tonnes each, were so accurately shaped that no mortar was needed or used in the joints. Two outstanding bridges built in the middle ages were the lovely Pont d'Avignon in southern France and, in England, Old London Bridge with its crowded street of shops and houses. It was the first major bridge built with masonry piers in a tidal river, but nevertheless lasted for more than 600 years.

One of the most beautiful stone arches was the Santa Trinita Bridge built over the River Arno in Florence, Italy, in the 15th century. It was the first "basket-handled" arch, so-called on account of its novel and effective shape.

Arches of brick, stone or concrete have to be supported, whilst being built, on a timber framework called centering, which puts a severe limit on the length of the span. The longest span yet built in reinforced concrete is 305 metres in the six-lane Gladesville Bridge at Sydney, Australia, completed in 1964.

The first iron arch was built at Coalbrookdale over the River Severn in 1779. Since then arches of mild steel and high-tensile steel have been built of ever-increasing spans. The greatest, because of its enormous carrying capacity and the difficulties overcome in building it, is the huge Sydney Harbour Bridge (1932), designed by Sir Ralph Freeman. The arch has a span of 500 metres and carries a 17 metre-wide roadway, four railway tracks and two footpaths.

Suspension Bridges

The first major suspension bridge, designed with chains made of wrought-iron links, was the Menai Bridge built by Thomas Telford, the renowned engineer who was the first President of the Institution of Civil Engineers. The bridge was completed in 1826 and carried roadway traffic over the straits for more than 100 years until it was reconstructed in 1940.

Many of the early suspension bridges were blown down or wrecked by storms. John Roebling was the first engineer to appreciate fully the importance of stiffening them by building the roadway as a rigid girder and also by bracing the roadway with cables anchored beneath. His last great work was the design of the famous Brooklyn Bridge. This was the first long-span suspension bridge over the East River at New York and was opened in 1883. After the foundations and anchorages had been constructed and the stone Gothic towers built on the two main piers, the cables were assembled. They were made up of thousands of parallel wires, each approximately 6 millimetres thick, which were "spun" in place. This was done by carrying individual loops of wire over the span by means of a spinning wheel fixed to a hauling rope, and then attaching them to the anchorages. Experience with this method has caused it to be used to spin the main cables on most major suspension bridges. When the wires of the cables have been placed, they are squeezed together and bound round with more wire and the hangers and roadway are suspended from them. The amount of wire used may be more than 160,000 kilometres, or long enough to go four times round the earth.

The longest suspension bridge yet built is the Verrazano-Narrows Bridge (1964) across the en-

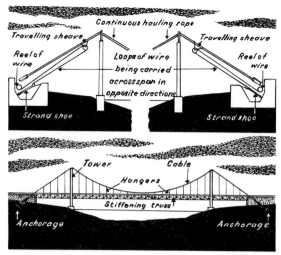

When a suspension bridge is being built, loops of wire are hauled across the span by a wheel fixed to a hauling rope.

trance to New York Harbour, which has a span of 1,298 metres between the main piers. Each of its two decks can carry six lanes of traffic. Next comes the much older Golden Gate Bridge (1937) at San Francisco, with a span of 1,280 metres.

Construction of the Bosporus Bridge in Turkey began in 1970; it is designed with a central span of 1,074 metres. An even longer span has been proposed for a four-lane bridge over the Humber at Hull: 1,396 metres. The Salazar Bridge across the River Tagus at Lisbon has a span of 1,013 metres and towers 190 metres high; it is unusual among suspension bridges because it is designed to carry a lower deck for railway tracks at a later date. The Severn road bridge (1966) has a span of 987 metres, which is only 18 metres less than that of the Forth road bridge (1964), but because of improvements in design the Severn bridge contains only about two-thirds the weight of steel in the Scottish one.

Movable and Military Bridges

Perhaps the best-known kind of movable bridge is the bascule, in which the arms are pivoted and counterweighted and can be swung upwards by means of machinery, as in the Tower Bridge in London. Another is the swing bridge, in which the opening span swings round horizontally, the two arms being balanced on a pivot, as in the Kincardine Bridge over the River Forth.

The third type is the vertical lift bridge, such as the Tees Bridge at Middlesbrough, with a span of 80 metres, which is lifted up bodily when the bridge is opened. In this type counterweights are attached to the lifting span by means of wire ropes passing over the tops of towers at either end.

For military purposes pontoon bridges are often used in which girders span between pontoons moored in the river. The most universally used military spans are the Bailey bridges invented during World War II.

BRIDGET OF KILDARE, Saint (453–523).
Bridget, or Brigit, was the daughter of an Irish chieftain and of one of his slaves, and it is said that she was sold to a wizard whom she later converted to Christianity. Bridget returned to her father, but made him angry by giving his wealth to the poor. He tried to sell her to the king of Ulster, who, however, was so impressed by her goodness that he set her free.

Bridget dedicated herself to God and founded a church and a convent at the place that afterwards became known as Kildare, "the church of the oak". It remained the most famous of the convents that she founded, and it was in Kildare that she was buried.

There are hundreds of legends about St. Bridget, who is one of the patron saints of Ireland. She is also known as St. Bride.

BRIGHT, John (1811–1889). John Bright was a great English politician who worked all his life for the things he thought were just and right. When he spoke, everyone listened, not only because he became a wonderful speaker—the greatest of his time, many people thought—but because it was clear that he meant and believed in everything he said.

John Bright was born in Rochdale in Lancashire. His father was a cotton manufacturer and when John was 16 he went into the business and eventually became a partner in it. He soon became interested in politics, however, especially in campaigning against the Corn Laws. These laws (which are described in a separate article) caused hardship to many poor people, for because of them the price of corn was kept high, and so bread was dearer than it need have been. Bright became very friendly with Richard Cobden, the leader of the Anti-Corn Law League, and largely through their work the Corn Laws were eventually repealed or done away with.

Bright was a member of parliament from 1843 to 1888. In whatever cause he supported, he was guided by three beliefs. He hated war and believed wars would not happen if countries were able to trade with each other, buying and selling without any control from governments; he believed that poor as well as rich should vote in elections; and he believed that a man should not be kept from having the kind of education and employment he wanted because his religion was not the same as most other people's. (Bright himself was a Quaker.) In parliament he showed his love of peace and justice when he spoke against the Crimean War, against flogging, against punishment by death and when he demanded a law to let Jews become members of parliament.

Bright held important posts in the Liberal governments of W. E. Gladstone in 1868 and from 1873 to 1882.

BRIGHTON is a famous seaside resort on the coast of Sussex, England. There were once Roman and Saxon settlements roughly where the town now stands and later it must have been quite a large fishing village, for the Domesday Book mentions a rent of 4,000 herrings being due on part of it. It did not start to become important as a resort until the 18th century when a doctor from Lewes persuaded many of his patients that the sea at Brighton was particularly salt and therefore good for them, whether they bathed in it or swallowed it. When the Prince of Wales, who later became George IV, began to visit the town from 1783 and built the famous Pavilion, Brighton became popular and has always remained so. In 1841 the construction of the railway line from London led to the rapid growth and development of the town. Much of the older part, with its narrow streets, can still be seen, however.

The Pavilion contains a museum and art galleries, while the nearby Dome, which used to form the stables for the Prince of Wales's horses, is used as a concert hall. On the sea front, near the eastern or Palace pier, lies the aquarium, containing thousands of living underwater specimens. The western pier is nearer Hove where there are also many hotels. Catering for holidaymakers is the main industry but there are also factories which make office equipment, automation machinery (see AUTOMATION), furniture and many other products. With its population of about 166,000 and the visitors besides, Brighton forms a large market for merchandise.

The University of Sussex is near by at Falmer.

Courtesy, County Borough of Brighton

The Royal Pavilion was built in the Indian style. Inside, some of the rooms had fantastic Chinese decorations.

BRINDLEY, James (1716–1772), became famous for planning canals in England. He was born in Derbyshire where his father had a small farm. Brindley had no schooling and, as soon as he was old enough, started work as a labourer. At 17 he was apprenticed to a millwright in Macclesfield, Cheshire, who made not only machinery for mills but any other kind for which he was asked. At first Brindley was not very successful, perhaps because no one bothered to give him much help. He was often left to carry on the business by himself while his master was away and then was blamed for making mistakes. Eventually his talents were recognized and when his master died he moved to Leek in Staffordshire at the age of 26. There Brindley set up as a millwright, making machinery for flour mills and water-driven silk mills and gained a reputation

Courtesy, Phoenix House Ltd.

Brindley astonished the people of Lancashire with the sight of canal boats passing high above the River Irwell.

for his originality and reliability.

Brindley's great chance came when he successfully drained a colliery at Clifton near Manchester by designing and building a tunnel through rock to lead the water away. A few years later he was called in by the Duke of Bridgewater to construct a canal leading from the Duke's collieries at Worsley to Manchester. This was a magnificent piece of work which he finished in two years. He carried it across the River Irwell on an aqueduct (see AQUEDUCT) 182 metres long and for a great part of its length built it between earth embankments.

This canal was such a success that Brindley was called upon to build many others. These included the Staffordshire and Worcestershire canal, the Oxford and the Chesterfield canals and also the Grand Trunk canal. This canal is now called the Trent and Mersey canal and goes through the Harecastle Tunnel, which is over 2 kilometres long. A builder of canals was called a navigator, and so Brindley was sometimes known as "Brindley the Navigator". It is from this word navigator that we get the modern slang word "navvy" which is used to mean a labourer. Brindley died in 1772, five years before this tunnel was completed.

Brindley could hardly read or write and did all his work without written plans or drawings.

BRISBANE is the capital of the state of Queensland, lying near its southeast corner, and is the third largest city in Australia. The site was selected in 1824 by the explorer, John Oxley, and was named after Sir Thomas M. Brisbane who sent a party from Sydney in the following year to establish the settlement.

Almost through the middle of the city runs the Brisbane River, whose mouth is about 22 kilometres away in Moreton Bay. From the port of Brisbane are shipped most of Queensland's exports of wool, beef, corn, dairy produce, sugar, coal and timber, and big ships can load at berths in the heart of the city. There are also two airfields. Industries include food-processing, engineering, shipbuilding, tanning, sawmilling and the manufacture of footwear, clothes, cement and motor cars. Coal is mined near by.

Brisbane has a wonderful winter climate which attracts many visitors. It has fine parks and recreation grounds and within easy reach are the Darling Downs, mountain holiday places, Pacific Ocean surfing beaches and the Great Barrier Reef (on which there is a separate article). The city has a population of nearly

Courtesy, Australian News and Information Bureau

The city hall of Brisbane with King's Square opposite.

800,000. Many of its streets are named after British kings and queens.

BRISTOL is a great seaport city on the east shore of the Severn estuary. Though it will form part of the new county of Avon, Bristol has for long had the dignity of being a county in its own right. It has more industries of greater variety, and more people—about 425,000—than any

Reece Winstone

Above: The gorge of the River Avon at Clifton is crossed by the suspension bridge built by Isambard Kingdom Brunel. The length of the central span is 214 metres. Left: The Cabot Tower on Brandon Hill was built in memory of John Cabot, who in 1497 sailed from Bristol with a crew of 18 men and discovered Newfoundland.

other place in the west of England.

The ancient city of Bristol was built on a small mound where the River Frome joins the River Avon, making a sheltered inland port which could easily be defended. One can still turn a street corner and find men loading and unloading ships, but the great modern docks are at Avonmouth, 11 kilometres away, where the Avon runs into the Severn estuary.

Bristol is connected with south Wales by the railway tunnel under the Severn. A road bridge over the Severn has been built about 20 kilometres north of Bristol. Main roads and railway lines join the city to towns in the midlands and the west of England, and the M4 motorway connects Bristol with London.

Bristol is, therefore, a great centre for the collection and distribution of goods, both those produced at home and those which come from abroad. However, its greatness is really due to the way its manufacturers have for centuries made use of the various raw materials brought from beyond the seas by the merchants. This explains the presence of the huge tobacco factories and the cocoa and chocolate factories. During the 20th century the local paper-making industry made use of imported timber, while printing grew up alongside. Similarly, it has been the hides and skins imported from abroad which have led to the development of the local shoe and leather industry.

Metal industries were started up early in Bristol, helped by the presence of lead in the Mendip Hills of Somerset and by Cornish tin; they were also greatly encouraged by the imported foreign ores. At Avonmouth there are important lead and zinc smelting works. Out of all this has grown a great engineering industry, of which the most important branch in modern times is the one producing aircraft.

Well over 1,000,000 tons of imported grain and other foodstuffs pass through the port each year and the enormous grain mills towering above the docks are a sign of Bristol's importance as a producer of flour, while there are great sheds built specially for handling bananas.

From the end of the 15th century Bristol captains and seamen played a great part in the voyages of exploration to distant countries. It was from Bristol that John Cabot sailed in 1497 on a voyage to North America and this is commemorated by the Cabot Monument on Brandon Hill. The same spirit of adventure inspired such daring Bristol seamen as Martin Pring, Captain Thomas James and many others whose names have been forgotten. These early voyages of discovery opened up new possibilities of trade for the merchants of Bristol. In the 16th century there began the trade in African slaves and in the following century thousands were carried from the Gold Coast of Africa to the sugar and tobacco plantations in the West Indies and the American colonies. The ships that carried them brought home sugar, rum (made from sugar) and tobacco. However, the slave trade was vigorously opposed by the Quakers, who had great influence in Bristol, and also by John Wesley. (See QUAKERS and WESLEY, JOHN.) It was Bristol seamanship which led to the phrase "ship-shape and Bristol fashion", meaning neat and tidy, with everything in its place.

Many of those made wealthy by the trade of Bristol have given buildings to the city or enriched others. There are almshouses founded by John Barnstaple and Edward Colston and many churches like St. Stephen and St. John on the Wall. Indeed, Bristol is famous for its churches. Elizabeth I thought the church of St. Mary Redcliffe "the fairest, goodliest and most famous parish church in England", and there is a cathedral which started as the church of an Augustinian abbey, built in the 12th century.

The new university buildings were a gift to the city by the Wills family and beside the massive tower can be found an art gallery and museum which are well worth a visit. The road opposite leads on to the suburb of Clifton and to the Clifton Suspension Bridge, spanning the Avon Gorge nearly 300 feet above the river. Beside this bridge is a *camera obscura*, made in 1829, in which can be seen the whole of the surrounding scenery. Clifton has a well-known zoo but is more important for the college whose "old boys" include such famous men as Earl Haig, a great British general during World War I, and Sir Francis Younghusband, the explorer, soldier and author. Other famous names connected with Bristol are those of Edmund Burke, its M.P. towards the end of the 18th century, and famous for his oratory, or speeches, and the great cricketer W. G. Grace, born at Downend a little to the north of the city; there are articles on both.

BRITAIN, BATTLE OF.
The Battle of Britain was the great air battle fought by the Royal Air Force against the *Luftwaffe* (the German air force) in the late summer of 1940 during the early part of World War II. After Germany had defeated France the German dictator Adolf Hitler planned to invade England, but he dared not attempt an invasion while the British air force was strong enough to destroy the German ships bringing troops and supplies across the English Channel. Hitler's aim, and the aim of the *Luftwaffe*, was therefore to crush the

British fighter force out of existence by attacking its aerodromes, radar stations (that is, bases from which the positions of approaching aircraft could be found by means of radio) and the aircraft factories. The Germans used Heinkel 111, Junkers 88 and Dornier 17 bombers, which were often escorted by Messerschmitt fighters. The British fighters opposing them were Hurricanes, Spitfires and a few Defiants and Blenheims.

Throughout July 1940 British bombers had been attacking the German invasion shipping which was gathered together in the Channel ports of northern France and British fighters had been shooting down German planes attacking targets on the English coast, but the real Battle of Britain did not begin until August 8. Seven days later, on August 15, particularly fierce fighting took place and the Germans lost 75 aircraft, the largest loss for a single day in the course of the battle. The following day, for the first time German aircraft reached the outskirts of London and for the next few days the British fighter pilots were in action almost every moment. Three fighter stations were made temporarily unusable by the Luftwaffe and three radar stations were severely damaged. There were many casualties in the 21 squadrons of No. 11 Group of the British Fighter Command and British fighter strength could be kept up only by bringing squadrons from less threatened areas as far away as Caithness in the northeast of Scotland and from the Fleet Air Arm. One Czech squadron and two Polish squadrons took part with the R.A.F., and so did a Canadian squadron. Even though the Allies' losses were heavy, on only one day did the Germans manage to inflict greater casualties than they suffered themselves.

On September 7 the main bombing attacks were shifted to London. On the afternoon of that day 300 German bombers, with an escort of 600 fighters, reached the centre of London, the only time they were able to do so in daylight. They caused heavy casualties and did much damage, but on that and several other days during the following weeks the Allied fighters made them pay heavily by shooting down over 50 German raiders. The main damage was done to the districts near the docks on both sides of the Thames. Many fires were started there and many of the people, who lived in closely packed houses and flats, were either killed or injured. Yet despite the loss of their families and homes, the people of London did not flinch and never lost their faith in victory. (See FIRES OF LONDON.)

By the end of September the *Luftwaffe* had failed both to crush the Royal Air Force and to break the brave spirit of the people. To the German commanders this meant that the chance of invading England had faded away and invasion was never again a serious danger to the Allies during the rest of the war. Heavy night attacks on London continued during the whole of the following month and until the end of the year the average number of German aircraft attacking England every night was about 200, but the actual battle to save Britain from invasion was really over by the end of October.

During the battle the Germans lost 1,733 aircraft, with another 643 damaged. The R.A.F. lost 915 aircraft, with 449 pilots killed and 450 wounded. (Many allied pilots were among them.) Among the civilians, 1,700 people were killed in day raids and 12,581 in night raids. In addition the fighter aerodromes and their warning organizations suffered badly and the squadrons were worn out with constant flying and fighting. Yet the anti-aircraft guns continued to shoot down the raiders, and the fighters never hesitated to attack the enemy.

Directing Fighter Command operations during the battle was Air Chief Marshal Sir Hugh Dowding. The main weight of the fighting was borne by No. 11 Group under Air Vice-Marshal Keith Park, and it may be truly said that during those weeks the fate of Great Britain, perhaps even of the world, rested on the shoulders of that handful of pilots.

One afternoon, at the height of the battle, Winston Churchill was in the operations room when a great force of German raiders was reported to be approaching London. The last available fighter squadron was ordered up to the attack and once more the German formation was broken up and sent scuttling back across the Channel. It was then that Winston Churchill, who was Prime Minister at the time, made the remark that best sums up the true spirit of the Battle of Britain: "Never in the field of human conflict was so much owed by so many to so few."

BRITAIN, EARLY. The story of Britain does not really begin until the time when it became an island. This happened about 8,000 years ago, in the last part of the Ice Age. The huge sheets of ice that had covered great parts of Europe for hundreds of years began to melt, and so seas grew larger and overflowed. Gradually the North Sea flowed westwards over the low swampy ground that joined Britain to the continent of Europe, until it met the waters that are now called the English Channel, and Britain was cut off. (See ICE AGE.)

In the last part of the Ice Age, the more southerly regions of Britain beyond the edge of the ice were open stretches of bare country, where a few savage hunters went after bison, reindeer, wild horses and other animals. Then as the climate grew milder, forests spread almost everywhere. At first they were pine forests like the ones that still cover many parts of northern Europe, but in time the weather became damper and oak and elm trees grew instead of pines.

So it was that when Britain became an island there were dense forests all over the country. The human hunters lived mainly on what are now heaths and moors, along the banks of rivers and lakes and by the sea. They hunted deer for meat and were skilful at shooting birds with bows and arrows. The ones who lived by the water were very cunning fishermen, using hooks, spears, nets and traps, all simply made. The rubbish heaps that some of the people who lived by the seaside left behind show that they ate huge quantities of limpets, mussels and other shell fish.

Although these hunting and fishing people lived in many parts of Britain, there were very few of them—perhaps only 1,000 or so in the whole country. (Roughly 54,000,000 people live in Britain now.) These few people did not make much difference to the look of the land; if it had been possible for anyone to fly over Britain 7,000 years ago, he would hardly have noticed the few little huts and the canoes moving on the rivers and sheltered waters near the coast. Man had hardly disturbed nature at all.

Above: City Museum, Bristol. Top right: Horniman Museum, photo C. M. Dixon. Centre right: Courtesy, Société Jersiaise. Below: Ashmolean Museum

Above: An earthenware bowl made by the farming people of the New Stone Age. It was found at Tom Tivey's Hole, in the Mendips. Top right: A polished axe of the New Stone Age, with delicately formed arrowheads from East Anglia and a spearhead from Yorkshire. Centre right: A gold torque (twisted neck ornament) made by Bronze Age craftsmen. It was found in Jersey. Below: Pottery, tools, ornaments and weapons of the Early Bronze Age.

Farmers Come to Britain

The first signs that a change was beginning came 5,000 and 6,000 years ago, when newcomers crossed the Channel to southern England, and others sailed up the coasts of western Britain and to Ireland. Their boats carried not only men, women and children, but also cows, sheep and pigs. These animals, probably with their legs tied to make sure they did not struggle about and sink the little boats, were landed safely; they were the first farm animals to set hoof on British soil. The boats must have been loaded with seed corn, too; perhaps the women looked after it, storing it in leather bags to protect it from the sea-water.

From that time to this, farming has gone on steadily, and these were the people who began in a small way to make the countryside of Britain what it is today.

In early days all changes took a very long time. There were very few workers, and they had nothing better than stone, bone and wooden tools to use against the huge stretches of forest and swamp. Because of this the farmers went to the hills and other small patches of land where the forests did not grow and where there was good pasture for the animals. Even the chalk downs then were not free from trees.

Some of the things the invaders needed most were good axes to cut down trees; they had to clear away trees from the land so that they could grow grass and corn, and they wanted wood, too, for making fences and the framework for their huts. The best material from which to make axes was the flint which lay embedded in the chalk far below the surface of the ground. To reach it, the men dug straight down through the chalk and then made tunnels along the beds of flint just as coal-miners follow the seams of coal under the ground. They did all this with picks made from antlers, and wedges and shovels made from the shoulder blades of oxen. The dark tunnels where the miners crouched struggling to lever out the big lumps of flint were dimly lit with lamps cut from chalk and filled with animal fat. Flint mines have been discovered at Grimes Graves in Norfolk, and there are many others on the Sussex downs. In the mountain country tough rocks were used to make tools instead of flint. Axes were made in large numbers at the mines and quarries, and then pedlars slung them on their backs and carried them all over the country to exchange them with farmers for their goods.

Yet some of the greatest efforts the farming people made were not in useful and practical tasks, but in building great tombs for their dead, so that the memory of them would live on. Some made immense long mounds of earth and timber, others built burial chambers from colossal blocks of stone and hid them below cairns of earth and small stones. These tombs were almost certainly more than mere burial places; probably they were places where religious ceremonies were performed, in some ways like the churches of much later times. Some of the ceremonies had something to do with the dead, and the idea that they would some day be born again; others were perhaps meant to make the corn grow and the flocks and herds increase. (The article PAGANS describes some of early man's religious beliefs.)

After about 2,000 years of toil by these early farming peoples the landscape of Britain at last began to change. Much of the higher ground, especially the chalk downs, was almost cleared of trees, and on it could be seen the marks of enclosures for cattle, burial places and flint mines. If an observer could again have spied on the island from the air, he might have been able to see huts on the hills and on the open river banks, and with his eye he might have followed the tracks that ran along the top ridges of the hills. No one could any longer mistake Britain for a desert island empty of people. (See STONE AGE.)

The Bronze-using People

It was about 2500 B.C. that new bands of invaders began to reach Britain. None of them, this time, followed the long sea route up the western coasts, but they landed at many places in the south and east. These invaders were probably a strong, warlike race who overcame the farming people and made them slaves. What perhaps helped them to do this was that they had a few tools and weapons made of bronze, which is a mixture of copper and tin, though at that time it was still so rare that only chiefs could afford to buy even small daggers and poorly made axes.

These new and energetic people who knew how to make things with metal made Britain prosperous. They mined copper in Ireland, north Wales and Scotland, and tin in Cornwall. There was also gold which could be washed from the water of streams in the Wicklow Hills in Ireland. So it is not surprising that the people of Britain built up their own metal industry, and within a few centuries they were even exporting their goods to the continent of Europe. The bronze-makers turned out strong and well-designed axes, spears, knives and daggers, and the goldsmiths made really magnificent necklets of twisted gold. Other craftsmen were skilled in designing complicated necklaces of jet and amber beads.

The clothes the bronze-users wore were made of woven wool and linen. The stone-using farmers had known how to make pottery and they had probably known how to weave, as weaving combs, but no clothes, have been found at their settlements.

In spite of the growth of these new skills and the beginning of trade with foreign countries, everyday life in Britain may not have changed a great deal. Most people still lived on the hills, kept cattle, sheep and pigs and looked after the corn crops by hand with a hoe. Cattle-breeding may have become even more important, and perhaps some tribes wandered from place to place leading their herds to good pastures, instead of living all the time in one place.

The bronze-users made one great change in Britain, however, for their religion and the ceremonies they performed were very different from those of the early farmer-people. They buried their dead under round mounds of earth, called round barrows (described in the article BARROW). These were sometimes quite large, and all sorts of food, weapons and ornaments were put in the grave to go with the dead person into his new life. Instead of holding their religious ceremonies at the burial places, as the farming people did, the bronze-users set up circles of gigantic stones or large wooden posts. Probably these circles were temples where the gods were worshipped—

gods very different from those who had been honoured at the ancient tombs. The most famous of the circles are those at Avebury and Stonehenge in Wiltshire. (See AVEBURY, STONEHENGE and also BRONZE AGE.)

The Celts Come to Britain

In about 1000 B.C., when the early farmers and their conquerors had long ago mingled together and become like one people, new invasions began. This was a time when many peoples in Europe were being driven out of their homelands by other invaders, and some of these landless peoples crossed to Britain. At various times during the whole of the last 1,000 years before the birth of Christ fresh groups of settlers reached the island. They came in at many points—east and west and north and south—sometimes having to fight for land to live on, sometimes fitting in peacefully with their neighbours who had been there for centuries.

These people are all known as the Celts, because they spoke Celtic languages—it was they who first brought to Britain the early forms of the Welsh and Gaelic languages, which some British people still speak now after more than 2,000 years. Even in England, where the speech of the Anglo-Saxons took the place of the Celtic speech, many of the names of cities, villages, rivers and mountains are from old Celtic words.

The early Celtic invaders still used bronze for tools and weapons, but later ones, after about 500 B.C., brought with them the knowledge of how to make things of iron. These later Celts—and we can now call them Britons—were very warlike. The tribes fought one another, and probably made daring raids on each other to carry off cattle, rather as the Scots and Irish did in more recent times. Their large and elaborate strongholds show that they had highly organized communities. The earth walls of these forts, overgrown with grass, can still be seen on many hills in Britain. (See FORT.) The best treasures of these British chiefs were their helmets, shields and swords and the trappings of their horses, all of them decorated with beautiful patterns.

The Britons would not have been able to afford their wars if they had not also been successful farmers. They completely changed the

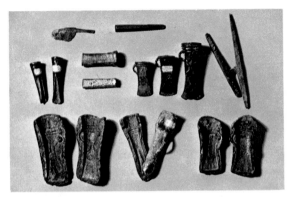

Top left: Ashmolean Museum. Top right and bottom left: Courtesy, Trustees of the British Museum. Centre: National Museum of Wales, photo Peter Boyce. Above: Guildhall Museum

Top left: Tools and moulds for casting axes, from the late Bronze Age in Britain. Top right: An Iron Age helm, dated from about 750 to 600 B.C. Centre: A reconstruction of an Iron Age chariot. It was drawn by two horses. Left: This bronze portrait of the Roman Emperor Hadrian (A.D. 76 to 138) was discovered in the River Thames. Above: A Roman silver canister, recovered from the Temple of Mithras unearthed at Walbrook in London.

old ways of farming by using ploughs drawn by oxen and by using the new iron tools such as axes, sickles and scythes to clear woodlands and open up new ground for cultivation. The earlier farmers had grown corn for themselves on little plots, and changed to new ones when the goodness had gone out of the soil. The Celts spread a permanent field system over much of the downlands and river terraces. They built round huts as farmhouses, very simple, but strong enough to stand up for hundreds of years. (See IRON AGE.)

Roman Britain

The Britons were still farming and fighting from these farms, villages and hill forts when the Roman army launched its attack on Britain in A.D. 43. The Romans had been planning to make Britain part of their empire since Julius Caesar and his army had fought in the island nearly 100 years before. Now, in the reign of the Emperor Claudius, they invaded with a strong army and within a few years they had conquered the lower parts of the country; the British tribes were enemies with each other, and did not join together against the Romans. The mountain tribes of Wales and the north held out longer, while the Scots were not conquered until the end of the first century.

Hadrian's Wall, the great stone wall that runs across the north of England from the River Tyne to the Solway Firth, still marks the frontier which long ago the Roman army held against the tribes of Scotland. The Romans also built fortresses for their legions at Caerleon, York and Chester to defend their new land against the Welsh and northern tribes. Inside these frontiers the Roman province of Britain was peaceful. The Britons gained peace and prosperity, but they no longer had their independence and the fine quality of the work of Celtic artists and craftsmen was gradually lost.

Though no one then realized what a great city London would become in the future, people came to recognize it as the capital of the province, and it was the centre of the good roads the Romans built to join up all parts of the country. (See LONDON and ROMAN ROADS.) There were Roman towns in other places, too, where the Britons could learn the civilized ways of their conquerors. Each important town had a dignified market place, a town hall, public baths and an amphitheatre where games and shows took place.

In the country villas took the place of the old rough timber farmhouses. The villas were large or small country houses which stood in well-kept farmlands belonging to the villa owners. They often had central heating, glass windows, plastered walls which were sometimes painted and floors of mosaic; that is, many small coloured stones arranged to make ornamental patterns or pictures. Most of the villa owners were Britons who after several generations of Roman rule had accepted the new way of life and begun to profit by it.

In spite of all these changes, the lives of the poorer farming people went on in the same way as before. They still lived in their huts and looked after their small fields on the slopes of the hills. The Romans did not introduce many new ideas in farming methods, but by their good management, which included large-scale drainage schemes in the Fens, the population must have increased considerably. However, when the Roman government collapsed in the 5th century A.D. the farming system also collapsed and wild animals returned to areas that had once been farmed. The Britons had to fend for themselves. For protection against raiders they hired Saxon mercenaries whom they paid in land. These early Saxon settlers took over much of Kent, Essex, East Anglia and east Lincolnshire. By 600 A.D. Angles and Saxons had taken over most of south and central Britain. They often made their homes in new areas and by the time of the Norman Conquest in 1066 Britain was a very different country. Settlement had begun to spread into the heavy clay lands that had previously been forest. (For more about these people see ANGLO-SAXONS.)

The Britons, among them the descendants of all the early peoples, lived on among the mountains of the west and the north of Britain. Even in England they survived, and mingled with their conquerors; and left the remains of their houses and fields, forts, tombs and temples. (See also ENGLISH HISTORY; IRELAND; SCOTLAND; WALES.)

☐ Read about EXPLORING ROMAN BRITAIN in the blue pages of this volume

BRITANNIA.

BRITANNIA. The figure of Britannia, which appeared on old pennies and is also on the 50 pence piece, is a symbol of Britain. Britannia is shown as a graceful woman wearing a helmet. The trident in her hand shows that she rules the waves and she has a shield with the Union Flag on it.

As a symbol of the British nation Britannia became popular after 1707, the year in which Scotland and England became united. A Scottish poet named James Thomson helped to make Britannia well known, for in a play of his performed in London in 1740 came the song "Rule Britannia!", which was at one time almost like a second national anthem. (See the separate article "RULE BRITANNIA!".)

The Britannia on coins has a long story. Britannia was the name of the Roman province of Britain, and there was a figure of a woman on the back of the brass coins of the time.

Not until Charles II's reign did the figure again appear on coins, but since then various designs of it have featured on copper and bronze coins, and occasionally on silver ones.

BRITISH ANTARCTIC TERRITORY.

This name was given in 1962 to the South Shetland Islands, the South Orkney Islands, the Antarctic Peninsula (Graham Land) and a section of the Antarctic mainland stretching to the South Pole. In 1914–1916 Sir Ernest Shackleton's expedition visited the area. During this expedition his ship "Endurance" was crushed by ice in the Weddell Sea. Later British scientific bases were set up which are now operated by the British Antarctic Survey. Parties of scientists live and work at the bases carrying out research into the geology, weather and other features of the Antarctic. (See ANTARCTIC REGION.) The territory is a British colony and is governed by the high commissioner in the Falkland Islands.

BRITISH ARMY.

BRITISH ARMY. Until 1660 there was no British army. From the 5th to the 11th centuries, under the Anglo-Saxons, anybody who owned land could be called out to defend the country against invaders and it was such a body of men, known as the *fyrd*, with which Harold defeated the Norsemen at Stamford Bridge before being himself defeated by William the Conqueror at the Battle of Hastings in 1066. Later, when the feudal system was established (see FEUDALISM), the feudal lords were responsible for providing men for the militia, the defence force which succeeded the *fyrd*. They also raised their own troops when they went on expeditions abroad. These men fought under the banner of their masters and usually wore their uniform. They formed the armies which went on the crusades and fought battles such as Crécy, Poitiers and Agincourt.

During the 16th century England began more and more to think of itself as a single nation, but oddly enough it was when the country was split in half by the great Civil War (1642–1652) that a beginning was made in building up a proper army. Oliver Cromwell realized that the untrained and ill-disciplined bands of men which made up the armies of both sides would never win a war, so he formed his Ironsides. They were the example on which he based the New Model Army, a force containing cavalry, infantry and artillery, properly trained, properly paid and all dressed in the same way—in the famous scarlet of the British army.

When Cromwell died, General George Monk marched with 6,000 men of the New Model Army from Coldstream, on the Scottish border, to London. He established order and in 1660, when Charles II was recalled to the throne, Monk's men were assembled on Tower Hill and ordered to lay down their arms as soldiers of Cromwell's Commonwealth and then to take them up again as His Majesty's Regiment of Foot Guards. They were known then, and still are, as the Coldstream Guards. New regiments were added—the 1st Foot Guards (now the Grenadier Guards) and the 1st and 2nd Life Guards, all of whom had been Royalists fighting for the king, together with the Horse Guards who had been soldiers of the New Model Army.

They were soon joined by other regiments, some returning from abroad like the 1st Foot (now the Royal Scots), which had been lent to the French King Louis XIII by Charles I, and the 3rd Foot, later the Buffs (Royal East Kent Regiment), which had been in Dutch service. There were others, like the Royal Dragoons and the 2nd Foot, later the Queen's Royal Regiment (West Surrey), which had been raised in 1662 to provide a garrison for Tangier in North Africa, part of the dowry received by Charles II when he married Catherine of Braganza. (A dowry is a present given by the parents of the bride to her husband.) From now on regiments were raised as they were needed—to deal with rebellions and the many wars in which England became involved—and were disbanded when the need passed. (There is a separate article REGIMENTS.)

Army Life in the Old Days

The British army of those days, and all through the 18th century, was very different from the army of today. Although as a whole it belonged to the king, the different regiments practically belonged to their colonels, who had been given a sum of money to raise them. Today an officer has to be trained and to pass an examination before he receives his commission, but in those days he purchased his commission and, if he wanted promotion, he purchased the rank next above his own. The officers, therefore, having spent this money to obtain their commissions, naturally wanted to get as much of it back as possible and the only way they could do so was out of the pay of the ordinary soldier. This pay was divided into two parts—"subsistence" and "off-reckonings". Subsistence money was what the soldier had to live on, but although he was supposed to have all of it the officers usually found some good reason for giving him only part. Off-reckonings were the amount left over from a yearly payment after the colonel had taken his share for the men's uniforms and one day's pay had been taken for the Royal Hospital for army pensioners. (See CHELSEA PENSIONERS.)

On top of this, the good example of the New Model Army was not followed in training and discipline, largely because regiments were hardly ever all together as units except in war. There were no barracks; instead, small parties of men were billeted, or housed, all over the country, so that they could not train together, or learn to know their officers or even do their drill in the same way. It is not surprising that recruits were hard to find or that many of them were bad characters.

However, it was this army which time and time again defeated France when that country was the greatest military power in Europe. In the type of battle fought then, the opposing armies marched in lines with bands playing and colours flying and then fired at each other until one side wavered and the other finished matters with a charge. It took courage and discipline to go through the long and complicated business of loading and firing muskets while men were falling all around, killed by the enemy infantry and artillery fire. Whenever it fought, however, whether it was in the Wars of the Spanish or Austrian Succession (1701–1714 and 1740–1748) or later in the Seven Years' War (1756–1763), the British army showed what determination could accomplish. In battle after battle, from Blenheim to Fontenoy and Minden, the British infantry behaved in a fashion which won the admiration of all Europe. British cavalry, too, became famous for the extraordinary dash it showed in charges like those at Emsdorf and Warburg.

In these battles casualties were usually heavy, but armies were small in size. Up to the time of the French Revolution not only battles but whole wars were fought on a fixed kind of pattern and with a number of well-accepted "rules". Armies fought each other during the summer and then retired into winter quarters during the bad weather, when the only men taking part in operations were those in outpost lines who watched to see that the other side did not break the rules. While in winter quarters, in whatever country it might find itself, the British army lived in very much the same way as it did at home. The men were either billeted in houses and inns or lived under canvas; they depended on the country for their food supplies and received only ammunition, arms and reinforcements from home. Nevertheless, there was a difference between home and foreign service. It was on foreign service, under such great leaders

BRITISH ARMY
from 1642 to 1775

◄1670
King's Troop of Horse Guards

▼1660
Musketeer, King's Foot Guards

▼1669
Foot Guards
Tangier

▲1642
Royalist trooper
Civil War

▲1642
Parliamentary pikeman
Civil War

◄1775
17th Light Dragoons
American War of Independence

◄1704
Foot Guards
Blenheim

▼1745
42nd Highland Regiment
Jacobite Rising

▼1756
Horse Grenadier Guards
Seven Years' War

▼1758
Light Infantry
North America

as the Dukes of Marlborough and Wellington, that the great regimental traditions and the feeling of pride in the regiment grew up, turning the army into a fighting force second to none.

New Regiments of Different Kinds

During the 18th century there were a number of changes in both the size and the structure of the British army, but in the long run it had to grow larger and more efficient as war spread farther afield and Great Britain began to have a colonial empire. Twenty-one new regiments were added in the Seven Years' War and parliament passed an Act under which every able-bodied man could be made to do three years' training. Twelve more regiments, mostly Scottish, were added towards the end of the century.

Although numbers were important, however, the most noteworthy changes were those introduced as the result of practical experience or in order to cut the cost of the army. At the beginning of the 18th century the cavalry had consisted of the "Horse" regiments, which were heavy cavalry, and "Dragoon" regiments trained to fight on foot as well as mounted. The dragoons were cheaper to maintain and so in 1746, to cut expense, all the horse soldiers except the household troops were turned into dragoons, though they were called Dragoon Guards. Ten years later light troops, specially trained in scouting and acting as outposts, were added to dragoon regiments, and later several regiments were converted entirely into light dragoons, though it was many years before they were allowed to act in war as they had been trained to do in peace.

Almost exactly the same change had taken place in the infantry. Fighting the French in the forests and mountains of North America was very different from fighting them in Europe and it became obvious that the army needed some lightly equipped men, trained in scouting and skirmishing (fighting in small parties) and chosen for toughness and intelligence. As a result light companies were added to every infantry regiment, and later some regiments were changed entirely into light infantry. Later still some of these light regiments were turned into rifle regiments, armed with muskets and dressed in uniforms of dark green which were much less easily

seen by the enemy than the scarlet coats of the ordinary infantry. They had special customs and words of command which they still preserve to this day, but rifle regiments have never had colours (special flags on which the regiments' past battles are inscribed).

As well as these changes in the cavalry and the infantry, there were two more of great importance. In 1787 the Royal Engineers were formed and in 1793 the first two troops of the Royal Horse Artillery Regiment were added to the army's slow-moving artillery, whose trains of horses had always been driven by civilians before that. However, of all the changes perhaps the most important were those made by the Duke of York, son of George III, when he was Commander-in-Chief of the army from 1798 to 1827.

The Duke of York had been on active service and knew exactly where many of the faults lay in the military system. In order to put these right he created a headquarters staff and the Staff College and he founded the Royal Military College at Sandhurst for the training of officers and also a school for the children of soldiers. Above all he tried to improve the conditions of the common soldier by providing the regiments with doctors and chaplains, by improving the way in which the army obtained and moved its supplies and by setting up a veterinary service to look after the horses. It took some time for his reforms to have much effect, however, largely because the country was then involved in the prolonged struggle with revolutionary France. The Duke of Wellington called the army he led against the French "the scum of the earth", but his soldiers deserved a better name. In Spain they were short of nearly everything—food, feed for the horses, boots, uniforms, pots and pans. They endured long periods of hardship, interrupted only by savage battles, retreats and sieges in which they suffered many casualties, and yet they fought their way through the Spanish Peninsula and eventually defeated Napoleon at Waterloo in 1815.

In spite of the great victories they had won, the old peacetime feeling that soldiers were "the scum of the earth" still remained after peace had been signed. They were cramped into dirty, unhealthy barracks in which, until 1827, each bed had to be shared by four men. They had the same small pay and they were still flogged as a punishment. They had only two meals a day and nowhere to spend their time off except the "wet canteen", where all they could do was get drunk. People said that these conditions were good enough for the bad characters who joined the army, and although some of the officers did their best for their men, few people seemed to realize that it was the conditions themselves which helped to create the bad characters. It needed another European war to show that something drastic had to be done about the whole army system. The necessary lesson was given by the war in the Crimea in 1854–1856.

Some Big Reforms

It was not a lesson in fighting that was needed, for the army had been kept in practice by the wars which took place in the 1840s and 1850s in India, New Zealand and South Africa. These wars had taught the officers and men better ways of moving against the enemy on various types of ground but gave no experience in the problem of providing the food, clothing, materials of war and hospitals required for a European war. Thus, when the British army found itself fighting in the Crimea, for every soldier lost in battle seven of his comrades died of sickness or cold, made worse by hunger. (The story of how Florence Nightingale looked after the wounded soldiers and improved conditions in the hospital at Scutari is told in the article NIGHTINGALE, FLORENCE.)

Edward Cardwell, who became Secretary of State for War in 1868, was given the task of reorganizing the army and he did it well. He increased the size of the army by recalling regiments which were guarding the colonies—some of them seemed to have been quite forgotten—and he created a real reserve of men by arranging for soldiers to be enlisted for 12 years—6 to be spent with the colours and 6 with the reserve. He also ended the buying of commissions.

His most difficult problem was how to maintain an army abroad without forcing the soldiers to spend years overseas. This he did by dividing the country into 70 districts, each with a regiment of two battalions, so that while one battalion was overseas the other could train its recruits and thus supply it with the men it needed.

At the same time other changes were taking place which improved conditions in the army. What were eventually to become the Royal Army Medical Corps and the Royal Corps of Transport were formed and the first of the great military camps like Aldershot were created (see ALDERSHOT). Most important of all was the change in the attitude of the country towards the soldier. With the better conditions offered to him, with his triumph in a multitude of tiny wars (in Queen Victoria's reign there were 40 expeditions overseas) and with the Queen herself taking an interest in his welfare, "Tommy Atkins" became a popular figure and his profession no longer one to be despised. (Thomas Atkins was the name chosen by the War Office when it issued a specimen to show how the soldier's pay would be recorded in the new pay books.)

Although a drab, or dull coloured, uniform had long been worn unofficially in hot countries, it was not till 1902 that khaki became the normal service dress. The last time the famous scarlet coat was worn in battle was in the Khartoum expedition of 1884.

From the Boer War to 1939

The army had still to learn to make the best of its new advantages. Most of all, its generals had to learn how to forget again some of the rules which had served in European wars and to adopt methods to suit the country and the way the enemy fought. This became clear during the Boer War in South Africa which, because it was being fought by the wrong methods, took two and a half years to win, from 1899 to 1902. The Boers were mounted on good ponies, had light equipment and were all excellent marksmen. Knowing that they would be defeated in open battle, they always did their best to avoid it and often slipped away from the British, who were hampered by long columns of supplies.

Many mistakes had been made in the South African War, and the government decided to improve the army. At the top it was completely reorganized, the supervision of all the armed forces being entrusted to the Committee for Imperial Defence (today, the Ministry of

Defence and the Chiefs of Staff Committee) and the command of the army being put into the hands of the Army Council, which included civilians as well as soldiers and now had a specially trained general staff to rely on. The post of Commander-in-Chief was abolished.

In 1906 Mr. (later Lord) Haldane became Secretary of State for War and he had the task of re-shaping the fighting part of the army. He decided to keep the same kind of system as Cardwell had introduced, under which one battalion in each regiment served overseas (India, Burma, South Africa or some other place) and the other was stationed at home. Those at home were organized into six infantry divisions and one cavalry division, complete with artillery, engineers and supply and medical services. It was this fine force—known as the British Expeditionary Force—which went to France in 1914 and fought so splendidly against the Germans in the retreat from Mons and at the battles of the Marne and Aisne.

At the same time the reserve forces were reorganized. The old Volunteers and the Yeomanry both went to form the new Territorial Force (renamed Territorial Army in 1921), consisting of 14 infantry divisions and 14 cavalry brigades. This force was organized on the same lines as the regular army but did its training in the evenings, at week-ends and at the annual camps. Service was for home defence only but within a few days of the outbreak of World War I in August 1914 practically every officer and man had volunteered for service overseas. During the war years, up to 1918, units of the Territorial Force served with great distinction in many campaigns—France, Palestine, Gallipoli, Mesopotamia (now Iraq) and elsewhere.

Under Lord Haldane's reforms territorial units became part of regular regiments. The old militia battalions, which had originally been trained for use when invasion threatened or actually occurred, were made into special reserve battalions to train men as reinforcements in war. Under this system most infantry regiments consisted of two regular battalions (one at home and one overseas), one special reserve battalion and as many as four territorial battalions. Each regiment recruited its men and had its depot in a particular place and many took their names from their county area—the Cheshire Regiment and the Argyll and Sutherland Highlanders for example. The method of linking together regular and territorial units was also carried out, as far as possible, in the cavalry and the artillery. This general system continued until 1967, when the Territorial Army was disbanded and regiments had been reduced to one regular battalion each.

In World War I the British army expanded to about 80 divisions. At first volunteers were called for, but in 1916 all men young and fit enough became liable for military service. This was the first war in which aeroplanes were used and as it went on many new inventions were made, such as tanks, deadlier kinds of bombs and heavier guns with longer ranges.

When the war ended in 1918 the army was quickly reduced in size to slightly below the 1914 level and both regular and territorial armies were reorganized on much the same lines as before the war. Although Great Britain had a number of small wars and there were disturbances in India, China and Palestine, nobody thought that there was likely to be another big war for many years and parliament was not willing to provide much money for the army. Consequently it had to make do with the weapons of World War I and was not able to develop many new ones. In 1933, however, Adolf Hitler and his Nazi party came into power in Germany and started rearming on a large scale. To meet this threat the British began to rearm their own forces, but at first much of the money was spent on the Royal Air Force. In the spring of 1939, only a few months before World War II began, the government introduced conscription (the first compulsory peacetime service in British history) and also doubled the size of the Territorial Army. Thus the men were provided, but most of them were untrained and the army was still short of modern tanks, guns and equipment when war broke out again in September 1939.

World War II and After

In World War II a great number of men served in the Royal Air Force and in the antiaircraft artillery which defended the United

BRITISH ARMY
since 1794

▶ 1854
11th Hussars
Charge of the Light Brigade

▼ 1857
93rd Highland Regiment
Indian Mutiny

▲ 1794
14th Foot
French Revolutionary Wars

▲ 1807
95th (Rifle) Regiment
Peninsular War

◀ 1815
Royal North British Dragoons
Waterloo

▼ 1864
Driver, Royal Artillery

▼ 1900
Infantry
Boer War

▼ 1944
Parachute Regiment
Arnhem

▼ 1970
Infantry

▼ 1916
7th Leicesters
World War I

Kingdom against the enemy's bomber aircraft. Consequently it was not possible to have such a large field army as in World War I; about 35 divisions were formed of which 6 were armoured and 2 airborne. (See the article ARMIES for an account of how modern armies are made up.) In the early years of the war, owing to the shortage of trained troops and of guns, tanks and other equipment, the British suffered a number of defeats, notably at Dunkirk and in North Africa, Burma and Malaya. In October 1942, however, General Montgomery and his famous Eighth Army won the great battle of El Alamein in North Africa and from that time there was a series of allied victories which led to the freeing of all Africa, France, Belgium, the Netherlands and Burma and the invasion of Italy and Germany. The land fighting in World War II was very different from the trench warfare of World War I. Airborne troops were able to land behind the enemy lines by parachute or in gliders, while columns of tanks and lorries could travel more than 100 miles a day, so that most battles were fast-moving ones. Nevertheless, in mountain or jungle country such as Burma and parts of Italy, the infantry soldier, fighting on foot, still played the most important part.

When the Germans and Japanese surrendered in the summer of 1945 most people thought, as they had done in 1918, that there would be many years of peace. Unfortunately after the war had ended, the countries of the world became divided into two opposing groups, and so Great Britain, like other western nations, felt bound to maintain large forces and spend immense sums of money providing them with modern equipment. The army kept about four divisions in Western Germany and in addition large numbers of troops were kept in India (until British rule ended in 1947), in the Middle East, Korea (1950–1953), Malaya, Kenya and Aden, together with garrisons in places like Malta and Gibraltar. In many of these countries the troops were on active service. In Korea they were at war for three years and there was also fighting against terrorists and raiders in Malaya, Kenya, and other places. (See the articles on those countries.) To keep the forces up to the strength required, the government had to continue

conscription and from 1945 about half the regular army consisted of "national servicemen" conscripted for 18 months or 2 years. After serving with the regular army, national servicemen had to do a year's part-time service with the Territorial Army or Army Emergency Reserve. Conscription ended in 1960, which meant that there were no more conscripts in the army after 1962.

Very big changes were made in the structure of the army between 1958 and 1968. Some famous regiments were disbanded and others amalgamated, or merged together. In 1967 the Territorial Army was replaced by the much smaller Territorial and Army Volunteer Reserve (T.A.V.R.). In 1968 the infantry regiments were regrouped to form six administrative divisions: Guards, Scottish, Queen's, King's, Prince of Wales' and Light. The strength of the army in 1971 was about 185,300 officers and men including about 14,200 enlisted outside Britain.

If a nuclear, or atomic, war had to be fought the army would use atomic and hydrogen shells, rockets, guided missiles and other new inventions. (See NUCLEAR ENERGY; ROCKET; GUIDED WEAPONS.) The army might, on the other hand, have to fight a small war of the old kind—what is now called a "conventional" war—with weapons like those used in World War II.

The Army as a Career

The modern regular army provides an interesting and adventurous life, with a fine chance to see the world. Living conditions, pay, leave and opportunities for sport are good and many civilian trades, such as that of mechanic, can be learnt. A boy up to 17 who wishes to join the regular army can enter an Army Apprentice School; after that age he may enlist at a barracks or recruiting office. Every man has a chance to become an officer and both officers and men receive a pension and also a lump sum of money when they leave the army after a certain number of years' service, according to rank.

The article WOMEN'S SERVICES describes the work done by the Women's Royal Army Corps and Queen Alexandra's Royal Army Nursing Corps and there are separate articles on many of the people and events mentioned in this article.

BRITISH BROADCASTING COR-PORATION.

The B.B.C., as it is usually called, is one of the world's largest radio and television organizations, and broadcasts every day to listeners all round the world in many languages. Originally called the British Broadcasting Company Limited, it was formed in 1922 and worked under a licence issued by the Postmaster-General, the minister who controlled all wireless communications in Great Britain. The company had to provide a service to the Postmaster-General's "reasonable satisfaction".

In its early days the B.B.C. worked from studios in Savoy Hill, off the Strand, in London, but it moved to Broadcasting House, near Oxford Circus, London, in 1932. At first, programmes were sent out only in the evenings, but gradually daytime broadcasts were added. At the end of 1922 there were 35,000 holders of receiving licences. When the first B.B.C. came to an end in December 1926 the number of licences had grown to more than 1,000,000.

In 1926 it was decided that broadcasting should be conducted by a public corporation which would make sure that all programmes would be chosen and prepared in the interests of the nation. The British Broadcasting Corporation was therefore created on January 1, 1927, by a royal charter, which laid down that the B.B.C. should be controlled by a board of governors appointed by the Sovereign in Council. Sir John Reith (later Lord Reith) was appointed the first director-general of the corporation. As a general rule the charter has been renewed every ten years with very few changes, although in 1952 the B.B.C.'s licence to broadcast was no longer referred to as exclusive, which meant that the B.B.C. no longer had the right to carry out *all* broadcasting. This was done because of the Television Act, which came into force in July 1954, and so for the first time the B.B.C. had a rival—commercial television. In 1971 the government decided that there should be local commercial radio stations also.

Money for the programmes the B.B.C. provides for viewers and listeners in the United Kingdom comes from the annual licence fees for television and radio sets. The sound broadcasts to other countries are paid for by an annual grant from the government.

The B.B.C.'s television service, opened in 1936 at Alexandra Palace in north London, was the first of its kind in the world. It closed in 1939 at the outbreak of World War II but reopened in 1946. In 1964, when a second service was started, the services were named BBC-1 and BBC-2. Since 1967 some programmes have been transmitted in colour, but these can be seen in black and white by viewers who do not have colour television sets. B.B.C. television programmes are produced at the B.B.C. Television Centre at the White City, in west London. There, also, Eurovision and other international link-ups are handled.

On average, three-quarters of the B.B.C.'s daily radio audience listen to Radios 1 and 2. Radio 1 provides continuous popular music, introduced by "disc jockeys", while Radio 2 concentrates on light music and sport. Radio 3 broadcasts serious music, drama, and programmes on the arts and sciences. Light entertainment, plays and talks can be heard on Radio 4. The coverage of news and current events

B.B.C.

The statue of Prospero and Ariel at Broadcasting House.

has been greatly increased. In 1969 plans were announced for the reorganization of radio services. Eight English regions would replace the old North, Midlands, South and West. The Welsh, Scottish and Northern Ireland regions, however, would remain. The B.B.C.'s daily radio output in 1969 was about 65 hours.

Local radio stations take some programmes from the national network and also transmit daily programmes of particular interest to the local community which they serve. In addition to the 8 stations originally set up, 12 more were being brought into operation in 1970. There were plans for 20 more by 1973.

The external services of the B.B.C. consist of two main branches—the European Services and the Overseas Services. Broadcasts are in English and in many other languages. They include news, music, English lessons and discussions about all kinds of subjects, some of them describing the British way of life. (See also BROADCASTING, RADIO and TELEVISION.)

BRITISH COLUMBIA is the western province of Canada which, with Yukon Territory to the north, includes practically all the mountainous region in the Canadian far west. The Rocky Mountains, on which there is a separate article, rise in jagged peaks to heights of up to 3,954 metres, dividing the province from its eastern neighbour, Alberta. On the western side of British Columbia is the Coast Range. In the great valley between the two main ranges are smaller ranges, the most important being the Selkirk Mountains, with their great glaciers, or moving rivers of ice. Deep valleys and gorges, clear, cold lakes and mountain streams which soon become tumbling, rapid rivers make all this wild inland country exceedingly beautiful. The rivers find their way to the many inlets which cut into the Pacific coast. Near the coast is a great number of islands, much the largest being Vancouver Island in the south, which is in fact the size of Belgium. The second largest is Graham Island, one of the Queen Charlotte group. North of this the province is cut off from the sea by a narrow strip of Alaskan territory, which is part of the United States. The whole province of British Columbia is more than three times as large as the British Isles. Much of it is still almost unexplored, but other parts, because of their great beauty and their fine roads and hotels, attract many holiday visitors.

The various parts of the province have different kinds of weather as well as different kinds of scenery. On the Pacific side, Vancouver Island and the coastal fringe of the mainland enjoy a delightful climate, mainly because of the mild westerly winds from the sea. At Victoria, the capital, which lies at the southern end of Vancouver Island, it is mild enough for flowers to bloom out of doors in winter. It is never very hot or very cold near the coast, but there is quite a lot of rain and some fog. In the interior, on the other hand, there is little rain and the temperatures vary a great deal; at Kamloops, in the southern part of the interior, the temperature falls below zero in winter to $-34°C$ and occasionally rises to $37°C$ in summer. In the extreme north the climate of British Columbia is almost arctic.

On the islands and along the coast of the mainland and the outer slopes of the Rockies are great forests of cedar, spruce and Douglas fir. Some of the giant firs and cedars were growing here when Christopher Columbus discovered America in the 15th century; they are as much as 90 metres tall, with trunks so huge that a motor road could be cut through a single tree. To keep some of the forest in its natural state, certain areas have been set aside as national parks; Strathcona Park is on Vancouver Island, Garibaldi Park lies near the city of Vancouver, on the mainland, Mount Robson is in the Rockies and Glacier Park is in the Selkirk Mountains. Hunting and fishing are not allowed in these great areas, but the man with a gun can find elsewhere many mountain goats, elks, caribou, black and grizzly bears, ducks, geese, pheasants and grouse, while the trapper can obtain the skins of fox and marten, otter, mink and muskrat. On the northern coast there is a fish called the candlefish which contains so much oil that when dried it will burn like a torch. In the mountain streams the angler can find trout, while salmon, which once provided the Indians with most of their food, still come up the rivers in

Indian totem poles in Totem Park, Vancouver. The totem poles of the North American Indians are not used in totem worship, but illustrate the history of a family. Some are grave markers and others illustrate ancestry and legendary or real events in the lives of their owners. The carvings were often scattered through an Indian village.

their thousands from the sea to lay their eggs.

Indians make up only a small part of the population; the government has set apart for them special areas, called reservations, although they are not forced to live there. Indian villages with their totem poles can still be seen and the Indians are very clever at making baskets and weaving. The once warlike Haidas, the Nootkas on the coast and the Shushwaps, who live inland, are the chief tribes. Near Nelson, in the south-east, is a settlement of Doukhobors, who are Russians with a special kind of religion; they are not very willing to fall in with the Canadian way of life. There are also Scandinavian, German and French people, but three out of every four of the inhabitants of British Columbia are of British descent, for it was the British who explored and developed the province, as described later on in this article.

The coastal region of British Columbia obtains some of its wealth from its fisheries, particularly the salmon fisheries, and some from its ports. The ports, most of them on inlets from the sea, are not frozen up in the winter and so all the year round ships can trade with lands as far away as South America, Australia, South Africa and Great Britain.

The forests of the province provide a very large part of Canada's yearly output of timber. From the Queen Charlotte Islands comes the finest clear-grain spruce, a softwood used for making parts of aeroplanes. British Columbia contains about one-third of all the softwood in the Commonwealth of Nations.

Valuable minerals including lead, zinc, gold, asbestos, copper and silver are mined. The area near Crowsnest Pass in the Rockies is a coal-mining district, with Fernie as its chief town, and Vancouver Island also is important for coal. Aluminium is produced with the aid of hydro-electric power at Kitimat, in the Coast Range, and the Peace River area produces natural gas.

Cattle and sheep ranching are carried on in the Kamloops region and elsewhere, while the breeding of animals such as mink for their fur is also becoming important. Apples and other fruits are grown in the Okanagan Valley. Northward, with the help of irrigation (see

National Film Board of Canada
A train goes through the Kicking Horse Pass.

IRRIGATION), an increasing amount of farming is being done in the interior of the province. The Peace River country produces much grain.

The railways, like the roads, are mostly found in the southern part of British Columbia. The visitor who comes from the east by railway travels through passes in the Rocky Mountains up to 1,622 metres above sea level. The main

Left: National Film Board of Canada. Right: Courtesy, Greater Vancouver Tourist Association
Left: Moving salmon to a cold storage plant. Right: Vancouver, the business centre of British Columbia.

line of the Canadian National Railways crosses at Yellowhead Pass, just south of Mount Robson, and other lines cross further to the south through Kicking Horse Pass and Crow's Nest Pass. At Rogers Pass the Canadian Pacific Railway tunnels through the Selkirk Mountains for some 8 kilometres.

Two of the main railway lines end at Vancouver, the chief city on the mainland, and enormous quantities of grain, fruit, mineral ores and other products reach the city from the country inland. Vancouver is also the main industrial centre of the province and has a splendid harbour with large dock areas. (See. VANCOUVER.) Vancouver Island opposite is sometimes called the Little Continent because it has developed its trade and industry so independently from the rest of British Columbia; Victoria has been called "the most English town outside England".

History and Development

Vancouver Island appears in history some years before the mainland part of the province. It was discovered by Juan Perez, a Spaniard, in 1774, but four years later Captain James Cook, on whom there is an article, landed at Nootka,

Courtesy, Canadian High Commissioner
A totem carving of a puma in an Indian village on the coast.

on the west side of the island. Between 1792 and 1794 Captain George Vancouver surveyed, or examined carefully, almost the whole coast; both Vancouver Island, named after him, and the mainland were then claimed as English territory. At about the same time a fearless and famous Canadian fur trader crossed the Rockies from the east and, reaching the Pacific at Cascade Inlet, wrote on the rocks there: "Alexander Mackenzie from Canada by land, the twenty-second day of July, 1793". The search for furs led other traders of his company, the North-West Company, to follow him and between 1805 and 1811 Simon Fraser and David Thompson started trading posts in the valleys of the Fraser and Columbia Rivers. In 1821 Mackenzie's company joined up with its great rival, the Hudson's Bay Company, on which there is a separate article, and for the next 28 years this was the only organization allowed to trade with the Indians in the country west of the Rockies.

In 1824 Sir James Douglas was made head of the Hudson's Bay Company in the west and he was the real founder of British Columbia, controlling for a time the entire region and ruling the scattered fur-trading posts with an iron hand. In 1843 he founded Fort Victoria on Vancouver Island and before long this island became a colony and he was made its governor. After gold had been discovered on the Fraser River in 1858 the mainland was also made a colony and given

Courtesy, Canadian High Commissioner
A mountaineer looks down at a camp in the Yoho Valley.

Left: Jack Cash. Right: George Hunter

Left: A sweeping road bridge leads to the centre of Vancouver. Right: Rafts of logs in the harbour of Port Alberni on Vancouver Island.

the name of British Columbia; Douglas then governed both colonies until 1863. Three years later the two colonies were joined together and in 1871 British Columbia (the name now used for the combined colony) agreed to become a province of Canada on condition that a railway was built between the Pacific coast and the cities on the St. Lawrence River, in eastern Canada. This railway was completed at great expense in 1885 and from then on British Columbia developed rapidly its mines and factories, its forestry and farming, so that this province now provides a considerable part of the wealth of Canada. It has a total population of about 2,100,000 people.

BRITISH EMPIRE. As the colonies, or overseas possessions, of Great Britain have one by one taken a larger share in their own government or become completely independent (see COLONIES), so the old name "British Empire" has come to be replaced by a new one, "the Commonwealth of Nations", the nature and history of which is described in the article COMMONWEALTH OF NATIONS.

BRITISH INDIAN OCEAN TERRITORY. Lying in the western part of the Indian

Ocean, the Chagos Archipelago and the islands of Desroches, Farquhar and Aldabra were in 1965 grouped to form a British colony. Formerly, the islands of the Chagos Archipelago had been controlled by Mauritius and the others by the Seychelles. Most of the islands in the Territory are atolls (see ATOLL) and their total land area is only 223 square kilometres. The biggest is Aldabra, which is one of the few places where giant tortoises live. There are turtles also, though their number is declining. The island has a rich bird life including a colony of frigate birds, some flamingos (see FRIGATE BIRD and FLAMINGO) and a species of flightless rail thought to be unique to the island. As it is also a breeding ground used by the sacred ibis, Aldabra is of great interest to naturalists.

The chief product of the Territory is copra (see COCONUT). There is no permanent population but labourers from Mauritius and the Seychelles are brought to work on the coconut plantations. Guano deposits are worked for fertilizer and the turtle industry also gives employment. The colony is governed by a commissioner whose headquarters are at Victoria in the Seychelles and the territory as a whole is well positioned for use as a British and United States defence base in the Indian Ocean.

BRITTANY is the large northwestern peninsula of France, stretching out into the Atlantic Ocean. The sea coast and the interior of Brittany are two distinct districts. Inland are two hilly plateaux, or tablelands, with some good grazing land and woodlands in the valleys. The coast, particularly on the English Channel, is rocky with many inlets and here the main industry is fishing. The Bretons, as the people are called, are famous as seamen and their fleets of fishing boats go every year to Iceland and Newfoundland for cod which is salted and dried for use. Many ships have been wrecked on the rocky coast during the centuries for the tides often run strongly and fog is frequent in places. Near the coast, however, the climate is mild enough, with warm winters, for early vegetables and fruit to be grown and market gardening has made great progress. Cereals are grown in the most fertile districts.

In Roman times the inhabitants of Brittany were Celts. In 56 B.C. Julius Caesar invaded the country, then known as Armorica, and it remained under Roman rule until the 5th century A.D. Then other Celtic tribes fled there from

Courtesy, French Embassy
Tall starched head-dresses are still worn in Britanny.

Britain so as to escape the Saxons and later more came over as missionaries who gradually converted the whole country to Christianity. The Bretons remained independent of French rule until 1491 when their duchess married Charles VIII of France. Even then they had considerable control over their own affairs until the French Revolution at the end of the 18th century.

The Bretons, like almost all Frenchmen, are Roman Catholic and are deeply religious. Every village has its local saint whose help is asked for in sickness and distress, and each year, on the saint's day, pilgrims from far and wide attend the "pardon", or religious services and processions held in honour of the saint. Roadside calvaries, or crosses, some large and elaborately carved, others small and simple, are also characteristic of Brittany. Of great interest to the archaeologist, who studies the objects left behind by the early people, are the ancient stone monuments, built singly or in rows during the New Stone Age. In a few districts a long way from the large towns the ancient Breton, or Brythonic language is still commonly spoken. (See the article CELTS.)

The principal cities of Brittany are Nantes and Saint-Nazaire on the Loire River; Rennes, the ancient capital and the home of the university; and the naval port of Brest, almost at the tip of the peninsula.

BRITTEN, Edward Benjamin (born 1913). Benjamin Britten is one of the most brilliant living British composers. He is known for his operas, orchestral works and songs, including versions of British folk songs. Many of these songs and other compositions are written specially for the singer Peter Pears. Benjamin Britten himself is a pianist and he and Peter Pears have performed many of his works together in concerts.

Britten was born at Lowestoft in Suffolk. He began to write music at the age of five and while he was still at school studied under the composer Frank Bridge. (In honour of his old teacher he wrote the *Variations on a Theme of Frank Bridge* in 1937.) Later he became a student at the Royal College of Music under another well-known composer, John Ireland.

Britten became very well known when his first opera, *Peter Grimes*, was performed in London in 1945. It is a grim and frightening story of events in a Suffolk fishing village based on a poem published in 1810 by George Crabbe; it contains some very fine music for the storm scenes. Britten's other operas include *Let's Make an Opera*, to be performed by children and written so that the audience can join in, and *A Midsummer Night's Dream.*

Britten is very fond of the music of the English composer Henry Purcell, about whom there is a separate article; the delightful *Young Person's Guide to the Orchestra*, which Britten wrote in 1946, is a set of variations on a tune by Purcell in which all the instruments of the orchestra are introduced in turn.

Camera Press

Benjamin Britten.

One of his most praised works is the *War Requiem*, for large choir and orchestra, first performed in Coventry Cathedral in 1962. It includes poetry by Wilfred Owen, written during and about World War I. Much of Britten's music has been written for the Aldeburgh Festival, which he helped to establish.

BROADCASTING, RADIO.

Radio programmes usually have to be planned many weeks or even months in advance. This is not only to allow time for the programmes to be prepared, but because actors, artists and orchestras are booked up in advance and might not be available nearer the date of the broadcast. Programmes are usually planned one week at a time, a complete week's broadcasting being thought out to make sure that it contains the right mixture of items. The programmes also have to be arranged round fixed points.

These fixed points include such things as news bulletins, which must be read at the same time every day so that listeners will know when to expect them, and a number of other regular programmes like weather reports, religious broadcasts, schools broadcasts and so on. The kind of programmes that will be sent out between these fixed points will depend on the time of day and the number and kind of people who will be listening. From Monday to Saturday more people use their radios between 7 and 9 a.m. than at any other time; there is also a peak listening period between midday and 2 p.m., especially on Saturdays. The early morning programmes are for people getting up and off to their work. Later ones will be for housewives, factory workers and, in term time, schools. Others who listen during the day are the old, the very young and the sick. Throughout the day and for much of the night music is broadcast, both serious and popular. Plays are often put on in the evenings.

When the programme planner has made his own preliminary scheme for the week he finds (if he is planning for a varied service, like B.B.C. Radio 4, and not an all-music service like Radio 1) that he needs so many talks, so many plays, so many concerts and so forth. He then goes to the special departments whose job it is to produce talks or plays or music, tells them what he needs and asks them to provide programmes to be broadcast at those times.

Producing a Talk

Suppose that the planner has asked for a particular talk to last for 15 minutes on a given day. This request will be discussed at a meeting in the talks department, an exact subject decided on and a number of possible speakers suggested. Some of them may be well-known broadcasters, others experts on the subject who may not have broadcast before. Finally a decision will be reached and a producer appointed. Sometimes, the producer himself may be left to decide on a suitable speaker.

If the speaker is not experienced the producer will explain to him the great difference between writing an article for a newspaper and writing a script for broadcasting. An article for a newspaper or magazine must be written so that it makes good reading—that is to say, so that it is pleasant and easy to understand when it is taken in through the eye.

A broadcast script on the other hand is intended to be heard. If it makes good reading it will seldom make good listening—or at best it will sound like somebody reading from a book.

It must be written in the words and phrases which men and women use in ordinary speech, and they are surprisingly different sometimes from the words used by the same people when they write.

There are many reasons for the difference between good written English and good broadcast English. One of the most important is that when people read they take in several words at a time —often a whole line at a time and they are usually looking, as well, at a little of the line above and a little of the line below. The listener to a broadcast talk cannot do that. He can only take in one word at a time as it comes to him over the air. If a sentence or a paragraph is too long, the beginning will have begun to fade from the listener's mind before he has heard the end.

Remembering all this, the broadcaster will get to work on his script and produce a rough copy, or draft. This draft will be studied by the producer, who will discuss it with the speaker and perhaps suggest certain changes. He will then ask the speaker to read it through so that he can be timed with a stop-watch. A talk that is meant to fill a 15-minute space on the air should not take the speaker more than about $13\frac{1}{2}$ minutes when he reads it during rehearsal. The extra one and a half minutes must be allowed for a margin of spare time and for the opening and closing announcements—read, of course, by an announcer, not by the speaker himself. Allowance must also be made for the fact that most speakers read a little slower when on the air than during rehearsal.

On the day of the broadcast the speaker will probably arrive at the radio station 30 minutes or more ahead of the time when he is due to go on the air. This will give him a chance to settle down in the studio, overcome any nervousness which even practised broadcasters are likely to experience and have a run through sitting at the microphone.

Next to the studio itself, and separated from it by a sound-proof double glass window, is the producer's cubicle. The producer sits in here with another man whose job is to operate the knobs which, among other things, regulate the volume and level up the differences between a speaker with a naturally loud voice and a speaker with a naturally soft one. During rehearsal the broadcaster can be heard in the producer's cubicle through a loudspeaker which picks up the sound going into the microphone. However, the speaker in the studio cannot hear what is going on or being said in the cubicle, unless the producer presses a special switch which enables him, in his turn, to speak into a small microphone and be heard over another loudspeaker in the studio. A blue light is switched on in the studio and outside the studio door during a rehearsal to indicate that the studio is in use. The moment the talk is about to be broadcast, however, the blue lights both inside and outside the studio turn to red ones.

Other Kinds of Broadcasts

From the producer's point of view, a talk by a single speaker is the simplest kind of broadcast which he has to put on the air. A discussion with four or five speakers, or a play or feature programme, will be much more complicated. A discussion may be put on the air in a number of ways. One way is by gathering all the speakers together some days before the broadcast and letting them argue at much greater length than they will be able to do on the air, everything they say being recorded. The producer then goes through the recordings and picks out the best arguments. The extracts he has chosen are pieced together and re-recorded. It is this recording which is finally transmitted as a programme.

Of course, the simplest way of producing a discussion is to bring the speakers to the studio on the evening of the broadcast, seat them round the microphone and put them straight on the air. If all are skilled broadcasters this will produce by far the most lively programme, but taking part in a discussion without a script places a considerable strain on the broadcasters and not all of them will prove good at it. Some people find themselves overcome by nerves and this often makes them forget all the convincing things they intended to say until after the programme has gone off the air.

Producing a play for broadcasting is even more difficult. There may be a large number of actors using different microphones which will have to be brought in at exactly the right

Left: A reporter interviews actress Vivien Merchant in Stratford-on-Avon for a World Service programme. Above: The sound control room in Broadcasting House, London. Right: A 725-foot transmitting mast. Below: A radio play on the air.

B.B.C.

moment. Besides the voices of the actors themselves there may be music, either "live" or recorded, to help create the right atmosphere and, of course, the sound effects.

Some of the sound effects in broadcast drama are produced very simply. The sound of a car door shutting is made by shutting a real car door, in its frame, which is kept in the studio for the purpose. Others are produced electronically or by tricks which are "trade secrets" among those whose job it is to think them out. Most broadcasting organizations keep a library of sound effects on records. If a play is to have as its background a carpenter's shop, the producer can go to the effects library and take out a whole stack of discs or sound tapes, from which he can select the sounds of planing or hammering or sawing he needs for the play.

The term "feature" programmes is used in radio for programmes which describe a subject (such as coal-mining or a visit to a foreign country) by building up a "sound picture". Material for feature programmes is often collected by means of mobile recording equipment which is taken to the spot and used to record more material than will be needed in the programme itself. The producer edits this recorded material to achieve the effect he wants.

The success of a comedy programme depends partly on the script writer who has to think out most of the lines, partly on the producer, and partly—perhaps chiefly—on the artists taking part. Some comedy programmes are built up around the personalities of individual comedians.

In all countries the most important broadcast programme is the news. Radio has the advantage

Radio Leicester

B.B.C.

Left: Inside the studios of Radio Leicester. Right: A fire-eater demonstrates for the B.B.C. African Service.

of enabling an event to be known to many listeners within a minute or two of its being reported. The news has merely to be written in an easily understood form and read at the microphone. In a newspaper the same news has to be set up in type, the paper printed and then distributed among newspaper sellers before it can be read by the public. As against this, broadcast news has to be comparatively brief, for only about as much can be put into a 15-minute news bulletin as can be printed in two columns of an average daily newspaper. News bulletins are often associated with current affairs programmes, the purpose of which is to provide explanation and informed comment on important items in the day's news—to give "the stories behind the news".

Although news is the most important item in a day's broadcasting, music of all kinds—classical, light "pop", folk and jazz—takes up more time on the air than any other item sent out by most broadcasting stations. Music requires little special production to make it suitable for radio, though skill is required in placing microphones to ensure correct balance between the instruments in an orchestra. One of the striking effects of broadcasting over the years has been to allow a wide variety of people, rather than a small circle of enthusiasts, to appreciate "serious" music. "Pop" record programmes are made from a special kind of studio. The presenter, usually a disc jockey (or "DJ"), sits surrounded by a bank of several turntables ("grams"), on which the records are set up ready to play. Sometimes the DJ puts on the records himself,

sometimes they are put on by an assistant while the DJ does the talking.

One part of radio, known as Outside Broadcasts or, more briefly, as "O.B.s", deals with the description of events while they are actually taking place—for example, a space flight, or the opening of parliament, or a football match. The great art of the outside broadcast commentator on radio is to make those who are listening feel that they are somehow present at the event themselves.

Often O.B.s are televised and broadcast at the same time—for example, the Oxford and Cambridge Boat Race. The Boat Race involves the use of portable radio links, micro-wave radio transmission links, a V.H.F. (very high frequency) two-way communication link and a central control room. In the bows of one launch is the television camera together with the television commentator and in another launch the sound commentator. When sound and television are covering the same event it is not satisfactory for one running commentary to be used for both because the radio commentator must describe many things which television viewers are able to see for themselves. The radio commentary is transmitted from a small radio set in the launch and picked up at points on the shore for relaying by cable to Broadcasting House.

Schools Broadcasts

From the earliest days of broadcasting it was recognized that radio could play a valuable part in the teaching given in schools, and in Britain an experimental series of schools broadcasts was given as early as the summer term of 1924 and was followed by a regular service in the autumn term. Although the radio is intended only to assist ordinary teaching, there are a number of special ways in which broadcasting can help. For example, it can bring into the classroom the voices of famous people of the day and it can enable school children to listen directly to those who have special knowledge or experiences to describe—travellers, artists, industrial experts and so on. Classes can listen to first-class performances of music, of plays or the reading of prose or poetry, which it would be difficult for them to hear by other means. It can widen children's understanding of the world around them by eyewitness descriptions of events and by feature programmes which give the listener the feeling of himself being present. In the same way broadcasting can provide commentaries, specially produced for children on current events.

The success of school broadcasting depends very much on co-operation between the radio organization and the school. In Britain the link between the two is provided by the School Broadcasting Council for the United Kingdom. This council has representatives from both the teaching and the broadcasting sides. Teachers in schools help the council too : for each series of programmes there is a panel of teachers who report immediately after each broadcast on the value of what they have heard. Teachers help also by returning questionnaires in postal surveys. Such questionnaires are normally sent to a "sample" of, say, 500 schools and from the answers it is possible to learn how many children listen, their ages and the way in which the broadcasts are related to the rest of the school's work on the same subject. Besides collecting evidence on paper the council employs education officers who spend the greater part of their time visiting schools and talking to teachers and children. The series of programmes broadcast for schools are accompanied by special notes for the teachers and illustrated pamphlets for the pupils, which the schools can obtain before the broadcast lessons start. For some series there are "radio vision" strips—that is, strips of film with still pictures which can be put on a projector in the classroom to illustrate the radio lesson. Many

B.B.C.

Children improvising background music to a poem after a Music Workshop programme course.

schools record the broadcast lessons and use them when they wish.

Broadcasting in Other Countries

The broadcasts which countries send out for their own people can often be heard by listeners in other countries as well. One of the pleasures which radio offers to a listener in Britain, for example, is the choice of many stations all over Europe broadcasting in their own languages for people in their own countries. Many countries also send out programmes which are meant to be heard by foreign listeners. These programmes are usually broadcast in the language of the country in which they are intended to be heard. France, for example, broadcasts in English for listeners in Great Britain, besides sending out programmes in many other languages as well. Britain broadcasts to listeners overseas in about 40 foreign languages.

During World War II foreign language broadcasting was used by each side. Broadcasts from the B.B.C. to countries overrun by the Germans did much to keep up the spirits of the people in occupied territories.

In the United Kingdom, radio broadcasting has been operated as a public service by the

British Broadcasting Corporation alone. (See BRITISH BROADCASTING CORPORATION.) The work of the B.B.C. is mainly financed by licence fees collected from listeners, but it also earns money with its publications, especially from the advertising in the *Radio Times*, and the local radio stations run by the B.B.C. are financed partly by the towns which they serve.

In 1971, however, the government decided to introduce a competing service of local commercial radio stations, financed by money from broadcast advertisements. To begin with, about 60 stations were planned for large cities and towns in Britain.

In the 1960s a number of unlicensed stations began broadcasting popular records and advertisements from ships moored just outside British territorial waters and from forts which had been built far out in the Thames Estuary during World War II and later abandoned. Millions of people listened to the "pirates" until legal steps were taken to stop their transmissions.

In most other European countries broadcasting is controlled by the state, but in some cases it is paid for partly by income from the broadcasting of advertisements.

In the United States broadcasting is highly competitive—that is to say, there are a great number of stations all competing to attract listeners—and it is commercially sponsored, which means that many programmes are paid for by firms who advertise their goods during the broadcasts. No direct charge, such as a wireless licence, is made to the listener. A small amount of government control is exercised through the Federal Communications Commission.

In Australia there are two systems. There is a public corporation, the A.B.C. (Australian Broadcasting Commission), run on lines similar to the B.B.C. and on which advertising is not allowed. There is also a commercial system in which over 100 stations are run on money paid by advertisers, or "sponsors" as they are called. These stations are supervised by a government body, the Australian Broadcasting Control Board. In Canada there is a public corporation, the C.B.C. (Canadian Broadcasting Corporation), financed from public funds, and at the same time there are more than 100 private sta-

tions which depend on revenue from advertisements. The Canadian system differs from the Australian system in that in Canada the corporation itself carries sponsored programmes.

In New Zealand the New Zealand Broadcasting Corporation controls the public service, in which no advertising is allowed; a number of local stations, which come under the Minister of Broadcasting, are financed by advertisements.

In the U.S.S.R. broadcasting is entirely under government control. It differs from that of Great Britain and other western countries in that many listeners do not have ordinary radio sets in their homes. Broadcasts are sent out by radio from the main cities, such as Moscow and Leningrad. The broadcasts are received by powerful central receiving stations in other cities and towns. From these central receiving stations the programme is sent to the homes of listeners by a line similar to a telephone line and joined to a loud-speaker in the home.

Finding out what listeners like is a special problem in broadcasting. There is no direct indication like the circulation of a newspaper, or box-office receipts at a theatre, to show whether listeners enjoy a programme. Therefore most radio organizations employ a system of listener research. In Britain "samples" of typical listeners are asked questions about each broadcast. In the United States an automatic device fitted to radio sets in a number of "sample" homes records what programme has been chosen. Another method used there is to telephone people and ask them which programme they are listening to.

History of Broadcasting

Broadcasting began as a direct development of the use of wireless telegraphy for sending messages from ships and from one place to another. (See the article WIRELESS TELEGRAPHY.) Such messages were, in effect, already "broadcast"; that is to say, they were flung wide upon the air and could be picked up by anyone in range with a receiving set. While they remained in Morse code, however, they were of no interest except to the few people who could read them. As soon as it became possible to send and receive by radio not only Morse code, but music, human speech and other complicated sounds, broadcasting had started.

In Great Britain the first notable experiments in broadcasting were made by the Marconi Company in 1920. A station was built at Chelmsford in Essex, and from February 23 to March 6 programmes of talks and music were put out for two hours daily. These broadcasts were only intended, however, to be experimental and were not continued regularly. On June 15, 1920, Dame Nellie Melba, the famous Australian singer, took part in a programme from the same station. At the same time much broadcasting and receiving was being done in Britain on low-powered stations by amateurs. At the beginning of 1921 the Post Office issued 150 amateur transmitting licences and over 4,000 receiving licences.

In May 1920 a series of broadcast concerts were sent out from a Dutch wireless station at The Hague, and were heard by listeners in Britain. Concerts heard in Britain were also broadcast, in 1921, from the Eiffel Tower in Paris. In February 1922 regular weekly broadcasts were begun by the Marconi Scientific Instrument Company from a transmitter at Writtle near Chelmsford in England, and were continued, for 15 minutes once a week, until January 1923. A regular daily service was introduced with the formation of the British Broadcasting Company at the end of 1922. Regular radio services began in the United States and other countries at about the same time.

As soon as broadcasting became widespread a new difficulty arose. Only a limited number of "channels" exist, on short waves, medium waves and long waves, on which radio programmes can be transmitted. Some of these possible channels are claimed by other users of the air—for radio-telegrams, for sending messages between ships at sea, for air navigation, for the armed forces and so on. International agreements were therefore made laying down which wavelengths could be used by each country for the purpose of broadcasting. In fact these agreements have not always been kept and listeners in many countries, particularly in Europe, have suffered from interference on overlapping channels. This was one reason which led to the development, in the 1950s, of sound broadcasting on V.H.F. which suffers less from interference. Another way in which this problem was overcome was by "rediffusion" of broadcasts by direct wire from a central receiving point.

BROADS. Old maps of the east coast of England show that at one time a great part of east Norfolk, now known as the Broads or the Norfolk Broads, was covered by the estuary of the Bure, Yare and Waveney rivers, but when sandbanks formed along what is now the coast and blocked the estuary it became a great marsh.

Centuries of drainage have turned most of the marsh into good land although drainage is still necessary and some of the windmills are busy

THE BROADS

pumping water into streams that lead to the sea. However, there are still about 200 miles of waterways suitable for boating, as well as a great number of lakes, called Broads, formed by the widening of the river beds. Just how many of these lakes exist is difficult to say, for some have become so overgrown with reeds that they have almost disappeared.

There is good angling for such fish as pike, roach and bream and a large variety of birds can be seen, including bitterns, harriers, grebes and bearded tits. At Reedham is a great heronry which has been used for hundreds of years. Horsey has a famous bird sanctuary, while at Fritton Lake there is a clever decoy into which wild ducks are enticed by dummies and specially trained tame birds.

Boating Holidays

The great attraction of the Broads, however, is that they form Britain's finest area for a boating holiday. For boys and girls who want to learn to sail it is one of the best areas they can choose. There are no currents in most places, and beginners get plenty of practice in learning to tack and manoeuvre a boat, because the rivers are not very wide.

The North Broads, made up of the River Bure and its tributaries the Thurne and the Ant, are more suitable for this type of holiday than the South Broads, and boats can be hired at all the principal places such as Acle, Horning, Wroxham and Potter Heigham.

Those who have never sailed before will do best to choose a boat not more than 22 feet in length, which will sleep three on board. It is best to have a boat with a single sail because a boat with a second, smaller sail (called a jib) is more difficult to manage.

There are also motor cruisers to be had, of course. The firms which hire out the boats—both yachts and motor cruisers—provide everything likely to be needed, bedding, saucepans, cutlery and some sort of cooking stove, and there are plenty of shops near the river banks where food can be bought.

Holidaymakers usually spend most of their time on the three northern rivers, but the broads that are deep enough to take a yacht are well worth a visit and fun to sail on. Up the Thurne lies Hickling Broad, and to reach it in a sailing boat it is necessary to know how to lower the mast at the bridge at Potter Heigham. Hickling is one of the larger Broads but is so shallow and overgrown by sponge weed that it is necessary to keep to the marked channels. From Hickling, if the boat does not draw more than three feet of water, one can sail through Meadow Dike to Horsey Mere, a good piece of water but shallow. From here it is only a mile to the sea and a salt water bathe.

Up the Ant—and again one has to be ready to lower the mast at the bridge near Ludham—is Barton Broad, one of the best and deepest of them all. On the Bure itself is South Walsham Broad, one of the prettiest, and Wroxham Broad, one of the best known and most crowded. It is also worth while sailing down Ranworth Dyke to Ranworth, for not only is the village attractive but in the church is a famous and very beautifully painted rood screen.

Only experienced people should take boats below Acle, because here the river is strongly affected by the tides and the currents are tricky. The Bure flows into the sea at Great Yarmouth. To the southwest of Great Yarmouth the rivers Yare and Waveney join to form Breydon Water, which at high water is the largest expanse of water on the Norfolk Broads. Further south, at Lowestoft in Suffolk, is Oulton Broad, which has plenty of hotels and boatyards for holidaymakers and yachtsmen, although it is perhaps less attractive than the North Broads.

BRONTËS, THE. The three sisters Charlotte Brontë (1816–1855), Emily Brontë (1818–1848) and Anne Brontë (1820–1849) were members of a family which has attracted people's curiosity and interest ever since it became known more than 100 years ago. Charlotte, Emily and Anne all wrote novels—*Jane Eyre* by Charlotte and *Wuthering Heights* by Emily are great ones—and the story of the family itself is as strange as any novel.

The three sisters were the daughters of a Cornish mother and an Irish father, the Rev. Patrick Brontë, who was the parson of the bleak hillside village of Haworth in Yorkshire. Their mother died the year after Anne was born, and, though her sister Aunt Branwell came to Haworth to look after them, they were lonely, dreamy children. Their father spent all his time in his study, sometimes even having his meals alone, and the children were left to themselves to read and to wander on the wild empty moors

Charlotte, Emily, Branwell and Anne. Branwell Brontë painted this portrait of his three sisters and himself.

surrounding their home. Two elder sisters died young at school, leaving the three girls who were later to become famous and also their brother Branwell.

Together the Brontë children made up stories of an unreal world, writing them in tiny handwriting on tiny sheets of paper, which they stitched together to look like real books. By the time Charlotte was 15, she had written 15 "novels" like this. Branwell became so absorbed in this make-believe world that in spite of his many talents he was never able to succeed in real life and he took to drink and bad company.

For one year Charlotte and Emily went to a school for the daughters of clergymen, but they were very unhappy there. They were given only poor food and the discipline was harsh and cruel —Charlotte later gave a terrible picture of this school in *Jane Eyre,* where she called it "Lowood".

Mr. Brontë was a poor man and it was necessary for the girls to earn their own living (an unusual thing in those days), so they first became governesses, but as they were always unhappy when away from home they decided to start a school of their own. To be able to teach foreign languages, Charlotte and Emily spent some months at a school in Brussels kept by Monsieur Constantin Heger and his wife. Monsieur Heger had a great influence on Charlotte and drew her away from her make-believe stories to think of real life. When the girls tried to start their school in the parsonage, however, no one would come to it because it was in such a remote place and also because of Branwell's bad behaviour.

In 1845 Charlotte found some very fine poems which Emily had written and in 1846 the sisters published a book containing poetry by all three of them, under the pen-names of Currer, Ellis and Acton Bell, names which had the same initials as their own real ones. Many of Emily's noblest poems are included in this book, but it

When they were young, the Brontës made up many stories, often about an imaginary land called "Gondal". They wrote them in tiny writing and bound them like real books. The penny laid against these three shows how small they were.

was not a success at the time; in fact, only two copies were sold. However, the girls were encouraged by seeing their work in print and began to write novels.

Charlotte first wrote *The Professor*, a story of an English professor in a Brussels school. It was refused by many publishers, but when she sent *Jane Eyre* instead, the publisher's reader was so excited that he sat up all night to finish it. When it was printed, "Currer Bell", who everyone thought was a man, became famous at once. In this book Charlotte tells what happened to her heroine, Jane Eyre, as an unhappy little orphan in her aunt's home, as a pupil in a harsh boarding-school and as governess to the little daughter of Mr. Rochester. Mr. Rochester wishes to marry Jane, but during the wedding service it is revealed that he is already married to a mad wife. Jane runs away and has other tragic adventures, but the story ends happily.

Emily's only novel, *Wuthering Heights*, is a very wild, strange, powerful book. Its scene is laid in the Yorkshire moors, which are beautifully described. The story concerns a little boy, Heathcliffe, who is found wandering in the streets of Liverpool and brought home to Wuthering Heights by Mr. Earnshaw. When the children grow up, Heathcliffe and Mr. Earnshaw's daughter Catherine love each other, but Catherine marries Edgar Linton, a rich man. Heathcliffe decides to ruin the Lintons and Earnshaws in revenge and almost succeeds.

Anne's two novels are much less exciting than her sisters', but very truthful and religious. *Agnes Grey* is the story of a governess and a curate. *The Tenant of Wildfell Hall* contains a terrible account of a drunkard, written from what Anne knew about her brother Branwell.

When Branwell died in September 1848 Emily caught cold at his funeral. She tried to control her illness without the help of doctors and died in December 1848. No sooner was she buried than Anne became ill and she died in May 1849.

After her sisters' deaths Charlotte was very lonely, even though by then she was famous and much admired. She wrote two more novels. *Shirley* is a story of the riots over the bringing of machinery for the first time into the Yorkshire cloth mills. *Villette* tells of a lonely governess in a Brussels school.

In 1854 Charlotte married her father's curate, the Rev. Arthur Bell Nicholls, but in March 1855 she also died.

The three sisters were very different in character. Anne was gentle and open, Charlotte quiet but with very deep feelings; Emily, perhaps the greatest of the three, had the strongest and the strangest character. She was silent and reserved, and endured pain of body and mind with determination; yet in her novel and her poems can be seen the fierce passions which she kept hidden inside her.

BRONZE. When two or more metals are melted together and then allowed to cool and harden the product is called an alloy. (See ALLOY.) Bronze is a tough alloy of copper and tin; it does not rust or corrode and wears well. For these reasons it is used for machine parts, for nameplates on buildings and for certain scientific instruments. It can also easily be worked into rods, wire, tubes and sheets. Its colour varies

Victoria and Albert Museum
A 14th-century bronze flagon from a house in Norfolk.

Roman chariot — Drinking vessels — Bells — Springs — Ship's propeller — Coins

from coppery red to primrose according to the proportions of metals present. If exposed in climates which are not too damp it acquires a thin protective covering with beautiful green tints : this is a carbonate of copper. In wet climates a crust of metallic compounds forms on its surface. This can be removed and the original surface restored by chemical treatment.

There may be as much as 40% of tin in bronze. The addition of zinc or nickel makes bronze of a lighter shade and reduces its lustre. A very small proportion of lead, say $\frac{1}{2}$%, makes bronze easier to cut. Three important kinds of bronze are made up in the following way :

	Gun Metal	Phosphor Bronze	Bell Metal
Copper	85.5%	85.4%	76%
Tin	10.5%	12.55%	24%
Zinc	3.5%	1.05%	—
Lead	.5%	.75%	—
Phosphorus	—	.25%	—

Gun metal is used for steam and water fittings ; phosphor bronze is used for springs and turbine blades and bell metal has the property of producing sounds of high quality. The modern alloys known as manganese bronze and aluminium bronze are more like brass than bronze.

The Romans used copper for their coinage. Nowadays bronze is used, so that what is called a "copper" is really a "bronze". The following figures show how the composition of the bronze used for the coinage in Great Britain was changed in 1939 owing to the shortage of tin :

	Before 1939	After 1939
Copper	96%	97%
Tin	4%	.5%
Zinc	—	2.5%

It is not known with certainty how or when bronze was first made. It is likely that malachite, a green copper ore, and cassiterite, a metal-like tin ore, were melted together, because these two are sometimes found together in Asia. Bronze began to be used instead of flint for tools and weapons as long ago as 5000 B.C. For many centuries, during what is known as the Bronze Age, it was the only hard metal known. Hoards of rough round cakes of copper which are believed to be relics of the crude furnaces of that time have been found in Europe. It was hammered into bowls, cups, cooking utensils and arrowheads. The first effective armour and weapons were made of bronze. Chinese bronze vessels dating from between 1700 B.C. and 250 B.C. were often inlaid with gold and silver. The early Greeks and Romans were also skilled in the art of working in bronze, which has been used by sculptors ever since. Some famous works in bronze are the three pairs of doors in St. John's Church (the Baptistery) at Florence, the four horses at the entrance of St. Mark's Church, Venice, and a 700-year-old Buddha, 10 metres high, at Kamakura, Japan.

BRONZE AGE is the name given to the time when men were using bronze to make tools and weapons, but had not discovered the use of iron. In the New Stone Age men had made tools and weapons from stone, flint, wood and bone. It was a great step forward when men first learnt to use metal.

Bronze is not a pure metal but a mixture of copper with various other metals, principally tin. Copper was the first metal to be worked and there was a short "Copper Age" before the

Bronze Age began. Copper is sometimes found in the ground as a lump of pure metal, and it was probably first beaten out cold. Then it was noticed that it could be hammered very much more easily if it was heated. Eventually it was heated more and more until it melted, and men then discovered that it could be poured into a mould shaped to make a particular object. Copper by itself has a poor cutting edge, but eventually the primitive smiths discovered that by adding tin they could make a much harder metal that still melted at a low temperature. This was bronze. The Bronze Age saw the rise of the first civilizations in the Near East and the Pharaohs of Egypt, Ur and Mesopotamia (Iraq), the Minoans in Crete and the Mycenaeans in Greece, were all Bronze Age civilizations. The Iron Age really began with the Assyrians, the Greeks and the Romans.

Beaker Folk

The Bronze Age in Britain lasted some 2,000 years, beginning around 2500 B.C. and lasting until about 500 B.C. But how did bronze come to Britain? The idea of metalworking first began in the Near East and gradually spread to other parts of Europe. It is difficult to be certain when it first arrived in Britain. At first bronze was very valuable and nobody could afford to lose it or even bury it.

In about 2500 B.C. Britain was invaded by a new people whom archaeologists call the Beaker Folk, after the very distinctive pottery drinking vessels they used. These were often shaped rather like a small bell, with a decoration sometimes scratched or more often pressed with twisted rope into the surface of the clay before it was fired. These beakers are found in graves all over northern Europe, stretching from Spain to Czechoslovakia. There is a dispute among archaeologists about whether they began in Spain and spread to Czechoslovakia, or spread out from Czechoslovakia. There is also a dispute about why they should be so widely spread. The people might have been religious missionaries, burying their dead with their distinctive beakers, perhaps filled with beer. Or they may have been prospectors for metal seeking fresh sources of the copper or tin which had suddenly

become so important. They might even have been a bit of both, the first smiths being looked upon as magicians.

From the time of the Beaker invasions onwards we begin to get slight evidence of first copper and then bronze being used both by the Beaker Folk and by the native inhabitants. Unfortunately we know very little about how people lived at this time. It is often assumed that they were mainly shepherds driving their flocks along the chalk ridgeways of southern Britain where their remains are most densely clustered. However, grain impressions are sometimes found on their pottery, so it seems that they were farmers as well. There is little evidence to tell what sort of houses they lived in but they were probably slight huts.

Most of our evidence about the Beaker Folk comes from their elaborate burials. They introduced a new type of burial, placing their dead in a crouched position under a round mound or barrow. (See BARROW.) They believed in the next world and they therefore buried their dead fully clothed, with equipment ready for their future life. Some of this equipment has sur-

Ashmolean Museum, Oxford

A group of Bronze Age barrows (burial mounds) south of Stonehenge in Wiltshire.

vived, and we can learn a great deal about their way of life from the equipment buried with their dead. Later, instead of burying the bodies they cremated them and placed the ashes in a large pottery urn also buried under a barrow. They had temples or assembly places, the best known of which is Stonehenge. These were areas enclosed by a bank and ditch, and inside them were circles of stone or timber uprights. Some timber circles may have had a roof over them which formed a council chamber where the chieftains met.

Bronze Age Burials

The most common remains are the pottery vessels that were buried with the dead. These are of several different types, for each tribe had its own traditions of pottery making. By studying the different types of pot it is possible to distinguish the different tribes that lived in Britain at this time. At first the dead were buried with a beaker that presumably contained a drink of some sort, possibly beer. Later these were replaced by "food vessels" which may have contained a sort of porridge to nourish the dead man in the afterworld. Then when burial gave way to cremation, the special large "cinerary urns" appear in which the ashes of the dead are buried.

From other objects buried with the dead we obtain some idea of their activities in life. The Beaker Folk, for instance, appear to have used the bow, for they were often buried with their archery equipment. Sometimes they had stone axes buried with them, though these appear to have been a symbol of authority, rather like the mace of today. In other graves buttons made out of jet or amber were found which show how their clothes may have fastened. The occasional gold ornament discovered may mark the grave of a king.

As the early Bronze Age developed and the Beaker Folk merged with the native inhabitants, it seems that certain tribes grew more powerful than the others. The immense work involved in building a structure like Stonehenge must mean that the leader of the local tribe had become powerful enough to be thought of as a king. How did the "king" who built Stonehenge grow so rich? Archaeologists often suspect that the wealth needed to build Stonehenge may have come from a trade in metal. Perhaps the king was collecting tin from Cornwall and copper or gold from Ireland, and exporting it to the Continent at a good profit.

Tools and Weapons

Around 1500 B.C. the organization that produced Stonehenge seems to have collapsed. The rich burials gradually grew poorer and then ceased completely. This is unfortunate for the archaeologist, for when the graves disappear much of his evidence vanishes too. However, bronze became more common, presumably because it grew cheaper and easier to produce. Sometimes bronzesmiths gathered too much material to carry round with them and would bury their surplus until they returned later to collect it. Sometimes they forgot to return or were killed, and archaeologists have discovered hoards of their used and broken tools. These hoards provide us with most of our evidence for the middle and later Bronze Age and we see how tools and weapons gradually grow bigger and better. For example, the simple daggers which seem to have been used in the early Bronze Age as an all purpose knife grow into long thin rapiers in the middle Bronze Age and then later are replaced by proper swords, often leaf shaped. With these it was possible to slash with the edge as well as thrust with the point of the rapier. A simpler progression can be seen with axes. The flat axe of the early Bronze Age resembles a stone axe : it could not have been very easy to fix a handle to it, and the handle would probably often fall off. In the middle Bronze Age they are replaced by winged axes, known as palstaves, where the wings prevent the handle from slipping off. In the late Bronze Age palstaves give way to socketed axes where the handle can be fixed firmly in the socket in the axe.

By the late Bronze Age we begin to get more information about the way people lived and a picture very different from the early Bronze Age appears. The late Bronze Age society seems to have been much less religious and much more warlike, for instead of lavishing their wealth on the dead, they began to build great hill forts,

A reconstruction by Alan Sorrell showing Stonehenge as it is believed it would have appeared in the final phase of its construction.

Top left, top right: C. M. Dixon. Centre left: City and County Museum, Lincoln. Centre right: Ashmolean Museum. Right: National Museum of Wales

Top left: The temple of Hal Tarxien, Malta, may have been built by people who had discovered the use of copper. Later bronze-using people used the Maltese temples as resting places for urns containing the ashes of their dead. Top right: Burial cairn of the Beaker Folk in the Bricklieve Mountains, Ireland. Centre left: A finely decorated beaker with a handle. Beakers were placed beside the dead, perhaps containing milk or beer. Centre right: Tools and weapons of the early Bronze Age, found in England and Ireland. Right: Flint arrowheads of the Bronze Age, found in Glamorgan. Flint remained in use, just as bronze remained in use throughout the Iron Age.

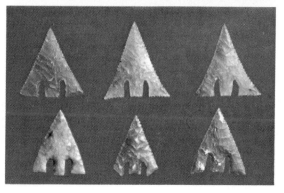

settlements on the top of hills, defended by an earthen bank and ditch. These are more characteristic of the Iron Age but many of them began in the late Bronze Age. The large roundhouses in which the Celtic farmers lived in the Iron Age also began to appear in the late Bronze Age, and small villages of roundhouses have been discovered in Sussex. Farming, too, took a step forward with the widespread introduction of a simple form of plough known as an "ard" which scratched the earth but did not turn the furrow as a proper plough does. In places it is still possible to see the outlines of small square fields, known as Celtic fields, which go back to this period.

BROOM. People sometimes talk of broom and gorse as if the two were the same thing, but they have only to walk on heaths and commons where the shrubs are thick to discover that it is the gorse and not the broom that scratches the legs. The broom is related to gorse, however, and to plants such as peas and vetches. The small lower leaves of the broom are divided into three parts, but there are no spikes on the long, dark green stems.

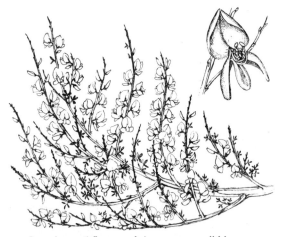

Branches and flowers of the common wild broom.

The flowers of the wild broom, appearing in May or June, are flaming yellow. Some of the garden varieties of broom are also yellow, while others are white or purple or a mixture of these colours. The flowers are fertilized and the seeds scattered by means of two "explosions". When the bee lands on the petals, the weight of the insect explodes the pollen on to its body, which in turn carries it to other flowers. The petals remain apart and the stamens that produced the pollen soon wither and die. The seed pods become dark brown and ripe in July and then they split along both sides and twist to make a second explosion, this time scattering the seeds over the ground.

The botanical name for the wild kind of broom, which grows up to 1·5 metres high in Britain, is *scoparius*, a Latin word meaning a "twig-broom", because the green stems can be tied together and used for sweeping.

Broom is often called *genista*, because at one time the botanists included it in the group of plants with that name. Geoffrey of Anjou, the father of King Henry II, used to thread the bright flowers in his helmet when he went into battle. That is how the *planta genista*, which came to be pronounced Plantagenet, became the emblem and the nickname of his family.

BROWN, John (1800–1859). Just before the American Civil War broke out, when men were still trying to settle the question of slavery peacefully, John Brown was fighting it as ruthlessly (pitilessly) as he could. He was violently opposed to slavery and, when local fighting started in Kansas between the settlers who wanted to free the slaves and those who did not, he became the leader in many fights. He decided that the best way of ending slavery was to arm the Negroes and give them a chance to fight for their freedom. To do this he planned to seize the arsenal, full of rifles and ammunition, at Harper's Ferry, Virginia. One night in 1859 he and 18 followers took it by surprise, expecting the slaves to revolt and join him. Instead, next day, a force of United States marines led by Robert E. Lee arrived and in the fight that followed 15 men were killed and Brown himself was taken prisoner. He was tried on charges of treason and murder and was hanged.

Although John Brown's raid and his execution roused great feeling in both the North and the South they did little to bring on the war which finally led to the end of slavery. During that war, however, one of the marching songs sung by Northern soldiers was "John Brown's body lies a-mouldering in the grave, but his soul goes marching on", a song still popular today.

BROWNING, Robert (1812–1889) and Elizabeth (1806–1861).

Robert Browning and Elizabeth Barrett were both poets, but perhaps nowadays more people know their names because of the romantic story of their lives than because of their poetry alone. Anyone who likes poetry at all, however, probably knows at least some of Robert Browning's poems, such as "The Pied Piper of Hamelin" and "How they Brought the Good News from Ghent to Aix", from which these lines come :

I sprang to the stirrup, and Joris, and he;
I galloped, Dirck galloped, we galloped all three;
"Good speed!" cried the watch, as the gate-bolts undrew;
"Speed!" echoed the wall to us galloping through;
Behind shut the postern, the lights sank to rest,
And into the midnight we galloped abreast.

Robert and Elizabeth were brought up very differently. Robert's father, an official in the Bank of England, was also a book lover and a scholar who wanted his son to enjoy books and painting as much as he did. Mr. Browning joined in the fun when Robert as a small boy shouted rhyming jingles, played the piano and painted with blackcurrant juice because he sucked his brushes. Robert became full of enthusiasm for music and painting and especially for books. Unlike many fathers, Robert's did not disapprove of his son wishing to be a poet—in fact, he encouraged him. When Robert's poems and plays began to be published, some of the famous literary men of the time took a great interest in him. It was then that Elizabeth Barrett, who at that time was better known as a writer than he was, began to be interested in him too.

Elizabeth Barrett was the eldest child of a family of 11, and her father's favourite. She was very clever and when she was still a child knew Latin, Greek and Hebrew. Her first book of poems was published when she was only 14. Elizabeth was never very strong, however, and when she was 15 she injured her back. After this her father treated her as an invalid and when the family came to live in Wimpole Street in London Elizabeth remained nearly all the time in

her room. There she went on studying and writing, and through her work she gained many admirers and made many friends.

Long before Robert and Elizabeth met they wrote letters to each other about their poetry, and in the end Elizabeth allowed Robert to come and see her. Mr. Barrett did not object to literary friendship, but he had forbidden all his children to marry or have friendships that took them away from the family. For this reason, when Robert at last persuaded the gentle Elizabeth to marry him, the marriage took place in secret one Saturday morning in 1846. A week later Elizabeth and her maid, with her dog Flush, crept down the stairs to set out with her husband for Italy. In the sunshine of Italy Elizabeth's health improved and the Brownings lived there in perfect happiness until her death in 1861.

After her death Robert returned to London and continued to write, having by then become very famous. His poetry is exciting to read, even though it is sometimes difficult to understand. He was very interested in people and in some of his best poems a historical or imaginary character is supposed to be speaking. As he talks the character often tells a dramatic and sometimes thrilling story. One of his greatest works is a poetical detective story called *The Ring and the Book*. It is about a real murder which was committed in Italy in 1698 and in each of the 12

Robert and Elizabeth Browning married secretly in 1846.

books of the poem a different person gives his account of the tragedy.

Elizabeth's poems are simpler and more gentle than Robert's. She always sympathized with people who were unjustly treated and one of her poems, "The Cry of the Children", protests against the dreadful conditions in which the children in factories and mines then worked and lived. In *Sonnets from the Portuguese*, perhaps her best book, Elizabeth described her love for Robert Browning.

BRUCE, Robert (1274–1329). Scotland has had no greater hero than Robert Bruce, who freed the Scots from the hated rule of the English. He is often best remembered now for his great victory over the English at the Battle of Bannockburn. (The battle is described in a separate article.)

Robert Bruce was from a noble family descended from a Norman baron who came to Britain with William the Conqueror. Bruce's grandfather had claimed the throne of Scotland, but he had a rival for it, named John Balliol. Edward I of England was asked to choose between them and chose Balliol, who was crowned King of Scotland in 1292.

Many of the Scots did not support the new king, however, and were angry that King Edward claimed to be their overlord. Robert Bruce took part in some of the struggles against the English but it was not until 1306 that he began to lead his countrymen openly against King Edward and Balliol. During a quarrel he killed one of Balliol's men, "the Red Comyn", in the Church of Greyfriars in Dumfries, and this deed made him an enemy to both kings and an outcast from the church. He gathered his supporters together and marched to Scone, where he was crowned king in March 1306.

Then he set out to win his kingdom, but he was soon badly defeated by the English and had to escape and hide in great danger of his life. Everything seemed hopeless for him and the story goes that he was saved from despair only by the example of a spider which kept on trying to fix its web to a beam in the roof and at last, after many failures, succeeded.

After many adventures and battles Robert Bruce succeeded too, and finally defeated the English at Bannockburn in 1314. After that, as long as he was alive, the English were forced to recognize Scottish independence.

When Robert Bruce died from leprosy in 1329 his body was buried at Dunfermline Abbey and his heart in Melrose Abbey in Scotland.

BRUEGHEL, Pieter (*c.* 1525–1569), a great and original Flemish painter, was born in what is now Belgium and may have studied first of all with a painter called Pieter Coecke van Aelst. In 1551 he joined the painters' guild in Antwerp and in about 1553 he went to Rome. He seems to have used his stay in Italy to gain more experience in the art of landscape painting, not to study classical themes and the works of the Renaissance as painters usually did.

In the ten years after his visit to Rome, Brueghel painted Flemish peasant life. These paintings are crowded with people, jolly, lively and coarse, who are dancing at weddings, eating huge meals and sleeping in the corn. In about 1563, Brueghel married the daughter of his first master and moved to Brussels where he lived for the rest of his life. Here he completed a great achievement in landscape painting, a series representing the months of the year. It was a familiar theme in mediaeval art, but Brueghel added an entirely new feeling for nature's various moods.

Brueghel's most important paintings all belong to the last few years of his short life. They are on the subjects which had always interested him—religion, as in the "Adoration of the Kings" and country life, in paintings like the "Wedding Dance". (The "Adoration of the Kings" is in the National Gallery, London.) The later paintings reveal Brueghel's particular view of the world where man's littleness, and sometimes his cruelty and stupidity are shown up against the independence of nature. This view is saved from hopelessness by Brueghel's humour and appreciation of every kind of natural beauty.

Brueghel is sometimes pictured as a rough peasant defending his own people against the Spanish who ruled Flanders, his country, during his lifetime. In fact, he was an educated towns-

"The Wedding Dance" by Pieter Brueghel the Elder captures the cheerful merry-making of the Flemish peasants.

Brunei has one of the world's most modern mosques. The dome and the tops of the towers are coated with gold leaf.

man who worked for intelligent clients, some of whom were Spanish. He was the most original Flemish artist of his day.

Brueghel's two sons, Pieter and Jan, were also painters. The younger one, Jan (1568–1625), became an assistant to another great artist, Sir Peter Paul Rubens (see RUBENS). For the next three centuries there were painters who were descended from Pieter Brueghel.

BRUNEI. The small country of Brunei lies on the north coast of the huge island of Borneo in southeast Asia, not far north of the equator. On the landward side it is surrounded by the Malaysian state of Sarawak. Brunei, which is not much larger than the English county of Norfolk, has a narrow coastal plain drained by several rivers flowing from the hilly interior. The climate is hot and damp with a heavy rainfall.

More than half the people are Malays and about one-quarter are Chinese. The remainder are native tribesmen such as Sea Dayaks and Muruts. The Chinese run most of the businesses and shops and a few Europeans manage the oil fields around Seria on the coast. Many of the people, however, work as peasant farmers or on rubber plantations. The chief product is petroleum. Others include natural gas, rubber and pepper. Most of the interior of the country is under forest which provides timber.

The capital is Bandar Seri Begawan in the east. Its mosque, with a dome covered with gold leaf, is one of the biggest in the Far East, for Islam is the national religion. (See ISLAM; MOSQUE.) Brunei was placed under British protection in 1888. It is ruled by a sultan, but Britain is responsible for defence and foreign affairs. The population is about 136,000.

BRUNEL, Sir Marc Isambard (1769–1849) and Isambard Kingdom (1806–1859), were two very famous engineers.

Marc Brunel was one of those who fled from France at the time of the French Revolution. He took refuge in the United States where he worked as an architect and civil engineer. His most important work was in Canada where he built a canal between the Hudson River and Lake Champlain. In 1799 he went to England and developed a method of building ships quickly in large numbers, or mass producing them as we say now. He had already learnt something about the machinery of ships as a young man in the French navy.

Marc Brunel occupied himself with many inventions until in 1821, due to financial difficulties, he was thrown into prison, regaining his freedom through a grant of £5,000 given to him by the government. His name is famous in history for one work started in 1825 which took him 18 years to complete under very great difficulties. This is the Thames tunnel between Wapping and Rotherhithe—the work for which Queen Victoria made him a knight in 1841. Tunnels had often been driven through rock and in a few cases through sand and clay, but never before had anyone been so wildly ambitious as to try to drive a tunnel through soft ground under a great river like the Thames. Work was abandoned several times and the partly finished tunnel could often only be passed through by boat, so serious was the flooding. This tunnel, which was originally for foot passengers, is still in use but now carries the Metropolitan Line of the underground railway.

In spite of all the accidents resulting from collapse of earth and sudden floodings, not more than seven men engaged on the work lost their lives throughout the whole weary 18 years, whereas in the building of the second London Bridge 45 men had been killed.

Sir Marc's only son, Isambard Kingdom Brunel, was born at Portsmouth in 1806 and after being educated privately was sent to a high school in France until he was 17. He then joined his father in the construction of the Thames tunnel, becoming engineer on the spot in charge of all the work. On several occasions he showed great leadership and courage in looking after the men working under him when water suddenly burst in during construction.

Isambard joined Thomas Telford as one of the pioneers of suspension-bridge design and construction. His design for the Clifton suspension bridge across the Avon gorge was preferred to Telford's, although the bridge was not completed until after Brunel's death.

In 1833 he became chief engineer of the Great Western Railway (now Western Region), which was then being built. He introduced the famous "broad" (seven-foot) gauge and built the Box Tunnel near Bath, as well as notable railway bridges at Maidenhead, Chepstow and Saltash.

Strangely enough Isambard's greatest work was in the field of marine engineering in which

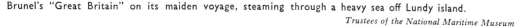

Brunel's "Great Britain" on its maiden voyage, steaming through a heavy sea off Lundy island.

his father had started as a boy. He designed and constructed several ships including the "Great Western" (1837), "Great Britain" (1843) and "Great Eastern" (1858). Each of these was the largest ship in the world when it was launched.

There is no other record in the history of engineering like that of the Brunels, where both father and son showed genius and character, each making a great name for himself through his own achievements.

BRUSH. There are two main kinds of brushes, brushes for "sweeping off" and brushes for "putting on". Among the first kind are all the brushes used to remove dirt and other unwanted matter—special brushes for scrubbing the hands and nails, tooth brushes for keeping teeth clean and white, hair brushes for making hair tidy, brooms for cleaning the house and countless others.

Brushes for putting on are just as important and range from the finest painting brushes used by artists for the most delicate work to the wide coarse brushes used by painters to put protective paint on huge surfaces like the side of a ship or a great bridge like the Forth Bridge in Scotland.

The word "brush" is also used to describe articles used in industry which, though they seem very different from the more familiar type of brush, are made of the same kind of materials and in much the same way.

All brushes, whether stiff or soft, are made from springy fibres of some kind. A fibre is a thin thread; it may be the hair of an animal or it may come from a tree or plant—these are called natural fibres—or it may be made by chemical means in a laboratory or a factory, in which case it is a man-made, or synthetic, fibre. Materials used in brushmaking include natural fibres, such as bristle (pig's hair) and horsehair and the fibres of certain trees and plants; wire made from steel or brass; whalebone; and man-made fibres such as nylon, which can be made into very stiff and springy brushes, and other plastics.

The animal hairs brushmakers use come from many countries. Bristle, for instance, comes from China, India, the U.S.S.R., Japan, South America and Europe; horsehair from South America, Canada and Australia, Europe, China

and the U.S.S.R.; squirrel from the U.S.S.R., northern Europe and Canada; badger from Turkey and other parts of southeast Europe, from China and many other countries. Vegetable (tree and plant) fibres come from the palm trees of Africa, India and Brazil, from the desert plants of Mexico and from the coconuts of India and Ceylon.

Some of the brushmaker's materials are very expensive and hard to get: sable hair used to make artist's brushes is sometimes more precious than gold, and even badger hair for shaving brushes, paint brushes and brushes used in industry is very valuable.

The backs of brushes are often made of wood, usually beech, sycamore, birch and alder. Other hardwoods of various kinds may be used. Among the other materials which can be used for the backs are plastics, ivory, tortoiseshell and silver.

Many animal hairs and vegetable fibres are thicker at one end, the root end, than at the tip. Thousands of bristles or fibres are needed to make a brush and these must be arranged in bundles with their roots all together at one end. When the material is removed from the animal's hide or from the plant's leaves, it is taken out in clumps, and the clumps are piled together with all the roots at the same end. Paint brushes are made from tapered fibres like these, but road brooms are made from fibres mixed in such a way as to give a solid bundle equally thick at both ends.

If the hairs are wanted for paint brushes, small bundles of them are usually tied on to rods or put into tubes and then steamed or boiled; this process straightens out the hairs. Bristles for shaving brushes or tooth brushes, and most animal hairs, are boiled or treated with chemicals to clean them and make them free of germs.

For most brushes hairs or fibres of different kinds or lengths are mixed together to make a more useful brush. For example, a paint brush may be made from two kinds of bristles, one kind which is soft and spreads paint easily and the other which is stiff and keeps a brush from becoming too limp when damp. These two kinds together make a better brush than either kind would when used by itself.

"Brushing-off" brushes, such as nail, clothes,

Here are a few of the many kinds of brush: (1) Scrubbing brush. (2) Toothbrushes. (3) Shaving brush. (4) Nail brush. (5) Clothes brush. (6) Hairbrushes. (7) Brush for carpet sweeper. (8) Paintbrushes of several different thicknesses.

scrubbing and tooth brushes, usually consist of many short tufts of fibre fixed in a handle or back. There are various ways of fastening them there. First, holes are drilled in the brush back. Smaller holes are drilled into the bottoms of these holes from the opposite side or the edge of the back. Loops of wire are then passed through the smaller holes and out through the larger holes; little bundles of fibres are threaded half way through the loops, and the loops are then drawn back again, carrying the bundles down into the larger holes. This is the way that expensive hair brushes are still made.

Another method is to drill holes into the brush back, take little bundles of fibres, dip them in pitch or some other cement, bind the dipped ends and thrust them into the holes. Many of the heavy brooms used to sweep the streets are made in this way. Sometimes the bristles are fastened in the holes with staples. Most brushes today are made by machinery. The machine bores the holes, selects the fibres, fits the staples and drives the fibres into the holes, all automatically and at great speed.

Most brushes which "brush on"—for instance, paint brushes—are made by securing one end of a bundle of fibres inside a metal band or ring and then attaching the band or ring to a handle. It needs great care and skill to prepare and fix the bristles or other materials properly since even if only a few of the many thousands of fibres are loose they will come out of the brush when it is being used and spoil the appearance of the paint-work. The most usual method of fixing the material in the holder is to "cement" it there with a special rubber preparation.

For long thin brushes—bottle brushes and brushes for cleaning tea-pot spouts, for instance —the fibres are twisted between two pieces of wire into a spiral shape.

Other brushes are made by pressing a layer of wire or bristle down into a long strip of metal with the edges turned up to make a narrow channel. This process makes brushes in long

261

BRUSSELS

strips, which are then wound on to rollers or
wheels.

The most unusual brushes are those used in
industry. For example, there are tentering
brushes, for stretching cloth. Cloth is made in
long strips which are wound on to rollers. During
the winding the cloth tends to pucker up and the
tentering brushes are used to prevent this. They
are fixed so that they touch the cloth as it runs
underneath them on its way to the rollers, and
the bristles are arranged in such a way that they
keep pushing the cloth outwards to the two
edges, so stretching it and keeping it free from
puckers.

Many other industrial brushes have this
wheel-like shape, with the bristles sticking out
from the rim. The brushes which a dentist uses
to polish the teeth of his patients are made like
this. They are tiny and are made to revolve very
fast in the dentist's machine. Many wheel-like
brushes are designed for use at high speeds in
machines.

Other industrial brushes are made like rollers,
with bristles or other fibres sticking out all round
them. Some are used for spreading the substance
which makes certain kinds of paper look glossy.
Others are used in carpet factories to give the
carpets a good cleaning after they are made.
Others are used for spreading dye on the metal
rollers which print the patterns on cotton
materials. Still others can be found in vacuum
cleaners, brushing the dust from the carpets so
that it can be sucked away by the fan.

BRUSSELS is the capital of Belgium, lying almost exactly in the centre of the country on the
banks of the Senne River. Its history goes back to
before A.D. 695, for in that year St. Vindicien,
Bishop of Cambrai, left a place called Brosella
to return to Cambrai. His "village of the
marsh" (Bruocsella) grew into the large and
beautiful city with the name of Brussels.

The city grew rapidly during the middle ages
as men developed their trades and industries on
the banks of the Senne. Then, from the 16th to
the 19th centuries, Brussels struggled under the
rule first of Spain and later of Austria, France
and Holland. Belgium finally became independent in 1830 and during the next century Brus-

Courtesy, Belgian National Tourist Office
The flower market in the spring. A market has been held
in the Grande Place, Brussels, since the 12th century.

sels recovered much of its prosperity. It was
occupied by German troops during both world
wars but was not damaged.

In the lower town are splendid modern shops,
banks and hotels and yet there is an open square
called the *Grande Place* near by with many old
buildings of the middle ages, wonderfully
carved and richly decorated with gilt. On one
side is the *Hôtel de Ville,* or City Hall, with its
delicate tower from which a statue of St. Michael
has been looking down for 500 years upon the
city that the saint protects. The other sides of the
square are occupied by guild halls (see GUILD)
which are like palaces, and one can almost picture the silk merchants, archers, carpenters and
bakers of hundreds of years ago going in and
out of them. In the early morning vegetables are
sold from many stalls. Near by is the long arcade
called the *Galeries St. Hubert,* with shops,
theatres and cafés.

Down one of the twisting streets that lead from
the *Grande Place* is the Manneken Fountain, a
little naked bronze boy whom the people of
Brussels call their oldest citizen because he was
put up in the 17th century. From another
corner of the square a street winds up the hill to

263

the great broad steps of the fortress-like church of St. Michael and St. Gudule, which was begun in the 13th century. Beyond the church is the upper town where the noblemen and their families have lived from the time the dukes of Brabant built a castle there 500 years ago. Where this castle stood is now the stately palace of the Belgian king, while the Parliament house —the *Palais de la Nation*—is to be seen on the other side of the large Royal Park. Near by are wide streets in which the fine houses look large and prosperous. At the opposite end of the upper town, overlooking the whole city, is the immense Palace of Justice (the law courts) and not far away is a gate called the *Porte de Hal,* which is all that remains of the 14th-century city walls.

Brussels is joined by canals with the North Sea and by railways with the great cities of Europe. Its lace and carpets have long been famous and there are, besides the iron and steel foundries and engineering works, a number of other industries; these include chemicals, clothing and textiles, leather, food, soap and motorcar bodies. The city is also a centre of the arts and sciences with its Royal Conservatory of Music and its university, opera house and art galleries. A scheme of underground roads and one overhead road was completed in 1958 in order to help with the problem of overcrowded traffic in the city. Greater Brussels, which includes all the modern suburbs, has a population of about 1,600,000.

BUCHAN, John, 1ST BARON TWEEDSMUIR (1875–1940). John Buchan is probably best known to most people as the author of a series of exciting adventure stories, but he was also a fine statesman, a man of action and a student of history. It would be hard to find anyone in modern times who led a fuller and more complete life. As a statesman he rose to the high position of Governor-General of Canada, while his books— *Prester John, The Thirty-nine Steps, Greenmantle, Mr. Standfast* and many others—are famous. In these he describes without any exaggeration the most thrilling events so that they seem very real. As well as these books Buchan wrote the life stories of several famous people in

history, such as *Montrose, Oliver Cromwell* and *Walter Scott.* These biographies show that Buchan had a good judgment and a clear understanding of history and literature. He also wrote some poetry of high quality.

Buchan was born at Perth in Scotland. His father was a Free Church minister and his mother a farmer's daughter. He went to Oxford University, where he did brilliantly, and after that he intended to become a lawyer. Then his ideas changed, for he was invited to become private secretary to Lord Milner, who was at that time, near the end of the Boer War, the High Commissioner for South Africa. This turned Buchan's mind to politics and more especially to Empire affairs. During World War I he worked in the Department (later the Ministry) of Information. He was a member of parliament for the Scottish Universities from 1927 to 1935 and held other important posts. He was given several decorations and received many honours from Scottish and other universities. In 1935 he was made Governor-General of Canada and was given the title of Baron Tweedsmuir. One of the honours he received in Canada came from a tribe of Indians in British Columbia—they made him their chief.

Although in many ways John Buchan's character was a romantic one, he felt also that it was important to be efficient and clear-headed in practical things, as he himself was. He suffered from an internal illness which caused him much discomfort and pain, especially as he grew older. In spite of this, however, he was very active, a daring rock-climber, a tireless walker, and he loved fishing and shooting. As a person he was rather like the heroes of his own books, who are brave, adventurous and honest. He made one of his characters say: "If we are playing our part well and know it, then we can thank God and go on. That is what I call happiness." Buchan's own life was happy in this way.

BUCHAREST is Romania's capital city. It lies in a slight hollow through which a small river runs; on one side there are flat plains and on the other only low hills, so there is little protection from the dry, hot winds of summer or the blizzards in the winter. However, although it can be very hot or very cold, Bucharest was for a long while one of the gayest capitals in eastern Europe and was proud of being called "the little Paris".

Bucharest was founded in about the 14th century and at the end of the 17th century became the capital of Wallachia, but it was not until 1862 that it became the capital of the kingdom of Romania, which was formed by uniting Wallachia and Moldavia. From then on, modern buildings started to take the place of the old villas and mansions and more and more people began to live in the city. The population is now about 1,450,000.

Decorated wooden buildings in the Village Museum, Bucharest.

Bucharest is a great centre of education. Apart from the schools and university, there are training colleges for engineers, scientists and artists. Many roads and railways meet at Bucharest and its many industries include petroleum-refining, engineering and the manufacture of soap, paper, textiles, leather goods, farm machinery, motor cars and many other products.

BUCKINGHAM PALACE has been the London residence of British sovereigns since 1830. Before that their London homes were the palaces of St. James, Kensington, Whitehall, and, still earlier, Westminster.

Buckingham Palace is at the western end of the broad road known as The Mall, which starts at Trafalgar Square and runs along the north side of St. James's Park. The Palace stands on the site of Buckingham House, built in 1705 for an 18th-century Duke of Buckingham who had been keeper of the Mulberry Gardens (now St. James's Park) and with whose silkworms James I hoped to start a British silk industry. George III bought it in 1762 as a house for Queen Charlotte. The architect of the present building, begun in 1825, was John Nash, who among other things designed the Marble Arch as a ceremonial entrance. Unfortunately this arch was found to be too small for the largest coaches to pass through and in 1851 it was removed to its present site at the western end of Oxford Street when the Palace was enlarged by Edward Blore. In 1913 the Palace was given a new front from designs by Sir Aston Webb.

When the sovereign is in residence (living in the Palace) the Royal Standard is flown from the flagstaff, high above the famous balcony on which members of the royal family appear on special occasions. During these periods of residence, the Mounting of the Guard takes place in the courtyard in front of the Palace.

Although the front of the Palace is near the road, at the back the large gardens, with a lake and many fine trees form a lovely setting for the garden parties and open-air receptions given by the Queen and Prince Philip in summer.

Only the Queen's guests and official visitors see the inside of the Palace, some of which is far more magnificent than the plain and dignified exterior. There is, for example, the Throne Room, with the two thrones occupied by the royal couple on ceremonial occasions, great crystal chandeliers and a band of sculpture in marble showing scenes from the Wars of the Roses. The picture gallery contains one of the world's finest collections and from time to time the Queen lends some of the paintings for public exhibitions. A separate picture gallery known as the Queen's Gallery is open to the public. The State Ballroom, used for investitures, and the Green Drawing Room are two other magnificent apartments but the rooms in daily use by the royal family are of a more simple kind.

Most boys and girls would find the Riding House (1764) and the Royal Mews (1825) on the southwest side of the Palace just as interesting as

A corps of drums of a Grenadier Guards battalion, marching down the Mall from Buckingham Palace with a detachment of the Queen's Guard.

Top: The White Drawing Room, one of the state rooms in Buckingham Palace.. Bottom: The palace in the reign of George IV, after it was rebuilt by John Nash. The main entrance was then through the Marble Arch. The palace looked very different in those days: the present east front was not built until 1913.

The Old Berkeley Hunt

Olney pancake race

Thames at Marlow

Jordans Quaker meeting house

film making

furniture making

Stoke Poges church

Eton

the state apartments. Up to 30 magnificent horses are stabled there, including the six splendid greys used to draw the great state coach, which is also kept in the mews. This coach, decorated with paintings by the artist Giovanni Cipriani of Florence, was built in 1762 for George III and since then it has carried every British monarch to Westminster Abbey for his or her coronation. The Royal Mews and Queen's Gallery are open to the public at certain times.

BUCKINGHAMSHIRE. The county of
Buckinghamshire, in England, is long and irregular in shape. In the north it reaches towards the midlands of England, while in the south it touches the Thames and the boundary of Greater London. Buckinghamshire remains a county in the reorganization of local government, but loses to Berkshire a small area including Slough.

Buckinghamshire is divided into two distinct areas by the Chiltern Hills, which are described in a separate article. These run northeastwards from near Henley, in Oxfordshire, to Ivinghoe

near the eastern border of Buckinghamshire. In spite of its many modern industries, Buckinghamshire is still a beautiful county where the different crops and the ploughed land and pasture give the gently undulating, or rolling, fields the appearance of a great patchwork quilt.

Three rivers of importance pass through the northern half of the county—the Ouse which runs towards the Wash on the east coast, its tributary the Ouzel, and the Thame on its way to join the Thames in Oxfordshire. All this northern part of the county is comparatively flat; the large fields are used mainly for dairy farming and there are fewer and smaller woods —mainly of oak and ash trees—than in the south. It is famous hunting country.

Right in the north, on the River Ouse, is Olney where on Shrove Tuesday housewives run their famous pancake race from market place to church, each carrying her frying-pan, with its pancake, in her hand. Farther up the Ouse, to the west, lies Buckingham which is no longer the county town—this is now Aylesbury—but above whose town hall stands a weather vane in the form of a really magnificent sculpture of the chained swan which is part of the coat of arms of the county. Near Buckingham is Stowe, a public school for boys founded in 1923 and housed in a stately mansion that was once the home of the Duke of Buckingham.

Set in the walls surrounding Hartwell Park, in the centre of the county near Aylesbury, there are large coil-shaped fossil shells called ammonites which were found on the estate.

Ivinghoe Beacon is well-known but is only one of the many wonderful viewpoints along the Chiltern ridge, which are very popular places for picnic parties. Along the northern slope of the Chilterns runs the ancient Icknield Way and this route, which was being used by people before the Romans came to Great Britain, is still a favourite one. Overlooking the Prime Minister's country house at Chequers is a hill with earthworks said to have been made by Cymbeline, or Old King Cole, while near High Wycombe there are earthworks called Desborough Castle and about a kilometre southeast of the village of Monks Risborough is the prominent Whiteleaf Cross cut into the chalk hillside.

The Chilterns fall less steeply on the London side than they do on the northwest. There is good road and rail communication for those who go to work in the capital every day, as many do, and for the use of Londoners when they visit the county at weekends. The Corporation of the City of London actually owns part of Buckinghamshire, for in 1883 it bought a large area containing the famous Burnham Beeches. People come to spend days here or to visit the model village of Bekonscot at Beaconsfield near by.

There are many lovely villages on the London side of the Chilterns. West Wycombe was judged to be so beautiful that the Royal Society of Arts bought it to prevent it being destroyed by the widening of the road and it is now the property of the National Trust. Above the village is a curious church, its tower capped by a great golden ball, into which anyone may climb. Below the church there are caves.

The Chess is one of the best and loveliest trout streams near London and only a short way away is the valley of the Misbourne, although the river bed is now almost dry. Old folk say that the Misbourne always goes underground in troublous times and certainly it has not been seen very much since the beginning of World War II, but this probably has something to do with the boring of wells which take its water.

In the south, along the Thames, there are holiday resorts such as Datchet, Taplow, Bourne End and Marlow where rowing and sailing boats and canoes can be hired or trips taken on larger river-boats. Opposite Windsor, which is on the Berkshire side of the Thames, stands Eton College, founded by Henry IV in 1440 and one of the world's most famous schools.

Many of the people who live in the northern part of Buckinghamshire are either farmers or concerned in some way with farming. The chief crops are wheat and oats but the main agricultural occupation is the raising of sheep and cattle. Aylesbury, the county town, is now more important for its engineering and printing works and light industries than for Aylesbury ducks, few of which are now seen there. In the north, Wolverton is noted for its railway workshops and Bletchley is a growing industrial centre. Both these towns adjoin the large area of Milton Keynes, one of the biggest of Britain's new towns.

However, the busier part of the county is on the southeastern side of the Chilterns and the busiest town of all is Slough where, on the trading estate alone, there are about 700 factories turning out all kinds of articles which are classed as light industry—clothes, radio sets and sweets for example. At Eton, Bourne End and Marlow boats are built, while at Chesham spoons, brushes and shoes are made. Watercress is grown in the clear stream of the Chess.

At Iver and Beaconsfield there are film studios and technical research stations at Westcott (concerned with rocket propulsion), Fulmer (mainly metal working), Princes Risborough (forest products) and Gerrard's Cross (aluminium). Paper is produced at Loudwater. At High Wycombe more wooden chairs are made than anywhere else in Great Britain. Wycombe also makes other furniture and has many industries.

Many great men have been associated with the county. At Great Hampden, is the home of John Hampden and nearby at Prestwood is the land on which he refused to pay ship money, a tax levied by the king to help pay for the navy's ships. (See the article HAMPDEN, JOHN.) Close by is Chequers, a country house built in the 16th century which since 1821 has been an official residence of each Prime Minister. (See CHEQUERS.)

At Chalfont St. Giles is the cottage to which John Milton came to escape the Great Plague of 1665 ; here he finished the great poem *Paradise Lost*. Not far away is Jordans Meeting House which played an important part in the history of the Quakers, and beside it are the graves of William Penn (founder of the American state of Pennsylvania) and his family.

Buckinghamshire was also a rallying ground of the Lollards (see LOLLARDS), the followers of the 14th-century reformer John Wycliffe, and at Amersham there is a Martyrs' Memorial commemorating some who were burnt at the stake. Not far away, and of happier memory, is the churchyard at Stoke Poges which the poet Thomas Gray made famous by his "Elegy written in a Country Churchyard".

Isaac Disraeli lived in the charming manor house at Bradenham and his son Benjamin, who was twice Prime Minister of Great Britain in the 19th century and became Lord Beaconsfield, lived at Hughenden Manor. Among others who knew Buckinghamshire well were Edmund Burke, one of the greatest names in the history of English political writing, and the poet Percy Bysshe Shelley whose works include the "Ode to a Skylark" and the sonnet "Ozymandias". Olney, in the far north of the county, was the home of William Cowper, the poet who wrote "John Gilpin" and "The Task" and co-operated with John Newton in composing the beautiful Olney Hymns. You may know the Olney Hymn "Glorious things of Thee are spoken". (There are separate articles on most of the people who have been mentioned in this section.)

BUDAPEST is the capital and largest city of Hungary. It has a population of about 1,940,000. The city grew up at one of the few places where people living on the Hungarian plains could cross the Danube River (there is an island in the middle of the river). The old fortress

and town of Buda were built on the steep hill on the right hand side of the river and the town of Pest grew up on the left. The two were joined as Budapest in 1872.

On the hill where Buda fortress was originally built, there was a fine Royal Palace with 860 rooms and also a 700-year-old church in which the kings of Hungary were crowned, but the palace was badly damaged by artillery and fire in 1944. Modern Buda covers many other hills besides this one, however, and near them can be found mineral baths fed by hot springs which are good for the health. To the north there are the remains of an ancient Roman settlement.

Buda hill gives the best view of Pest. Below is the Danube, where Margaret Island is covered with cafés and mineral baths. There are many

Hungarian News and Information Bureau
Many bridges join Buda to Pest across the Danube.

bridges linking Buda with Pest, the most famous being the suspension bridge built by an Englishman, William T. Clark.

On the opposite bank from Buda are quays and landing stages, and there stand the smartest hotels and the Parliament House, which was built to imitate the British Houses of Parliament. Behind them is Pest with its beautiful university and opera house. The houses where most of the people now live are even further back from the river while on the outskirts of the city are many industrial firms, including steelworks.

Buda was captured by the Turks in the 16th

century, when Pest was just a suburb. About 150 years later, however, Buda was retaken by the Austrians. From the time when the two towns were united as Budapest the Hungarians did all they could to attract rich and clever people to the city so that they would not depend any more on Vienna, the capital of Austria, to which Hungary was then joined in the Austrian Empire. On the Pest side of the river the city began to grow quickly and many factories were built there.

After World War I Austria and Hungary were made into separate nations. In 1918 Budapest suffered a revolution and in the next year it was occupied by the Rumanian army, but it survived these troubles and continued to grow. Towards the end of World War II it suffered severely from Allied bombs and Russian shells and many of the beautiful old buildings in Buda were destroyed. When the Germans retreated they blew up all the bridges.

In 1956 Budapest was the central point in the Hungarian uprising against the Russian domination and control of their country. (See HUNGARY.) It was a public march of protest by Budapest university students which brought into the open the demand of the Hungarians that their country should be free. In the capital the crowds tore down Russian flags and destroyed the statue of Stalin and there were pitched battles with Russian troops in the streets. Men, women and even children threw home-made bombs at Russian tanks and put water in their petrol. The Russian troops put down the rising with great brutality, often running over people with their tanks and bombarding their homes. Thousands of lives were lost and even more damage was done to this fine city.

BUDDHA AND BUDDHISM. About one
in five of all the people in the world follow the teachings of Buddha, who lived in the 6th century before Christ.

"Buddha" is a title, not a name, and it means the "Enlightened One", "the One who Knows". The Buddha's name was Siddhartha, of the clan of Gautama. He was the son of a chieftain in northern India and he and his family were all Hindus. (See HINDUS AND HINDUISM.)

He was brought up in luxury and saw nothing of the outside world until he was a young man. Then he saw three sights which altered his whole life: a man feeble with old age, another with some terrible disease, possibly leprosy, and a corpse.

These sights filled him with a longing to find some way to help his fellow men and to discover the true meaning of life. Therefore, although he was married and had a baby son, he left his home to devote himself to finding some way of overcoming suffering.

First of all, Gautama went to two Brahmans, or Hindu priests, but they could not answer his questions about suffering. Then he tried to live like a Hindu holy man and for six years he tortured himself in an attempt to become indifferent to pain, but he eventually realized that this was foolish and useless. At last he seated himself under a bo-tree (a type of wild fig-tree) and waited there until he found his answer, or attained Enlightenment.

The cause of suffering, Gautama said, is desire; that is, the wish to live and to possess various things. Strong feelings, such as love for other people, also cause suffering. Following this idea, he laid down the Four Truths. The first Truth is that pain accompanies all the normal happenings of life—birth, sickness, old age and death are all pain. The second Truth is that desire causes pain. The third Truth is that to overcome pain it is necessary to get rid of all desire and selfishness.

The fourth Truth is how to do this, and the method that Gautama taught is known as the Eightfold Path. There are eight "right" principles to be followed: right beliefs, right aims, right speech, right conduct, right occupation, right effort, right thinking and right meditation.

Gautama, now known as the Buddha, spent the rest of his life wandering from place to place teaching his discoveries to the people of India. He disregarded the Hindu caste system (see CASTE) and preached to all who would listen to him. As the Eightfold Path is difficult to follow while living a normal life among other people, many of Buddha's followers became monks and nuns. Gautama died at the age of 80.

The aim of all Buddhists is to attain Nirvana, which is a state of perfect peace and freedom

A Chinese painted wood sculpture from the Sung Dynasty. It shows Bodhisattva Kuanyin, the compassionate future Buddha.

Left: Courtesy, University of Pennsylvania.
Above: Museum of Fine Arts, Boston

Buddhism has been an inspiration of much Chinese
art. The gilt-bronze figure of a standing Buddha
was made nearly 1,500 years ago. The painting on
silk shows "Buddha under the Mango Tree". It
was painted in the 11th century.

efforts. In Buddhist monasteries and temples are great images of the Buddha, usually sitting cross-legged. Before his image Buddhists kneel, not in worship or prayer, but in meditation on his example and teaching.

Many legends have grown up about Buddha, who is regarded by some of his followers as more than human. His teachings are recorded in the Tri-pitaka, or "threefold basket". This is divided into three parts. The first states the rules for the monks, the second contains the sermons of the Buddha and the third deals with the Buddhist system of thought.

Buddhist monks wear robes of an orange-yellow colour called saffron and go barefoot. They shave their heads and carry bowls, known as begging bowls, in which they carry the gifts that other Buddhists give them.

Buddhism spread very quickly in central India during the long lifetime of Gautama. In about 250 B.C. the Emperor Asoka became a Buddhist and tried to rule his kingdom by the Buddha's teaching. He sent out missionaries to other countries, including Ceylon. Buddhism also spread to Burma, Thailand, Laos and Cambodia. Today Ceylon is mostly Buddhist while Burma, Thailand, Laos and Cambodia are almost entirely so and these five countries claim to keep faithfully to the original teaching of Gautama.

Buddhism also spread to other countries, but it often became mixed with other religions. In Tibet, for instance, it is known as Lamaistic Buddhism (see LAMA), while in China it absorbed some of the ideas of Confucius and in Japan it became mixed with the Shinto religion. (See CONFUCIUS and SHINTOISM.) So although there are millions of people in China and Japan who call themselves Buddhists, theirs is not the pure Buddhism taught by Gautama.

Strangely enough there are very few Buddhists left in India itself, though there is still a great reverence for the Buddha as a religious teacher. Buddhism seems to have been gradually absorbed into Hinduism.

Courtesy, Thailand Information Service

Many shrines and temples decorate Thailand. The Buddha footprint shrine is at Serabusi.

from suffering. One of the chief beliefs of Buddhism is that every person has lived other lives in past years and when a person dies he will later be born again. By this means the events of life are explained as being the punishment or reward for something done in an earlier life. These earlier actions are known as Karma, and it is by wiping out the bad Karma by good deeds and meditation that Nirvana may be reached.

One of the most important teachings of the Buddha is that it is wrong to take any kind of life. This is because he believed that everyone begins life in a very humble way and lives hundreds of lives, sometimes as an insect or an animal and later as a human being. Thus all life is sacred.

Gautama Buddha did not claim to be a god or a saviour but simply a teacher who could show men the true way of life to follow. Therefore Buddhists do not worship God but believe that men can attain Nirvana by their own

BUDGERIGAR. This beautiful Australian parakeet has become the most popular of all the cage birds in Great Britain and indeed in the world. The wild budgerigar has pale greenish-yellow upper parts, with many dark brown, curved bars on the wings, bright green under parts and rump and bright blue cheek patches and central tail feathers. It is usually found in desert areas covered with saltbush (a kind of plant), and it lays its three or four eggs in the hollows of rotted gum trees.

The budgerigar's scientific name is *Melopsittacus undulatus*. It is also known as the shell, grass and zebra parakeet and is sometimes, and wrongly, called a lovebird. Budgerigars usually live in large flocks. They feed on grains and grass seeds and often fly long distances in search of food and water. It is when a flock is moving about in this way that the birds can be trapped for the market. The first pair was brought to England in 1840 and now huge shipments arrive in Europe from time to time. By careful selection and breeding many attractive colours have been produced, such as sky blue, cobalt blue, violet, mauve and olive green.

The budgerigar has become so popular, not only because of its beauty, but also because it is easy to keep as a pet in the home (better still in an aviary, or large bird enclosure, in the garden,

John Markham
Careful breeding from the green wild budgerigar has produced many varieties of many different colours.

however) and it makes a pleasant companion. The article PETS, CARE OF tells about the cages suitable for both budgerigars and canaries and the proper way to feed and look after them. You should be sure to read this if you intend to keep a bird as a pet. There are also many books on the keeping of budgerigars.

Most children can afford to keep a budgerigar out of their pocket money and if you are given, or can buy, a bird when it is quite young (preferable six to eight weeks old) you may be able to train it to talk, or rather to imitate the words you use yourself. At this stage, however, the bird will still have its baby feathers and there is no need to worry when these start to come out for they will be replaced by the adult plumage. It is an advantage to buy a bird with a Budgerigar Society ring on its leg, for this will have a registered number which may help to trace it if it is ever lost. Budgerigars appreciate such tit-bits as a small piece of apple, besides their normal needs of seed, clean water and a little grit.

BUDGET. Every year the Chancellor of the Exchequer tells parliament how much money will be needed by the government in the coming year and how this money will be obtained. When he does this he presents his budget.

First of all, during February and March, the government gives parliament figures showing how much it expects to spend on, for example, defence, schools, hospitals and so on. These are called the estimates, because it is hard to be exact about the future.

Early in April, the Chancellor "opens his budget". He does actually open the *bougette* or small leather bag in which he keeps his papers. Then he makes his budget speech. This takes much less time than it used to. Mr. Gladstone, a famous politician of the last century, often spoke for four hours when he was Chancellor of the Exchequer.

Nowadays, in his budget speech, the Chancellor talks a good deal about economics—for example, what the country must do if it is to be able to pay for what it buys from other countries. He also tells parliament whether they should feel content or anxious at the way the nation's money matters turned out in the past year.

While he is saying this, the members of parliament are waiting impatiently to hear what changes he is going to make in the taxes people will have to pay. For the changes made in the budget are always kept secret until the end of the Chancellor's speech. At last he tells them. The tax on petrol is to be raised 2p a gallon perhaps, or income tax is to be lowered by $2\frac{1}{2}$p in the £; he may also say that there will be one or two new taxes. The reporters rush to the telephones and soon the taxpayers themselves are reading all about it in the newspaper headlines.

If new or higher taxes are announced they usually come into force at once. This is to stop people rushing out to buy things before the price goes up. All the Chancellor's proposals have to go in a bill, called the Finance Bill, which is passed by parliament, and the government's ideas for spending money also have to be agreed upon. You can read more about government finance in TAXES AND TREASURY.

Although this article has been about the budget for the whole country, you may hear your parents or other people you know talking about their budgets. They mean the amount of money they are able to spend each week or month and what they plan to spend it on.

BUENOS AIRES, whose name means "fair winds", is the capital of Argentina in South America and one of the largest cities on the whole American continent. It has a population of about 3,600,000.

Spanish colonists first settled where the city now stands in 1536, but they suffered from lack of food and were harassed by the Indians, so they finally moved away. No other colonists arrived until 1580 and this time they stayed.

Although Buenos Aires is the chief port of Argentina it lies 200 kilometres from the sea on the estuary of the Plata River. There is no natural harbour—an artificial one had to be made—and when ocean-going ships became too large for the shallow river, channels were dredged to allow them to pass in and out. The citizens of Buenos Aires call themselves *porteños* ("people of the port").

The city has many important business streets. The narrow Calle Florida is a well-known shopping street and is closed to wheeled vehicles at all times so that people can gaze into the shop windows at leisure without having to get out of the way of traffic. The Avenida 9 de Julio is one of the widest streets in the world (130 metres).

Another important street is the tree-lined Avenida de Mayo (Avenue of May) which seems as if it might have been transplanted from Paris. It is bordered with many clubs, hotels and business houses, all of the same height, while the cafés have tables on the pavements where people can eat and drink while watching the passers-by, just as they do in Paris. At one end of the avenue is the palace of the Argentine Congress, or parliament, and at the other stands the square called the Plaza de Mayo. In the Plaza are the headquarters of the president of the Argentine Republic, called Casa Rosada (Pink House), and the old Spanish cathedral in which the remains of the national hero, José de San Martin, lie buried. In the part of the city where people live, the finest street is the Avenida Alvear, where there are palaces owned by millionaires who made their money by selling meat, wheat and wool to Europe.

Picturepoint

The Avenida 9 de Julio, one of the widest streets in the world.

BUFFALO

Courtesy, B.O.A.C.
Malaysian water buffalo. Domesticated animals are used for farm work and provide milk, meat and leather.

More than half of Argentina's industries are in Greater Buenos Aires. Near the waterfront are many grain elevators, and there are meat packing establishments which prepare the carcasses of sheep and cattle for the home market and for export. Other large modern factories make cement, paper, glass, shoes and clothing.

Besides being the business and trading centre of Argentina, and the terminus of the principal railways, Buenos Aires is a centre of education and the arts. It has a well-known university and some fine schools. Apart from New York and London, no other capital in the world has so many theatres as Buenos Aires. There are many beautiful parks which add to its charm. Every July a great agricultural show is held in Palermo Park, where the finest pedigree cattle and sheep are exhibited.

BUFFALO. Although the bison of the American prairies is often called the buffalo, the true buffaloes come from much warmer lands in Asia and Africa. The best known of them is the Indian water buffalo. The wild kind, often called the arna, is found in various forms from India and Burma to Borneo in the East Indies; several thousands of years ago it used to live as far away as Mesopotamia (now Iraq). It is called the water buffalo because it lives in the tall grass on the flat land not far from the rivers. Buffaloes love to lie in water or to wallow in mud, to help to avoid the flies as well as to keep cool. They are sociable animals, who live in large herds.

The water buffalo has been tamed for very many centuries, and is most valuable as a working animal. It can stand wet conditions and for this reason is much used in the flooded rice fields. Many millions of them are at work in India and over 1,000,000 in the Philippines. The buffalo is used as a domestic animal far from its real home and even today it can be seen in parts of southern Europe, including Italy. It gives good milk as well as meat and very useful leather. The water buffalo is larger than most domestic cattle of the east and may reach a shoulder height of nearly two metres, though it is generally rather less, with horns as much as two metres long.

The African or Cape buffalo is sometimes thought to be the most dangerous of all wild animals. It has never been domesticated. It is found in many parts of Africa, from the far south to the Gambia in the west and the Sudan in the north. The biggest are found in East Africa and may be as much as 1·5 metres high at the shoulder and very heavy. The horns are widespread and sometimes over 1 metre across. In West Africa they are much smaller and may be less than 1 metre high, with poor narrow horns. This form is often called the "bush cow" and is reddish instead of black, which is the general colour. African buffaloes like dense cover, especially near rivers, and are difficult to shoot for the head is well protected by the broad, nobbly bases of the horns which almost form a shield. Buffaloes also have the unpleasant habit of waiting for the hunter and turning on him unexpectedly, especially if wounded.

The smallest of all the buffaloes is found in the island of Celebes in Indonesia. It is called the anoa and is usually about 90 centimetres at the shoulder. It is almost black all over, except sometimes for some small white patches on the head and feet. The horns are short and nearly straight and not at all like those of most other buffaloes.

BUFFALO BILL (1846–1917). William Frederick Cody, to give him his real name, was born in Iowa, in the United States, and took his first job at the age of 15 as a member of the pony express. This was a team of horsemen who carried mail a distance of 3,140 kilometres from St. Joseph, Missouri, to Sacramento, California, by relays of ponies, each rider covering about 120 kilometres every day. When the American Civil War broke out in 1861 Cody left the pony express and became a scout for the Northern army and after that spent many years fighting the Red Indians. He was given the name Buffalo Bill in 1867 when he made a contract to supply buffalo meat to the workmen building the Kansas Pacific Railway; it is said that in 18 months he himself killed over 4,000 buffaloes. (The animals called buffaloes in America are really bison.) In 1883 he organized the first Wild West show with cowboys and Red Indians. It was exciting and spectacular and with it he toured Europe, appearing before royalty. It is said that he once gave five royal visitors a thrilling experience when he took them for a ride round the arena in the famous Deadwood coach.

BUG. It is quite usual for all sorts of insects to be called bugs, but this name should really be given only to one particular group of insects, known scientifically as the Hemiptera. True bugs have one thing in common: instead of having jaws to bite with, like beetles for instance, they have a sharp, tube-like beak through which they suck up their food. They are nearly always found upon plants, the various parts of which they pierce with their beak in order to feed upon the sap. Some kinds, especially in warmer parts of the world, are serious pests. In Great Britain, a little bug called the apple capsid does damage in orchards by piercing and spoiling the fruits.

Young chinch bugs (top) do great damage by sucking the sap of plants, especially that of wheat and other crops. Capsid bugs (bottom) are a menace to fruit.

Bugs are among the most brightly coloured of all insects, many of those found in the tropics being as showy as butterflies. They also vary a great deal in size and shape ; for instance cicadas are among the largest known insects. There are bugs that look just like thorns and others with delicate outgrowths on their body that make them look like pieces of lace.

Unlike butterflies and beetles, bugs do not pass through a grub and chrysalis stage. The nymphs, or young, differ from their parents chiefly in having no wings until they have moulted for the last time. Most bugs fly well and have two pairs of wings. The front pair are thicker and tougher than the hind pair which lie folded and hidden beneath them when not in use.

The "assassin" bugs, as their name suggests, prey upon other insects. They often overpower insects much larger than themselves by injecting a tiny drop of poison with the first sharp thrust of the beak. The poison acts so quickly that the victim is paralysed before it can struggle free.

The unpleasant bedbug has a remarkably flattened body which makes it possible for it to hide away in cracks and crevices in dwellings. At night it creeps out to feed upon human blood, crawling into beds and biting the sleepers. The bedbug is found, as a rule, only in houses that are dirty and neglected.

BUGLE. The musical instrument called the bugle is a tube made of copper, about four feet six inches long. This tube is coiled so that the bugle is easier to handle. The mouthpiece of the bugle is small and the tube widens out at the other end, which is called the bell. The different notes on the bugle are produced according to how hard the player blows and the way in which he stretches his lips across the mouthpiece.

Today the bugle is used only in the drum and bugle bands of the services, the Scouts and similar organizations, and in signalling in the armed forces. The British Army has its bugle calls for every occasion from "Reveille", the signal for getting up, to the "Last Post" and "Lights Out". (See BUGLE CALLS.) Only five notes are needed for these calls.

The word bugle in mediaeval English meant

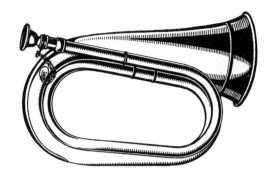

The bugle has no valves or keys, but few notes are needed.

"young ox", and the earliest bugles were, in fact, made from the horns of animals. Indeed, the bugle is a very ancient instrument : in the Biblical story of the capture of the city of Jericho by Joshua, bugles of cow's horn were blown to make the walls fall down, and another Jewish leader, Gideon, used a band of bugles to frighten his enemies the Midianites.

BUGLE CALLS. Until about 250 years ago, orders were given to the cavalry by trumpet and to the infantry with the drum, but when soldiers were trained as light infantry, moving spaced out over rough ground, they could not always hear the drum. So the bugle was introduced, for its notes carry clearly over a long distance. The drum was still used, however, to give orders to soldiers who were on parade and so well within earshot.

What are bugle calls used for now? They tell the soldier when to get up, when to come to meals, when to go on parade, and when to put out the lights at night. There are many British bugle calls, but none uses more than five notes. They were first collected and published in 1798, and some of them may have been composed by Franz Joseph Haydn, for he was on a visit to England at about that time. Bugle calls have been introduced into works for orchestra by Sir Charles Stanford and Ethel Smyth.

The best-known and most beautiful calls are the "Reveille" and the "Last Post". These are sounded at military funerals and on Remembrance Day, although they are really just the first and last bugle calls of the day. Another call you are sure to know is the one to which you

278

Captain Tom Tayler, R.M.

Royal Marines.

can fit the words "Come to the cook-house door, boys; come to the cook-house door." Others call soldiers to their daily duties, tell them to stand still or give them the alarm.

Similar calls are sounded in the Royal Navy, the Royal Air Force and in organizations such as the Scouts and the Boys' Brigade.

BUILDING. When someone decides to have a house built to suit his own wishes the first thing he ought to do is consult an architect. A site for the house has to be found, and permission to build there has to be obtained from the planning authorities. The architect will first survey the site, noting the differences in level and general slope of the ground and obtaining the other information he needs when deciding upon the exact position of the house. He draws a map of the site and on this he plans the house, producing finally a plan that satisfies the owner's wishes about the numbers of rooms, their size and arrangement, the general appearance of the house and the way in which it fits in with its surroundings.

The architect next produces the drawings which give full details of the way in which the house is to be constructed. The general drawings are to a scale of an eighth of an inch representing one foot (or 1 centimetre representing 1 metre) but certain details are drawn much larger than this, sometimes actually full-size. Many notes of the materials to be used are written on the drawings but a full description of the work to be

done and the materials to be used are put down in another very important document called the specification. The architect makes sure that every question which may be asked about the building of the house can be answered from the specification and the drawings.

When the drawings are ready the architect must apply to the local authority (which is responsible for approving plans) for permission to begin building. With his application he must send a set of drawings and a copy of the specification so that the local housing authority can make sure that the building does not break any building regulations. All buildings must be safe and must be up to certain standards in other respects such as keeping out dampness, providing enough natural light and ventilation and having proper drainage and sanitation.

The Building Contract

The architect may now approach the firms that do the actual building and he usually asks several of them to state a price for doing the work. This preparation of estimates, or tenders, by highly skilled estimators forms a very important part of the work of building firms. Copies of the drawings and specification are obtained from the architect and carefully studied.

For all but the smallest job, the architect usually arranges also for a bill of quantities to be available. This document sets out the amount of all the various types of work involved in the building and its main purpose is to make sure that all firms estimate for exactly the same work and that no misunderstandings of the drawings or specification can afterwards cause argument.

Beside studying the various drawings and documents provided, a firm that is making out an estimate will usually visit the site to see whether difficulty in getting to it, or any other obstacle, is likely to increase the cost of the work. The estimators will also be in touch with the firms that supply materials and will find out their prices. An efficient building firm will go to a good deal of trouble to find out how much labour it will take to do the various jobs on the building such as excavation, brickwork, carpentry and so on. Tenders have normally to be prepared in about a fortnight and so the estimators

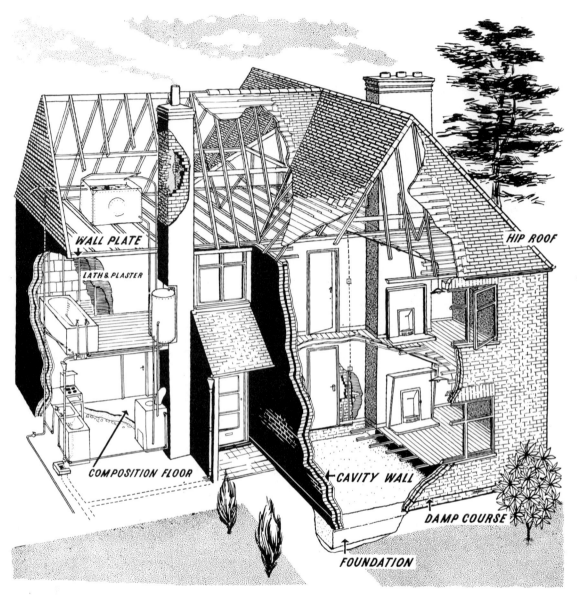

WALL PLATE

LATH & PLASTER

HIP ROOF

COMPOSITION FLOOR

CAVITY WALL

DAMP COURSE

FOUNDATION

How a modern house is built. The purpose of the damp course and the hollow wall is to keep the house dry and warm.

have to work hard to get them ready in time.

The tenders from the various building firms are opened by the architect at the same time and usually the lowest one is accepted. The owner of the building and the firm which is to build it are said to "enter into a contract"; the firm says that it will do the work and the owner agrees to pay the price asked.

A building job of this type is often known as a contract and building firms are known as building contractors. The drawings, specification and bill of quantities are known as contract documents because they contain the official description of the work to be done. The actual form of contract will also set down the date by which the work is to be completed, the method of making payments and the various ways in which the contractor must safeguard the interests of the building owner while the work is being done.

From time to time as the work proceeds, the contractor is paid a proportion of the value of the work he has already done. Usually about

The Sydney Opera House as it appeared while under construction. The construction of a large and imaginatively-designed building such as this can be a long complex job.

Courtesy, Wates Ltd.

Top left: The first stage in the construction of a building. Materials are brought to the site in trucks and the foundations are begun. Bottom left: The skeleton takes shape with foundations complete and metal rods in position as concrete reinforcements. Centre: Glass, woodwork, plumbing and electricity can be installed once the outer structure is in place. Right: The building is now complete and ready to be occupied.

10% of the value is kept by the building owner to cover the repair of any defects in the work which may appear later. Half the amount of the money the owner keeps is usually paid to the contractor when the work is finished. The contractor is made responsible for putting right any defects which occur within a certain period, usually between three months and a year, after the completion of the work. The final payment is made at the end of that period.

The contractor gets to work as soon as he is given the contract, before actual building begins. He has usually to enclose the site and erect huts and other buildings for the use of the workmen and of the staff that supervise them. A timetable for the work is drawn up showing the labour that will be required at various times and when materials should be delivered. Materials are ordered and, if special sections of the work are to be carried out by other firms (called subcontractors), these subcontracts are arranged.

The first work on the building site itself is the "setting out"; that is, the marking of the position of the house on the site. The corners of the build-ing are marked by pegs and short lengths of board are set up with marks to show the lines of foundation trenches and the faces of walls. The architect is usually responsible for seeing that this first setting out is correct, but after that the contractor must see that the work is accurate.

Foundations and Brickwork

Brick walls are usually built on concrete foundations placed 60 to 90 centimetres below the surface of the ground. Trenches are, therefore, dug equal in width to the concrete foundation and deep enough to give a good bottom for the concrete. Concrete is poured into the bottom of the trench and finished level at the required thickness. The brick walls are begun on these strips of concrete. When the brickwork has been brought above ground level the sides of the trenches are filled in. The turf is stripped and the top soil removed from the whole site to be covered by the house; this area is sometimes covered by a layer of concrete so that there is a clean foundation space below the floors.

Considerable thought is given to laying the

first courses, or layers, of bricks (see BRICKLAY-ING) so that the bricks are arranged to "bond" properly and need to be cut as little as possible. The openings in the brickwork for windows and doors higher up in the walls have to be taken into account when deciding on the arrangement of bricks to be adopted. When the brickwork has reached about 15 centimetres above ground level a layer of waterproof material (damp-proof course) has to be built into all walls. This prevents moisture from the ground being drawn up by the bricks and making the floors and lower walls damp.

To form the ground floor a layer of brick rubble, or similar material, is rammed down firmly and a layer of concrete is placed above it. This is made level and left ready for a finishing surface to be added at a later stage. Sometimes ground floors are made of timber boarding laid on floor joists which form a bridge between the walls. The ground below timber floors should be covered with a layer of concrete, and gratings or air bricks should be built into those parts of the walls that lie below the timber floor. This provides ventilation of the space below the floor and is necessary, for otherwise dampness would cause the timber to rot.

Frames for doors and windows are built into the walls as the brickwork proceeds and the beams or lintels, which go over the top of the doors or windows, must be placed above the openings to carry the brickwork and other loads which come from the upper part of the building. When the upper surface of the wall forms the bottom of a window opening it is protected by a sill of stone, wood or other material capable of keeping out the dampness. Special construction is also necessary at the threshold of an outer door. Window frames, without glass, may now be put in but the doors are hung later.

Upper Floors and Roof

The walls are now too high for men to work at them when standing on the ground and it is necessary to provide a raised platform, or scaffold, all round the building at a convenient height for the bricklayers. The scaffold is supported on a framework of steel tubes, and ladders are provided so that the men can get to the working platform. Materials such as bricks and mortar used to be carried up the ladders by builders' labourers but it is now usual to provide mechanical hoists.

Upper floors are made in much the same way as the timber ground floors. Wall plates (lengths of timber 75 millimetres by 50 millimetres) are built into the walls to form a support for the joists which are to bridge the walls. Boards are then nailed to the joists to form the floor. The upper walls continue to rise, windows to upper rooms being built in, until the eaves are reached. This is the top of the wall where another wall plate is fixed to support the ends of the rafters which form the roof. Sometimes the end walls are carried right up to the ridge, so forming a triangular gable end. Alternatively, a roof may slope down to the ends as well as along the side, so forming what are called hipped ends.

When the rafters are fixed they are covered with boarding or smaller strips of timber known as battens so that tiles or slates may be laid as a roof covering.

Finishing the Inside

The contractor usually completes the outside shell of the building as rapidly as possible since, until the roof is finished, bad weather may interfere with the work. Once the roof is finished the inside of the house is protected and work can proceed. The glass is put into the windows to provide additional protection.

Plumbers fix the water pipes, heating and hot-water services and make connections for sinks, lavatory basins and sanitary fittings. Joiners fix the stairs and cupboards. The bricklayers fix fireplaces and stoves, and floor and wall tiling is laid. The electricians and gas fitters run their conduits and pipes for lighting, cooking and heating. At this stage the job calls for special skill in organizing the work so that the various craftsmen come in the best order and avoid interfering with each other or spoiling one another's work or causing delay.

When as much as possible of this work has been completed, the plasterers plaster the walls and ceilings. Heavy fixing work, involving hammering and vibration, is best done before the plastering, otherwise the finished plaster work may be spoiled by cracks. When plastering is completed the joiners fix the skirtings and hang the doors, and plumbers put in the sanitary fittings.

Last Touches Outside

If the house is in the country, it may be necessary to build septic tanks to deal with the drainage from the house, but in towns and most larger villages a system of sewers is provided and the house drains are connected to the nearest convenient point in a sewer. Drainage is made up of rainwater from roofs and yards, wastes from sinks, lavatory basins and baths and also from sanitary fittings. These are taken from various points round the outside of the house and run through earthenware drain pipes sloping down to a central collecting point with an inspection pit ("manhole"). From this, one drain leads to the sewer. (See DRAINAGE; SEWER.)

Trenches must be dug along all these lines for the drains to be laid and the manhole is constructed in brick. Roof gutters are fixed and rainwater and waste pipes are attached to the side of the house, leading down to the drainage points. All underground work in the drainage system is tested by inspectors from the local authority before the drainage trenches are filled in. These tests ensure that water flows properly down the drains and that the drains do not leak.

All wood and a good deal of metal has to be painted in order to be preserved. At least three coats of paint should be applied to new work. The walls of the rooms may either be painted or covered with paper in order that a decorative finish may be given. The house is then ready for furnishing.

Out of doors, in the space provided for the garden, fences and gates are put up and drives and paths laid. The contractor removes the last of his plant and temporary buildings from the site and after a final inspection by the architect the house is handed over to its owner.

Large Buildings

Large commercial and industrial buildings are built in much the same way as a house. The most important differences are connected with the methods of carrying the loads from the floors.

In houses, the floor beams rest on the walls; larger buildings are usually constructed as a framework of beams and columns, the loads on the floors being carried by the beams whose ends are supported by the columns. The walls are then no more than screens supported on wall beams at each floor.

The frameworks may be either of steel or of reinforced concrete and when the foundations of the building have been completed the framework rises rapidly. The floors are made before walls, and much of the interior work can be begun before the walls are finished.

Timber-framed construction has been much used for houses in the past and is still used in parts of the world where timber is plentiful. A number of attempts have been made in recent years to apply other systems of frame construction to house building in Britain.

Courtesy, Wates Ltd.
A 12-storey block built from pre-cast concrete units.

Pre-cast concrete units are also widely used for building. Pre-cast panels of interlocking walls and floors are often used in the building of high and low rise blocks of flats. In "system building" like this, the floors, walls, staircases and even refuse chutes are cast in standard steel moulds in factories. Some are transported to the building site, others are made in a factory on the site itself. Cranes are used to erect the parts which usually weigh up to 4 tonnes each. The standard concrete units can be adapted to various designs.

EXPLORING ROMAN BRITAIN

by Graham Webster

THE PEOPLE OF BRITAIN

Many people think that most of the inhabitants of Roman Britain were Romans – soldiers and officials who had all left Italy and had come to live here. But there must have been many people living in Britain before the Romans came. Who were they, and what happened to them when the Roman army invaded this island in A.D. 43?

These Britons belonged to many different tribes and the tribes had different customs and languages from one another. In the south of this island the tribes were descended from people who had migrated from Gaul, just across the sea, in the previous hundred years. The ancestors of the tribes in the north and west of Britain had reached these shores even earlier. They had come from different parts of the western seaboard of Europe. And when these people arrived in Britain they pushed the tribes already living here into remote areas of Wales and North Britain, where they lived a nomadic, or wandering, existence with their herds, hunting and fishing to add to their resources. Britain was, therefore, inhabited by quite a large number of people when the Roman army arrived. Most of those who survived the early struggles continued to live in Britain under the Roman occupation and so made up the greater part of the population.

Who came with the Romans? The Roman army itself must have contained the greatest number of newcomers; but these were not all from Italy. About sixty or seventy thousand of the soldiers would be men from many parts of the Roman Empire, such as Gaul, Spain and Germany. As well as the army there would be civilian officials – civil servants who ran the country, collecting taxes, administering the law and so on. Then the merchants would have come. Hearing about this newly discovered land with its mineral resources they would see Britain as a rich field for buying raw materials and for selling their merchandise – pottery, bronze vessels, glass and the gaudy trinkets which would have delighted the eye of many a Briton.

But the Britons were faced with great changes. They had previously lived in a kind of feudal society. This means that they owed allegiance to their overlord and their priests. There were often wars between neighbouring tribes. When the Romans came all this was changed, for the Romans set up a government to control the whole of Britain as one province, and made people settle down peacefully with one another. This also introduced the idea of towns. Most Britons had never seen a town. They lived in small communities, in round wooden huts with thatched roofs, clustered together in their hill-top fortresses, or scattered as farms over the land they cultivated. There were no paved or cobbled roads along which carts could take heavy loads – only winding tracks.

Although some of the British tribes had their own coinage, there had been no development of trade on a large scale, and the farmers produced only sufficient grain for their own needs and for those to whom they owed their allegiance. But the Romans had been brought up to quite a different idea of existence. For a very long time the town had been a centre of organized life in the Mediterranean world. People lived there in houses built along streets, and in the centre there were the shops, taverns, great markets and public buildings where people came together to buy and sell and to conduct their business. Joining the Roman towns was a system of highways, so that goods could easily be transported to market from the farms and factories.

It probably took the Britons a long while to get used to the idea of having roads and towns and markets. But slowly the road system was built up, at first to enable the army to move about the country with speed, and later for the movement of goods. Thus towns came into being just like those in other parts of the Roman world. In the countryside however, little was changed except that farmers needed more and more land to grow corn, since so much of their corn had to be paid to the Roman authorities to feed the army. So more land came under cultivation.

While the towns were growing up as centres of trade with many fine buildings and houses, the Britons continued to live in the same kind of houses as before, cultivating their land in much the same way. But their lives were affected by the new system of government. They no longer looked to their old tribal chieftains for help and support, but suffered under new landowners who probably sent stern bailiffs to extract as much tax and corn from the peasants as they could.

It is difficult for us to realize how slowly these changes and developments took place. The Roman occupation of Britain extended over four centuries. If *we* look back over the last four centuries we are looking back to the reign of Queen Elizabeth I. This seems to us now to be a very long time ago. Things have changed a great deal in that time, and they have changed very gradually. So it is difficult to condense the history of Roman Britain into one small book, when we need to look at the growth and development of the towns, the countryside, the army and many other aspects of people's lives over a period of 400 years.

The main aim of this guide, therefore, is to show you where to look for signs of this long occupation, and where to study it in more detail.

THE ROMAN FORCES
The Legions

In A.D. 43, the year in which Britain was invaded, the Roman Imperial Army had a main fighting force of nearly 30 legions stationed throughout the Empire. Each legion contained between five and six thousand men, organized in cohorts and centuries, something like this:

$$\begin{aligned} 80 \text{ men} &= 1 \text{ century} \\ 6 \text{ centuries} &= 1 \text{ cohort} \\ 10 \text{ cohorts} &= 1 \text{ legion} \end{aligned}$$

The legions were an élite corps, and only a Roman citizen could become a legionary.

A legionary had steel body armour arranged in plates and strips to protect chest and back. Each man carried two seven-foot *pila* (javelins). The *pilum* had a wooden shaft with an iron head. This had a soft shank so that when it was thrown and stuck into something, it bent over and became difficult to remove. The *pila* would be thrown in volleys at the advancing enemy, who would raise their shields to protect themselves. The *pilum* would become firmly embedded in the shield and bend over. A seven-foot *pilum* dangling from his shield was a serious encumbrance, and the man was forced to abandon the shield.

With the enemy thus checked, the legionaries then drew their

A Roman legionary.

double-edged swords which were about two feet long and two inches wide. These were short, thrusting weapons, quite different from the long swords used by their Celtic enemies. Now the legionaries raised their shields before them and thrust themselves into the enemy in wedge-shaped formations, pushing them down vigorously with the shields, and thrusting the short swords into their unprotected bodies. The enemy were now so crowded together that they were unable to wield their long swords effectively.

With their superior body armour and equipment, their professional training and discipline, the legions could defeat great numbers of less well trained men. The Celtic peoples were great fighters, brave and tough, but they always preferred individual combat, and were rarely organized to use such intricate tactics as the well-trained, professional Roman soldiers.

At Maiden Castle in Dorset, you can see the site of one of these battles. Here the Britons withdrew behind the earthworks of the great hill fort, but were heavily defeated by the Romans. In their war cemetery was found the body of a Briton with the Roman weapon still in it.

The Auxiliaries

Units which assisted the legions were known as *auxilia*. These were recruited from the provinces outside Italy. They were usually 500 strong – the size of a legionary cohort, and each had a special way of fighting.

For horsemen in particular, the Romans always had to rely on their allies. From the earliest times cavalry was levied from conquered countries as part of their annual tribute to Rome. The horses were small and the horsemen wore light armour. They were normally stationed on the wings of the battlefield, and held back until the enemy was broken by the legionaries who took the main shock of the onslaught. As the enemy turned to flee, the horsemen rode forward, cutting the enemy down, and so completed the victory.

There were various kinds of horsemen and foot soldiers fighting in their own native traditions. There were specialists such as the slingers, who were recruited from the Balearic Islands, the archers with their short bows who came from Syria, and the men with long heavy spears who came from Gaul. The Batavian cavalry, from the Low Countries, were specially trained to swim across rivers, fully armed and with the horses, to outflank enemy forces who might be guarding a river crossing.

Cavalry parade helmet with face mask, found at Ribchester, Lancashire.

290

The Fleet

This formed a third section of the Roman army. It was used for transporting troops, equipment and supplies in the Mediterranean and along the great European rivers. Naturally this arm was very important for the invasion of Britain, and after the Roman conquest, a special British fleet was created to patrol the coast. The lighthouse at Dover remains to remind us of the Roman ships crossing the Channel.

HISTORY OF ROMAN BRITAIN

The Roman Invasion

The invasion army of A.D. 43 consisted of four legions: II *Augusta*, IX *Hispana*, XIV *Gemina* and XX *Valeria*. This would be about 25,000 men, with probably another 25,000 in 50 or 60 auxiliary units.

The conquest of the lowlands of Britain was very rapid, and it was not long before the army was stretched out on a frontier between the Humber and the Bristol Channel. It may not have been the intention of the Romans to advance any further at this stage, but they were forced to do so because the British prince, Caratacus, had placed himself at the head of the tribes in Wales and was harrying the frontier. The troops in the centre then moved forward up to the River Severn to bring Caratacus to bay, and he was defeated in a great battle somewhere in central Wales. The new frontier was however very unsatisfactory to the Romans because the Welsh tribes carried on a vigorous guerilla warfare in the very difficult country of the Welsh Marches, the present-day border area. Eventually the situation became so bad that it was decided to move forward and take over the whole of Wales.

Soon after this, the Brigantes (the people of Yorkshire and Lancashire) started to be troublesome under their king Venutius, and an advance had to be made northwards. This continued under the

THE PRINCIPAL TOWNS AND INDUSTRIES
OF ROMAN BRITAIN

famous general Julius Agricola who eventually took the Roman army right up into Scotland and overcame the Caledonian tribes. But the Romans felt that Scotland was not worth occupying so they gradually retired to a frontier between the Tyne and Solway, which during the reign of Hadrian they fortified with a great wall, known as Hadrian's Wall. It stretched from coast to coast and along it were constructed forts, milecastles and turrets. Behind this frontier, in the mountain areas the army now occupied, forts were spaced out in a network with communicating roads.

The Settlement of Britain

In the 1st century A.D. it had been the practice of the Roman army to build everything with timber, but by the beginning of the 2nd century it was necessary to provide more permanent defences and buildings. A vast programme of work was started, rebuilding most of the timber buildings on stone foundations, building some of the more important buildings entirely of stone, and providing the defences with solid stone walls.

The military situation never remained the same for very long and the northern frontier was always a difficult problem. Hardly had the great wall of Hadrian been completed when it was abandoned and the frontier moved forward to the Clyde–Forth line, where a new barrier was built, known as the Antonine Wall. This was made of turf instead of stone, but only lasted until the end of the second century, when it was abandoned and Hadrian's Wall brought once more into operation. There was, however, yet another great campaign in Scotland under the Emperor Severus which appears to have subdued the Caledonian tribes for at least another century.

Another change in the army strategy became necessary when bands of pirates began to raid the east coast from the Baltic and the Low Countries. To deal with the new threat special forts were built on the coast from the Wash to the Solent. These forts are known as the Saxon Shore Forts, and housed garrisons which not only protected the fleet, but also dealt with any of the pirates if they managed to make a landing.

The Roman army changed a great deal during the course of the occupation and the troops tended gradually to become more and more a kind of garrison force permanently attached to a station. Their sons grew up to be soldiers of the local garrison and families were given land which settled them permanently in a district. This meant that by the 4th century there had developed two kinds of soldiers, the permanent garrison troops and the mobile forces. The latter consisted of picked men, mostly mounted, since cavalry had gradually become more and more appreciated. They had their bases well behind the frontier zones so that they could move forward and deal with any serious trouble when it arose.

The End of Roman Occupation

Britain in fact never had a field army permanently stationed in it, but during the course of the 4th century it was necessary several times to bring one over from Gaul to deal with the troublesome raiders. One of the most serious occasions was in the year A.D. 367 when several different groups of barbarians got together and made a concerted attack from Ireland, Scotland and the North Sea. On this occasion a Roman field army was defeated and many historians have assumed that this marked the end of Roman Britain. But while this may have been a serious disaster, there is no archaeological evidence of any widespread destruction, either in the towns or the countryside, and life seems to have continued much the same. Soon, however, with increasing pressure on the Rhine and Danube, the Roman government was forced to take away more and more of the better troops from Britain, and finally in A.D. 410 the British tribes were told to look after themselves.

This they did by hiring their own soldiers, mostly Saxon mercenaries from Germany, but the people of Britain could not maintain the standard of culture even in the towns and they became more and more barbarized. It must be assumed that eventually the mercenaries took over. So Roman Britain gradually merged into Saxon England. There never was a moment of time when the new invaders swept through the land with fire and sword. The battles described in the *Anglo-Saxon Chronicle* (a collection of Anglo-Saxon and early mediaeval writings) give only the Saxon side of the story. It seems likely that the Celtic population survived, exchanging one kind of overlord for another.

THINGS TO SEE

There are many remains of Roman Britain to be seen in all parts of the country. In many museums there are the pottery, glass and metal objects which have survived in the ground, but one has always to remember that there must have been many more things made of cloth, wood and leather which have perished. So in looking at the objects in museums, one needs help from diagrams, illustrations and imagination to clothe the people of this time and see them in their everyday life. There are many remains above ground and others which have been excavated and preserved so that they can be visited and studied. But it is very difficult to understand some of these buildings merely by looking at the foundations and the task of re-construction is not always an easy one. I will now try to select places where you can go and see some of the best of these military and civil remains in different parts of the country.

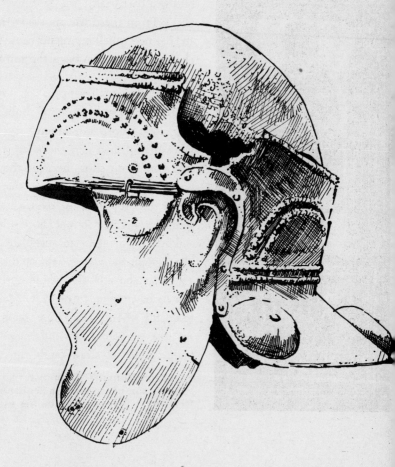

Bronze helmet found near Ely.

Remains of the Roman Army

TOMBSTONES. There are few remains of the 1st century to be seen, but there are some tombstones. In the museums of Lincoln and Gloucester, where there once stood great legionary fortresses, you can see some of these. They record the man's name, rank, birthplace, age and years of service. Occasionally the stones have a carved relief of the soldier himself in his best parade equipment, as he would have wished to be remembered. Two of the best of these stones are to be seen in the Castle Museum at Colchester. One tombstone, in memory of Facilis, a centurion of XX Legion, was erected by two of his slaves who gained their freedom on the death of their master. The other is to Longinus, a horseman of the First Thracian *ala* or regiment. There is another fine stone in the Corinium Museum at Cirencester, and one in Hexham Abbey, Northumberland, showing a soldier killing a barbarian.

From these we can study the dress and equipment of the army and deduce which regiments came to Britain. Can you think of anything else we might learn from the tombstones?

FORTS. Actual remains of 1st-century forts have not survived because they were built of timber and turf. Most timber has rotted away long since, and, in any case, as the army advanced the buildings were demolished and the sites were levelled off. However, we can still find these sites, because the crops above the old ditches grow taller and stay green longer than the crop in the rest of the field, while the crop growing over a long-forgotten Roman road will grow shorter and ripen sooner. So if a field has the right kind of crop in it, and if we go up in an aeroplane at the right time of year, we can photograph the whole field, and study the pattern of the crop-marks. This may show us the whole outline of a fort with a ditch round it, and roads running through it. Such crop-marks help the archaeologist to decide where to dig, if he wants to find out when the fort was in use. As you go round the museums you may see some of these aerial photographs on show, and you can try picking out the crop-marks

Tombstone found at Cirencester and now in the Gloucester Museum.
"Philus, son of Cassavus, a Sequanian of Gaul aged 45.
Here is the place [where he lies buried]."

Crop-marks, seen from the air, reveal the site of a fort.

for yourself. A Roman fort is usually shaped something like the one in the illustration, so this is the shape to look for. The archaeologist can tell where the timber buildings once stood by carefully studying changes of colour in the subsoil when the topsoil has been removed.

Although later forts were built of stone, all surface traces of these may have disappeared. One reason is that later people came and took away the stone to build their own houses and churches. Hexham Abbey and St. Albans Cathedral are good examples of this. Another reason may be that later people have simply built on top of the old Roman towns. At Chester (Deva) and York (Eburacum) for example, it is very difficult to find the great legionary fortresses, although in both places it is possible to walk round some of the walls which have survived. The third great legionary fortress at Caerleon (Isca) has survived in better state, and although there is a modern village in the centre of it, you can trace the outline and see some of the barrack blocks inside which have been excavated and exposed. Outside the fortress you can see a fine amphitheatre. The sites of many Welsh forts can be found, with the help of an Ordnance Survey map, but there is little to be seen except the outline of the defences and the levelled plateau where the fort stood. At Segontium, near Caernarvon, many of the buildings have been excavated and preserved. There are some splendid remains of forts on or near Hadrian's Wall.

HADRIAN'S WALL. This is the greatest Roman monument in Britain, and indeed in the whole of the world. It is 72 miles long, stretching from Wallsend, on the Tyne, right across England to Carlisle, and along the coast to Bowness-on-Solway. But this was in no way the end of the frontier – the Cumberland coast was protected by a series of forts spaced out down to St. Bee's Head, and there were probably similar forts on the east coast down to Tynemouth. Much of this remarkable wall has been preserved where it crosses the hills, and the best way of seeing it is by going on foot, following its track along the crests which dominate the countryside.

The Wall as you see it today is only a fraction of its former height. Though originally it stood at least 16 feet high, today only a half or a quarter still stands in some places. In front of the wall was a ditch 20 feet wide, and behind the wall is an earthwork known as the *Vallum* which has been a feature arousing much controversy. The *Vallum* is thought to have been a barrier to control the passage of goods and to delimit the strictly military zone, into which civilians were presumably not allowed. Incorporated into the Wall at about every Roman mile (1,620 yards), was a milecastle. These were little fortlets about 70 feet by 75 feet, each with two barrack blocks for the patrolling garrison. Between each milecastle were two turrets spaced out at intervals of about 540 yards, measuring 14 feet square internally. The main garrison was housed in 15 forts. Much is known about the history of the Wall and its forts from the many excavations which have taken place and the large collections of inscriptions which tell us often the names of the units in the forts. There are also many inscribed building stones which were originally part of the stone wall and these show which particular legion and cohort constructed a given length.

It is well worth while planning a trip along the Wall. There are youth hostels and camp sites for those who walk along it. The best place to start from is the Museum of Antiquities at the University of Newcastle, where you can study a model of the Wall and see many of the inscriptions and finds. There is also a full-scale model of the

Model of a milecastle
on Hadrian's Wall.

The milecastle at Castle Nick, on Hadrian's Wall.

temple of Mithras, mentioned below. You can obtain an Ordnance Survey *Map of Hadrian's Wall*, and all the information one can possibly need is in the *Handbook to the Roman Wall*. (There is a book list on the last page of this activity guide.) At the western end of the Wall you should visit Tullie House Museum, Carlisle, which has a fine collection of objects from the Wall and round about. There are Roman remains to be seen in both Newcastle (Benwell Fort) and Carlisle (Museum Garden), but on the Wall itself you should try to visit the forts at Chesters (Cilurnum), Carrawburgh (Brocolitia), where the temple of Mithras has been excavated and preserved, and Housesteads (Vercovicium), which is the only place where you can see the whole of a fort with its barracks, headquarters, granaries, roads and gateways. Here you can stand in the north gate and look out over "barbarian" country.

Another military site associated with the Wall but some distance to the south of it is Corbridge (Corstopitum). This site had a long and

The milecastle at Castle Nick as it is today.

complicated history and at one stage was a great store base and military workshops. Much of this site has been excavated and is preserved as an ancient monument, but one needs ample time to see it and its many interesting remains.

Chesters, Housesteads and Corbridge have museums with many fascinating objects in them – brooches, hairpins, coins, statues, cooking pots and so on.

SAXON SHORE FORTS. During the 3rd and 4th centuries a threat appeared to the safety of Britain from a different quarter. The North Sea was crossed by bands of raiders from the Baltic area. They landed on the shores and in the estuaries of the east coast and caused trouble in these unprotected areas. The answer was a series of strong forts along the coast from the Wash to the Solent. There were probably at least 12 of these forts, but some have disappeared entirely into the sea. They are square in plan and have very thick stone walls and projecting bastions. They show very clearly the change in ideas about defences in this late period when it became necessary to keep large bands of raiders at bay with fairly small forces. These fortresses operated in close touch with the fleet, which tried to intercept the raiders before they reached land, although there was an unscrupulous commander who found it more profitable to do this when they were returning laden with booty which he seized for himself.

The finest of these forts is Richborough (Rutupiae) near Sandwich. This is one of the most interesting sites to visit in Roman Britain, for here one can see the ditches of the first base constructed by the Invasion Army of A.D. 43, and also the foundations of a great memorial which commemorates the conquest of Britain, and the great Saxon Shore Fort, some of the walls standing almost to their original height. There is another at Reculver (Regulbium), but here one side of the fort has slipped down the cliff. Similarly there has been damage at Lympne (Lemanis). Perhaps the two best for preservation are at Pevensey (Anderita) and Portchester (Portus Adurni), but there is another very fine one at Burgh Castle (Gariannonum) near Yarmouth.

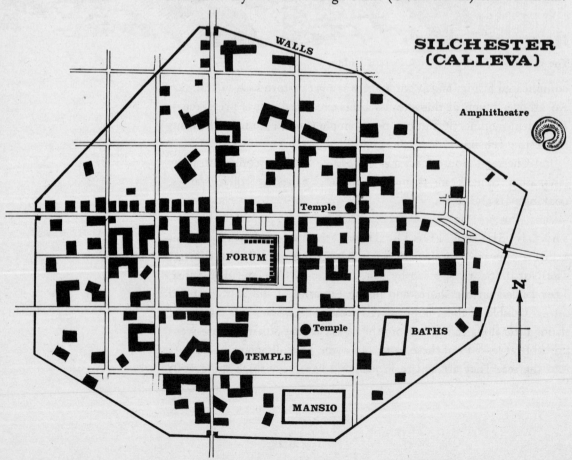

WALLS

SILCHESTER
(CALLEVA)

Amphitheatre

Temple

FORUM

Temple

TEMPLE

Temple

BATHS

N

MANSIO

Civilian Life

TOWNS. It was Roman policy to introduce town life into the barbarian areas they conquered. The towns were the markets where commerce could develop, and there was also the sound idea that these warlike barbarians could be made into respectable citizens. Then they would be less danger to the Romans, and would live in the Roman manner and pay their taxes regularly.

Like the principal towns all over the Roman world, those in Britain were laid out with a street grid, with the chief public buildings in the centre. Round the town was a circuit of walls with fine gateways where the main roads entered. The main public buildings were the forum and the bath-house. The forum was the market-place with its shops and booths around a great central courtyard. At one end stood the town hall, an enormous building supported by two rows of columns down the middle which must have looked very much like one of our great Norman cathedrals. Here the citizens could meet and law could be administered. Behind this building was a range of offices where the business of the town was carried out. The bath-house was a very large and complicated building, and the Romans introduced the idea of the daily bath as a social occasion. All the rooms were large enough for groups of citizens to congregate for talk and games as well as go through the ritual of the bath. The rooms were all of different temperatures and humidities, and people could pass from one to the other in any way they wished. Thus the more well-to-do citizens could spend much of the afternoon there and emerge clean and refreshed for the evening meal. Most of the towns had an amphi-theatre, a great arena with banks of seats all the way round. One could not have seen in Britain the great spectacles which were common in Rome, but there must have been wild beasts like bears, wolves and boars in mock hunts. Sometimes gladiators would perform, but these would have been expensive, something like our professional boxers and wrestlers. Criminals due for execution were also brought into the arena and cruelly attacked by wild animals or armed men in the semblance of a hunt or fight. The only town amphitheatres which remain visible today are at Cirencester (Corinium) and Dorchester (Durnovaria) in Dorset, although there is the same kind of structure outside the legionary fortresses at Caerleon (Isca) and Chester (Deva).

Unfortunately there is little to be seen of these monumental buildings in the towns of Roman Britain. This is because most towns continued to be occupied into Saxon, mediaeval or modern times, and these buildings have gradually been replaced. There are four towns where for different reasons the site was abandoned, and one can visit these and get some appreciation of their extent and layout. Perhaps the most interesting is Verulamium (St. Albans), where there has been much excavation which has told us a great deal about the houses and the life of the people and made the museum there one of the richest and most important in the country. Another town which is now under open fields is Silchester (Calleva) near Reading. This was partly excavated at the the end of the last century and the finds are now in the museum at Reading. Then there is the small town in East Anglia at Caistor St. Edmunds (Venta Icenorum) near Norwich, while in the west near Shrewsbury is the large and important city of Viroconium (Wroxeter), which was originally 200 acres in extent and where aerial photography has revealed the foundations of many buildings below the soil.

There are some important fragments of buildings that can be seen in the towns which have become some of our important modern cities. Even in London where there has been so much development through the ages, a fragment of the town wall can still be seen at the Tower of London. At Lincoln there is the Newport Arch still spanning the northern entrance into the town, and at Leicester there is a large piece of wall known as the Jewry Wall which was probably part of the bath-house. Elsewhere fragments of the town walls can be seen embodied in the later mediaeval ones, as at Canterbury (Durovernum), Dorchester in Dorset, Cirencester, Caerwent (Venta) and Chichester (Noviomagus). At Caerwent there is a fine length of walling with its projecting bastions which is well worth seeing.

One of the most important towns was Camulodunum (Colchester). Like Lincoln (Lindum) and Gloucester (Glevum) this was a *colonia* specially built for army veterans. They were given large grants of land in the area around the town and here they lived as models of citizenship for the Britons to imitate. Unfortunately many of these veterans were as barbarian in their habits as the Britons themselves. Their callous and brutal behaviour at Camulodunum was one of the causes of the great revolt under Queen Boudicca (Boadicea)

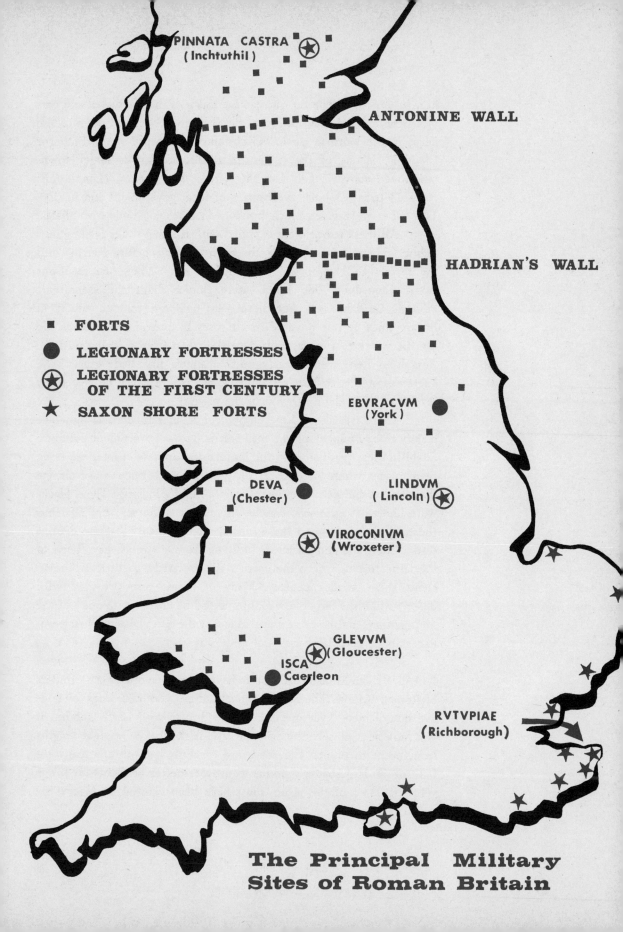

PINNATA CASTRA
(Inchtuthil)

ANTONINE WALL

HADRIAN'S WALL

■ FORTS

● LEGIONARY FORTRESSES

✪ LEGIONARY FORTRESSES
OF THE FIRST CENTURY

★ SAXON SHORE FORTS

EBVRACVM
(York)

DEVA
(Chester)

LINDVM
(Lincoln)

VIROCONIVM
(Wroxeter)

GLEVVM
(Gloucester)

ISCA
Caerleon

RVTVPIAE
(Richborough)

The Principal Military
Sites of Roman Britain

in A.D. 60. At Colchester one can see much of the town wall and part of a very fine and elaborate gate, the Balkerne Gate, and the museum here, in the Norman castle built round the temple of the Emperor Claudius, is one of the richest in the country. The larger towns mentioned above, other than the *coloniae* and London (Londinium) were all tribal capitals, the centres of local government and justice. The tribes were given much freedom in managing their own affairs.

All these towns were supplied with running water feeding into public fountains and supplying the main buildings before pouring into the sewers and helping to keep them clean. When one mentions Roman aqueducts one immediately thinks about the stone-built Pont du Gard in Gaul, but there were no large stone aqueducts in Britain since it was possible in all cases to provide sufficient slope for the water to run naturally into the town from a spring outside. Aqueducts here were merely open channels like little canals. The finest example is at Dorchester in Dorset where it can be traced for several miles to the northwest of the town.

There was also a large number of smaller towns and these are mainly to be found along the main roads. It was government policy to establish these roads all over the Empire and provide at intervals along them places where messengers on government service could change their horses and get refreshments and a night's lodging. These places were known as *mutationes* (stables for change of horses) and *mansiones* (hostels). It was around these official establishments that the Britons settled for trade and business. Most of the excavations have been in the larger towns where there are richer rewards, so little is known about these smaller centres. Many of them were provided with defences like the larger towns in a period of unrest at the end of the 2nd century, and bastions were added in the 4th century when it was necessary to keep large bands of raiders at bay.

ROADS. The Roman road system has always been one of the wonders of Roman Britain. The Saxons thought they were the work of gods and not of men. Everyone knows the Roman road is straight but if you look at it closely you will see that it consists of straight lengths from point to point. The roads are carefully laid out and many are built up on large banks (*aggera*) to provide better gradients for heavy vehicles. Most of the rivers must have been crossed by bridges or fords but none of these survive. Although one can see the original surface in only one or two places, like Blackstone Edge across the Pennines, the great banks can often be seen striding away across the fields like railway embankments.

TEMPLES AND RELIGION. The Romans brought with them all the gods of the classical world but allowed the Britons to worship their own Celtic deities, the two often being linked. There must have been temples in all the towns and many in the countryside. One of the largest was at Colchester and the foundations of this were preserved when the Normans built their great castle. There must have been another impressive temple at Bath (Aquae Sulis). This was a special religious centre around the hot springs. The Romans realized the wonderful curative properties of these waters and it became a centre of healing but connected with the goddess Sul Minerva. When the Roman drains became blocked up the water level at Bath rose in the early middle ages and this preserved many of the Roman structures, which became visible again when the drains were rediscovered and emptied in the 18th century. Bath is well worth a visit. Some temples had theatres attached to them like the one at Verulamium.

In museums all over the country one can see altars which came from these temples and smaller shrines in the countryside. They show from the inscriptions that they were usually put up as a result of a vow. A promise was made to the gods that if a business prospered or if a journey was made safely, a sacrifice would be made and an altar erected. These altars are the visible remains of many of these wishes and hopes fulfilled.

Apart from these simple cults there were others which were imported from the Near East like Mithraism and Christianity. The excavation of the temple of Mithras in London in 1954 created a great sensation. The foundations of this building have been rebuilt at present ground level and the important sculptures and other remains are to be seen in the Guildhall Museum in London. Mithras was popular with the soldiers and most of the forts must have had a temple. The best one to see is at Carrawburgh on Hadrian's Wall, beautifully preserved by the Ministry of Public Building and Works. There are no certain Christian churches of this period, but a little building at Silchester which still remains buried below the soil was probably one. Usually the Christian communities took over other buildings and worshipped in converted temples or private houses like the villa at Lullingstone in Kent.

FARMS AND VILLAS. All the lighter subsoils would have been under cultivation in Roman times and many woods cleared to provide timber for building. The expert Roman engineers drained the marshy areas of the Fenlands and the rich soils there were brought into intensive cultivation. At one time one could see on the chalklands of the south many traces of the small Celtic fields of this period, but alas they are now almost all entirely ploughed away in the intensive cultivation of the last few years. All over the lowlands of Roman Britain there were small communities and farmsteads. These modest establishments built mainly in wood have not survived; they are difficult to find and excavate with any understanding, but they resemble very closely the farms of the late prehistoric period. It is obvious then that most of the people in the countryside continued to live much as they had done before but prospered and multiplied in the peace the Romans brought. Only in the mountain areas can one see their little settlements. Some of the best of these are in the island of Anglesey. Another in the hills of North Wales is Tre'r Ceiri, and although remote it is well worth a visit. There are other sites in Westmorland and Cumberland and on the hills round Grassington in Yorkshire.

The remains that have attracted the most attention are the villas. People investigated these in bygone centuries mainly for their wonderful pavements. These large and elaborate buildings must have been the houses of the great landowners living on their estates in great splendour and leisure, but of course they are buildings of varying size and the smaller ones are merely where the well-to-do farmers or the bailiffs lived. There are quite a few of these buildings which can be visited, and perhaps the most famous is Chedworth near Cirencester in a remote but beautiful situation. There is also Bignor in Sussex, Brading on the Isle of Wight, and Lullingstone in Kent. Although the last of these was a very small building it is one of very great interest since it was here that a small Christian chapel was discovered. It was identified by its wall paintings and the excavator has written an interesting popular account of his excavations – see the list of books at the end.

A Roman villa similar to the one at Chedworth.

There are probably 600 similar villas scattered all over the lowlands of Britain but although the sites are known, there is little to see on the ground. A building of outstanding interest, quite different from the rest, is at Fishbourne near Chichester. This is a great palace built towards the end of the first century A.D., possibly by Cogidubnus (a client king who did much to help the Romans in their conquest) or more likely by one of his descendants. It is very large, has some interesting mosaics and every indication of monumental grandeur. It has now been almost completely excavated and one wing has been preserved inside a modern building. The site has become one of the showpieces of Roman Britain.

INDUSTRY. The most important industry in Roman Britain was agriculture and it was this that gave the wealth to the countryside and the towns.

Britain has never been very rich in ores producing metals (except ironstone) but the Romans developed the silver mines in the Mendips and those in North Wales. The only things which survive from this activity are pigs of lead. (Lead was a waste product of the industry.) There was also a little gold mine at Dolaucothi in South Wales and one can see a few remains of the water channels and tanks where the ore was broken and washed. In many areas there must have been extensive iron workings, particularly in the Weald of Kent and in the ironstone areas of Lincolnshire.

Where there was clay there may have been potteries and tile works and these are scattered all over the lowlands zone. There were important centres at Water Newton (Durobrivae) near Peterborough, in Oxfordshire and in the New Forest, but all these remains are now below the ground. Their products and occasionally their reconstructed kilns can be found in museums.

Some of the stone quarries date back to Roman times but they are difficult to identify. Along some of the Roman roads one can also find the little pits dug to obtain the gravel for the road surface.

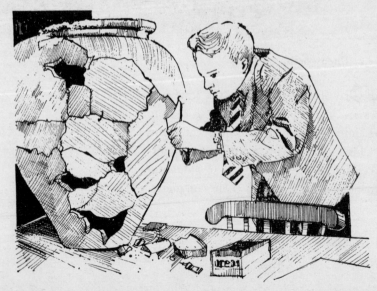

Piecing together a large jar from a Roman villa.

THINGS TO DO

Visiting Sites

We have already discussed those sites which can be visited where actual remains can be seen in position. Some of them are in towns, although of course there are quite a number in the open country where public transport may be difficult, so one needs to have a bicycle or some other means of travelling independently. All the sites mentioned above are accessible and most of them are ancient monuments looked after by the government and where you pay a small charge when you go in. These sites are usually very well kept. Some of them have small museums where many of the objects found on the sites there can be seen, together with photographs, diagrams, models and other things. Before visiting any of these monuments you need to know what there is to be seen, so instead of just going along without any preparation is is very desirable that you should obtain guide-books and any other literature you can find which will tell you all about the site before you get there. Then the remains you see will be far more meaningful. On Roman sites in this country one sees little more than foundations and it is often difficult to see how these fitted into buildings. Unfortunately very little care has been taken to provide diagrams and models showing what the buildings looked like when they were occupied.

What to look for in Museums

In museums which contain Roman remains you will see the same things over and over again. Why not start making a list of all the things you are likely to find? There are the different types of pottery for example, from the red glossy samian ware imported from Gaul and Germany, to the rougher, coarser, buff and grey wares, most of which were made in Britain. See if you can distinguish various kinds of vessels and work out what they were used for. Some are fairly obvious, like the flagons with big globular bodies, small necks and handles – these were of course for holding and carrying liquids. But what about the bowls studded with grits on the inside and known as *mortaria*? It is generally thought that these were used in the kitchen for breaking down food, pulverizing it into a kind of paste or mixing it with liquids so that it could be prepared for the meal. Then there are cooking pots, store jars, bowls, dishes, platters and even colanders. All these things would be used in the kitchen of a normal household and would have a definite use. Find out all the different kinds, draw them and see if you can discover what they were used for and whether their materials would be suitable for this purpose. Then of course you can find different kinds of glass vessels, but these are not so common since, being fragile, they are broken in the ground and very rarely found complete. Metal objects are also difficult since in many cases they belong to things like doors and boxes and all you have left are pieces of the fittings. It is useful to go through a collection in a museum and try to work out exactly what each piece could have been and see what they tell you about the everyday life of this particular period.

Always be on the look-out for inscriptions on tombstones and altars, because these sometimes tell us quite a lot about the people themselves. They tell us their names, and in the case of tombstones their ages as well and where the people came from. The inscriptions are all in Latin and with practice you may be able to work out what they mean and what all the abbreviations stand for. Perhaps the most exciting find is where someone has scribbled his name or something on a piece of tile or pottery. Here you feel you are actually in contact with a person living in the period who just felt like jotting something down. Perhaps it was his name, or perhaps he was just practising the alphabet, or he might even have left a message for somebody.

Helping in Museums

Seeing things in cases is after all only half the fun; it is far better to be able to handle material for yourself. In museums you might be allowed to do this by going behind the scenes and looking through boxes of broken pieces of pottery. In some cases you might be able to help by washing pottery which has just come from an excavation, and perhaps even restore it to its original shape. If you do this you will learn a great deal about the pottery of the period. There are plenty of other odd jobs one can do in a museum, but of course there is very little room and few facilities in most. Museum curators have not always the time to give to this sort of thing either, so when going into a museum to offer to help in this way, only go in one or two at a time.

Measuring up a
Roman pottery kiln.

Helping on Excavations

Most people of course want to excavate – this to them is what archaeology is all about. The idea of just going into a field and digging a hole may appeal to some people but I am afraid it only leads to destroying the site. An excavation these days is a much more careful scientific operation and has to be done by someone who really knows what it is all about. Of course there is a great deal that can be done on an excavation providing it is properly conducted, but work has to be very closely supervised, so no excavator can have large numbers of people all at once. For this reason it is necessary to go along in small groups of three or four at a time and be placed under the care of someone who can instruct you about exactly what you can do. You have to be very patient and do just what you are told. Be careful where you walk, because if you start running around you will only disturb things and probably destroy fragile objects in the ground. If you can accept the discipline necessary on an excavation, it can be a very interesting and rewarding experience, but it must never be treated as a kind of lark or holiday, for it is quite a serious matter. Just as you would never be let loose in the science laboratory at school, you should never be let loose on an excavation.

Field-work

Far more useful work could be done in field-work. At first sight this is nowhere near so exciting as digging things up, but there is plenty to be found actually on the ground itself by walking over the fields, especially after they have been ploughed or after heavy rain when things have been washed out. You can pick up pottery and objects and may even be able to discover completely new sites in this way by recognizing the date of the pottery. This is why it is important when you go round museums to look very carefully at all the different kinds of pottery of different periods. Then when you find tiny fragments on the ground you should know what they represent, what kind of settlement was there, and at what date or period it existed. To do field-work properly you need a set of maps, perhaps six inches to the mile. You take them out and work through the fields, very carefully plotting on the maps exactly what it is you discover. If you find a large site you have to work out its area. Then there are all sorts of bumps, hollows and features on the ground where the fields are not ploughed but are under grass or in woods. Many of these things may be completely unknown. You have to check up in the history books to find out if someone has noted them before, and you may find they are well-known sites. They all need to be looked at carefully, and it is necessary to learn to make a survey on the ground to measure up these bumps and hollows so that you can make a map of them.

This recording is all very useful work and has its own rewards because you may be finding completely new and unknown sites anywhere in this country. But, like excavation, it has to be done carefully and systematically and you must not just rush in and do the odd hour or so at it. Above all, remember that all the fields of our country are owned by somebody and most of them are cultivated. It is necessary to obtain permission from the farmer before walking about on his land, otherwise you will be very unpopular. If you explain what you want to do and are serious about it, farmers very rarely prevent you from going around, providing you shut all the gates you come to, do not disturb any animals or game birds, and obey any other instructions.

Where to Obtain Information

These activities may be difficult to organize at school since there are not many teachers who know enough, but during the holidays there are many excavations going on all over the country, some of them very large and some quite small. It is possible that you might be able to help on some of these. If you want to find out more about this you can obtain information concerning excavations from the *C.B.A. Calendar* which is published every month during the summer by the Council for British Archaeology, 8 St. Andrew's Place, Regent's Park, London N.W.1.

BOOKS TO READ

General

Ordnance Survey	*Map of Roman Britain*	
Ordnance Survey	*Map of Hadrian's Wall*	
I. A. Richmond	*Roman Britain*	The Pelican History of England
A. L. F. Rivet	*Town and Country in Roman Britain*	Hutchinson University Library
Antony Birley	*Life in Roman Britain*	Batsford
J. Liversidge	*Britain in the Roman Empire*	Routledge

The Army

Graham Webster	*The Roman Imperial Army*	A. and C. Black
Graham Webster	*The Roman Army*	Booklets published by the Grosvenor
F. H. Thompson	*Deva, Roman Chester*	Museum, Chester
G. Boon	*The Roman Fortress at Caerleon* (plan published separately)	Booklet published by the National Museum of Wales, Cardiff
J. C. Bruce (ed. I. A. Richmond)	*Handbook to the Roman Wall*	Harold Hill, Newcastle-upon-Tyne
Anne S. Robertson	*The Antonine Wall*	Handbook published by the Glasgow Archaeological Society

Towns

J. S. Wacher (ed.)	*The Civitas Capitals of Roman Britain*	Leicester University Press
G. Boon	*Roman Silchester*	Max Parrish
R. Merrifield	*The Roman City of London*	Ernest Benn

Roads

I. D. Margary	*Roman Roads in Britain*	John Baker

Countryside

C. Thomas (ed.)	*Rural Settlement in Roman Britain*	C.B.A. Research Report

Villas

G. W. Meates	*Lullingstone Roman Villa*	Heinemann

Furniture

J. Liversidge	*Furniture in Roman Britain*	Tiranti

Excavation

Graham Webster	*Practical Archaeology*	A. and C. Black
Ordnance Survey	*Field Archaeology*	
J. X. W. P. Corcoran	*The Young Field Archaeologist's Guide*	Bell